Puerto Rico
& Virgin Islands
Guide

Travel Guides to Planet Earth!

OPEN ROAD TRAVEL GUIDES SHOW YOU
HOW TO BE A TRAVELER – NOT A TOURIST!

*Whether you're going abroad or planning a trip in the United States, take Open Road along on your journey. Our books have been praised by **Travel & Leisure**, **The Los Angeles Times**, **Newsday**, **Booklist**, **US News & World Report**, **Endless Vacation**, **American Bookseller**, **Coast to Coast**, and many other magazines and newspapers!*

Don't just see the world – experience it with Open Road!

About the Author

Janet Groene and her husband Gordon changed directions while in their young 30s, leaving behind Gordon's career as a professional pilot in Illinois. They sold everything, loaded Janet's typewriter and Gordon's cameras aboard a small sloop, and lived happily ever after cruising in the Bahamas and the Caribbean.

Now based in Florida, they travel worldwide and have written more than a dozen books and thousands of newspaper and magazine features. They won the NMMA Director's Award for boating journalism and Janet is a recipient of the Distinguished Achievement in RV Journalism Award.

Open Road - Travel Guides to Planet Earth!

Open Road Publishing has guide books to exciting, fun destinations on four continents. As veteran travelers, our goal is to bring you the best travel guides available anywhere!

No small task, but here's what we offer:

• All Open Road travel guides are written by authors with a distinct, opinionated point of view – not some sterile committee or team of writers. Our authors are experts in the areas covered and are polished writers.

• Our guides are geared to people who want to make their own travel choices. We'll show you how to discover the real destination – not just see some place from a tour bus window.

• We're strong on the basics, but we also provide terrific choices for those looking to get off the beaten path and experience the country or city – not just see it or pass through it.

• We give you the best, but we also tell you about the worst and what to avoid. Nobody should waste their time and money on their hard-earned vacation because of bad or inadequate travel advice.

• Our guides assume nothing. We tell you everything you need to know to have the trip of a lifetime – presented in a fun, literate, nononsense style.

• And, above all, we welcome your input, ideas, and suggestions to help us put out the best travel guides possible.

Puerto Rico
& Virgin Islands Guide

Travel Guides to Planet Earth!

Janet Groene
with Gordon Groene

open road publishing

Open Road Publishing

We offer travel guides to American and foreign locales. Our books tell it like it is, often with an opinionated edge, and our experienced authors always give you all the information you need to have the trip of a lifetime. Write for your free catalog of all our titles.

Open Road Publishing
P.O. Box 284, Cold Spring Harbor, NY 11724
E-mail: Jopenroad@aol.com

3rd Edition

To Robert Irving Hawkins, my brother and first travel buddy.

Library of Congress Control No. 2002108179
ISBN 1-892975-76-9

Maps courtesy of Magellan Geographix.
    The author has made every effort to be as accurate as possible, but neither she nor the publisher assumes responsibility for the services provided by any business listed in this guide; for any errors or omissions; or any loss, damage, or disruptions in your travels for any reason.

Puerto Rico & Virgin Islands Guide

contents

Sidebars

Maps

Puerto Rico & the Virgin Islands

Chapter 1

i
n
t
r
o
d
u
c
t
i
o
n

Spellbinding is the first word that comes to mind when we remember our first sail into Caribbean waters and the sight of a sandy bottom clearly seen forty feet under our small sloop. Except for the Dry Tortugas west of Key West, there are no waters like them in the US mainland because silt, carried to the sea by rivers, clouds even the cleanest seas. It isn't uncommon in Puerto Rico and the Virgin Islands for visibility to be 100 feet or more.

In later years we were to see the islands time and again from airplanes large and small. We cruise them in tiny cockleshells and aboard huge ocean liners. We trudge their rain forests and rutted roads. We luxuriate in the best hotels and delight in funky guest houses. We sun on beaches that are alive with families and fun seekers. Best of all, we like finding a lonely stretch of sand with no footsteps but our own. We salute the islands for the sophistication of the dining in even the smallest settlements, yet we can also be happy with a native breakfast of johnnycake and pawpaw and a lunch of rice and beans. Most of all, we love the people of the islands whose bloods have blended to create a unique beauty in many skin colors.

Don't forget that Puerto Ricans and US Virgin Islanders are Americans. Compared to other parts of the Caribbean where you have non-citizen status, this is home with a zip code, American currency, American fast food, telephones and ATMs that work most of the time, plus the stars and stripes fluttering over a courthouse that assures justice under the US Constitution. We have included the British Virgin Islands in this guide because they are so closely combined with St. Thomas, St. John and St. Croix.

Say hello to Puerto Rico and the Virgin Islands, where you can combine an exotic island in the sun with all that is familiar and good about Hometown USA.

Overview

Chapter 2

The **Caribbean Sea** is ringed with a diadem of islands that starts with Cuba, which is only 90 miles off Florida, and spirals southwards through Haiti and the Dominican Republic, Puerto Rico, the Virgin Islands, the Leewards and Windwards, and Trinidad. Below Cuba are Jamaica and the Caymans; afloat in the Caribbean north of Venezuela are the Dutch Leeward Islands of Aruba, Bonaire, and Curacao as well as some resort islands owned by Venezuela.

If you are confused about what to call them, you're not alone. Even longtime Caribbean visitors have their own favorite ways of calling, categorizing, and collating the islands. All of them are the **West Indies**, called that because Columbus thought he had found India, not a new world. They are also the **Antilles**, called the Lesser Antilles below the U.S. islands and south to Trinidad, and the Greater Antilles from Cuba to Puerto Rico including the U.S. Virgin Islands, which are also the start of the string known as the Leewards.

To make things even more confusing, they are also grouped according to political loyalties such as the British Virgin Islands, the British Windwards, the French West Indies, or the Dutch Windwards in the Leewards. You're always safe in referring to any of the islands in this book as the West Indies, the Caribbean, or the Antilles. Briefly, the American Virgins are called the **U.S.V.I.** and the British Virgins are the **B.V.I.**

Puerto Rico

As colorful as a serape and as warm as a freshly baked tortilla, **Puerto Rico** offers American can-do and

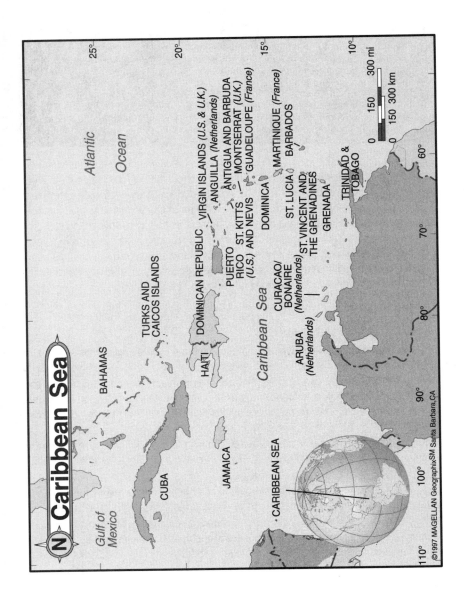

N

Caribbean Sea

Gulf of Mexico

BAHAMAS

CUBA

JAMAICA

TURKS AND CAICOS ISLANDS

HAITI

DOMINICAN REPUBLIC

PUERTO RICO (U.S.)

VIRGIN ISLANDS (U.S. & U.K.)

ANGUILLA (Netherlands)

ANTIGUA AND BARBUDA

ST. KITTS AND NEVIS

MONTSERRAT (U.K.)

GUADELOUPE (France)

DOMINICA

MARTINIQUE (France)

ST. LUCIA

BARBADOS

ST. VINCENT AND THE GRENADINES

GRENADA

CURACAO/ BONAIRE (Netherlands)

ARUBA (Netherlands)

Caribbean Sea

TRINIDAD & TOBAGO

Atlantic Ocean

CARIBBEAN SEA

25°

20°

15°

10°

110° 100° 90° 80° 70° 60°

0   150   300 mi

0   150   300 km

©1997 MAGELLAN GeographixSM Santa Barbara, CA

Currencies

U.S. dollars are the currency of Puerto Rico and the U.S. Virgin Islands, and you won't need anything else in the B.V.I. for everyday meals, accommodations and purchases. In Puerto Rico and the U.S. Virgins, U.S. postage stamps will send your postcards home through the U.S. Post Office system. Drop them in any mail box. If you're receiving mail in Puerto Rico or the U.S.V.I., you'll have a U.S. zip code, the same as at home. Just remember that U.S. stamps can't be used in the B.V.I.

convenience, gregarious Latin gaiety, and the kinds of beaches and clear waters for which the Caribbean is richly famed. **San Juan** is a major airline hub that hosts dozens of nonstop flights each day from North America and Europe, so it's a logical choice for a quick, weekend stay in the sunshine. If you can stay longer, vacation in the mountains in a rustic parador or take a suite in a four-star resort patronized by celebrities from around the world.

For dining, golf, watersports, a romantic getaway or a family holiday, it's hard to beat America's "shining star," found just east of Cuba and west of the U.S. Virgin Islands.

U.S. Virgin Islands

St. Thomas and **St. John** are just east of Puerto Rico and can be seen from there on a clear day. Sister islands, they are polar opposites. St. John is mostly national park land, focusing on eco-tourism and the outdoors. St. Thomas too has picturebook bays and beaches, but its cash registers jingle and its streets stream with cruise ship passengers and day-trippers in search of "duty-free" bargains. Ever since the days when the islands belonged to Denmark, St. Thomas has been a commercial center. To find the "real" St. Thomas means getting out of Charlotte Amalie and into country lodgings that range from charming inns to the plush Ritz-Carlton.

The third of the American islands, **St. Croix**, is in a world of its own well away from the other U.S. and British Virgin Islands. It was here that crops were raised for shipment to St. Thomas; the island is still largely farmland. Its scuba diving and underwater national park are alone worth the trip, but St. Croix also has historic plantations, picturesque settlements at Frederiksted and Christiansted, and great beaches and resorts, all under the U.S. flag.

British Virgin Islands

They're only a brief boat ride from American shores. They're tiny and unspoiled. Yet they are British, lending a sense of "foreign" travel to your vacation in the U.S.V.I. So closely tangled with the U.S. Virgin Islands that we couldn't leave them out of this book, they are known as the **B.V.I.** to loyal visitors who come back year after year.

Tortola is the chief settlement but travelers can also sample the sunbleached beaches and limpid seas of **Virgin Gorda**, **Jost Van Dyke**, and some thirty other rocks and islets plus the worlds-end island of **Anegada**. It lies north of the B.V.I. in the boundless Atlantic, creating a resting place for seabirds and world-weary humans.

itineraries

Chapter 3

This is a book about islands, so itineraries will be governed by airlines and ferry schedules, cruise departures and arrivals, tides and winds. On cruises, ports of call provide only a short look at a small patch of each island, but you'll have enough of a taste of each to help decide which ones you want to return to for longer stays. If your introduction to the Caribbean is aboard a cruise ship, don't make too quick a judgment. Cruisers who hate St. Thomas or San Juan find when they fly in that the "real" island isn't at all the border-town frenzy they saw at the pier.

Aboard a charter boat, you can see strings of islets and cays in a week. In two weeks you can make voyage through a briar patch of islands, stopping at some on the way out and the rest during your return sail. Even if you sail no more than a few miles each day, you'll see dozens of coves, villages, good snorkeling reefs, and shoreside attractions.

If You Have Three To Four Days

When all you need is a quick trip to re-charge your batteries in the Caribbean sun, minimize travel time by choosing an island that has the fastest, most direct service from your home city. This will vary according to where you live, the season, and whether charter flights are available in addition to scheduled airlines. Some islands have direct flights only once or twice a week, so careful planning is essential to getting in and out when you want to go.

Islands that have nonstop flights from the United States and Canada include Puerto Rico, which is a major hub for the entire Caribbean, St. Croix, and St. Thomas. Getting to St. John or any of the British Virgins takes a little longer.

We also recommend that, on a visit this brief, you stay in a full-service resort or guest house where you'll get the pampering you long for. Condo living and bareboating are fine for longer stays, and in fact it's part of the fun to provision at local markets. For a power vacation, however, don't waste time shopping, cooking, making beds, and trying to find your way around.

Among our suggested itineraries are:

!Fly into **San Juan** and check into one of the beach hotels within an hour of the airport. This gives you a choice of prices from the regal Hyatt in Dorado and the Westin Rio Mar to smaller hotels and guest houses in metropolitan San Juan itself. In the resorts, spend days reading in a hammock, walking the beach barefoot, sailing a small boat, or playing golf or tennis. If you stay in the city, walk Old San Juan and spend your time in museums and great restaurants.

!Fly to **St. Thomas** or **St. Croix**, where a drive of less than 30 minutes from the airport brings you to a hotel, resort, condo, or guest house. Just as in San Juan, you won't waste time in lines for customs, immigration, and currency exchange. Bring your golf clubs or a suitcase filled with good reading, and let the sun shine in.

If You Have a Week

• Fly into San Juan and take a **week-long cruise** aboard one of the ships that starts and ends its itineraries there. They vary seasonally, but a cruise-savvy travel agency can find the right package for you. For example, **Royal Caribbean's** *Adventure of the Seas* does seven-night cruises out of San Juan in winter, calling at such ports as Aruba, Curacao, St. Martin, and St. Thomas and its *Radiance of the Seas* cruises Saturdays out of San Juan to the southern Caribbean. **Princess** offers two itineraries out of San Juan. If you can spare a few days for a pre- or post-cruise stay in St. Thomas or San Juan, so much the better.

• Fly into Beef Island Airport in **Tortola** and enjoy a week-long package at the Bitter End Yacht Club. You can stay on land every night or get a land-sea package that includes some nights aboard a boat. Learn to sail, go snorkeling or scuba diving, hike nature trails, or scoot over to a deserted island in a Boston Whaler and have a picnic.

• Book into **St. Croix** and a stay at the Hotel Caravelle downtown. It's the perfect headquarters for diving, boating, island exploring, shopping and dining around Christiansted, meeting some yachties, and catching rays around the pool. Many of your fellow guests will be from Denmark, lending an international mood to dining and nightlife. On Sunday morning, attend services at the old Danish Lutheran church across the street for a heartwarming welcome from a multi-racial congregation. Never will you feel less like a tourist, more like a traveler.

• Take a week at Sapphire Beach Resort & Marina **St. Thomas**. It's one of the closest resorts to the airport and is also handy to the Red Hook ferry if you want to take a day trip to St. John. There's a full menu of activities and watersports, fine dining, a children's program, and plenty of packages to choose from. Kids under age 17 sleep free and under age 12 eat free too.

• Fly into **San Juan** and transfer to one of the island's elegant golf resorts such as the Hyatt Regency Cerromar Beach Resort & Casino, El Conquistador Resort & Country Club, Westin Rio Mar Beach Resort, or the Wyndham Palmas Del Mar Resort & Villas. Then golf your brains out for a week. Non-golfers in your family will enjoy sunning, beachcombing, sightseeing, shopping, tennis, and horseback riding. The island is known for its fine dining. After dinner, the resorts offer casino gambling. If you're bringing the children, stay at the Caribe Hilton near San Juan or the Ponce Hilton & Casino, and book the kids into the fun-packed Hilton Vacation Station (contact for any of these Hiltons: *Tel. 800/ HILTONS* or *www.hilton.com/families)*. They'll get a welcome gift and free use of age-appropriate "loaner" toys and games. Parents too get a welcome packet explaining the program for children ages 12 and under. Children's menus are available in the hotels' restaurants and family activities include scavenger hunts and hula dancing. Children under age 18 stay free in the same room with parents and grandparents.

If You Have Two Weeks or More

• Book a charter boat with The Moorings out of **Tortola** for a week, starting and ending your vacation with a couple of days ashore at the company's own inn. Check into the resort for a day or two to rest up and to plan provisions. Under sail you can seek out lonely beaches and seaside bars patronized by yachties from all over the world. Build the ultimate sand castle. Snorkel over pristine reefs. Have a rum swizzle on deck in a quiet anchorage, and hope to see the green flash.

After your cruise when you return to the inn, you'll be grateful for long showers, restaurant meals, and the company of other returning sailors to swap tales with. Explore the rain forest on Mount Sage, drive to beaches you didn't get to by boat, ride horseback on Cane Garden Bay, and shop the quaint boutiques of Road Town. The Moorings also has fleets based in St. Martin, St. Lucia, and Grenada. Try them all later, but start with the user-friendly BVI. .

• Fly into **St. Thomas** and then catch the ferry to **St. John** to camp Virgin Islands National Park. Spend days hiking, snorkeling the underwater trail, cooking on a camp stove, and enrolling in ranger-led nature programs. Then reward yourself with a few days in an air conditioned hotel on St. Thomas before flying home.

• Fly to **Puerto Rico**, rent a car, and stay a night or two at each parador, or government guest house. Built in scenic areas and points of interest such as beaches, mountains, forests or hot springs, these accommodations aren't fancy but they have the basics including wholesome, delicious, native food. By the end of two weeks, you will have savored a Puerto Rico that few visitors see.

Chapter 4

Land & Sea

The lands and seas of the Caribbean make up one of the most geologically interesting places on Earth. Much of the Caribbean Sea is on the continental shelf with great expanses of clear, shallow waters where small boats can cruise for days without losing a view of the bottom 50 or 60 feet below. Yet vast valleys plunge to ocean depths of 29,000 feet and more in the Puerto Rico Trench.

Much of the land is volcanic, rising to peaks that are, in some cases such as Saba, the entire island. The total land area of all the Caribbean islands is only about 90,000 square miles, half the land mass of the United Kingdom, yet only a handful of cities have a population of more than 100,000 people. Among them are San Juan, a major metropolis, and other Puerto Rico cities including Ponce, Bayamon, Mayagüez, Arecibo, and Guaynabo.

The islands of Puerto Rico and the U.S.V.I. are a combination of low mountains and plains, rimmed with sandy beaches and surrounded by coral reefs. Around them, waters shoal so gradually that the white sand bottom shines through, creating a neon luminescence in the turquoise waters. St. Croix has a sort of rainforest but only in Puerto Rico do you find the American Caribbean's highest mountains and lush, craggy rainforest.

The beaches alone are a geology lesson. All of them are formed by nature's grindstone, the sea, which pulverizes volcanic rock to make black sand beaches, or grinds up limestone or chalk to create sands in shades of white, pink, beige and brown. Regularly they are rearranged as storms suck away all the sand from some shores and deposit it somewhere else. New islets are formed, sometimes to be swept away in the next storm. Others grow, rooted with mangroves whose roots capture more sand, and become real islands.

Geology has also played a role in the animal life found in the Caribbean, where species often evolved independently for centuries. A cheerful tree frog called coqui, found only on Puerto Rico, is the island's symbol. Where mongoose were introduced to control rats in the cane fields, they bred in the wild and themselves became a problem. Non-native monkeys brought in by settlers escaped into the wild and formed large populations in some rainforests. Creatures such as whales and turtles, hunted almost to extinction, are making a comeback in Caribbean waters.

The larger islands, including Puerto Rico, offer the largest variety of vegetation, ranging from savannah to tropical scrub. Woodlands include mangrove swamps, dry forests, and jungles euphemistically called rainforests. Crops native to the Americas thrive in Puerto Rico and the U.S.V.I. They include tobacco, ackee, mango, avocado, cacao and sisal. Settlers introduced crops, some of them still commercially portant, including sugar cane, coffee, bananas, coconut, rice, cotton, pineapple, nutmeg, citrus, and many produce crops ranging from cabbage to tomatoes.

The People

Except for a few islands down the chain, the Caribbean including the U.S. islands and B.V.I. are predominantly black and tan, with a sprinkling of Amerindian, Asian, and East Indian blood. Puerto Ricans are a blend of proud Spanish blood, Amerindian, and African. Everywhere you'll find beautiful people with skin colors in all hues.

Most islanders are **Christians**, often with an undercurrent of African Voodoo, Obeah, Santeria, or Shango (also spelled Xango). Roman Catholic and major Protestant churches are found on almost every island. Puerto Rico is primarily Roman Catholic; the Danes left a legacy of Lutheranism in the Virgin Islands. Judaism has made an important contribution in the Caribbean since the 16th century and it remains a tiny but vital force in the U.S. Caribbean, especially on St. Thomas.

Rastafarianism, which hails the late Ethiopian emperor Haile Selassie as its messiah, took root in Jamaica and has some adherents in most other islands. Its members are usually recognized by their beehive "dreadlock" hair, usually covered in a black, red, gold, and green cap indicating traditional Rasta colors.

For all their shades of color and belief, the peoples of the Caribbean have much in common. Except for Puerto Rico, where Spanish or Spanglish is the first language, the West Indian accent has minor variations but it shares a softness, lilt, and range of octaves that is captivating. A question in a man's deep voice can start in a basso profundo and lift at the end to soprano range. A woman's silvery laugh can turn harsh and scolding. A balladeer's voice can

Don't Call Them Natives

You are always safe in saying West Indian or Islander, but the word native is offensive to many people in the Caribbean. We have also encountered situations where locals were offended by the terms "boy" and "guy."

People who live in...	Are called...
St. Croix	Crucians
St. John	St. Johnians
St. Thomas	St. Thomians
Puerto Rico	Puerto Ricans

turn to gravel or velvet. If you have an ear for language, you'll find yourself falling into its rhythms and convoluted sentence structure.

Culturally, the Caribbean is on a fast track that began with the realization that its own unique cultures need to be cherished and preserved. Dance groups, art galleries, theater and musicals celebrate ancient African, French, English, and Spanish forms. New forms, such as reggae and salsa, have been exported around the world.

Modern arts are welcomed in the islands. San Juan is as sophisticated as any other American city when it comes to symphony, opera, theater, and the internationally famous Casals Festival. Old San Juan has become the Greenwich Village of the tropics. Every island in the U.S. Caribbean has at least one painter, scultor, or photographer who has won international recognition. Maria Henle on St. Croix, daughter of the late photographer Fritz Henle, is a second-generation artist of international renown. Husband and wife team Jan D'Esposo and Manuca Gandia in Old San Juan, Deborah Broad and Mark Austin of Christiansted, and dozens of artists "out on the island" in Puerto Rico make up a who's who of artists.

The annual arts and crafts show held in Old San Juan in late April attracts top artists and crafters from around the island including the gifted Cotto family made up of Sixto, his wife Ana María and their teenage son, Miguel Ángel, whose his first serigraph edition, created when he was eight, quickly sold out.

Music of the Caribbean

The sounds pound and punish, puzzling tourists who are trying to sort out such music forms as dubbing, reggae, calypso, salsa, plena, and bomba. They are as familiar in the Caribbean as rockabilly, heavy metal, and leadbelly are to North American ears.

The music and dance of the Caribbean have a language all their own, a patois born in the gavottes and quadrilles of ancient Europe, tempered in torrid Africa, and spun into unique, New World rhythms and harmonies. Early Spanish explorers told of graceful dances performed by Arawak slaves who, with the warlike Caribs, had populated the Caribbean before the first European explorers arrived. Their traditions were added to those of British, Dutch, French, Spanish, and Danish settlers.

Most compelling of all were the contributions of African slaves, who soon outnumbered the combined total of whites and Amerindians, and whose dances and drumbeats were a lifeline of familiarity to captives in a strange land. Even in manacles, they sang and danced. Some say that the languid movements of the merengue are based on the limping gait of a slave wearing a ball and chain.

Pulsing sounds rise from the villages to serenade hilltop hotels. **Calypso** singers stop by diners' tables to improvise outrageous rhymes that are made up on the spot. Television star Wayne Brady, beloved for his improv ditties, comes from a St. Thomiam family. In Puerto Rico, your table is serenaded by mariachis. When anyone turns on a boom box or brings out a guitar, a spontaneous "**jump-up**" erupts. On Sunday mornings, joyous **Gospel** music rings out from open-air churches in every island hamlet. Every community in Puerto Rico has its patron saint, and the music and feasting go on for more than a week to honor that saint once a year.

As you travel the islands and sort out their great diversity of cultures, the differences in music become clearer. **Reggae**, which evolved from forms called ska and mento, began in Jamaica in the 1920s and '30s when Jamaican cane cutters were sent to Cuba to help with the sugar harvest and Cubans came to Jamaica to return the favor. They sang together, adding a Latin tinge to mento street songs. Radio programs bounced in from Miami and Memphis adding American boogie, blues, and jazz to the mix. Bluesy songs with a mento rhythm formed a short-lived movement called rock steady, which grew into reggae.

Puerto Rico's music has a strong Latin air. Trinidad gave us calypso. In Jamaica, musical instruments called abengs are made from cow horns. **Goombay**, the Bantu word for rhythm, was born in the Bahamas as African tribal rhythms mated with British colonial patterns. The melody is usually played on a piano, guitar or saxophone accompanied by bongos, maracas, or "click sticks." Traditionally performed only by males, it's passed down from father to son.

Goombay in turn has become **Junkanoo** (sometimes spelled Jonkanoo or Jonkunnu), a word used to describe festivals in some islands but now also used to describe the music itself. In Puerto Rico, ballads of 18th and 19th century Spain were performed on native Caribbean instruments used by pre-Columbian Taino Indians. Today part of the Puerto Rican sound are the six-stringed

Spanish classical guitar, the 10-string cuatro, tambours made from hollowed-out trees, and guiros made from hollow gourds.

To the trained ear, each form is unique but to newcomers there is a quaint and compelling sameness. Common to almost all Caribbean music is a pattern of call and response and the hypnotic repetition of the same phrase dozens and even hundreds of times. In music, it's called ostinato, from a root word meaning obstinate. One of the best examples is cariso, which evolved among slaves on St. Croix. Before newspapers, these newsy ballads were a way of communicating local news. A classic cariso tells the story of the sale of a plantation known as Wheel of Fortune to an unpopular manager named Dunlop. One couplet goes: Dunlop sell all de potato, He sell all de guinea grass...

Also common to St. Croix is a **storytelling music** known there as **quelbe**. Evolved from a rap-like African storytelling to the beating of a drum, quelbe gradually added European music and whatever instruments were at hand—pots, pans, a sardine can on a stick, dried gourds, plus any available conventional instruments—guitar, ukelele, bongo drums, tambourines. If it's amplified, it's not authentic quelbe. Annual events involving the music include the Fungi Music Fiesta during the Christmas holidays and the Scratch/Fungi Cultural Awards on Emancipation Day in August. Both are held on Tortola.

In addition to their own music, people of the Caribbean embrace the finest music and dance from throughout the world. The annual **Casals Festival** held each June in Puerto Rico and named for immortal cellist Pablo Casals, attracts an international who's who of classical music artists. Traditional Puerto Rican folkloric music is kept alive by groups including the **Compania Musical Perla del Sur**, who perform locally and overseas. Puerto Rico is also home of the annual **Heineken JazzFest**, held in late May. The island's best jazz musicians join international jazz stars for four days and nights of music at the Parque Sixto Escobar.

The Island Center amphitheater on St. Croix and the Reichold Center of the Performing Arts on St. Thomas host programs ranging from ballet to opera, folk dance, to folk rock. The **Caribbean Dance Company** performs at special events on St. Croix. Puerto Rico, with its glittering casinos, has dazzling cabaret shows blaring the brightest new show tunes from New York and London. Monthly musicales at Whim Plantation on St. Croix bring in internationally acclaimed musicians who play unamplified music in an intimate, living room setting.

Most tourist hotels have lounges offering a variety of music from mellow piano bar and easy listening to floor shows and disco as well as combos playing rousing rhumbas and merengues for dancing. Adventurous travelers also like to sample local nightlife, which is often found at its best in tiny, thatch-roofed bars or right on the streets.

The Caribbean has a music all its own born of sunshine and pounding surf, a bonding of many peoples of all colors and backgrounds, and a welcome as wide as the sea itself. Listen. Then let it carry your feet away.

It's best to write each island for tourist information and music festival dates, but some general information is available from the **Caribbean Tourism Organization**, c/o Kahn Travel Communications, 77 North Centre Avenue, Suite 215, Rockville Centre NY 11570, *Tel. 516/594-4100.*

The Caribbean's Jewish History

Jewish settlers came early to the islands and added yet another golden thread to a tapestry of African, European, and Asian immigrants. Jews, most of them fleeing persecution starting with the Spanish Inquisition and continuing through the Nazi years, began settling in the islands with the earliest Europeans, some directly from Europe and others from other refuges such as Brazil. From here they brought sugar cane, the first to be introduced into the islands. For centuries, other Jews came to the islands from Israel, bringing their expertise in irrigation. Many others were merchants or ship chandlers.

Many of them settled in St. Thomas, where a Jewish congregation was founded in 1796. Tombstones in the island's Jewish cemetery date as early as 1792. The present synagogue was used in recent years by a congregation of Palestinian Arabs until their mosque could be built – one more example of the mellow melting pot that is the Caribbean.

Alexander Hamilton, who was Secretary of the Treasury under George Washington, was born in the West Indies to a Jewish mother. Impressionist painter Camille Pissarro was born to Marrano Jewish parents in St. Thomas. The story is told in Irving Stone's novel Depths of Glory. Victor Borge fled the Holocaust in Europe to settle on St. Croix. Other famous Jews from the islands have included Judah Benjamin, secretary of state for the Confederacy, and U.S. Senator David Yulee.

Chapter 5

For thousands of years before European settlement, the Caribbean islands were roamed by canoes carrying peoples who came to be known as **Caribs** and **Arawaks**. Although other tribal names such as Ciboney, Caiqueto, and Taino crop up, the people who met Christopher Columbus were primarily the warlike, cannibalistic Caribs and the peaceful, agrarian Arawaks.

Tragically, most Amerindian tribes disappeared within a few decades. Many were taken as slaves; others caught European diseases such as measles and pox because they had no natural immunity. Indians died in droves from disease, hunger, oppression, and massacre. Only a few pockets of Caribs remain.

Let's Start with Columbus

Modern history is considered to have begun on October 12, 1492, when Christopher Columbus landed on an island that the aborigines knew as Guanahani and the Spanish called San Salvador in what we now call The Bahamas.

Between then and 1504, Columbus made four trans-Atlantic voyages, discovering and claiming island after island for Spain. By 1504 he had found Trinidad, the coast of South America, and the Central American coast, which he still called the **Indies** because he thought he had found a route to Asia. However, the first maps using the name America began appearing in 1507, taking the name from a Florentine explorer, Amerigo Vespucci, who had discovered the Amazon River.

It wasn't until 1513 that Florida, which he thought was yet another island, was sighted by Juan Ponce de Leon. His ornate tomb is now a tourist attraction in San Juan Cathedral.

Almost from the beginning, powerful struggles and intrigues marked Caribbean history. The 38 men left in the Dominican Republic in 1492, supplied only with what they could salvage from the wreckage of the *Santa Maria*, disappeared by the time the next vessels arrived. Spain worked quickly to fortify its holdings, founding settlements in Hispaniola in 1496, Puerto Rico in 1508, and Cuba in 1515.

The Caribbean yielded some gold, which was quickly pounced upon by the conquerors and their queen back in Seville, but by 1521 greater riches were discovered in Mexico and the islands were left to chart their own riches the hard way, by planting sugar and raising cattle.

By 1536, all Europe wanted a piece of the action. The seas were aboil with mighty warships belonging to nations, pirates, and privateers. The Dutch plundered Santiago de Cuba in 1554; Havana fell in 1555; Santo Domingo surrendered in 1586. The British won San Juan in 1595 and the Dutch captured the Spanish silver fleet off Cuba in 1628.

Only part of the battle was fought in the Caribbean. The fortunes of many islands rose and fell according to European treaties resulting from wars thousands of miles from the Caribbean. Some islands changed hands 20 times or more. Meanwhile in the islands, wars were fought on land and sea among Europeans and between Europeans and the few surviving Caribs.

The total land area of all the islands is less than that of England and Scotland, but each harbor was a precious resource and every arable acre of land an economic battleground. Battles roared on, almost always in favor of the British, whose fleet based in Antigua ruled the seas. The plot thickened during the American revolution, when the West Indies were a smuggling crossroads for munitions on their way to the rebels led by General George Washington. A century later, during the American Civil War, the islands would again become havens for smugglers and blockade runners sympathetic to the Confederacy.

In addition to the battles sanctioned by European monarchs, honest settlers throughout the islands had to endure raids by pirates such as Henry Morgan, who operated out of Nassau, and Edward Teach, known as Blackbeard, whose hideaway at Port Royal, Jamaica, was destroyed in an earthquake of Biblical proportions. Two French pirates headquartered in the little Dutch island of Saba. Pirate Piet Heyn, a Netherlander, is said to have taken $5 million in booty back to Holland. The islands were a no-man's land, worked by slaves who were being brought in at the rate of as many as 75,000 persons a year and exploited by anyone who had ships and cannons.

The End of Slavery

The first major slave rebellion came in 1801, when blacks led by Toussaint Louverture rebelled against the Spanish and set up a free society. Haiti declared itself independent in 1804 under the emperorship of former slave Jean-Jacques Dessalines. By 1834, slaves in all the British islands were free; freedom in the Dutch islands came soon after.

With the introduction of sugar beets into European agriculture, the continent's sweet tooth no longer had to be satisfied by Caribbean plantations. Without slaves to work them, many lands weren't replanted. Experiments in cotton, pineapple, and other crops were tried, often ending in disaster after a blight, a drought, hurricane, or a market collapse.

Suddenly the Caribbean was hardly worth fighting over.

After the Treaty of Paris ended the Spanish-American War, Cuba and Puerto Rico were ceded to the United States, which also bought the Danish Virgin Islands to protect the Americas against the Germans in World War I. Even as late as 1983, when Cuba's building of a major landing field on Grenada was halted by American intervention, the strategic value of the lands and harbors of the Caribbean was realized. Today the same coves that sheltered pirates long ago are transfer points for illegal drugs. The French have a saying: the more things change, the more they stay the same.

Stepping Stones of Caribbean History

3000 BC Settlers begin arriving on the island now known as Puerto Rico.

Circa 1100 BC Taino Indians establish a ceremonial center south of Arecibo.

700 BC Shell heaps grow on St. Croix, discarded by shellfish-eating tribes.

1492-1504 Christopher Columbus makes four voyages to the New World. Within 50 years, most Amerindian inhabitants of Puerto Rico have died of disease, hunger, enslavement, and execution.

1493 The Spanish begin settling Puerto Rico.

1496 Columbus' brother Bartolomé Colon founds Santo Domingo; the first written description of the tobacco plant reaches Europe.

1504 Columbus returns from his last voyage; Isabella of Castille dies.

1518 The first slaves are brought to Puerto Rico three years after sugar cane is introduced.

1521 San Juan is founded; its walls will be completed by 1630; Hernando Cortez destroys the Aztec state and claims Mexico.

1523 The first Christian church in the Americas, San Jose Church, is built in Puerto Rico by the Dominican order; the first marine insurance policies are issued in Florence.

1555 Spanish forces defeat and soon annihilate the native population of the Virgin Islands.

1580 Sir Francis Drake returns from a circumnavigation of the globe; Dutch painter Franz Hals is born; coffee is introduced to Italy. In England, the hit tune of the day is *Greensleeves*.

1593 Bermuda is discovered; Shakespeare debuts *The Taming of the Shrew*; Izaak Walton is born. **1595** Britons Sir Francis Drake and Sir John Hawkins take San Juan; Hawkins dies. The Dutch begin to colonize Indonesia; Sir Walter Raleigh reaches a point 300 miles up the Orinoco River in South America.

1596 Sir Francis Drake dies; the first water closets come into use; tomatoes are introduced to England and soon make their way to the New World.

1650 Holland and England reach an accord about their turf in the New World; Harvard College is founded.

1672 Danes settle the Virgin Islands.

1728 James Cook, who would later introduce breadfruit to the Caribbean, is born; Spain stops its 14-month siege of the English at Gibralter.

1732 A rum factory is built at Gallows Bay, St. Croix. Today it is the Hilty House Inn.

1735 A Lutheran church, now known as the Steeple Building, is built in Christiansted.

1738 Fort Christiansvaern is built on St. Croix.

1779 Captain James Cook dies.

1785 A hillside mansion is built overlooking Charlotte Amalie to become, in modern times, L'Hotel Boynes.

1791 Slaves revolt on Santo Domingo, sending shock waves throughout the Caribbean. The first guillotine is set up in Paris; gaslights appear in England.

1796 Napoleon marries Josephine de Beauharnais, who was born in the West Indies; Spain declares war on England.

1797 Spain captures some bronze cannon from the British and, as a final insult, melts them down to cast a statue of Ponce de Leon. It can now be seen on San Jose Plaza in San Juan.

1808 importation of slaves from Africa is outlawed in the United States but the slave trade continues in the Caribbean and in Florida, which is not yet a state.

1834 Britain frees its Caribbean slaves. Abraham Lincoln wins his first election and becomes an assemblyman in Illinois.

1841 The Grand Hotel opens in Charlotte Amalie; English travel agent Thomas Cook books his first trip.

1843 The slave population of Cuba is estimated at 436,000. The first telegraph line is installed between Washington and Baltimore; Wagner's opera *Flying Dutchman* debuts in Dresden.

1844-1930 The Dominican Republic has 56 revolutions.

1848 France frees its Caribbean slaves; serfdom is outlawed in Austria; Wisconsin becomes a state. **1863** Holland frees its Caribbean slaves; the American Civil War rages; construction of the London subway is begun.

1887 Paul Gauguin lives in the French West Indies, while in England the first Sherlock Holmes story is published.

1898 Spain cedes Puerto Rico, the Philippines and Guam to the United States and agrees to free Cuba.

1909 Victor Borge, who would become a resident of St. Croix, is born in Copenhagen.

1911 The University of Puerto Rico is founded at Mayagüez.

1915 Herman Wouk, whose book *Don't Stop the Carnival* remains one of the best yarns about the Virgin Islands, is born in New York City. In 1998, filming of a pilot film "Walking on Sunshine", based loosely on the book's theme, is shot on St. Croix while a musical version of *Don't Stop the Carnival* takes shape in New York.

1916-1917 Kaiser Wilhelm of Germany has his eyes on the Panama Canal. To protect American interests, the United States buys the Virgin Islands from Denmark for $300 an acre, or $25 million. The United States and Cuba declare war on Germany; John F. Kennedy is born.

1919 400 people die when the Mayagüez Theater burns in San Juan.

1929 World markets collapse, bringing increased suffering to the Caribbean; Kodak introduces 16mm film. In Chicago, a gangland hit becomes known as the St. Valentine's Day Massacre.

1945 Singer José Feliciano is born at Lares, Puerto Rico.

1952 Puerto Ricans vote for Commonwealth status with the United States.

1954 five members of Congress are wounded when supporters of Puerto Rican independence shoot randomly from the spectator gallery in the U.S. House of Representatives.

1955 Hurricane Janet kills 500 in the Caribbean.

1962 The University of the Virgin Islands is founded at Charlotte Amalie.

1965 An uprising in the Dominican Republic brings intervention from the United States.

1967 Antigua, Barbuda, Redonda, Anguilla, St. Kitts, Nevis, St. Lucia, St. Vincent, and Dominica form the West Indies Associated States; in Puerto Rico, voters choose to remain associated with the United States.

1973 The Caribbean Common Market, or Caricom, is formed.

1981 Bob Marley, whose reggae music galvanized Jamaica and spread through the Caribbean and around the world, dies.

1983 American and Caribbean troops land on Grenada to restore order after a coup d'etat that followed four years of leftist rule.

1988 The first St. Croix Triathlon is held. The annual event now attracts top athletes from throughout the world.

1989 Hurricane Hugo devastates St. Croix.

1992 Tourism brings $792 million to the U.S. Virgin Islands.

1993 Spanish and English are proclaimed joint official languages in Puerto Rico.

1995 Hurricanes Luis and Marilyn deal a one-two punch to the Virgin Islands and Puerto Rico.

1996 The first Ritz-Carlton opens in the islands at St. Thomas; a second opens in 1997 on Puerto Rico. Puerto Rico produces $31.1 million in portland cement and $15.7 million in commercial fishing.

1997-1998 Recognizing the increasing popularity of the islands for foreigners' weddings, the islands one by one liberalize their marriage rules to allow easier, quicker licensing and documentation. Water Island becomes the fourth U.S. Virgin Island. Improvements begin to its beaches and parks and rumors arise about future development.

1999: Hurricane Lenny hits in late November, weeks after hurricane season was thought to be over, and does substantial damage.

2000: The first casino in the U.S. Virgin Islands opens at St. Croix. In San Juan, the Museum de Arte de Puerto Rico opens.

2001: Princess Cruise Line's *Grand Princess* introduces year-round, grand class, "love boat" cruising to Puerto Rico and the U.S.V.I. out of Fort Lauderdale.

2002: While most cruise ships leave the islands in summer, Holland America responds to steady demand by keeping at least one cruise ship in the Caribbean all year.

Chapter 6

planning your trip

When to Go

Weather doesn't vary much in Puerto Rico and the U. S. V. I. winter and summer, but when it does hit the news, it makes headlines. After your first visit to the islands, where you'll see buildings that have stood for hundreds of years, you'll have a better perspective. Yes, hurricanes can cause horrendous destruction, but they are also so infrequent in any given spot that they are barely worth considering when planning a vacation. Unlike earthquakes, they also give plenty of warning in most cases, giving you the option of leaving the island or moving to a shelter. With modern weather forecasting, most hurricanes take little or no human toll.

We once met the elderly caretaker of a half-ruined mansion on a remote island. Hungry to hear the history of this mysterious place, we pressed for dates but she said gently, "I can't read, you know. " It was obvious that she couldn't relate to the events of the outside world. The best she could do for a time reference was "the storm. " Births, deaths, and the building of the mansion were all before or after The Storm.

Researching it later, we deduced that she was probably talking about the hurricane of 1936. Obviously, it had been decades since a hurricane had touched her life. Although some islands get the occasional one-two punch, as the Virgin Islands got with Luis and Marilyn, this woman's story is more typical. When it's bad, it's bad, but it's so rare in any one family that histories are written around it.

Generally, hurricane season starts June 1 and ends on November 1, a day that on some islands is celebrated as Hurricane Deliverance Day. An exception was Hurricane

Lenny, which took the Caribbean by surprise in late November 1999 and did extensive damage.

Most storms hit in August and September, which are hotter and rainier than November through May. In exchange for the heat and humidity, travelers get a whale of a discount on summer rates—and who cares about the weather when you spend most of the time in the water anyway? Daytime highs at sea level range from the 80s or 90s by day to the low 60s by night, all year. Rarely, a very strong cold front from the United States will reach as far south as the U. S. islands, where the thermometer might plunge as low as 50 degrees for a few hours. We were on St. John during the December "Christmas winds," a time of screaming winds and temperatures that were no lower than the high 50s but were piercingly cold.

Only in the mountains is there substantial variation, and only in Puerto Rico among the American islands are there any mountains high enough to find substantially cooler air. On an 85-degree day on the beach, it can drop 10 degrees as you climb to 1,800 feet. At 3,000 feet it can be downright chilly. Take a light jacket when you visit the American Caribbean in winter or are going high into the hills in summer.

Many islands have minor micro-climates that are unique. For example, Puerto Rico's north coast has such an even rainfall that it has no real "wet" season. The west end of St. Croix has enough rain to create green forests filled with vines and ferns while the east end can be dry as a desert.

During **hurricane season**, June through October, the air is sultrier and breezes less constant in Puerto Rico and the U. S. V. I.. September and October can be obscenely still and sticky, and many restaurants and hotels – especially those that are not air conditioned – close at this time. These months are, however, among the best for scuba diving unless, of course, there's a big storm.

According to Stanley Selengut, president of Maho Bay Camps on St. John, annual sunrise temperatures on the island range from 72 to a high of 78. Afternoon temperatures average from a low of 82 in winter to a high of 88 in August and September. Rainfall averages 1. 6 inches in dry months and as much as 5. 8 inches in the wet season, August through September. Relative humidity averages a 62 in February, the driest month, and 68 July through September, the most humid months.

The Caribbean has become a year-round vacationland. The chief change in summer, aside from quieter winds, is the cost. Rates plunge and resorts add sweeteners such as free greens fees, airport transfers, meals, and much more.

Into each life some rain must fall, but I can't remember a day when we didn't see at least some sunshine. In Puerto Rico and the U. S. V. I. , even the liquid sunshine is warm and sweet.

Booking Your Trip

One of the organizations below might be useful for you:

American Association for Nude Recretaion, 1703 North Main Street, Kissimmee FL 34744, *Tel. 800/TRY-NUDE, Fax 407/933-7577, www.aanr.com.*

International Gay Travel Association, *Tel. 800/448-8550, Tel. 954/776-2626, www.iglta. org, E-mail iglta@iglta. org.* In the U. S. and Canada, this membership organization offers networking and travel packages for homosexuals and Lesbians.

Society for Accessible Travel & Hospitality, 347 Fifth Avenue, Suite 610, New York NY 10016**,** *Tel. 212/447-7284, Fax 725-8253.* www.sath. org. Provides information and aid for travelers who have physical challenges. A website that is a goldmine of information for special-needs travelers, including those who have a handicap-accessible home and want to make a vacation swap with a similarly equipped home, is *www.independentliving. org.*

Travel Companion Exchange, P. O. Box 833, Amityville NY 11701, *Tel. 631/454-0800, www.whytravelalone.com.* Phone Monday-Friday, 9am-5pm, Eastern time. For more than 20 years, this highly respected exchange has been matching singles of all ages with travel companions. A number of other websites for singles travel exist, including *www.singlestravelintl, singlesvacations.com,* and *singlescruise.com.* When choosing a service, note whether it serves people in your age group. Note too that most cruise lines and some resorts also offer solo accommodations or a deal in which you're given a same-sex, non-smoking roommate and each of you pay half the doubles rate. If no match can be made, cruise lines usually give you the cabin at the same rate.

Going Solo

Single supplements are the bane of solo travelers who see what appears to be an attractive rate and then find it is charged per person, based on two people sharing a room or ship cabin. If you want to have that room to yourself you may have to pay 20-100% more than the per-person fee.

In most cases, that's only reasonable. You think of yourself as using only half the towels and only one of the twin beds, but management sees you as occupying a room that must be cleaned, air conditioned, insured, and maintained pretty much the same whether it's occupied by one, two, or three persons.

Tour Packagers

Start with your home-town travel agent and local newspaper travel pages, where you'll find news of Caribbean packages that start at your nearest airport. Often, charters are organized once or twice a year from cities that don't usually have non-stop service to the Caribbean.

Countless packagers in North America and Europe offer Caribbean trips, usually focusing on some theme such as diving or adventure travel, senior travel, or general travel. With the explosion of Internet use for booking travel, resorts offer packages that include airfare and dives, airlines offer packages that include accommodations and a rental car, and almost every travel provider offers some sort of multifaceted deal. It takes far longer to put together your own package by researching dozens of Internet sites, and it's likely your savings will be less.

Note: while it has been big news that travel agencies no longer handle airline bookings, or do so only for a fee because airlines no longer pay travel agent commissions, it is less well known that airline vacation desks *do* pay commissions for packages. If you ask your trusted travel agent to book your Caribbean vacation through an airline's vacation planning service, it's likely you won't be charged an agency fee.

Booking agencies include:

Abercrombie & Kent, Box 305, Oak Brook IL 60303, *Tel. 800/323-7308 or 630/954-2944; www.abercrombiekent.com*. Only the finest and most unique vacations are booked by this exclusive company. Among its Caribbean offerings are voyages aboard the legendary yacht *Sea Cloud*, but each year's schedule is different so call for current brochures.

Air Jamaica, *Tel. 800/ 523-5585, www.airjamaica.com.* Ask for the vacation packages desk.

American Airlines Vacations, *Tel. 800/433-7300*, offers complete vacation packages. Ask for the international tour desk.

BWIA, *Tel. 800/538-2942; packages 877/386-2942; www.bwee.com.* British West Indies Airways offers packages that include airfare, accommodations, and other features.

Continental Airlines Vacations, *Tel. 800/634-5555, www.coolvacations.com*

Delta Vacations, *Tel. 800/221-6666, www.deltavacations.com*

Grand Circle Travel, 347 Congress Street, Boston MA, *Tel. 617/350-*

Vacation Link

Your house or vacation home anywhere in the world could be traded with someone who has a house or vacation villa in Anguilla, the Virgin Islands, Jamaica, St. Martin, Barbados, or the Dominican Republic. A two-year membership in the program costs $295. Call **Vacation Link**, *Tel. 404/843-2779 or 800/750-0797, www.vacationlink.com.*

Other websites that match homeowners who want to make a vacation swap include www.holi-swap.com and homelink.org. Home swaps among seniors can be made through *www.wiredseniors.com.*

7500 or 800/248-3737, is a highly regarded packager of escorted, upscale tours for active senior citizens.

Holland America Line-Westours, 300 Elliott Avenue West, Seattle WA 98119, *Tel. 206/286-3441 or 800/426-0327, www.hollandamerica.com*

US Airways Vacations, Suite 241, 7200 Lake Ellenor Drive, Orlando FL 32809, *Tel. 407/857-8533, 800/455-0123, www.usairwaysvacations.com*

Cancellations

Reservation and cancellation policies in most resorts and hotels in Puerto Rico and the U. S. V. I. are much tighter than in other parts of the world. To confirm a reservation you may have to make a deposit weeks and even months in advance. The most popular accommodations in the most popular weeks are booked a year or more in advance. To get a refund, advance notice of 4-8 weeks may be required and even then you may not get all of your money back.

Before providing a deposit or a credit card number to make confirmed reservations, make sure you understand the hotel's cancellation policies. It's always wise to buy trip cancellation insurance.

Travel Checklist

According to the National Tour Association, the following tips will assure a more carefree vacation:

• Verify that the travel agent or tour company is a member of a professional association such as the National Tour Association (NTA), United States Tour Operators Association (USTOA), or the American Society of Travel Agents (ASTA).
• Make sure the company offers a consumer protection plan.
• Carefully read the company's cancellation and refund policies.
• Use a credit card. If you pay cash, get a receipt. Get everything in writing.
• Verify that the tour company has errors and omissions insurance and protectional liability insurance coverage.
• Ask for a reference from a client with whom you are familiar.
• Avoid high pressure sales with limited time to evaluate the offer.
• Beware of companies sending a courier for a check or requesting a direct bank deposit or certified check.
• Decline offers requiring a property sales presentation.
• Prior to payment, review written details of the trip.
• Request specific hotel and airline names. Terms such as "all major hotels" or "all major airlines" are a warning flag.
• If you are given a toll-free number, insist on getting the local number too. This establishes that the tour company has a central office. Never use 900 numbers.
• To report travel-related fraud, call the **National Fraud Information Center**, *Tel. 800/876-7060,* or the **Federal Trade Commission**, *Tel. 202/326-*

2000, as well as your local and state consumer agencies.

Generally, the lowest single supplements are at all-inclusive resorts where meals, sports, and drinks are included. Rates are quoted for two but hosts realize that you're eating and drinking only for one and they give you a price break–sometimes as much as half the per-person, double occupancy rate. A few resorts and ships, and they will be included in individual listings in this book, have single accommodations with one bunk and no extra charges.

Often the single supplement is waived for special seasons or promotions. Still other resorts guarantee to match you with a same-sex roommate. You take your chances that you'll be able to get along with a stranger but, if a roommate can't be found, you get the room or cabin at the "double occupancy" rate. Many travelers think it's worth the gamble. If you prefer to find your own roommate, you can join a club such as **Travel Companion Exchange**, *Tel. 631/454-0800, www.whytravelalone.com.*

If you're going to share accommodations anyway, think big. The best buys in Caribbean accommodations are not doubles but triples and quads. A typical two-bedroom condo sleeps six, with two in each bedroom and two on a sofabed in the living room. Each twosome pays less than the cost of a double hotel room and you get a full kitchen to boot.

It can be crowded, but some ship cabins also sleep two or more extra people. Or, consider renting an entire villa, chartering a yacht, or even renting an entire island such as Peter Island. Per-person costs go down as numbers go up. Just arrange the deal so that others can't back out at the last minute, leaving you with the entire bill for a five-bedroom mansion or a ten-villa island.

Getting to Puerto Rico & the Virgin Islands
By Air

The airfare nightmare seems to get worse every year. Our personal rule is to call any airline at least three times. Invariably, we get three different stories so we take the best deal. If we are shopping between two or more airlines, we make several calls to each.

Two big changes are occuring in the travel business. Most air lines have eliminate their commissions to travel agents, so you may have to pay a fee now for services that used to be free. A travel agent might be more willing to help, fee free, if you book a large packages that include a cruise or resort plus air fare, but the days are past when a travel agent would spend hours on the telephone to find you the lowest air fares. Try calling the air line to find the best package including a hotel, rental car, meals, airport transfer, spa treatments, and so on. We say it time and again in these pages. Packages are always worth investigating and are almost always the best buys—even better in most cases than you can put together yourself on the Internet.

The second big change is the use of the Internet for self-booking on the air lines either through the line itself or through one of the online discount services. Most airlines offer Internet-only fares, some of them available with advance booking and others at the last minute. They are available only at the airline's website. Some websites, such as www.site59.com also specialize in last-minute bargains. Look too at resorts' and airlines' websites for last-minute package deals.

A few pointers:

Get to the airport two hours early as instructed. Experienced travelers with no check-in luggage used to be able to beat this by an hour or more, but new security measures make it much chancier to shave the time limit. Some airlines will give your ticket away if you don't check in as required and if you are not seated on board within the required limit your luggage will be removed from the plane and your seat sacrificed.

Put new luggage tags on every piece including carry-ons, with the address of your destination in the islands. On the return trip, use tags with your home address. Since 9-11 this is more than protection against lost luggage; it is a security requirement.

Don't buy second-hand tickets or frequent flyer coupons that were issued in someone else's name. Tighter security means a great chance of having your ticket confiscated, leaving you stranded.

Package tours are almost always a better buy than a la carte travel, but before signing up for air add- on, call airlines and compare. If you have frequent flyer points or are a senior citizen, you may do better than add-ons offered by cruise lines or resorts.

U. S. Numbers for Airlines Operating in the Caribbean

Numbers for large carriers may vary in your city. Check your local phone directory or, to get a different toll-free number that applies in your area, *Tel. 800/555-1212.* Calls to Information are not free.

- **AOM**. **French Airlines** *Tel. 800/8 92-9136*
- **Access Air** *Tel. 877/ 462-2237, www.accessair.com*
- **Aer Lingus** *Tel. 800/ 223-6537, www.aerlingus.ie*
- **Aeroejetivo**, *Tel. 800/ 735-5396*
- **Aeroflot**, *Tel. 800/ 736-4192, www.aeroflot.com*
- **Aerolineas Argentinas**, *Tel. 800/ 333-0276, www.aerolineas.com*
- **Aeromexico**, *Tel. 800/ 237-6639, www.aeromexico.com*
- **Air ALM** *Tel. 800/ 327-7230, www.airalm.com*
- **Air Aruba**, *Tel. 800/ 882-7822, www.airaruba.com*
- **Air Canada** *Tel. 800/ 800/630-3299, www.aircanada.ca*
- **Air France** *Tel. 800/ 237-2747, www.airfrance.com*
- **Air Jamaica** *Tel. 800/ 523-3515, www.airjamaica.com*
- **Air Sunshine** *Tel. 800/ 327-8900*

- **AirTran Airways** *Tel. 800/ AIR-TRAN,www.airtran.com*
- **American Airlines/American Eagle** *Tel. 800/ 433-7300, www.americanairlines.com*
- **Atlantic Airlines**, *Tel. 800/ 879-0000, www.atlanticairlines.com*
- **Avianca**, *Tel. 800/ 284-2622,www.avianca.com*
- **Bahamas Air** *Tel. 800/ 222-4262*
- **British Airways** *Tel. 800/ 247-9297, www.britishairways.com*
- **BWIA International**, *Tel. 800/ 538-2942, www.bwia.com*
- **Cayman Airways**, *Tel. 800/ 441-3003, www.caymanairways.com*
- **Chalk's Ocean Airways** *Tel. 800/ 4-CHALKS, www.chalksairways.com*
- **comair**, *Tel. 800/ 354-9822, www.compair.com*
- **Condor** *Tel. 800/ 524-6975, www.condorair.com*
- **Continental Airlines** *Tel. 800/ 525-0280, www.continental.com*
- **Copa Airlines**, *Tel. 800/ 359-2672, www.copaairlines.com*
- **Delta Air Lines**, *Tel. 800/ 221-1212, www.delta.com*
- **Gulf Air**, *Tel. 800/ 433-7300, www.gulfair.com*
- **Gulfstream International Airlines**, *Tel. 800/ 992-8532, www.gulfstreamairlines.com*
- **Horizon Air**, *Tel. 800/ 547-9308*
- **Island Air**, *Tel. 800/ 323-3345, www.islandair.com*
- **JetBlueAirways**, *Tel. 800/ 538-2583*
- **KLM Airlines**, *Tel. 800/ 374-7747, www.klm.com*
- **Lacsa Costa Rica Airlines**, *Tel. 800/ 735-5526, www.lacsa.com*
- **Martainair Holland**, *Tel. 800/ 627-8462*
- **Mustique air** *Tel. 800/ 526-4789*
- **Northwest Airlines**, *Tel. 800/ 225-2525, www.northwestairlines.com*
- **Pan Am**, *Tel. 800/ 359-7262, www.panamairlines.com*
- **St. Vincent Grenadines Air**, *Tel. 784-456-5610, www.svgair.com*
- **Southeast Airlines**, *Tel. 800/ 222-1201, www.southeastairlines.com*
- **Southwest Airlines** *Tel. 800/ 435-9792, www.southwest airlines.com*
- **Spirit Airlines**, *Tel. 800/ 772-7117, www.spiritairlines.com*
- **Suriname Airways** *Tel. 800/ 327-6864*
- **TACA Airlines** *Tel. 800/ 535-8780, www.taca.com*
- **TWA**, *Tel. 800/ 221-2000, www.twa.com*
- **United Airlines**, *Tel. 800-241-6522, www.ual.com*
- **Vieques Air Link**, *Tel. 340/775-0183*
- **Winair** *Tel. 340/775-0183*

See also individual sections for lists of airlines that serve Puerto Rico, St. Thomas, St. Croix, and the B. V. I. . Watch your local newspapers travel pages for news of charter trips from your area to one of the islands. They may be offered seasonally or only once or twice a year, but can be an economical, easy way to get to the islands from your home town.

Travel Insurance

Travel insurance plans are always recommended. What if you get sick and have already paid for an expensive cruise? What if your luggage is lost? What if you are injured and have to be air-lifted home from a remote cay? It's usually best to get trip cancellation and lost luggage insurance from your travel agency, packager, or cruise line. As with most travel purchases, there is no substitute for doing your homework.

First, know what coverage you already have through existing policies (homeowner, personal liability, and collision damage waiver). Confirm that this coverage applies in the islands, not just in your home country. (Coverage may also be different in the BVI from that in the U. S. V. I. or Puerto Rico.

Second, know what protection is automatically extended to you by the airline, resort, travel agency, or resort and what is required to be bought from the company that rents you the villa, car, or boat.

Last, look into several policies to see what features make sense for you. If you travel often, year-round coverage is a better buy. Most travel policies bought through airlines or travel agents are for trips of a few days or weeks. Policies range from a simple refund of your deposit in a medical emergency to such premium coverages such as the Love Boat Care Gold policy from Princess Cruises, which allows credit if you cancel even for a non-emergency reason. Available as add-ons to this policy are higher limits for lost baggage and medical coverage.

Medical insurance coverage is available from:

AirEvac International, 28193 Skywest Drive, Hayward CA 94541, *Tel. 510/293-5968 or 800/854-2569.*

Health Care Abroad, 107 West Federal Street, Middleburg VA 22118.

International Association for Medical Assistance to Travelers, 417 Center Street, Lewiston NY 14902, or 40 Regal Road, Guelph, Ontario, Canada N1K 1B5, provides its members a list of English-speaking doctors in other countries.

International SOS Assistance, Box 11568, Philadelphia PA 19116, *Tel. 215/244-1500 or 800/523-8930.*

International Medical Assistance, *Tel. 800/679-2020, Fax 510/293-0458*

Medic Alert, *Tel. 800/825-3785,* provides body-worn identification that reveals to health care workers your allergies or chronic health problem even if you can't speak for yourself. Also offered is a booklet "Hot Weather Survival Guide."

Near, Inc. , Box 1339, Calumet City IL 60409, *Tel. 708/868-6700 or 800/654-6700.*

World Access, Inc. , 6600 West Broad Street, Richmond VA 23236, *Tel. 804/673-1522 or 800/482-0016.*

MedJet, Box 610629, Birmingham AL 35261. *Tel. 800/963-3538 or 205/595-6626, www.mednetassistance.com*. This worldwide company offers emergency consultation and emergency evacuation. While some insurers offer only evacuation to an "adequate" facility, this company flies victims to their home hospital. Coverage is $195 or $295 per family for a year's coverage. If you're between the ages of 75 and 81, ask about the Diamond Plan.

Wallack & Co., 107 West Federal Street, Middleburg VA 20118, *Tel. 800/237-6615*. This company offers long- and short-term insurance for travel in and outside the United States and for U. S. travel by foreign nationals. Included are medical evacuation, a 24-hour emergency service that can be accessed toll-free or collect anywhere in the world, and repatriation of remains.

Passports & Visas

Puerto Rico and the Virgin Islands do not require U. S. citizens to have a passport, but a passport is one of the most powerful travel documents you can have and we recommend getting one. To get back into the mainland, you need a copy of a birth certificate, green card, naturalization papers, or an expired passport not more than five years old, plus a government-issued photo ID such as a driver's license. A driver's license alone won't do. Rules for Canadians are the same as for U. S. citizens but Britons need passports for Puerto Rico and the U.S.V.I.

Customs

Things have changed a lot since the days when some islands didn't even permit travelers to bring portable radios with them. You can bring in almost anything except drugs, which are dealt with severely. Leaving Puerto Rico and the U. S. V. I., you pre-clear on that end by going through a brief, easy customs line. You're allowed to bring back purchases worth up to $1,200—twice the allowance in the other Caribbean islands, and up to six bottles of good Virgin Islands or Puerto Rican rum.

Getting Around Puerto Rico & the Virgin Islands

Aviation has replaced the old mail boat as the means of getting around the islands, but ferries are still an affordable way to go and sometimes the only choice. Hundreds of islands and cays in the U. S. islands and B. V. I. can be reached only by private boat, scheduled ferry, or water taxi. If you're flying all the way, the most economical, reliable way to get to a remote destination is to book your ongoing flight with your primary carrier, which will do its best to arrange the most convenient times and connections.

Packages that include airfare, accommodations, and inter-island connections or side trips can be arranged through **American Airlines Vacations**, *Tel. 800/321-2121*; **British West Indian Airways (BWIA)**

> ## Rental Car Alert
> If you are younger than 25 or older than age 65, check age limits before counting on renting a car. Some car rental agencies have minimum or maximum age limits.

Vacations, Tel. 800/247-9297; **Delta's Dream Vacations**, Tel. 800/872-7786; **TWA Getaways**, Tel. 800/GETAWAY; and **United Airlines Vacations**, Tel. 800/328-6877. **LIAT**, Tel. 246/495-1187, offers multi- island tickets. See individual chapters for information on getting between islands by ferry or air.

Cruising the Caribbean

No waters on the planet are more inviting than the clear, cradling seas that surround the islands. Choose among dozens of ways to get out on these waters: liveaboard dive boats, bareboating (you're the driver), crewed charter yachts (with captain only, captain and cook, or captain, cook, and crew), and leviathan "love boats" sailed by almost every major cruise line in the world.

Cruise ships are best booked through travel agents, especially cruise-only agencies. They're found in every major city, so check your Yellow Pages. A time-proven travel agency that books only cruises is **Cruises, Inc.**, 5000 Campuswood Drive, East Syracuse NY 13057, Tel. 800/854-0500 or 315/463-9695. The company is always abreast of the latest bargains, especially for early or last-minute booking. **Cruise Planners**, Tel. 888/820-9197, are also cruise specialists who can offer exciting deals. An excellent guide to small and specialty cruise ships is www.smallshipcruises.com.

Some cruises originate in St. Thomas or San Juan; others sail from mainland ports to Puerto Rico and/or the Virgin Islands. Among ships or lines that call at one or more islands are:

Carnival Cruise Lines, Tel. 800/327-7373, has several ships that sail the Caribbean out of San Juan, Miami, and Fort Lauderdale.

Costa Cruises offers seven-night luxury Caribbean cruises December through April. Ports of call include San Juan, St. Thomas, Nassau, Key West, Cozumel, Ocho Rios, and Grand Cayman. Tel. 800/GO-COSTA.

Crystal Cruises, Tel. 800/446-6620, is a luxury line offering cruises with the finest service.

Cunard's Sea Goddess 1, carrying only 116 pampered guests, offers occasional sails to the Virgin Islands. Tel. 800/5-CUNARD. One of the most luxurious ships in the world, Sea Goddess offers round-the-clock complimentary caviar and champagne in an atmosphere of an ultra-luxurious resort without canned activities, deck sports, assigned seating nor gratuities. Cunard also sails a variety of other ships in and out of the Caribbean.

Holland America, *Tel. 800/426-0327,* is one of our favorite cruise lines because of its tipping- optional policy. Indonesian crew are so eager to please you may want to tip sometimes, but it's not like other cruise lines where you're told not just to tip but how much is expected. Enroll the children in Club HAL, which has a pod for ages 5-8, another for ages 9-12, and another for teens ages 13 to 17. They'll have their own playmates, supervisors, and play, joining you for lunch and dinner and for family events such as movies and shore excursions.

Norwegian Cruise Line, *Tel. 800/327-7030,* brings out the Viking in you. Handsome Nordic officers bring spit-and-polish to big, comfortable ships that have all the luxuries as well as superb cuisine that cruising is known for.

Peter Deilmann Ocean and River Cruises roam the world constantly, sometimes bringing its exclusive, small, luxury ships through the U. S. islands. The *MS Deutschland* and the line's other ships sail in Edwardian opulence on itineraries worldwide. The best part, for many travelers, is an international guest list of people from all over the world. For information, *Tel. 800/348-8287, www.deilmann- cruises.com.*

Princess Cruises, *Tel. 800/LOVE-BOAT, www.princesscruises.com,* the line that cruised the original Love Boat, offers seven- and ten-day Caribbean cruises aboard a half dozen luxurious ships. Ports of call include San Juan, St. Thomas, St. Croix, Sint Maarten, Guadeloupe, Dominica, Martinique, St. Lucia, Barbados, Grenada, Caracas, and Aruba.

Royal Caribbean Cruises sail the Caribbean in season in some of the largest, most luxurious cruise ships on the seven seas. *Tel. 800/327-6700 www.royalcaribbean.com.*

Royal Olympic Cruises sail out of San Juan, stop at St. Croix and continue down the islands to Venezuela, arriving back in San Juan 10 or 11 days later. The ship carries guest lecturers, and enriches the experience with discussions and seminars on the area's flora, fauna, and culture. Cruise-only fares start at under $1,000 per person, double occuypancy. Air add-ons and airport-ship transfers are available. *Tel. 800/ 872-6400, www.royalolympic.com.*

Star Clippers (see *Best Places to Stay*) are authentic clipper ships built in modern times, offering the silence of sail and the luxury of a fine yacht or small cruise liner, *Tel. 800/442-0551, www.starclipper.com. .*

Windjammer Barefoot Cruises, *Tel. 305/672-6453,* are barebones on the luxuries but laidback and youthful, with a heavy accent on fun and eco-tourism. Five classic sailing ships, the largest fleet of tall ships in the world, sail to more than 60 ports of call in the West Indies and Yucatan, *www.windjammercruises.com.*

Windstar Cruises, *Tel. 800/258-7245, www.windstarcruises.com,* offer the best of sailing and the best of cruise liner luxury in small ships that really sail (see my *Best Places to Stay* chapter).

Yachts of Seabourn are known for balcony suites and small, ultra-luxury cruises. *Tel. 800/929-9391,* www.seabourn.com.

About Cruise Prices

Cruise ships offer a dozen or more cabin categories with hundreds of dollars difference in cost, but that isn't the end of the story. First, there is the cabin. Usually the largest, lightest, airiest cabins are those on top decks, which means the disadvantage of greater motion in rough seas. Thanks to new stablizers, however, new ships don't have the problems with roll and yaw that were once guaranteed to give you *mal de mer.* In mid-to-best cabins, you get a suite with king-size bed and sitting area and big windows. The most expensive cabins have a a private balcony, mini-bar, personal steward, full-menu room service around the clock, and other perks.

Second is extras, which can add up to $100 or more per day if you have a soft drink or beer with lunch, a couple of cocktails before dinner, a bottle of wine, and drinks in the lounge after dinner. Look closely at that is included and what is extra. Top-of-the-line cruises, those costing the most per day, usually provide unlimited alcohol and soft drinks, trips, shore tours and other extras.

At the bottom end of the rate scale are windowless, inside cabins deep in the hull. Small and furnished with narrow bunk beds, they aren't for the claustrophobic but in rough seas the lowest cabins amidships have the least

Cruising Solo

The best way for a solo traveler to see the Caribbean is aboard ship, but most cruise and charter lines charge a hefty single supplement. You'll save by finding a roommate to share a cabin, each paying half the double occupancy fee.

One of the best ways to find a fellow traveler is through Jens Jurgen's **Travel Companion Exchange**, Box 833, Amityville NY 11701, *Tel. 800/392-1256, 631/454-0880, Fax 454-0170, www.whytravelalone.com.* Your travel agent can also match you up with the occasional singles cruise (make sure it's in the age bracket you want). Senior citizens can also travel solo on singles excursions organized by **Grand Circle Travel**, 347 Congress Street, Boston MA 02210, *Tel. 800/221-2610 or 617/350-7500.*

Caribbean cruises are also organized by **American Singles**, 205 Mark Twain Avenue, San Rafael CA 94903, *Tel. 415/479-3800 or 800/469-0091, Fax 415/507-9832, www.americansingles.com.* You are guaranteed a roommate if you need one to avoid paying the singles supplement.

motion. A good compromise is an outside cabin two or three decks from the top, as close to amidships as possible for the least movement. Incidentally, the most expensive and cheapest cabins sell out first. For either, book as early as possible.

In addition to the basic rate, customs and port charges can add up to $200 per week to the cost of a cruise. Most lines also make it crystal clear that tips are not only expected but should amount to $X per passenger per day for the cabin steward, $Y for waiters, and so on. If this sticks in your craw, sail a tips-optional line such as Holland America or Windstar.

Other extras include optional shore excursions plus tips for drivers and guides, bar drinks including soft drinks and an automatic tip for bar bills, and personal needs such as laundry, gambling, babysitting (children's programs are usually free but individual child care is not), beauty salon and spa services, and much more. It's easy to spend twice as much on a cruise as the cost of your initial fare, so be sure to comparison shop for the best total deal. Ask about packages that include airfare and pre- or past-cruise accommodations and tours. They're almost always a better buy than deals you put together by yourself.

Booking a Charter Boat Cruise

Travel agencies, especially those that specialize in cruises, are the best places to shop the vast and confusing Caribbean cruise market. However, travel agents rarely book charters, which are another market entirely. Your best bet is to get copies of *Yachting, Sail*, and *Cruising World* magazines, where crewed and bareboat charters are advertised. You'll see dozens of ads for owner-operated, crewed charters. Also advertised here are charter brokers who match up travelers with the right ship and crew. If you're a qualified sailor and want a boat all to yourself, look for ads run by large fleets, such as **The Moorings**, which can book your entire vacation including the charter, airfare, pre- and post- charter overnights, and provisioning.

Charters are also found on the Internet. See *www.1800sailaway.com, Tel. 800/sailaway, www.top-yacht.com* or *www.nicholsonyachts.com.* Unless you're an experienced charterer, don't deal directly with a boat owner or owner-crewed charter. In a one-on-one deal, you could arrive to find that the boat is dirty or mechanically suspect. Go through a charter broker who can give you a choice of boats and locales, who has personally seen the boat, and can give you the names of some recent clients. If you're going to spend a week or more alone with crew, personality matches are crucial. Generally, owner-crew are the most eager to please but, even here, there are a few weirdos in the business. If the boat is absentee-owned and managed, crew could range from rude to unqualified. Check it out thoroughly.

Two of the best charter outfits in the business, both with long track records, are **The Moorings**, 19345 U. S. 19 North, Clearwater FL 34624, *Tel.*

800/535-7289, www.themoornings.com; and **Nicholson Yacht Charters**, 78 Bolton Street, Cambridge MA 02140, *Tel. 800/662-6066*, *www.nicholsonyachts.com*. The Moorings has fleets in Tortola, St. Martin, Guadeloupe, Martinique, St. Lucia, and Grenada. Boats are available without crew, with captain only, or with captain and cook. Nicholson's is based in Antigua but has listings throughout the islands. Either outfit can arrange a pre- or post-charter land stay and, because they have multiple home ports, it's sometimes possible to arrange a one-way sail.

Live-Aboard Yachting

Let's sort out the lingo of **chartering**, a verb that means both to hire the yacht and to allow your yacht to be hired. You can charter a live-aboard boat three ways:

Bareboat means with no crew. If you have sufficient credentials as a sailor to satisfy the fleet owners and their insurance company, you and your family or crew may take command and sail away. Navigation, provisioning and cooking, swabbing the decks, sailing, and all other responsibilities are yours.

Captained charters have a captain aboard to take charge of the boat's sailing, navigation, and maintenance. Cleaning and cooking are still your responsibility.

Crewed charters let you play the guest while others do all the chores and sailing. You can still decide on destinations and schedules, pending the captain's approval and safety factors, and the captain will be glad to teach you as much about sailing and piloting as you care to know.

Things to Know Before You Go

• Get recent, firsthand knowledge of the boat and its crew before you book it. Most owner-crews are liveaboards who take great pride in their boats and their hospitality. They charter part of the year to support their own sailing the rest of the year. Corporation-owned boats may or may not have this personal touch.

• If you're bareboating, take the provisioning package, at least for the first day or two. It's far easier than running all over the island to round up a grocery list of staples.

• Most crewed yachts provide all food and drink, and some provide airport transfers, but others do not provide alcohol. On a captained cruise, you will probably be asked to pay for the captain's food as well as your own. Know exactly what is provided for the price you are paying.

• Not all yachts are suitable for very young children, and some skippers do not accept them. Check ahead. Among our friends are many charter couples who tell horror stories about guests who were warned against bringing pets or very small children, but showed up with them anyway knowing that it was too late for the skipper to turn them away. In most cases—

including one instance where a poodle fell overboard and was grabbed by a shark – they wished they had heeded the hosts' advice.

• If possible, get a pre-charter package including a night or two in a hotel before you move aboard, especially if you're bareboating. It's just too much to reach the island, move aboard, stow provisions, get checked out, and set sail all in the same day.

Dive Cruising

Princess Cruises in cooperation with the **Professional Association of Diving Instructors** (PADI) offers a cruise add-on scuba course in which a passenger can become fully certified for $299 plus the cost of a luxury cruise. The program includes an open water dive manual, workbook, dive log book with carrying case, class and video instruction, four supervised dives in the ship's pool, four supervised open water dives in port, and a written exam. Most of the cruise lines listed above offer scuba diving as an extra.

Windstar, for one, has a divemaster on board. You might also find a liveaboard dive charter through ads in diving magazines, through a charter broker, or through scuba websites such as *www.paradiseconnections.com*, *bvicrewedyachts.com* or *charternet.com/diveboats*.

Accommodations

Accommodations in the islands range from some of the world's most palatial hotels to seedy inns, but we've found that even the most humble hostels are usually clean and are furnished with at least the basics. In fact it's rather heartwarming when we see a small inn, struggling to accommodate its guests in the aftermath of a hurricane, doing the best they can with futons and plastic lawn chairs until full refurbishing can be done.

A caveat: bugs are a fact of life in the islands. Hosts battle them constantly, and the sighting of the occasional ant or cockroach shouldn't be taken as poor housekeeping. Indoors, we have rarely found bugs to be a problem even in open-air lodgings that have no glass nor screens in the windows. Many areas are surprisingly mosquito-free. The smart traveler always brings bug repellent just in case, and doesn't leave unwrapped food and crumbs hanging around a hotel room.

Low-budget travelers can usually find a guest house, usually with breakfast laid on. It probably won't have a private bath, or even hot water at all, let alone a telephone, radio, or television. No matter how much you pay for a room, however, don't take it for granted that it will be air conditioned. Many travelers dislike AC even on the hottest days, but it's our opinion that you can always turn if off if you don't want it. Puerto Rico and the Virgin Islands are hot and humid winter and summer. Countless innkeepers have looked us straight in the eye and said that "we really don't need air conditioning here" even though we were all sweating like stokers. A good fan is a must; air conditioning is a plus even if only during the mid-day heat. When in doubt, ask.

After hotels, the most common accommodations are privately-owned homes, condos, apartments, or villas. Many are built by overseas investors – usually American, Canadian, or British – as a tax shelter. They are booked through word of mouth, with happy customers returning year after year, but don't book blindly. Unless the place is professionally managed, you could arrive to find things broken or uncleaned. It's best to get a unit that has full-time, on-site management. Ask too about what is provided. Often, you must bring your own soap, shampoo, hair dryer, and other amenities that you expect to find in a hotel, and maid service may be limited to once a week or no service at all. Rarely, you may be asked to bring your own linens, and sometimes a non-refundable cleaning fee is required.

Many of the best private accommodations are part of a large resort with a restaurant, swimming pool, and other hotel-like features. You may not even know that you're staying in a time share or in a privately-owned villa.

Wheelchair access isn't always good in the Caribbean, but thanks to the Americans With Disabilities Act it is making excellent progress in the U. S. islands. Even in places where there aren't ramps and other aids, however, we have seen young paraplegics in agile chairs go everywhere if they're willing to accept a little help. It's willingly given everywhere – in and out of little airplanes, off and on dive boats, up and down steps, and in and out of hotels that cling to steep hillsides. The same problems faced by persons in wheelchairs also apply to strollers and luggage carts. They just don't work on sand, so don't count on wheels to help with your luggage or to carry the kids. .

As you read these pages, you may be surprised at what constitutes Expensive, Moderate, and Budget in various islands. Among the highest priced are the U. S. and British Virgin Islands. Among the least expensive is Puerto Rico. However, we've given the widest possible choice of accommodations in all price ranges. Live like a prince or a pauper. The sunshine, sand and surf are free.

Rating the Rates

Even though we have listed hotels under Expensive, Moderate, and Budget, it isn't always easy to make the call because all-inclusive resorts cost much more per day but that is the total cost of your vacation except, perhaps for gambling and gift shopping. When comparing rates, consider what you're getting for the price. **Full American Plan** (FAP) means three meals daily; MAP, which means **Modified American Plan**, provides breakfast and dinner. Many resorts offer FAP or MAP for an extra $50 or so per person per day. **European Plan**, or EP, means accommodations only.

The trend at all-inclusives has been to go well beyond FAP and MAP and to also include all meals, drinks, watersports, and entertainment. Many such resorts throw in unlimited bar drinks and wine with meals; others serve wine or beer with meals but charge extra for bar drinks or for premium brands.

To get to the bottom line, add up the cost of eating, drinking, tennis or golf, watersports rentals, scuba tank refills, spa services, airport transfers, tips or service charges, and hotel taxes. Tips and taxes alone can add 15-20% to a hotel tab, and some resorts are still sneaking in energy charges that became popular in some long-ago energy crunch. You may also be billed a per-person, per-day "resort fee" to cover evening turndown, local phone calls, beach chairs or other nonsense.

In an effort to leave happy surprises on the down side, **this book quotes winter rates**. In spring and fall, you might save 20-30% and in summer as much as 50% off high season rates. However, there's a trend in the Caribbean to keep rates higher but to offer more features, such as free greens fees or breakfast, or one free night for every so-many nights booked. The word "package" is solid gold in any season, but especially during the dog days. You may be able to get a week's vacation with all the bells and whistles for the cost of accommodations alone at the height of the season.

Note that the definition of "low-season" can vary widely among islands, and among resorts on the same island. The only way to know for sure is to contact each resort individually. By delaying or advancing your trip just a few days, you may save hundreds of dollars.

Hotel Chains

Chains, alliances and groups that have Caribbean properties that can be booked through toll-free numbers in the U. S. and Canada include:

Best Western International, *Tel. 800/528-1234, www.bestwestern.com*
- **CHARMS (Caribbean Hotel Association Reservations Management Service)**, *Tel. 800/74-CHARMS*
- **Choice International Hotels (Comfort Inns and Suites)**, *Tel. 800/4-CHOICE, www.comfortinn.com*
- **Days Inn**, *Tel. 800/325-2525, www.daysinn.com*
- **Econo Lodge**, *Tel. 800/555-2666, www.hotelchoice.com*
- **Embassy Suites**, *Tel. 800/362-2779, www.embassysuites.com*
- **Forte Hotels**, *Tel. 800/225-5843, www.forte-hotels.com*
- **Four Seasons Resorts**, *Tel. 800/332-3442,www.fourseasons.com*
- **Hilton Hotels**, *800/HILTONS, www.hilton.com*
- **Hyatt Hotels**, *Tel. 800/233-1234,www.hyatt.com*
- **Holiday Inn**, *Tel. 800/HOLIDAY, www.holiday-inn.com*
- **Leading Hotels of the World**, *Tel. 800/223-6800*
- **Marriott Hotels**, *Tel. 800/228-9290, www.marriott.com*
- **Meridien Hotels**, *Tel. 800/225-5843, www.lemeridient.com*
- **Preferred Hotels & Resorts**, *Tel. 800/323-7500*
- **Quality Inn**, *Tel. 800/228-5151, www.qualityinn.com*

- **Radisson Hotels**, *800/333-3333, www.radisson.com*
- **Ramada Inns**, *Tel. 800/2-RAMADA, www.ramada.com*
- **Relais & Chateaux**, *Tel. 800/735-2478, www.relaischateaux. fr*
- **Renaissance Hotels & Resorts** *Tel. HOTELS-1, www.renaissancehotels.com*
- **Ritz-Carlton**, *Tel. 800/241-3333, www.ritzcarlton.com*
- **Sheraton Corporation**, *Tel. 800/325-3535, www.sheraton.com*
- **Small Luxury Hotels of the World**, *Tel. 800/525-4800*
- **Westin Resorts**, *Tel. 800/WESTINS, www.westin.com*
- **Wyndham Hotels**, *Tel. 800/996-3426, www.wyndham.com*

Recommended Reading

Books that are set in the Caribbean or have Caribbean flavor:

!A Cruising Guide to the Caribbean by William T. Stone and Anne M. Hays is published by Sheridan House, 145 Palisade Street, Dobbs Ferry NY 10522, *Tel. 888/743-7425.* The book is invaluable as a guide to cruising the islands by boat, but it also makes fascinating armchair reading before and after any Caribbean visit whether by land, air, or sea. The book covers many of the islands in this guidebook as well as ports along the Latin American coast of the Caribbean. The authors' personal anecdotes call for reading and re-reading over the years.

- *A Small Place* by Jamaica Kincaid
- *Caribbean* by James Michener
- *Caribbean Guide* by Janet Groene, with Gordon Groene
- *Caribbean with Kids* by Paris Permenter and John Bigley.
- *Caribbean Mystery* by Agatha Christie
- *The Comedians* by Graham Greene
- *Church and Des*, a book of short stories by Philip Wylie
- *The Deep* by Peter Benchley
- *Don't Stop the Carnival* by Herman Wouk
- *Far Tortuga* by Peter Matthiessen
- *Golden Rendezvous* by Alistair MacLean
- *Islands in the Stream* by Ernest Hemingway
- *Mosquito Coast* by Paul Theroux
- *Murder on the Atlantic* by Steve Allen.
- *The Oxford Book of Caribbean Short Stories* (Oxford University Press)
- *Wide Sargasso Sea* by Jean Rhys

Specialized guides:
- *Caribbean With Kids* by Paris Permenter and John Bigley (Open Road Publishing, distributed by Simon & Schuster)
- *Caribbean Guide* by Janet Groene, with Gordon Groene (Open Road Publishing, distributed by Simon & Schuster)

- *Caribbean Hideaways* by Ian McKeown (Prentice Hall Travel) covers 100 romantic places for couples.
- *Caribbean Afoot* by M. Timothy O'Keefe (Menasha Ridge Press) is a walking and hiking guide to 29 islands.
- *World Guide to Nude Beaches and Resorts* by Lee Baxandall
- *Cruising Guide to the Leeward Islands* and *Cruising Guide to the Windward Islands* by Chris Doyle (Cruising Guide Publications, Box 1017, Dunedin FL 34697; available through yachting book stores or *Tel. 800/749-8151.*)
- *St. John Feet, Fins, and Four-Wheel Drive* by Pam Griffin (American Paradise Publishing, ISBN 0-9631060-7-4).
- *Yachtsman's Guide to the Virgin Islands and Puerto Rico* (Yachtsman's Guides Publications, Box 281, Atlantic Highlands NJ 07716, *Tel. 800/749-8151, www.floridacruising.com.*

Chapter 7

basic information

Banking

Banks throughout the Caribbean keep abbreviated hours and, on the smallest islands, may be open only one or two days a week. On the plus side, currency exchanges, and sometimes full-service banks, are often open when flights arrive, even at odd hours. Most have Automatic Teller Machines, which are found throughout the region, but, as with anything else in the islands, it's best not to bet the farm on finding a machine where it's supposed to be, and in working order.

Before leaving on your trip, check with your home bank to see if you need a different PIN in the islands. Your home bank may also be able to give you a list of ATM addresses in the island you'll be visiting.

Business Hours

The **siesta** is a time-honored tradition, especially in Puerto Rico, where "only mad dogs and Englishmen go out in the noonday sun."

Stores may be closed through the lunch hour and many museums and other attractions will be closed for as long as two hours in the middle of the day. Shops' hours are also influenced by cruise ship arrivals and departures. When the fleet's in, they open earlier, stay open later, and open on Sundays and holidays when they are usually closed.

Carnival!

Carnival (spelled Carnaval on some islands) in the Caribbean can take place any time of year.

Puerto Rico celebrates most of its carnivals just before Lent, but regional dates vary. Each community celebrates its saint's days for a week or more. In the **Virgin Islands**, Carnival is two days before Ash Wednesday, when it's celebrated with bambooshay , kill t'ing pappy and roas-a-time, all meaning "live it up". There's a carnival queen, prince and princess, calypso singers, street vendors, high hats, horse racing, food fairs, masquerades, parades. mocko jumbies, and enough excess and insanity to last through Lent.

Credit Cards

MasterCard and Visa cards are accepted in almost every tourist shop, hotel, and restaurant in Puerto Rico and the Virgin Islands. Discover has some acceptance, with American Express and Diners Club in a distant fourth place.

Currency

U.S. currency is in use in the British Virgin Islands as well as in the American territories, so there is no worry about currency exchange. However, we recommend carrying a good supply of ones and fives for tips and small purchases at roadside stands and backwoods shops where vendors may not have change. Travelers' checks and credit cards can take care of the big bills in resorts and restaurants. We usually carry travelers checks no larger than $50.

Electricity

Electrical service in the U.S. islands and the British Virgin Islands is American-style 110-volt, 60-cycle. Many hotels have built-in hair dryers.

Emergencies

When you arrive in your hotel, review emergency procedures. They will include the usual things about what to do in case of fire, and may also include hurricane instructions. Power outages are a fact of life, so locate the candle(s) and matches that are usually provided. On some islands it's also wise to draw a pitcher of water to provide a rinse in case the water fails when you're soapy. The 911 system is in use throughout most of Puerto Rico and the U.S.V.I., but check with your hotelier.

Health Concerns

People from northern climes often picture the islands as hurricane-lashed sandspits inhabited mostly by boa constrictors, clouds of mosquitoes, and spiders the size of Siamese cats. The good news is that the U.S. Caribbean and most of the other islands are highly advanced in terms of safe drinking water, the availability of emergency medical care, and food sanitation. See individual chapters for specific warnings.

The Caribbean does have its pests, but its chief danger by far is Ol' Sol, the faithful sunshine that brings most of us here in the first place. Sunglasses are crucial, according to Dr. Wayne J. Riley of Baylor College of Medicine in Houston, "especially in...equatorial sand beaches."

Bring with you a supply of high-SPF sunscreen, preferably a waterproof brand that won't come off with perspiration or swimming. Some of the worst sunburns are suffered by swimmers and snorkelers who don't realize they're getting burned right through the water. If you're especially sensitive to sunburn, bring a lightweight, long-sleeve, long-leg outfit such as pajamas to wear while snorkeling, and wear waterproof sunscreen too.

Don't forget sensitive spots such as a bald head, the nose, and the back of the neck. Our rule is to apply sun block after showering, while still slightly wet. The goo goes on more evenly, dries better, and you don't miss spots, such as under the wristwatch or the top of the feet, that are easy to miss once you're dressed or in your swim suit. "Remember," say the Coppertone folks, "that if your shadow is shorter than you are, you are more likely to sunburn. No shadow? Seek shade!"

Mosquitoes can always be a problem in the tropics, and the World Health Organization now admits that they can't be eradicated. Travelers should bring their own spray-on protection; if you're staying in primitive surroundings, bring your own mosquito netting too. Various designs of drapings for beds or sleeping bags are available from **Magellan's**, Box 5485, Santa Barbara CA 93150, *Tel. 800/962-4943, www.magellans.com*. Request a free catalog. Another superb source of travel clothing and accessories is **TravelSmith**, 60 Leveroni Court, Novato CA 94949, *Tel. 800/950-1600, www.travelsmith.com*.

Many people find "no-see-ums" to be far peskier than mosquitoes. They can fly through screens and are not deterred by all mosquito sprays. They can cause a watery blister that itches for weeks and can leave scars that last for months. Occasionally, visitors have had such severe reactions they had to be hospitalized. Since different repellents work on different body chemistries, take two types in hopes that one of them will work on your skin against no-see-ums. Many people swear by Avon's Skin-So-Soft bath oil, but it doesn't work for everyone. Deep Woods Off gets top marks for most uses on most people. If you have very small children, check with your pediatrician about products that contain DEET.

The same precautions that apply anywhere are also wise in the Caribbean. When in doubt about water, ask. Don't drink water in remote streams and waterfalls; giardia are found throughout the world. Wash or peel fruit before eating it just as you would at home.

Fish poisoning isn't unique to the islands, but one toxin that occurs here is not destroyed by cooking. It's **cigatuera**, sometimes found in fish that feed on reefs. It's rarely a problem in hotels and restaurants but could be a threat if you cook your own catch. Ask locals for guidance before eating barracuda, amberjack, or colorful reef fish.

Cigatuera is a neurotoxin that causes tingling in the mouth, fingers, and toes. Often an initial dose produces only mild symptoms, which get worse with each exposure. So locals, who could be made sicker than a newcomer who is getting cigatuera for the first time, are usually very savvy about what fish to catch and where to catch them.

In years of traipsing through the bush, we've never had an allergic reaction to vegetation. Fortunately we never tangled with the **manchineel tree**, found throughout the Caribbean, which is so poisonous that people have gone temporarily blind just by breathing smoke from a manchineel fire. The trees are not uncommon; ask a local to point one out so you'll always recognize them. Don't touch. Don't even stand under one in the rain. Drips could give you a nasty rash.

As long as you don't taste strange plants or tangle with thorns or cactus, it's likely you won't have severe reactions to plants. You also won't see many snakes in the U.S. Caribbean, thanks to a creature that is even scarier and more slithery. The mongoose was introduced eon ago to kill rats in the sugarcane fields and proved to be a natural control for snakes. Now they've multiplied in the wild until the mongoose is more a pest than snakes ever were. Looking like a cross between a dachshund and an alley cat, it's startling more than harmful. Once you've seen one and realized it's not an oversize rat, you'll know what to expect.

In the water, most dangers look dangerous. Black, spiky sea urchins can stick in your skin and are almost impossible to pull out. Give them a wide berth. Don't swim near enough to touch coral of any kind. Aside from the fact that you could get scraped, it's bad for the coral.

CDC Health Advisories

Get the latest information from the **Centers for Disease Control & Prevention**, *Tel. 888/232-3228, Fax 232-3229, www.cdc.gov*. It's a 24-hour automated line that can provide recorded information, brochures by mail, or information via fax if you have the patience to work your way through all the steps. AIDS and hepatitis are a threat anywhere, but sunburn is the most common health problem in the U.S. Caribbean. Use sunscreen and wear a long-sleeve shirt, even while snorkeling in shallow water.

Postal Service

Mail to the U.S. Caribbean travels with a U.S. zip code and at U.S. rates. If you'll be there for a long time, mail can be forwarded free. UPS and Federal Express are commonly used throughout Puerto Rico and the Virgin Islands.

Religious Services

The most "insider" thing you can do as a visitor in the Caribbean is to attend local worship services. Dress in your best and act responsibly even if you don't know what is going on. We'd suggest sticking to mainstream denominations, which are found on every island, rather than unusual cults and sects that might consider you to be a snoopy intruder. In fact, some of the darker rites (voodoo, obeah, some Mormon sacraments) are not open to outsiders and it would be a gaffe to try to attend.

We can promise you a warm welcome in church, and a new dimension to the friendships you make on the island. Attending a tiny, open air Baptist church on one cay, we found ourselves the subject of a lengthy sermon, the gist of which was a prayerful request for our safety at sea. In another, a translator was provided just for us. We've never felt so loved and honored.

Service charges

Instead of tipping, many hotels and restaurants automatically add 10-20 per cent to bills. Check your bill before leaving additional money under the plate. There's no point in tipping twice.

Taxes

Hotel taxes seem to be soaring in recent years at a pace that is hard for an annual guidebook to keep up with. When asking for rate information, always ask whether taxes and tips are included. If not, be sure you know how much they add because it's not uncommon for tax and service to add another 20-25 per cent to the room rate. Ask to if any other charges apply, such as so-called resort fees, amenities charges, or an energy surcharge.

Tipping

Tips are always welcome, so tip the same as you would at home. Tipping for the taking of photographs hasn't caught on widely here and we're hoping you won't start a trend. Locals either allow you to take their picture or they don't.

Telephones

Hotel phone charges for overseas calls are excessively high in most cases so, even though you can dial anywhere in the world from most hotel rooms, ask the cost first. Pre-paid cards are used almost exclusively in the Caribbean; many pay phones accept nothing else. Before leaving home, check with your long distance carrier to get the access code you'll use. Different codes may be required in Puerto Rico, the Virgin Islands and the B.V.I. Check too with your wireless telephone provider about whether service is available in the islands you'll be visiting.

Note that hotels and pay phones may charge you for connection to an 800 number. Each time you dial your credit card's 800 access code, you incur a charge *even if your party doesn't answer*. As far as the hotel or phone company is concerned, your call was completed with the 800 number answered. Where possible, have calls made from home to you rather than the other way around. We make sure we have the resort's local number (not the toll-free reservations line) and tell family and business contacts that we can be reached in our room at a certain time each day, e.g. just before we leave for breakfast or when we are dressing for dinner. In an emergency, of course, a message can be left any time but this method works well for everday chats.

Time Zone

Most of the Caribbean covered in this book is on **Atlantic Time**, which is the same as **Eastern Daylight Savings Time**. When the East is on Standard Time, the island time is one hour later than New York time.

Troublespots & Sour Notes

Crime varies among islands but it is an increasing problem. In fact, petty crime became so bad in St. Croix, several major cruise lines announced they would not call there for the 2002-3 season. Don't bring unnecessary credit cards or expensive jewelry. Keep close tabs on electronics, laptops, cameras, and other items that are easily lifted and sold. Don't take valuables to the beach, not even to be locked in the trunk of the car.

Firearms are generally verboten in the islands, even if you arrive in your own airplane or boat. Penalties are swift and severe.

Driving in the U.S. and British Virgin Islands is on the left. British style. Unlike in the United Kingdom, where steering wheels are also on the left and serve as a constant reminder to drive on the left, the most cars found in the islands were built for the North American market and have right-hand steering. Add to this the poor roads on most islands, and the absence of good maps and road signs, and you have a heads-up situation. Log some time as a passenger before attempting to solo. Puerto Ricans drive on the right, yanqui-style.

Drowning is one of the leading causes of accidental death for Americans visiting the Caribbean. Unwary tourists get in over their heads, literally, with watersports equipment or on surf-pounded beaches that have no warnings nor lifeguards. Sea conditions can change suddenly. Respect local advice.

Drug laws are strict in the islands, but they catch North American visitors unawares because of the lazy, laidback pace of life. If you carry prescription medications, keep them in the original container labeled with the doctor's name, pharmacy, and contents. In the British Virgin Islands, British law applies.

Shopping can be a waste of money if you buy products that will be confiscated on your return. Don't rely on locals to tell you, or even to know, what items cannot be brought into the United States. They include any products made from sea turtles including cosmetics and turtle shell jewelry, fur from spotted cats, feathers and feather products, birds stuffed or alive, crocodile and cayman leather, and black coral. In fact, it's best to avoid buying any coral either in jewelry and au naturel, according to the U.S. Department of State.

Sour Notes

Every vacation has its grace notes but also its clams, those sour notes that can detract from an otherwise perfect vacation. Under individual chapters we've listed warnings but some generalities apply.

In most of the Caribbean be prepared for such things as:

Arrogant airlines – as more airlines come on the scene, competition is resulting in a kinder, gentler airport scene. Still, Caribbean baggage handlers are some of the roughest in the world. If you travel with a pet, don't ship it as cargo. In any case, most airlines won't accept pets as cargo during the hot months. Take only pets small enough to go as carry-ons.

Bold birds can turn outdoor dining into a swatting war. It's common for greckles or bananaquits to perch at your elbow, waiting for a chance to steal a morsel. And, as soon as you leave the table, they're on your plate. The more they're fed by tourists, the worse things become. At first, you think it's cute but the constant pestering, not to mention the goopy messes, can cure you forever of sharing your table with poultry.

Bloody sports such as cockfights are part of the Latin culture. While opposition exists, they are still legal in Puerto Rico.

Food attitudes are different in the islands, where family loyalty and sharing are a way of life. Taking food is not a crime, so a cook may maneuver cleverly to minimize what you are fed and to maximize the leftovers that she, by common practice, takes home. If you are paying for food that is prepared by someone else in your lodgings or charter boat, take a close look at where your money goes and make sure the menu served is the menu you paid for.

Island time is a way of life in which nothing ever happens at the appointed hour. Except for official schedules such as closing time for government bureaus (which may close early, but never late) most things start many minutes later than the announced time. Nothing steams North Americans more than the feeling that locals are doing this just to get your dander up. It isn't you. It's the culture. Relax and enjoy it.

Weddings

Most islands welcome the increasingly popular trend among visitors to get married in paradise, so they have streamlined the procedure as much as possible. Nevertheless, it's essential to allow plenty of time because all the paper work must be done during government business hours. Each island has its own holidays; government offices usually close earlier than other businesses. Start by rounding up all the paper work that will be required, including copies of any applicable divorce or death papers and parental consent for underage applicants.

Choose a hotel that has a full-time wedding planner, who can work miracles with the paper work as well as ordering flowers, a photographer, music, and the reception. Usually, residence in the islands of two or more business days is required before application can be made. If the wedding is to be performed by a clergyman, it will be helpful if your home clergyman coordinates with the island-based clergyman who will preside. This is especially important in Catholic rites.

Bring your wedding clothes in carry-on baggage or ship them ahead via FedEx. Murphy's Law requires that if luggage is to be lost, it will be the bags with the wedding gown, veil, tux, and all the matching shoes.

Chapter 8

Sports & recreation

The Caribbean has been one of the most sports-mad areas on earth since before European settlement. Ball courts used by the Arawaks and Caribs have been excavated and it's now known that games similar to those played by the Mayans were played here. Archaeologists traced the progress of South American Indians up the Caribbean chain by the ball fields because the game was played with a rubber-like ball made from chicle that could be harvested only on the South American mainland.

Puerto Ricans are passionate baseball players, so North American ball fans will have no shortage of teams to cheer. Golf and tennis came to the islands with Scottish and British settlers. Today's sophisticated golf courses were designed by the biggest names such as Donald Ross, Robert Trent Jones, Jr. and Sr., and Pete Dye. Locals have their own favorite sports, and it's always fun for a visitor to see a spirited local game of soccer, rugby, or cricket. Most islands have large gyms, teams, and coaches for all the Olympic sports. See individual chapters for more coverage of the local sports scene.

Beaches

The best beaches in the U.S. Caribbean and, many of us believe, in the world include **Cane Garden Bay** on Tortola, **Trunk Bay** on St. John, and **Luquillo Beach** in Puerto Rico. When photographers what to shoot the quintessential beach, they often choose **Magens Bay** on St. Thomas. It's a perfect seascape of sand and cerulean waters. **The Baths** on Virgin Gorda are a spectacular spread of sand and cathedral-size boulders. Most of the north shore of St. Croix is a picture postcard beach; so are the beaches at **Hibiscus Beach** Hotel on St. Croix, **Caneel Bay** on St. John, the **Ritz-Carlton** on St. Thomas, and hundreds more too numerous to name. Find your own favorite beach, and keep it secret. We did.

Biking

See individual island listings for names of local bicycle rentals. Mountain biking is a popular sport and bicycling is a way to sightsee in the slow lane. Roads can be narrow and traffic heavy, however, so wear a helmet and take all precautions.

Birding

Birding tours worldwide are offered by **Field Guides Incorporated**, Box 60723, Austin TX, *Tel. 512/327-4953, Fax 327-9231; toll-free 800/728-4953.* Their Caribbean tours focus on Trinidad and Tobago but ask about trips to the U.S. Caribbean.

Boating

There are more ways to get out on the water than can be mentioned here, but of special interest is **Club Nautico** at Villa Marina Yacht Harbor near Fajardo, Puerto Rico, *Tel. 800/628-8426 or 787/860-2400.* A worldwide membership organization, the Club rents powerboats to its members at a highly discounted price. Many travelers join by the year because it means a big savings on boat rentals at home and anywhere travels take them.

Diving & Snorkeling

Even though there is a big difference between the training and equipment needed by scuba divers and mere snorkelers, both require the clearest waters with the furthest visibility. Some of the best dive and snorkel spots include:

Buck Island on **St. Croix** is a national park completely surrounded by waters filled with dive and snorkel sites. **Cane Bay** on St. Croix has spectacular drop-offs favored for wall diving.

The **Wreck of the Rhone** off **Salt Island** in the **Virgin Islands** is one of the most famous, most photographed dives in the Caribbean. Off **Dead Chest Island** in the B.V.I. where Blackbeard is said to have marooned 15 men, a coral reef is electric with color and motion. The Caves on **Norman Island** are an exciting place to snorkel or make a night dive. Only 10 miles from Virgin Gorda, the wreck of the *Chikuzen* lies in 75 feet of water. She was scuttled in 1981 to attract reef fish. Today the wreck is home to giant octopus and rays against the ghostly backdrop of the old ship's rigging. **Trunk Bay**, St. John, has a marked, underwater snorkel trail.

Fitness

For muscle building, slimming, toning, and other specialized workout vacations, try **Spa Finders**, *Tel. 212/924-6800 or 800/ALL-SPAS*. Resort spas are such a rage that the spa you visited last season has probably doubled in size for this season, and the resort that had no spa last year is likely to have just opened one the size of Penn Station. Virtually all resorts either have spas or at least a masseuse on call and the new spas that are coming online offer eye-popping menus of exotic treatments from around the world.

Among the biggest and best spas in the Virgin Islands and Puerto Rico are the Golden Door Spa at the AAA Five-Diamond Wyndham El Conquistador in Puerto Rico and the Journeys Spa at the Wyndham Sugar Bay in St. Thomas.

Golf

Favorite golf resorts in the U.S. Caribbean include:
- **Carambola Golf Club**, St. Croix. *Tel. 340/778-5638*
- **Wyndham El Conquistador Resort & Country Club**, San Juan, Puerto Rico, *Tel. 787/863-1000* or *800/468-5228,* has an18-hole championship golf course.
- **Hyatt Dorado Beach**, Puerto Rico, *Tel. 787/796-1234* or *800/233-1234,* is one of two resorts (the other is the **Hyatt Cerromar Beach**) that offer memorable golf to guests. Between the two resorts, which are side by side, you can play four courses.
- **Palmas del Mar**, near Humacao in Puerto Rico, offers outstanding golf in an outstanding resort setting, *Tel. 787/852-6000* or *800/468-3331.*
- **Westin Rio Mar**, Puerto Rico, *Tel. 800/WESTINS*, has three 18-hole championship golf courses in the shadow of El Yunque rainforest.

Hiking

According to outdoor writer M. Timothy O'Keefe, author of *Caribbean Afoot* (Menasha Ridge Press), one of the ten top hikes in the Caribbean is the entire island of **St. John** in U.S. Virgin Islands. In the national park that covers most of the island, join ranger-led hikes for bird watching, exploring historic ruins, and other explorations.

In the B.V.I., eleven areas are managed by the National Parks Trust. They include the 92-acre **Sage Mountain National Park** with its 1,780-foot peak, the highest point in all the Virgins. **The Baths**, Virgin Gorda is a tourist attraction, but hikers can walk the entire area beyond the crowds. **El Yunque**, Puerto Rico is also touristy, but once you get away from the bus stops there are miles of rainforest trails to explore.

GPS

More and more tourists are relying on **Global Positioning Satellites**, long known to sailors and pilots as a navigation aid and now coming into land use in trucking fleets, auto travel, and even for hiking. GPS receivers, now available for about $200, fit in a shirt pocket. Taking their reading from three or more satellites, they can tell you exactly where you in relation to a known destination, such as your hotel or the place you parked your car at the airport.

Until all maps and guidebooks are geo-coded to give the exact longitude and latitude of every hotel and point of interest, GPS won't replace street addresses. However, once you reach a spot, note your location, and program it into your receiver, you can always ask it how to get back there. It will point the right direction and tell you how far it is as the crow flies. And it's accurate to a matter of meters! If you'll be doing a lot of hiking and exploring, you're ready for GPS.

Horseback Riding

Puerto Rico is especially well known for its paso fino horses. Many other islands also offer riding on mountain trails or beaches. Outfitters are found throughout Puerto Rico and the Virgin Islands.

Kayaking

Sea kayaking is one of the most popular sports throughout the islands, so it's likely that your hotel has kayaks for rent or can arrange a kayak expedition for you. At all-inclusives, non-motorized watersports are usually free.

Sailing

Most beach resorts have Sunfish and other small, non-motorized sailboats for guest use, often at no added cost. Fleets are also available at almost all of the all- inclusive resorts.

The two best places to get a bareboat are **The Moorings**, *Tel. 800/353-7289*, which has a base at Tortola, and **Nicholson Yacht Charters**, *Tel. 800/662-6066*. Although it's based in Antigua, the firm can arrange charters anywhere in the Caribbean. **Steve Colgate's Offshore Sailing School** in Tortola offers sailing instruction for future racers and cruisers, *Tel. 941/454-1700 or 800/221-4326*.

For crewed charters, contact the **Virgin Islands Charterboat League**, *Tel. 340/774-3944 or 800/524-2061*.

Tennis

Virtually every large resort offers tennis, usually at no added cost. See individual chapters for many more choices.

Biras Creek Estate on Virgin Gorda is the perfect hideaway for people who love tennis, sailing, the beach, and nature walks, *Tel. 340/494-3555 or 800/608-9661.*

Sunterra Resort on St. Croix offers tennis on Laykold courts and a pro shop to non-guests as well as to guests. *Tel. 340/778-3800 or 888/503-8760.*

The Wyndham El Conquistador in Puerto Rico has a full-service tennis facility with a tennis pro, pro shop, clubhouse, and Har-Tru courts, *Tel. 787/863-1000 or 800/468-5228.*

Hyatt Dorado Beach, Puerto Rico, *Tel. 787/796-1234 or 800/233-1234* is one of two resorts (the other is the Hyatt Cerromar Beach) that have plenty of tennis courts for day or night play.

Wyndham Sugar Bay Resort, St. Thomas, has a dozen Laykold courts, a stadium tennis court, a tennis pro, and plush resort facilities, *Tel. 340/777-7100 or 800/927-7100.*

Windsurfing

Most beach resorts offer board sailers for guest use and, on good surfing beaches, concessions often offer board rentals. See individual island listings.

shopping

Chapter 9

Thanks to a growing network of international alliances such as NAFTA and the European Union, the words "duty free" are fast losing their magic around the world. Where once the traveler could save smartly in the Caribbean by buying duty-free French perfumes, English porcelain, Irish crystal, and Scottish cashmeres, today's bargains lie only in the fact that you are not paying whatever sales tax or VAT might have applied in your hometown.

For the canny shopper who buys on sale or at discounts, which are rarely seen in Caribbean duty-free shops, the savings can be unimpressive. Add to this the expense of shipping or the hassle of packing and carrying things home and the luster of old-fashioned Caribbean shopping fades. However, it's still possible to buy everything from Wedgewood to Waterford, and American visitors to the U.S. islands can bring back twice as much tax-free merchandise as from the other islands.

If you're shopping for specific items, such as your flatware pattern or a Kosta Boda vase, make note of hometown prices and compare them with what you find in the islands. According to travel shopping expert Suzy Gershman in *Travel Holiday* magazine, big savings in the Caribbean are rare. "In my experience, 10 to 20% discounts are the norm," she says. Often you can do better than that at home during a sale.

You can still shop the U.S. Caribbean for South American amethysts and South African diamonds, but you can also get unique keepsakes that are found only here. For meaningful souvenirs, take a closer look at the works of a growing network of local artists, crafters, writers, chefs, sculptors, wood carvers, potters, ironmongers, goldsmiths, basket makers, photographers, publishers, ceramists, weavers, fabric designers, batik artists, knitters, lace makers and seamstresses.

Locals have learned that it is more profitable to work with locally available products. Tropical flowers are turned into floral perfumes more compelling than any found in Paris. Locally-grown hot peppers end up in fiery sauces that travelers love to take home to try on their friends. Exotic fruits end up in jams and preserves, allowing visitors to introduce seagrape or guava or nutmeg jelly to the folks at home. Local sugar cane ends up not only in time-proven rums but in other alcoholic drinks enhanced by such tropic flavors as coconut, guavaberry, coffee, and spices. Hand-picked mountain coffees from Puerto Rico are world famous. Shop tourist stores for the popular Alta Vista brand, or visit local supermarkets for great buys on robust blends used in local kitchens.

Island-grown spices turn up in liqueurs, cosmetics and soaps, preserves, jerk mixtures, and spice blends for everything from cakes to pot roast. Whole spices and native seashells are strung into necklaces. Local earths are turned into museum-quality pottery pieces. Shards of broken glass are fished from the sea after being tumbled into smooth-edged jewels, and are mounted to make brooches and earrings.

Wood Carvings

The islands of the American Caribbean, especially Puerto Rico, now have North American-style shopping centers with spacious parking lots and all the familiar chain stores. If you're visiting by cruise ship, you'll also find large malls at quays and, in St. Thomas, St. Croix, and Old San Juan, tiny shops crammed together in centuries-old buildings in a merry jumble

Throughout the islands, woodcarvers ply their craft and offer it at prices that are, for the most part, hard to resist. Whether you're a serious collector or a novice, the biggest misstep is in buying a piece that is perfect in context but looks simply silly in your living room back in Manchester or Minneapolis. Many carvings are large, crude, and almost impossible to get into your luggage. They may also be (1) made in China or Africa, (2) made from green wood that will split when you get it back to the dry heat of your home, (3) full of worms – look for tiny holes – or (4) all of the above.

Another thing to check for is balance. If the piece is to be hung up or displayed on a flat surface, try it that way. It may sit or hang quite differently from the way it looks in the carver's hands in the village bazaar. To get a serious sculpture as a serious investment, it's better to pay a little more to buy from a trusted gallery.

On almost every island, local palm fronds, straws, grasses and barks are made into basketry unique to that culture. Each island has its own laces too made from ages-old patterns passed from mother to daughter. Plantation-era antiques are sold in many island shops, and it's also possible to shop for new furniture made by local artisans from native hardwoods.

The more you know about Caribbean cultures, the more fun it is to bring home souvenirs that capture some element of it: carnival masks, dolls in native costume, pottery bearing ancient symbols, and santos, the carved saints so loved by Puerto Ricans. Great varieties of music come out of the Caribbean and now the islands have their own recording studios producing tapes and CDs. Bring home the best in reggae, salsa, quelbe, calypso, and steel drum, performed and recorded in the islands by island artists. And, if you insist on tee shirts, they are being printed in the Caribbean now too.

The Caribbean now has North American-style malls, some of them in special shopping centers built at quays where cruise ship passengers debark. By contrast you can also shop in scores of tiny shops sardined into centuries-old downtown buildings. Throughout the islands, entire new merchant classes have taken root, from the Indians and Pakistanis who operate many of the shops, to ex-patriot painters and sculptors who came to the islands and never left. Some sell from their own galleries; others; works are found in general galleries.

Write the **Superintendent of Documents**, Mail Stop SSOP, Washington DC 20402-9328, for information on the booklets *Tips for Travelers to the Caribbean* and *Know Before You Go*. Ask too about booklets covering other of your interests and concerns such as relocating to the islands, working abroad, travel health, and so on.

The Best Islands for Power Shopping

For Megabucks Shopping: if you're shopping for a really costly jewel, set of china, or watch, keep in mind that you can bring home more than twice as much in duty-free merchandise from the U.S. Virgin Islands than from other islands. From Puerto Rico, you can bring in unlimited merchandise tax free.

For Convenient Malls: the concentration of shops in downtown Charlotte Amalie, St. Thomas, makes for some of the Caribbean's most interesting browsing in old warehouses that have been selling goods for 400 years. Big supermarkets and chain stores are outside the city. Puerto Rico has many well-stocked, modern, American-style malls, or browse boutiques and galleries in Old San Juan. Quayside shopping is also good at St. Thomas and San Juan. St. Croix also has a concentration of good downtown shopping at Christiansted, and supermarkets and discount stores outside the city.

For Native Goods: shop Puerto Rico for art with a Latin flavor and St. Croix for unique Cruzan bracelets. Almost all the islands have local rums and liqueurs, artists, sculptors, crafters, and cooks who produce jams, jellies, preservves and so on.

For Imported Goods: St. Thomas, St. Croix, and San Juan have excellent selections of luxury goods from around the world.

taking the kids

Chapter 10

West Indians love their children, and family is a strong and loving force here. Resorts that don't have children's programs can always find a capable babysitter for you. Those resorts that do cater to families with kids do it with a capital C. At family-friendly places you can expect all the usual features such as a crib, children's pool, children's program, high chairs, and kiddy menu plus oodles of things for kids to do with other kids and with parents.

If your children are old enough to be tempted by drugs, drill into them how thoroughly a vacation can be ruined by one misstep. The islands seem so easygoing and laidback, visitors can be lulled into thinking that anything goes. At best you could all be thrown off the island after payment of a big fine. At worst, a young person could be jailed. We saw a teenager pulled out of line for drug possession just as he was re-boarding a cruise ship. You can bet that his family's vacation was ruined and his immediate future a nightmare. Remember too that in the B.V.I., British laws apply, and laws in the U. S. territories may be different from those in your hometown.

It takes some planning to find the right resort for all children. Even those resorts that cater to children may not have programs for toddlers under the age of three or four, for children who are not potty trained, or for teenagers. Some resorts welcome children only in summer; some have separate sections for families, away from couples and senior citizens who don't want to be disturbed by the patter of little feet. Exclusive **Caneel Bay**, for example, added a children's program after years of childlessness, but family accommodations are well removed from areas designed for couples.

Some children's programs operate all year; others are in session only during school holidays. Some resorts welcome children but don't want them in the dining room after 6:30 or 7pm. Do your homework and you'll have the time of your life.

Keeping Kids Safe

The tropics hold few unique hazards for children. However, if your toddler is at the age when everything goes into its mouth, don't let it get hold of any plants, beads, seeds, sticks, or flowers. Even the beautiful oleander, a common landscaping shrub, can be poisonous when eaten. The manchineel tree, found on many tropical beaches, is so poisonous that rain dripping from its leaves can raise skin blisters.

As long as your child's shots are up to date, the Caribbean holds no special fears. Malaria and other tropical diseases are found only in the more remote areas of the most undeveloped island nations, not in the U.S. Caribbean. Thankfully, rabies is virtually nonexistent here, which is one reason why pet restrictions are so tight. Small dogs and cats in carry-on containers make wonderful travel mates on a trip to the U.S. islands (providing they are allowed at your hotel or resort) but you'll need papers and up-to-date shots.

Mosquito and sandfly bites are a nuisance, easily avoided through the use of bug repellents. Teach children not to touch coral, sea urchins, or pretty jellyfish. They can sting. Wasps, scorpions, and spiders may be seen in the West Indies, just as they are almost everywhere, but aren't worth worrying about unless your child is subject to anaphylactic reactions. In years of tropic travel we have rarely seen them and have never been stung.

The tropics' chief threat is its greatest blessing: the sun. In fact, a tropical tree with red, peeling bark is known by locals as the Tourist Tree. Bring a good supply of a strong waterproof or water resistant sun block as well as light, coverup clothing and a hat with a brim. If the child is old enough to wear sun glasses, bring them too.

A bad burn can occur even on cloudy days. In a white boat on bright sea on a clear day, a burn takes only minutes. Apply sun block before leaving your lodgings, and re-apply it according to manufacturer directions, especially if you're in and out of the water. According to *Travel Holiday* magazine, a sun block with the SPF of 15 blocks 96 per cent of the sun's burning rays and a 30SPF blocks 98.5

Caribbean with Kids

If you're looking for a guide book catering to families, pick up a copy of Open Road's *Caribbean With Kids*, by Paris Permenter & John Bigley. The authors guide you to the best of the family-friendly resorts that are growing throughout the Caribbean, as well as kid-focused activities, sights, travel planning tips and lots more.

per cent. While a 45 SPF blocks less than three percent more than a 15, it lasts about three times as long, says the magazine.

Seasoned island visitors bring light cotton pajamas with long sleeves and trousers to wear while snorkeling. In clear, shallow water, you may not feel the sun's heat but it can give a bad burn even underwater. Bring a big umbrella to shade tender young skin from sun and rain. Socks help protect bare feet from sun when swimming, and they cushion the fit of rented snorkel fins. Adopt the siesta habit, staying out of the sun at mid-day.

Take beach shoes (jellies, reef runners) for the whole family to protect feet against sharp coral, stones, and broken glass on the beach. Most resort beaches are sandy and clean, but even some of the best beaches have rocky patches.

Drink lots of water, avoiding sugary drinks, making sure that babies who can't talk also get frequent drinks. In the Indies' cooling breezes, perspiration is blown away and both adults and children can become dehydrated before anyone realizes it.

Additional Tips

- Don't board the airplane first even though people with children are invited to do so. Why confine restless kids any longer than necessary?
- Ask cabin attendants if any of the bathrooms have changing tables. Usually at least one does.
- Until the children are older, avoid islands that are reached by multiple transfers involving small airplanes, ferries, and other delays. For now, the big bird and direct flights are best. Remember that after your arrival you still have to get to the hotel, often on bad roads and in torrid heat.
- In the Caribbean, you can't count on wheels as you do at home. Strollers and wheeled luggage are no help where you must negotiate stairs, deep sand,

How to Handle a Jellyfish Sting

For jellyfish stings, "Do not rub the wound," says Dr. Wayne J. Riley, director of the Travel Medicine Service at Baylor College of Medicine in Houston. Soak it in salt water, apply baking soda, and remove the animal's tentacles. For a man-o-war, use the same procedure but substitute vinegar for the baking soda. "In treating (these) wounds, do not use fresh water," says Dr. Riley. "The change in salt concentration will increase the toxin release."

Discomfort usually lasts only a few hours but if you have any reason to think a severe reaction is occurring, such as nausea or weakness, get professional help, urges Dr. Riley.

and unpaved roads. Even in the U.S. islands where the Americans with Disabilities Act applies, wheelchair/stroller access is sometimes poor or unavailable. Consider getting a backpack to carry a small child. You'll need your own child safety seat for the airplane(s) and rental cars. Rental agencies may not have them or may offer out-dated models that aren't up to your personal standards.

- Disposable hand wipes are lifesavers, but they're quickly gone. Instead, seal wet wash cloths in zippered plastic bags and use them to clean up sticky hands and faces. Each time you can get to a bathroom, soap and rinse them for the next use.
- Disposable diapers are available in all but the smallest island stores. Pack extra zip-top plastic bags for sealing up nasty diapers until they can be disposed up properly.
- A 36-inch inflatable swimming pool packs in less space than a rain coat, yet it can be blown up with a few puffs to provide hours of splashy fun for a toddler. If your lodgings have no baby pool, take your own.
- Take plenty of medicated baby powder for heat rash and, if the baby is susceptible, a good salve for diaper rash.
- Don't forget a plastic pail and shovel for building sand castles. The pail can serve as a catch-all for carrying small toys.
- Don't bring home seashells unless you know them to be empty and dry. Even an old shell may contain a hermit crab. Sealed in your luggage, the smell is indescribable.

Best Resorts for Children

Resorts that are especially recommended for children include the **Hyatts** that have Camp Hyatt, **Wyndham El Conquistador Resort & Country Club** or the **Westin Rio Mar** in Puerto Rico, the **Caribe Hilton** in San Juan, **Chenay Bay Beach Resort** on St. Croix, and **Sapphire Beach Resort & Marina** on St. Thomas.

When you're choosing a resort, ask questions about the children's program. Is there supervised play in a variety of places, or are the kids just plunked down in front of a video screen to watch old cartoons? What is the ratio of counselors to kids? Is the children's program included in the price or does it cost extra? Are kids fed free or is their lunch and snack added to your room tab? Is there an evening program at least some nights each week, so parents can dine and dance in peace?

The Puerto Rican Advantage

In Puerto Rico, teenagers can learn Latin dances and conversational Spanish. Youngsters can learn to snorkel. Children of all ages can discover nature on their own level. Parents, grandparents, and children romp on beaches and in swimming pools. Children can stay happy in a supervised "camp" where they make crafts, play games, and hear stories. At most hotels, children under age 18 stay free in a room with two paying adults.

CARIBE HILTON, *Tel. 800/HILTONS, U.S. and Canada.*

Camp Coco operates only during school holiday periods, when it is open every day 8am-4pm at a cost of $35 per child daily or $125 weekly. Included are lunch and two snacks. Ages 4-12 have a wide choice of play, contests, field trips, lessons and fun. One activity each day is for the entire family.

CONDADO PLAZA HOTEL & CASINO, *Tel. 800/468-8588.*

Features Camp Taino for children ages five to 12. The $25 fee includes lunch and camp fun from 10 a.m. to 4 p.m. The hotel also offers teenagers a video room, tennis courts, putting greens, and organized activities.

WYNDHAM EL CONQUISTADOR RESORT & COUNTRY CLUB, *Tel. 800/468-5228.*

Offers Camp Coqui for $38 per day including lunch. Age groups of three to nine and nine to 13 go on adventures to the resort's own Palomino Island, take nature hikes, learn crafts, and much more.

EL SAN JUAN HOTEL & CASINO, *Tel. 800/231-3320.*

There's a daily camp for ages five to 12 at a cost of $28 including lunch and gifts such as a disposable camera, tee shirt, and "sand dollars" for use in the game room.

HYATT RESORTS, *Tel. 800/233-1234.*

At Dorado Beach there are bilingual, certified counselors who direct children's activities 9am to 4pm. The daily fee of $40 includes lunch and gifts such as a hat and, after the fourth visit, a Camp Hyatt backpack. Night camp is $28 per child.

WESTIN RIO MAR RESORT & COUNTRY CLUB, *Tel. 800/WESTIN-1.*

Put the kiddies in Camp Iguana, where "kids are kings." The three-room camp center has arts and crafts room, playroom, and a TV room that converts to a sleeping room for late night campers. For older children, the Westin offers sailing, tennis, and golf clinics for beginners through advanced. The price is $35 per day for 9am to 3pm including lunch and snacks. A half-day program from 9am to noon without lunch is $20.

WYNDHAM PALMAS DEL MAR RESORT, *Tel. 800/WYNDHAM.*

They provide a long list of children's groups, activities and discounts depending on the time of year. The Adventure Club plays daily 8:30am to 4:30pm with groupings for children ages four to 13. The rate of $95 weekly, $25 daily, and $15 per half day gets your child lunch, snacks, and a tee shirt.

Chapter 11

ecotourism

Environmental or **ecological tourism** is hot worldwide and Puerto Rico and the Virgin Islands have caught the fever for good reason. These islands have some of the world's most pristine beaches, the most unspoiled waters, the most virgin reefs, and ruins and rainforests that have yet to be fully explored. In few other regions of the earth can you find more a sense of ground-floor discovery and wise leaders want to keep it that way.

Most islands have climbed aboard the ecotourism bandwagon early, and often with such zeal that old-timers caught by surprise if they try to hike alone into the bush or pitch a tent on a remote beach. Gone are the days when you could set up camp or drop anchor just anywhere and spear dinner. All sorts of new laws, permits, and prohibitions apply. Welcome to the new, environmentally-sensitive Caribbean. See individual chapters for the names of hiking guides, dive operators, and nature tours.

Ecotourism

Agencies that can book your trip include:

Backroads, 801 Cedar Street, Berkeley CA 94710, *Tel. 510/527-1555, Fax 527-1444; toll-free 800/GO-ACTIVE* is a group that organizes walking, bicycling, hiking, and multi-sport adventure tours in the Caribbean for a few weeks in November and December. Featured are unspoiled islands known for their scenic beauty.

Ecantos Tours, *Tel. 800/272-7241* or *787/272-6696*, offers trips to Puerto Rico's Mona Island where only 100 visitors are permitted at a time. A camping permit must be obtained, and all food, water and camping gear brought with you. All waste must be packed out. If you want to camp

Mona Island on your own, a permit must be obtained from the Puerto Rico Department of Natural resources, *Tel. 809/724-3724.* Camp fees are $4 nightly for adults and $2 for children.

Texas River Expeditions, Box 583, Terlingua TX 79852, *Tel. 800/839-7238* or *915/371-2633, Fax 915/371-2993, www.texasriver.com.* Ask about family ecotours in U.S. Virgin Islands National Park, St. John. Specialties include 4-wheel drive, birding, sea kayaking, and photo workshops. Expeditions are for five or seven days.

Spa Vacations

With the explosion of interest in spas, healthful living, weight loss, muscle building, and other lifestyle-enhancing vacations has come a mushrooming of spa choices in the Caribbean. Some focus on total pampering with massage and therapy; others specialize in a lifestyle change such as heart attack rehabilitation or weight loss; still others accent a skill such as muscle building or toning.

Your key to finding the right package is **Spa Finders**, 91 Fifth Avenue, New York NY 10003, *Tel. 212/924-6800, Fax 212/924-7420, toll-free 800/ ALL-SPAS.*

Chapter 12

Lucky the Caribbean traveler who gets into local neighborhoods to seek out small restaurants that are frequented by the islanders themselves. Foods here are made by cooks who learned island ways from their parents. Stop at roadside stands, where sanitation standards are god-knows-what, to buy fresh fruit, homemade drinks such as mavi, or an icy jelly nut, sizzling jerk chicken fresh from the fire, fish tea, or goat water. An entirely new language is to be learned here for every island group you visit.

A Caribbean Food Dictionary

Love 'em or hate 'em, the key to discovering different cultures is to try their foods, the more traditional the better. Take every opportunity to try them in restaurants, where they have been prepared by expert hands, and stop in the outback at roadside stands where a local person can tell you how to eat or prepare strange fruits and vegetables.

Here are some words that will help you in your search:

Accra: a fritter known in Jamaica as stamp and go, in Puerto Rico as **bacalaito**, in the French islands as acrat de morue, and in the Dutch islands as cala. The batter is made from ground beans and a meat or fish, usually salt cod.

Annato: a seed used as flavoring and coloring in Latin dishes.

Asopao: a Puerto Rican soupy stew usually made with rice plus chicken, pork or fish.

Bacalao is the Spanish word for salt cod, which persists as an island favorite centuries after refrigeration made it unnecessary to smother fish in salt as a preservative. It's found on many menus under its English or Spanish name.

Bakes: in Trinidad, baking powder biscuits that are fried. They may be served in the U.S. islands as a starch course, usually with fish.

Bananas, which are known as figs on some islands, come in so many shapes, colors, and sizes in the Caribbean that it's fun to try them all. Don't confuse them with plantains, which never soften and sweeten. They are cooked as a starch.

Blaff is named for the sound made when live fish are thrown into a big pot of spiced boiling water.

Boterkoek are Dutch butter cookies.

Boucan: another word for barbecue and the source for the word buccaneer.

Breadfruit: literally a staff of life in some islands, it's a starchy fruit that shows up on almost every dinner plate fried, baked, or boiled. It has little taste of its own.

Calabaza: any of several varieties of squash, usually called pumpkin.

Calas are bean fritters.

Callaloo: the word refers to the green, which could be compared to spinach, and also to a soup made with the greens plus crabmeat. It spelled many different ways, sometimes with a k.

Capsicum: another name for peppers, which are found in huge variety and abundance, from sweet to fiery, in Caribbean kitchens.

Carambola: a very tart citrus often called star fruit because of its shape. It's sliced thinly and used as a garnish, usually in drinks.

Cashew apple: the part of the cashew that produces the nut, this apple-size red fruit may be stewed or made into jelly.

Cassareep is a flavoring ingredient made by reducing grated cassava root.

Cassava, also called manioc, yuca, or mandioca. More familiar to us as tapioca, this starchy root can be poisonous if eaten raw. It's said that many of the native Arawaks and Caribs committed suicide by eating it to avoid being taken and enslaved by the Spanish.

Chayote is a pear-like vegetable that has little taste but adds a nice crispness to a salad. It can also be cooked and buttered like squash. In French restaurants it's called christophene and may be served stuffed. In other islands it's called chocho.

Cherimoya is a sweet, juicy fruit.

Cocido: stew in Spanish speaking areas.

Coconut is a basic staple, served in countless main dishes, drinks, and desserts. If you buy from a roadside stand, let the seller remove the husk and either crack it for eating or hole it for drinking. Coconut water is cool and refreshing but if the nut is too green its water can cause diarrhea in some people. Cold "jelly" nuts are sold along roadsides.

Conch: pronounced conk. Picture the seashell that sounds like the sea when you hold it to your ear. The delicate white meat from this shell is served in fritters, chowder, or "cracked," which means pounded, dipped in cracker crumbs, and fried. In conch salad, it's served raw and marinated in lime juice. It can be compared to breast of chicken. In French restaurants it may be called lambi.

Coo-coo: a buttery cornbread or polenta studded with okra.

Crapaud: a large frog that tastes like chicken.

Dolphin does not refer to Flipper, the bottle-nose dolphin, but to a meaty, iridescent fish known in the Pacific as mahi-mahi and in the Spanish Caribbean as dorado.

Djon djon: small Haitian mushrooms.

Duckanoo, spelled many ways, is a steamed cornmeal pudding served as a sweet.

Dumb Bread: a dense, crusty, non-yeast bread popular in the Virgin Islands. It derives its name from Dum, which refers to an Indian way of baking bread.

Dumplings are a common starch accompaniment for a Caribbean meal. They can be made with flour or cornmeal, with or without leavening, and are cooked in boiling water, broth, or stew. In Jamaica, they're also called fufu or spinners.

Escabeche: Fish and sometimes poultry that is cooked, then pickled. In Jamaica it's called escovitch. Not to be confused with seviche, which is marinated raw fish.

Festival is a fritter made with flour and cornmeal, deep fried, and sold to go with fried fish. It is flavored with vanilla and allspice.

Frio-frio: means cold-cold and refers to a snow cone, a paper cone filled with crushed ice and dosed with a fruit-flavored syrup.

Fungi, also spelled funchi or fungee, is a creamy cornmeal pudding usually served as a starch course..

Genep, spelled many ways but pronounced gah-NIP, is a common dooryard fruit rarely served in restaurants or sold at road stands, but you may be offered some. It has a large seed and a sweet, gluey flesh. Pop it into your mouth and smoosh it around for a while, then spit out the seed.

Goat is as familiar to island tables as lamb is to North American menus. It looks and tastes much the same too. It may be called mutton or goat mutton. In Spanish islands it is called cabrito. **Goat Water** is actually a hearty soup.

Grizzadas are coconut tarts, sold at almost every market and served at every church bazaar.

Groundnuts is the old African name for peanuts, which are used here in main dish recipes.

Guava is a tartly astringent fruit, lumpy in appearance and loaded with Vitamin C. It appears in ice cream, tarts, and other sweets but especially in firm, sweet guava jelly that is served with cheese and crackers as a dessert. Guavaberry is a cranberry-size red or yellow fruit that grows on trees and is used to flavor liqueurs.

Jack fruit: also called jaca or jaquier, it looks like a huge breadfruit and has a terrible smell. Its flesh, however, is sweet and its seeds, like breadfruit seeds, can be roasted like chesnuts.

Johnny cake: a cornbread in the United States, Johnny cake in the islands is made with white flour and may be baked or deep fried. Its name derives from "journey" cake because it's a good travel staple.

Kachoiri is a fritter made with garbanzo flour and green onions.

Land crab: anyone who has encountered one of these sci-fi nightmares on a dark beach immediately discards any romantic notions about making love on moonlit sands. The idea of eating these scavengers is even more repulsive, but in skilled hands they're a succulent sensation. The crabs are captured and put on a diet of clean corn for several days until they lose their gamey taste. Only then are they served in the shell, in chowders, and in other traditional crab recipes.

Langouste: also called langosta or lobster, the spiny lobster provides a chunk of sweet, rich meat in its tail, which is the only part that is eaten.

Loquat: also called Japanese plum in the United States, it's a small, sweet fruit the size of an apricot.

Mamey apple: a colorful favorite on fruit plates, this juicy red fruit is similar to mango.

Mango: a peachy, juicy, very sweet fruit that comes in many shapes, colors, and sizes. Press it with the thumb. When it yields gently, it's ready to peel and eat. Some people are allergic to the skin, so peel it with caution.

Mofongo: a Puerto Rican favorite made from boiled, mashed plantains. They have little taste of their own and are seasoned to the chef's whim.

Old sour: the juice of sour orange trees (you haven't tasted sour until you've tried wild oranges) is salted and allowed to age. It's a popular sauce, shaken over foods much as you'd use vinegar.

Papaya is a sweet, melon-like fruit ranging from deep orange to delicate yellow, often served for breakfast. Papaya, also called pawpaw, lachosa, or fruta bomba, can be peeled, boiled, buttered, and served as a vegetable when it is unripe.

Pasteles: also called ayucas, it's a mixture of meat and some starch such as cornmeal plus raisins, almonds, and other flavorings and then steamed in a plantain leaf.

Patty: pronounced pahtty in Jamaica, and called pastelitis, pastelillos, or pastechi, these are meat pies, perfect for lunch on the go. **Rotis** are somewhat the same. Think of a Cornish pasty, an inexpensive and filling dish.

Peas: could refer to any number of beans, usually dried, such as kidney beans, habichuelas (red kidney beans), gandules (also called pigeon peas, goo

goo, or gunga peas) or frijoles negros (black beans). Some form of peas/beans and rice is a staple dish in most islands. When referring to the familiar green peas that North Americans served steamed, often with carrots or tiny onions, islanders usually say English peas.

Pepper Pot or pepperpot is one dish in Trinidad and another in Jamaica because of the different seasonings favored. In the U.S. islands it is usually a spicy, thick soup.

Picadillo is a Cuban classic that is a favorite in Miami and Key West as well as in Cuba itself. Made with ground beef, it's somewhat like sloppy joe with raisins and sliced, stuffed olives.

Pilau is also called pilaf or pelau, a rice dish that often includes meat, poultry, or fish. It may also be just rice and peas.

Plaintains look like bananas, but don't try to eat them raw. They're cooked as a starch or are thinly sliced, fried in oil, salted, and served as a snack. Boiled in a stew, they have only the faintest banana taste and tend to take on the flavor of whatever they are cooked with.

Rotis are dough wrapped around a mixture of meat and potatoes, often spiced with curry.

Rundown is pickled or salt fish cooked with coconut milk, usually served with boiled bananas.

Sanchoco is a Spanish stew, made differently in each stewpot but basically a blend of meat and vegetables.

Sapodilla have a short season, so be sure to try them if you have a chance. Furry green or brown skin peels away to reveal a sweet pulp that tastes like a very juicy pear. Also called naseberry.

Scotch bonnet is one of the hottest peppers under the sun.

Sea urchin: the spiny menace that you try to avoid when swimming or diving produces delicious, caviar-like eggs. Also called sea eggs or, in the French islands, oursin.

Shaddock: also called pomelo, is a pungent, grapefruit-like fruit named for the Captain Shaddock who first brought seeds to the islands from Polynesia.

Sofrito: a sauce that is central to many Latin dishes. It's made with onions, garlics, spices, tomatoes, peppers, and a little ham.

Sopito: a rich chowder made with fish and coconut milk.

Soursop: a horrible looking fruit with a heavenly taste somewhat like kiwi.

Stamp and go refers to codfish fritters, a Jamaican favorite.

Star apple has a short season and is tricky to harvest, so count yourself lucky if you get a chance to try one. Under its purple flesh is a jelly-like sweetness.

Sweet potato or boniato comes in many colors and may not look at all like the familiar sweet potato eaten in North America. One type of sweet potato is called tannia.

Taro is also called dasheen, tannia, malanga, or elephant's ear. It looks like a baking potato, has a bland taste, and is used as a starch or filler. Taro leaves are also called callaloo or elephant's ears. Fritters made from taro leaves and split-pea flour are known as sahina.

Ugli fruit: sometimes seen now in North American supermarkets, this cross-bred fruit was developed in Jamaica by joining orange, grapefruit, and tangerine. It's ugly to look at, sweet and citrusy to eat. Jamaicans, whose language borrows from Cockney and Irish, pronounce it *whoogly*.

Yam: different botanically from what we call the sweet potato, this enormous tuber has a furry skin and starchy meat that may be white, orange, or red.

Drinks of the Caribbean

A wise mother once cautioned her children never to drink anything with an umbrella in it. Caribbean drinks tend to be sickly sweet and fruity, laced with rum, and capable of delivering a delayed knockout that catches newcomers unaware. At one all-inclusive resort where all drinks are on the house, we asked how they could afford to serve unlimited bar drinks. "It only takes one day," chuckled the manager. "Drinking drops off dramatically after that. If fact, some guests never drink again."

Rum punch, called *planteur* in the French islands, is every bartender's pride, and each has his or her own secret recipe. Most are largely a blend of sugary fruit juices. The more subtle, untouristy punches combine light and dark rum with a little lime juice and ice.

Every islander has a favorite rum, often tied in with loyalty to a local distillery or bottling plant, and they love it when tourists ask for their recommendations. Reputable bottlers put the country of origin on their labels, so you'll soon be able to make a wise choice. **Cruzan** comes from St. Croix, **Westerhall** from Grenada, **Gosling's** from Bermuda, **Bacardi** mostly from Puerto Rico. **Pusser's Rum**, sold in its own bar in Tortola, was the official rum of the Royal Navy. Although some of the cheaper, no-name rums taste like kerosene, it's possible to get a superb rum for less than the cost of the Coke you mix it with.

It's fun to try light rums n drinks where gin or vodka might be used, such as martinis. Fruit-infused rums, such as Bacardi's orange, are also coming into popularity. Medium dark rums are the color of bourbon or scotch and are good in almost any drink. Myers dark rum is in a class by itself – inky, acrid, and the finishing touch in most good rum punches.

Caribbean Drinks

Carib beer comes from St. Kitts and Trinidad.

CSR is a clear, sugar cane-based liquor from St. Kitts and Nevis. Often mistaken for rum, it is really more like vodka with a faint hint of white rum. It's usually mixed with a grapefruit-flavored Caribbean soft drink called Ting.

Guavaberries are harvested in the islands and made into a liqueur best known in St. Maarten.

Mauby or Mavi: made from tree bark, spices, and sugar, this drink is non-alcoholic or may be lightly fermented. It's sold along Puerto Rican roadsides.

Mistress Bliden: a specialty of Little Dix Bay on Virgin Gorda and served only during winter holidays, this potent liqueur is made from prickly pear cactus.

Purple Rain is a blend of vodka, blue Curacao, and fruit juices.

Shrob: more likely to be called shrub in English islands, this is a French island liqueur made from rum and bitter oranges.

Coffees of the Caribbean

The world's new love affair with coffee brings new awareness of the variety, quality, and subtle shadings of the coffees to be tasted in the Caribbean. The best known Caribbean coffee is Jamaica's Blue Mountain coffee but even more rare is the small harvest of Puerto Rican coffee. It is so cherished that it is sent to the Vatican.

Legend says that the first coffee plants, which are native to Yemen and had been introduced into Europe, were sent to Martinique by France's Louis XV in 1723. Of the three plants, two died. Whatever the true story, Jamaica's governor brought seedlings in from Martinique in 1728 and encouraged coffee planting as an alternative to sugar, on which the island economy was totally dependent.

It takes at least five years to get the first cash crop from trees that produce the intensely fragrant arabica bean, which has not only a compelling flavor but only a third the caffeine of the more common *robusta* coffee harvested in South America. Then the beans must be hand picked one at a time, like delicate cherries.

**b
e
s
t

p
l
a
c
e
s

t
o

s
t
a
y**

Chapter 13

These are our picks for the best places to stay in Puerto Rico, the U.S. Virgin Islands, and the British Virgin Islands. Rates are for a double room in high season. Check the destination chapters for further information about these hotels in their island context.

Puerto Rico

RITZ-CARLTON SAN JUAN HOTEL, SPA AND CASINO, *6961 State Road 187, Isla Verde, Carolina PR 00979. Tel. 800/241-3333 or locally (787) 253-1700, Fax 253-0700. Rates are from $509 nightly in holiday season, European Plan, but lower rates and packages are available other times. The hotel also has a club floor with rooms and suites. It's five minutes from the international airport and 15 minutes from Old San Juan. Through the hotel, get airport transfers for $85 for a limousine or $65 for the van each way. Cab fare is $8.*

A bustling business hotel with a ballroom, meeting rooms and a business center, the Ritz is also ideal for the leisure traveler who wants unabashed luxury in rooms lavished with works by local artists. Each guest room has a stocked honor bar, personal safe, marble bath with hair dryer, scale, and telephone, individual heat and air conditioning control, terry robes, three telephones with dual lines and data port, and AM/FM radio with digital clock/alarm. Enjoy the 450-foot beach, a full-service spa, and a city location handy to the airport, financial district, Old San Juan, and shopping at Plaza Las Americas. Nightlife and dining at Condado are ten minutes away. Dine in the Vineyard Room, the hotel's signature restaurant serving

California and continental cuisine or in more informal restaurants indoors and out. Room service answers 24 hours a day.

Swim in the supersize, 7,200-square foot pool, soak in the whirlpools, play tennis on the hotel's courts, and gamble late and luxuriously in the 17,000 square foot Monte Carlo by the Sea Casino. The hotel's 12,000 square foot spa is created by the Sonoma Mission Inn and Spa, featuring life-enhancing Sonomotherapy treatments. Hotel guests have golf privileges at nearby courses. The Fitness Center offers aerobics, exercise equipment and free weights. Three fishing clubs are nearby; horse racing is 20 minutes away. View are of the sea or of El Yunque rainforest.

On the Club floor with its private lounge and personal concierge staff, guests get complimentary continental breakfast, light lunch, afternoon tea, hors d'oeuvres, and a variety of beverages throughout the day and evening. New in 1998, the hotel is surely destined for five-star status with its twice daily maid service, 24-hour room service and valet parking, child care, and much more.

WESTIN RIO MAR BEACH RESORT & COUNTRY CLUB, *6000 Rio Mar Boulevard, Rio Grande PR 00745. Tel. 787/888-6000; U.S. and Canada 800/ 4-RIO-MAR OR 800/WESTIN-1. Rates start at this 600-room start at $395 and range to $3,500 for an ocean villa. The hotel is 19 miles (one hour in most traffic conditions) east of Luis Munoz Marin International Airport, or about $65 by cab. Take Route 3 east to Rio Grande, then left on PR 968.*

This exclusive golf resort is built around an earlier country club development anchored by a Fazio- designed golf course. Two more courses have been added. Sprawling across 481 acres framed by miles of beach on one side and El Yunque National Forest on the other, the property has largely been left *au naturel* with manicured lawns surrounded by swampy lagoons and tangled woodlands bangled with birdlife. Rooms are more cozy than cavernous, filled with comfortable furnishings in Mediterranean moods and colors accented with classic and modern pieces. Balconies look out over the beach or gardens. Even the tiniest balconies have a table and two chairs, just perfect for a breakfast serenaded by coquis.

Rooms have key-lock safe, hair dryer, lighted magnifying mirror, remote control cable television, clock radio, two telephones with voice mail, 24-hour room service, mini-bar with refrigerator, triple sheeting, and other appointments of an outstanding, deluxe hotel.

Choose from two signature restaurants for gourmet fare or enjoy the casual mood of the buffet, the cafe, or the poolside restaurant. For tapas before dinner or cigars and brandy after, visit Bolero with its sensuous basketweave leather furniture. The Lobby Bar is the resort's nerve center, serving continental breakfast each morning, drinks all day, and entertainment nightly.

The casino opens at noon and buzzes until 2am on week nights, 4am on Friday and Saturday. Le Spa is one of the island's most sophisticated, offering a long menu of services and products. Workout facilities feature the latest machines; a daily activities schedule provides group aerobics as well as games and outings.

Put the children into the Kid's Club; let the teens play the video room; shop the 6,000 square feet of retail space; make an appointment in the beauty salon; use the guest laundry if you like. Car rental, a complete tour desk, and savvy concierge services are all in the front lobby.

All the features of a fine resort are here, but it's staff attitude that provides the final flourish in a winning combination of Puerto Rican warmth and Yanqui can-do.

CANDELERO RESORT AT PALMAS DEL MAR, *Kilometer 84.6 on Road #3, Route 906, Humacao; mailing address: Box 2020, Humacoa, Puerto Rico 00792-2020. Tel. 787/852-6000 or U.S. 800/725-6273. A 45-minute drive from the San Juan airport, the resort has 250 rooms and suites. Rates are from $195 nightly for a double room and range to $480 nightly for a three-bedroom villa in high season. Ask about packages.*

Developed in the 1960s by Charles Fraser, known for his ecologically-sensitive developments, the resort is a complete city with branch banks, churches, school, shops, casino, beauty services, restaurants, lounges, and permanent residents living in homes costing $225,000 to $1 million. Once registered, you can charge everything in "town" to your account.

Your domain includes a Gary Player-designed, 18-hole golf course said to have more scenic holes than any other course in the world, and a comprehensive tennis center. Snorkel right off the beach; take a horse from the Equestrian Center and cantor off through the surf. Scuba dive with the resort's own dive masters.

Choose a spacious hotel room with a private balcony or a villa to house the entire family. Furnishings are tropical and bright; accessories are drawn from Puerto Rican folk art. The kids' program gives children, ages 3 to 13, the time of their lives while adults sun, read, or play golf or tennis. Every day finds a new list of planned activities.

Dine in your choice of a dozen restaurants. Use the workout facilities, scuba, go deep-sea fishing, sail, swim in pools galore, bicycle, and enjoy the camaraderie or keep to yourself. The grounds, graced with 3,000 coconut palms, cover 2,750 acres. If you like a big resort with all the bells and whistles and enough to do for weeks without having to traipse all over the island, this is the place.

HOTEL EL CONVENTO, *100 Cristo Street, Old San Juan 00901. Tel. 787/ 723-9020, Fax 787/721-2877, toll-free 800/468-2779, www.elconvento.com. Rates, which include continental breakfast, are from $265 for a room to $1200 for the Gloria Vanderbilt Suite. Ask about the many packages. It's a $6 cab ride from the pier and $16 from the airport.*

You're not just in the heart of history, you are part of history when you stay in a building that was built as a convent more than 400 years ago. Now lavishly restored, it's one of the city's most talked-about showplaces not just for overnighters but for locals who patronize the shops and meet in the smart restaurants such as El Picoteo, famed for its tapas menu, and Blue Agave Tequila Bar & Grill, a Mexican room where you can get superb gazpacho, totopos and mole poblano. An especially popular suite with families is Room 404 with two doubles in the bedroom and a convertible sofa in the living room. It's next to the pool terrace, radiant with great views. If you're coming to San Juan to join a ship, ask about pre- and post-cruise packages.

U.S. Virgin Islands
St. Thomas

RITZ-CARLTON, *699 Great Bay, St. Thomas 00802. Tel. 340/241-3333, Fax 340/775-4444; toll-free 800/241-3333. U.S. and Canada 800/241-3333. Rates start at $400 per room. Packages are available in some seasons. The 148-room, four-suite hotel is 30 minutes from the airport or about $10 per person by taxi. Airport transfer by limousine can be arranged by the hotel, which is found on the island's eastern tip.*

Surely the *ne plus ultra* of St. Thomas resorts and the first Ritz-Carlton in the Caribbean, this one has all the five-star features of other Ritz-Carltons around the globe. From the moment you're welcomed at the portico and ushered across gleaming marble floors to the check-in desk, the coddling from perkily-uniformed staff is complete. Built in the fashion of a grand palazzo, the property rims a fine beach and overlooks a brimming pool with an "infinity" edge that makes you think you're swimming on the horizon.

The main building houses some guest rooms, the lobby, meeting rooms, and The Cafe for fine dining. Additional buildings, preferred for their privacy and nature sightings, cluster around a salt pond nature preserve filled with waterfowl. Even from the farthest building, it's only a brief walk to the main hotel through meticulously groomed grounds and gardens. If you prefer to ride, a driver is only a phone call away. If you'd rather dine in your room, order room service around the clock. It's brought in wicker hampers and set up with starched linens, fresh flowers, shining silver, and Villeroy and Boch tableware.

Everything about the hotel spells quality, from upscale amenities to the waffle weave robes and slippers provided for guest use. Spacious rooms are done in bold royal blue and gold, accented with plaids and colorful prints on the walls. Rooms have hair dryer, iron, mini-bar with refrigerator, telephones in the bath, at bedside, and on the desk, and a private balcony or terrace. Some are roofed and others have a lattice covering, so specify sun or shade when you book the room.

Plan your days around swimming, the beach, sailing excursions aboard the resort's own boat, or the tennis courts. The fitness center offers cardio-vascular and advanced strength equipment, private trainers, and aerobics classes. Scuba, deep sea fishing, golf, picnic sails, and in-room massage can be arranged. The hotel has its own beauty salon, and shops selling designer clothing and accessories. We didn't see neckties, and jackets are not required, but this resort calls for your very best resort wear.

SAPPHIRE BEACH RESORT & MARINA, *Route 6, Smith Bay, St. Thomas 00801. Tel. 340/775-6100 or 800/524-2090. Rates at the 171-unit resort start at $395 for a suite with full kitchen. Rates are plus 8 percent tax, 7 percent resort fee and an energy surcharge of $4 per suite or $6 per villa per day. Suites sleep four; villas sleep up to nine. Ask about packages and meal plans. Children under age 17 sleep free in their parents' accommodations, and children up to age 12 eat free. The resort is 8 miles from the airport, 30 minutes from Charlotte Amalie and five minutes from the Red Hook ferry.*

Check into a spacious suite decorated in cool whites and pastels. Each has a private balcony with ocean view, air conditioning, microwave, coffee maker, full-size refrigerator, satellite television, telephone, ceiling fans, air conditioning, and a living-dining area where the maid leaves fresh flowers daily. The beach is a picture postcard of white sand and turquoise water. In the Kids Klub, activities, crafts and meals keep little ones happy 9 a.m. to 4 p.m. for $20 per child, with a discount for multiple children. Leave kids for the evening, 5:30-10 p.m. for $25 and they'll be fed and entertained.

The resort is 15 minutes from the famous Mahogany Run golf course but, unless you're an ardent golfer, you won't want to leave the resort. It has its own gift shop, marina and dive center where you can connect with scuba lessons or dives, a power yacht for excursions to the most colorful reefs for snorkeling, sea kayaking or deep sea fishing. Use of non-motorized watercraft is free. Play tennis or volleyball. For a small charge, shuttle service into Charlotte Amalie or Red Hook is available one way or round trip. Be at Red Hook in five minutes, hope on the ferry, and spend the day on St. John.

Casual dining is in the PrittyKlip Pavilion and Bar or dressier in the Seagrape Restaurant. Room service is available during breakfast and dinner hours. The bar, where live entertainers play most nights, is open until 2am. A Budget Rent-a-Car desk is in the lobby; a coin-op laundry is available for guest use.

St. John

HARMONY RESORT at *Maho Bay, mailing address 17 East 73rd Street, New York NY 10021. Tel. 800/392-9004 or 212/472-9453, Fax 861-6210. Locally, Tel. 340/693-5855. Doubles are $95-$150 nightly plus $15 each additional person. A shuttle from the ferry costs about $5 per person.*

This is the place to rough it next to nature, without air conditioning, room service, or any other luxuries. This resort was once chosen the World's Most Environmentally Friendly Hotel by 18,000 travel agents. In second place was a hotel in Bali. A step up from the same management's Maho Bay Campground, these tent-cottages are made from recycled materials and are sparsely but adequately furnished. Solar panels provide energy to heat bath water and operate the microwave. The design scoops in any trade winds, but on a calm day we wished for some high-voltage air conditioning. Furnished are kitchen gear and all linens. Your camp will have its own bathroom and deck. Use the same transportation, restaurant, cultural events and water sports as Maho Bay Campground.

While St. John has more luxurious resorts, this one is chosen for our Best Places listing because it's unique.

St. Croix

BUCCANEER HOTEL, *Gallows Bay, mailing address P.O. Box 25200, Christiansted 00824. Tel. 340/773-2100 or 800/255-3881, www.thebuccaneer.com. Rates in this 150-unit resort start at $280. Take East End Road east out of Christiansted for two miles. The resort is a $14 taxi ride from the airport.*

A historic treasure founded in 1653 by a French settler, this charming property is on ground that was once planted to sugar. Its lobby is in the remains of an old mill. The resort has been in the same family since 1947. Our deluxe beachfront room was as big as a ballroom, with cavernous closets, a big bathroom with double sinks, refrigerator and ceiling fans as well as air conditioning and remote control cable television. Butter yellow and Danish blue fabrics complement the blue and white tiles, vaulted pine ceiling, mellow rattan furniture, and mahogany woodwork. The window seat overlooking the beach is a bookworm's delight.

Swim in the pool, which has its own bar, or choose one of three surrounding beaches. Play the 18-hole golf course or eight tennis courts, choose from four restaurants, use the fitness center, or make an appointment in the spa. In addition to the beachfront units, other rooms, suites and a guesthouse are high on the hill with soaring views. Take a hike, or call for the shuttles that are always available. This resort is listed in our Best Places because of its country setting. The next listing is chosed for its downtown location.

HOTEL CARAVELLE, *44 Queen Cross Street, Christiansted, 00820. Tel. 800/524-0410, www.hotelcaravelle.com. Rates at this AAA Three-Diamond Hotel are from $110. It's in the heart of downtown on the water, a $10 ride from the airport for one or two persons.*

A European-style boutique hotel has been transplanted in the tropics, blending the sunny airiness of a Cruzan resort with modern amenities. It has been generations since the Virgin Islands were Danish, but Danes continue to come to this user-friendly hotel. Rooms, many of them overlooking the harbor, are air conditioned and have mini-refrigerator and cable television. There's a freshwater pool, gift shop, and free parking— a plus if you have a car because it's almost impossible to find parking anywhere in Christiansted.

The staff love innkeeping, and it shows. This hotel has one of the highest rate of repeat guests in the islands. The restaurant here is a St. Croix favorite for locals and visitors alike, and the hotel is also within walking distance of dozens of great eateries, clubs, bars, and shops. Ask about dive packages year round and family environmental study programs in summer.

British Virgin Islands

BITTER END YACHT CLUB & RESORT, *Box 46, Virgin Gorda. Tel. 284/ 494-2746, U.S. 312/944-5855 or 800/872-2392, www.beyc.com. Rates start at $450 including all meals. Airport transfers, which are included, involve a taxi ride then a 10-minute boat ride.*

Many Caribbean resorts are as yachty as they are landlubberly, but this one is especially salty because you can sleep on a boat or in one of the rooms for about the same price. You'll still get maid service, meals in the Yacht Club and, if you want to anchor off for a night, the boat will be provisioned with enough food to tide you over. Sea and sails are part of the scene everywhere, whether you're overlooking them from your hilltop villa, trading tall tales with sailors in the bar, or actually sailing one of the big fleet of Sunfish, Lasers, JY15s, Rhodes 19s and J-24s. Introduction to Sailing is a popular course for resort guests.

Zone out on your private veranda overlooking the verdant grounds, or plug into a carnival of good times: island excursions to The Baths and Anegada, snorkeling in reef-sheltered coves, swimming at the pool or one of the resort's three beaches, or joining a group to study marine science. A dive operator based at the Club can do a complete dive package from beginner to advanced, Ginger Island to the wreck of the *Rhone*. Dine in the Clubhouse Steak and Seafood Grille or the English Carvery, then dance under the stars at Almond Walk. Provision at The Emporium, which has staples as well as baked goods and takeout dishes.

LITTLE DIX BAY, *P.O. Box 70, Virgin Gorda, British Virgin Islands. U.S. mailing address, P.O. Box 720, Cruz Bay, St. John, VI 00831. Tel. 284/495-5555, Fax 495-5661, U.S. and Canada 800/928-3000, www.littledixbay.com. Rates start at $375 and range to $1,100 for a one-bedroom suite. Children age 16 and under sleep free and ages 5-12 get the meal plan at half price. MAP (breakfast and dinner) is $90 per person extra or pay $110 per person for three meals daily. Ask about packages and escorted airport transfers.*

Lying serenely behind a barrier reef, Little Dix Bay has a half-mile crescent of beach surrounded by 500 acres of forest, seagrape, tamarind, and palms. Founded in 1964 by the Rockefellers it is now a grand resort with three employees for every guest, assuring a level of pampering that's impressive even in the service-savvy Caribbean.

From the moment you are met at the airport or ferry dock, you're in a world of seabreeze, sun, and luxury. Airy, spacious rooms are furnished with wicker and bamboo, soft pastels and brightly contrasting tropic bouquets. Most rooms are air conditioned but not all are, so specify air if you want it. All have telephones, balconies or terraces. Hike nearby **Gorda National Park** or the resort's own nature trails. Walking sticks are provided in each room, and they come in handy on Cow Hill, the Savannah Trail, or the Pond Bay Trail.

Sightsee by boat or Jeep, play tennis, or enjoy a full menu of watersports. The resort has its own 120-slip marina where boats are waiting to take you sailing, deep sea fishing, or sunset cruising. Ferries run regularly to a sister resort, Caneel Bay on St. John, where you can eat if you're on the Little Dix meal plan. Dining here is in the Pavilion, in the Sugar Mill with its tropical bistro look and wood oven-baked pizzas, or the nautically themed Beach Grill featuring seafood and sandwiches. After dinner, dance to live music on the Pavilion Terrace and walk home along paths lit by tiki torches and scented with frangipani. In season, there's a children's program at additional cost.

Best Cruises

Cruise ships can't be ignored as among the Caribbean's Best Places to Stay. These have luxurious cabins, memorable dining, attentive service staff, and all the romance of the golden age of sea travel.

STAR CLIPPER, *4101 Salzedo Avenue, Coral Gables FL 33146, Tel. 305/442-0550 or 800/442-0551, Fax 305/442-1611, www.starclippers.com. Cruise for about $1,400 per person per week.*

"The noblest of all sailing vessels...these were our Gothic cathedrals," wrote historian Samuel Eliot Morison in describing the great clipper ships that once danced around the globe at speeds never before seen at sea. It was thought that their kind would never be seen again. Now clipper ships have entered a luxurious new era with two four-masted barkentines, *Star Clipper* and *Star Flyer*. Classic clippers in the tradition of the majestic clippers of old, the ships are designed from the keel up to house pampered passengers in enormous hulls once destined to hold cargoes of tea and crates of Chinese porcelain.

World trade was transformed with the introduction of spritely, seakindly clipper ships. Their names made history: *Cutty Sark, Flying Cloud, Sea Witch.* Then suddenly, it was over. In 1869, the Suez Canal opened. Steamships replaced sail. A railroad crossed the United States. The splendor of sail was silenced. Until now.

The two new clippers bring all the romance of sail into a twentieth century cruise scene where haute cuisine, air conditioning, spacious cabins, and private baths are expected by even the saltiest of sailors. These ships have it all. Don't confuse them with the many old, wooden windjammers that offer no-frills cabins and shared baths. Swedish yachtsman Mikael Krafft has built authentic, all new clipper ships in a gamble that affluent travelers will pay "love boat" prices to live in luxury while tacking, heeling, luffing, and furling.

Don't worry about jargon. You don't have to know a spanker from a mizzen staysail to bask in all the breezy good fun of a Star Clipper cruise. However, the more you know about sailing, the more you'll be surprised and pleased. All the traditional touches abound: wooden belaying pins, bronze winches, teak decks, miles of brightwork, shrouds surrounded by baggywrinkle, and neat coils of line. Yet the ships also sport high-tech touches: roller furling, self-tailing winches, sparkling white sails in tough new synthetic sailcloths, satellite navigation, and a television in every cabin. Star Clipper has a modest diesel engine, but make no mistake. This sister sails.

Itineraries vary with each trip, but generally sail from St. Maarten or Barbados, calling at many islands including the British Virgins. *Star Clipper, Star Flyer* and the new *Royal Clipper* roam the world, also offering itineraries in Europe and the Pacific Rim. Once you become a part of the Star Clipper family in the Caribbean, you'll want to try them all.

An international staff serves an international passenger list. Half the 200-odd guests aboard a typical clipper cruise are from Europe; many others are yachtsmen; a few are landlubbers in search of an offbeat vacation. Like cruise ships, *Star Clipper* and *Star Flyer* have a couple of swimming pools and plenty of deck chairs. Like charter boats, they carry a full watersports inventory of board sailers, SCUBA and snorkel gear, and inflatable runabouts. Sports operations are directed by professional, multilingual staff. Unlike the ocean-going leviathans, the clippers are able to nose into shallow bays and tie up at smaller docks.

There's a cozy library with fireplace, but that's about the end of the entertainment menu. Passengers are invited to heave halyards, spin the big mahogany wheel, or check charts if they like. A versatile singer-instrumentalist plays for nightly Happy Hour, and on Amateur Night talented crew members and willing passengers put on a show. There's even gambling aboard, if you don't mind betting on crab races. This old pirate ship tradition has been revived aboard the clippers. Aside from that, nightlife consists of stargazing on deck before retiring to a bunk that jostles gently with the seas, heeled to port or starboard as the winds decree.

WINDSTAR CRUISES, *300 Elliott Avenue West, Seattle WA 98119. Tel. 206/281-3535, 800/258-7275 in U.S., 800/626-9900 in Canada; www.windstarcruises.com. Book through your travel agent. Week-long Caribbean cruises start at under $2,000 per person per week including port charges. Ask about early booking discounts.*

No cruising grounds in the world can compete with the Caribbean's clear waters, faithful trade winds, and a United Nations of islands only a few hours sail from each other. Aboard a Windstar ship, passengers have the best of all worlds: a ship that really sails, cabins as plush as a small hotel room, a different island each morning, and knockout cuisine that's included in one price. A Holland America Line company, Windstar is a slick, savvy operation that offers the best airfares, shore tours, entertainers, and special events thanks to its international network of hospitality professionals.

You'll join your ship in Barbados or St. Thomas depending on the itinerary. Ports of call include the Tobago Cays, Bequia, Barbados, Martinique, Grenada, St. Barts, Iles des Saintes, St. John in the U.S. Virgin Islands, and Tortola, Jost Van Dyke, and Virgin Gorda in the British Virgin Islands. Aruba, Curacao, and Bonaire are included in a 15-day Panama Canal itinerary.

A typical cabin has a queen-size bed that can be converted to two twins, a full-length hanging locker, big portholes, twin vanities, and a private bathroom with shower. Your cabin attendant makes the bed, tidies up, and fills your ice bucket while you're at breakfast. While you're at dinner, your attendant leaves fresh towels, turns down the bed and puts a treat on your pillow. Most activities and watersports, endless meals including beach barbecues, and entertainment are included. The only extras are shore excursions and drinks. These ships cruise the world, sailing the Caribbean only in winter. Plan your cruise as far in advance as possible, both to get the week you want and to take advantage of early booking discounts.

Puerto Rico & the Virgin Islands

Chapter 14

p u e r t o r i c o

Puerto Rico – America's "Shining Star of the Caribbean" – lies between St. Thomas and the Dominican Republic, its north shore on the Atlantic Ocean and its south on the Caribbean Sea. The island is 110 miles long and 35 miles wide. Among its many treasures is El Yunque, the only tropical rainforest in the eastern United States. Only 3 1/2 jet hours from New York and two from Miami, Puerto Rico offers all the spicy Latin flavor of a foreign country, yet you're still at home where U.S. dollars and postage stamps are in use.

Christopher Columbus carried the Spanish flag to island after island but eventually Spain lost most of her Caribbean holdings to the English, French, Dutch, and Danes. Puerto Rico is the only Caribbean island under the U.S. flag where you can still capture the Latino legacy left by the original Conquistadores. For adventurous vacationers, it means a chance to taste mofongo, mavi, juicy tropical fruits, dizzying rum drinks, and lush seafood harvests fresh from the sea. Yet for those who like a touch of home, it also means McDonald's, Pizza Hut, Kentucky Fried Chicken, Sears, Radio Shack, Ma Bell coin telephones, and driving on the right side of the road.

Let's start with the beaches because they rim the island like a necklace of sugar cookies – sandy, sweet, fragrant and warm. The beach resort areas nearest **San Juan** include **Condado**, **Miramar**, **Ocean Park**, and **Isla Verde**. Drive the coast roads around the big island, stopping at every pretty beach you see. For a real getaway, take a ferry to the islands of **Culebra** or **Vieques**, which lie east of Puerto Rico.

Puerto Rico's spine of mountains is a magnet for hikers and nature lovers. It is here in lofty coffee plantations that a special harvest is made each year of rare coffees to be presented to the Vatican. Plan at least three days if you want to explore inland Puerto Rico along the mountain road. You'll probably get lost a few times, meet a lot of friendly natives, stop at a pineapple stand, and eat wonderful food at rundown shacks.

No matter when you go, there's likely to be a fiesta somewhere on the island. It may be a religious or folk festival, a tournament in any sport from auto racing to baseball, or a seasonal harvest celebration. Other festivals such as the Casals Festival each June and the Puerto Rico Heineken Jazz Fest at the end of May, are cultural events that attract world class artists and musicians. Most of the smaller towns are a fiesta in themselves on Friday nights when people dress up and take to the streets. The best blowout in each town is the feast day of its patron saint, when parties go on for a week or more. The largest are those in San Juan (June 23-24), Loiza (June 25), and Ponce (December 6-15).

Waves of settlers arrived on Puerto Rico starting around 3,000 B.C. including Arawaks, followed by the Tainos, whose culture was one of the most advanced in the Americas. Within 50 years of Columbus' first call here in 1493, they had almost disappeared, victims of enslavement and disease.

A Spanish stronghold almost from the beginning of Spanish exploration in the Americas, San Juan was fortified in the early 1500s by **Juan Ponce de León**, who is buried in the San Juan Cathedral. By the 1630s it was a walled city sprawled under the imposing **El Morro**, a 200-acre fort that repelled the most savage English attacks. Only in 1598 was it taken by the English, and then only briefly. Its stones seemingly indestructible through the ages, it's still one of the Caribbean's most majestic forts.

The Spanish quest for gold had some success in Puerto Rico, with meager findings along the rivers, but soon the cash crop became sugar cane harvested on fields tended by slaves brought in from Africa. Their language and lore, and to some extent the color of their skin, melted seamlessly into local culture.

When the world sugar market collapsed, Puerto Rico slumbered through the ages, eking out an income from exporting coffee and tobacco. Running for office in 1929, Luis Muñoz Marin described it as a "land of beggars and millionaires." In 1940, per capita income was only $120. Then came the end of World War II, the building of a Hilton hotel, and the island was transformed forever. The natural hospitality of the people, sunny winters, clear waters, and a continuing building boom in hotels has turned Puerto Rico into a world-class player in leisure and business travel.

When you first hear the ear-piercing cry of the coqui tree frog, which is found only on Puerto Rico, it's a shock. Then this nightly chorus gets into your blood until it's a lullaby. Soon, you can't imagine nights without the coqui's chirp echoing through flower-scented breezes. *"Soy tan puertoriqueño como el coqui"* means "I'm as Puerto Rican as a coqui." The little fellow is pictured everywhere as a symbol of the island.

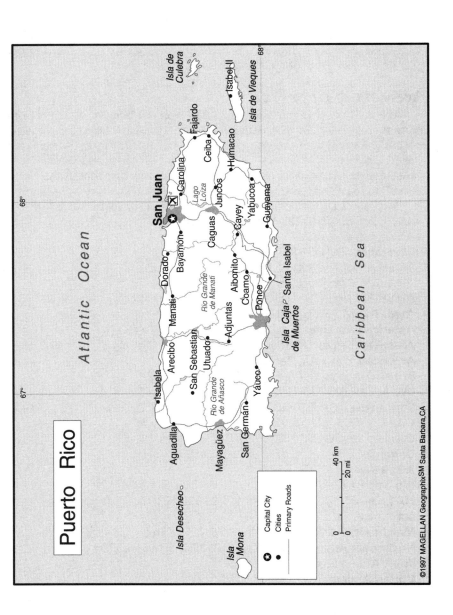

Puerto Rico

Isla Mona
Isla Desecheo

Atlantic Ocean

Aguadilla
Isabela
Arecibo
Mayagüez
San Sebastián
Manatí
Dorado
San Germán
Utuado
Adjuntas
Yauco
Río Grande de Añasco
Río Grande de Manatí
Bayamón
San Juan
Carolina
Lago Loíza
Caguas
Aibonito
Coamo
Ponce
Santa Isabel
Isla Caja de Muertos
Juncos
Cayey
Yabucoa
Guayama
Fajardo
Ceiba
Humacao
Isla de Culebra
Isabel II
Isla de Vieques

Caribbean Sea

40 km
20 mi

Capital City
Cities
Primary Roads

©1997 MAGELLAN GeographixSM Santa Barbara,CA

67°
68°
68°

Climate

The northern coast of Puerto Rico, exposed to the northeast trade winds, is wetter than the south coast. There is no dry season, just a pleasant spread of sunshine and showers throughout the year. Daytime temperatures in San Juan rarely reach above the low 90s; nighttime lows get no cooler than the low 60s. Be prepared for light, cooling showers in the mountains.

Arrivals & Departures

The Caribbean's main airline hub, San Juan is a beehive of flights from more than a dozen North American cities including New York, Los Angeles, Boston, Baltimore, Detroit, Hartford, Miami, Dallas-Fort Worth, Washington Dulles, Orlando, Philadelphia, Tampa, Toronto, Chicago, and Dallas. From here American Eagle flies to another 40 destinations throughout the Caribbean. San Juan also has direct flights from London, Frankfurt and Madrid.

San Juan's **Luis Munoz Marin International Airport** is served by:
- **ACES**, *Tel. 800/846-2237 or 787/791-5840*
- **Air Caraibes**, *Tel. 787/253-0933*
- **Air France**, *Tel. 800/237-2747*
- **Air Jamaica**, *Tel. 800/523-5585*
- **Air Santo Domingo**, *Tel. 866/288-3939*
- **Air St. Thomas**, *Tel. 800/522-3084 or 787/791-4898*
- **ALM**, *Tel. 800/327-7230*
- **American Air Lines**, *Tel. 800/433-7300 or 787/749-1747*
- **American Eagle**, *Tel. 800/433-7300 or 787/749-1747*
- **American Trans Air**, *Tel. 800/883-5228*
- **British Airways**, *800/247-9297 or 787/723-4327*
- **BWIA**, *Tel. 800/538-2942*
- **Continental**, *Tel. 800/525-0280 or 800/231-0856*
- **COPA**, *Tel. 800/981-8284 or 787/722-6969*
- **Condor**, *Tel. 800/524-6975*
- **Delta**, *Tel. 800/221-1212*
- **Iberia**, *Tel. 787/725-7033*
- **Isla Nena**, *Tel. 787/741-6362*
- **LIAT**, *Tel. 800/468-0482 or 787/791-0800*
- **Lufthansa,** *Tel. 787/764-0777*
- **Martin Air**, *Tel. 800/981-9448 or 787/253-0167*
- **Northwest Airlines**, *Tel. 800/225-2525 or 787/253-0206*
- **Spirit Airlines,** *Tel. 800/756-7117*
- **United Airlines** *Tel. 800/426-5561*
- **US Airways**, *Tel. 800/842-5374 or 800/428-4322*
- **Vieques Air Link**, *Tel. 787/722-3736, 888/901-9247*

Agricultural Inspection

Even though U.S. citizens have no customs and immigration problems in Puerto Rico, there is an agriculture inspection for checked baggage. Allow time at the airport to put your bags through it before checking in at the counter or gate; bags won't be accepted without the inspection sticker.

Frequent air service is also available from San Juan to Vieques, from Vieques to Fajardo, from Fajardo to Culebra, and from Vieques to St. Croix. Mayagüez has an airport served by **American Eagle**. **Carnival Air** flies from New York to Aguadilla and Ponce.

Ferries depart every half hour from **Pier Two** in Old San Juan for Cataño and Hato Rey, *Tel. 788-1155*. For schedules, rate information, and reservations for passenger ferry service among Fajarado, *Tel. 787/863-4560*, Vieques, *Tel. 787/741-4761*, and Culebra, *Tel. 767/742-3161*. Transportation for cars is available on the cargo ferry, *Tel. 863-0852*. Allow at least a week for planning and reservations. San Juan is the second largest cruise ship port in the Western Hemisphere, hosting 28 ships that make 748 home port sailings each year. If you are cruising out of San Juan, take as much time as you can afford for pre- and post-cruise stays in Puerto Rico, the true "shining star" of American tourism.

Orientation

Metropolitan San Juan has spread like a giant amoeba that has gobbled up Toa Baja, Cataño, Bayamon, Trujillo Alto, Carolina, and Guaynabo almost as far as Caguas, which will probably soon be part of the megalopolis. **Old San Juan**, an island that forms half the rim of San Juan Bay, is a time machine frozen in the 16th century. It's a place to roam and sightsee, and rest in shaded plazas paved with centuries-old stones. East of Old (or Viejo) San Juan are the high-rise tourist hotels of Condado and Miramar. Hato Rey is the city's financial and commercial hub. In Guaynabo and Hato Rey, you're in the 'burbs with their real estate developments and American-style shopping malls and supermarkets.

From San Juan, Route 3 goes east past **Luquillo** with its famous beach to **Fajardo**, where ferries leave for offshore islands. South of Route 3 spreads **El Yunque,** the magnificent rainforest covering the **Sierra Luquillo**.

Driving south from San Juan takes you through **Caguas** and on to the colonial city of **Ponce**. Or you can head east from Caguas to the resort area of **Humacao**.

It's possible to drive around almost the entire perimeter of the island, going west from Ponce, skirting inland through **San Germán**, and back to the coast at busy **Mayagüez**. Then north to **Aguadilla** and east along the coast to the attractions of **Arecibo** with its radio telescope and the caves of **Rio Camuy**, through the resorts of **Dorado** and back to San Juan. An alternative route, if you have plenty of time, is to drive the spine of the **Cordillera**, the mountain range through the middle of the island.

Getting Around Puerto Rico

White-painted taxis participating in the **Tourism Taxi Program** operate on a zone system. Fare from the airport to nearby districts including Isla Verde and Puntas las Marias is $8. In Zone 3, from the airport to Condado and Ocean Park, the fare is $12. From the airport to Old San Juan, tourism piers, Puerta de Tierra nd Miramar, is a $16 fare. A Zone 5 fare of $6 applies from the piers to Puerta de Tierra.

Metered cabs have a $1 initial charge, then charge 10 cents for each additional 1/13 mile plus additional fees for baggage, waiting time, reserved rides, and night travel. Charter taxis charge $20 per hour. If you have complaints about taxis, call the Public Service Commission, *Tel. 787/756-1919,* or the airport police, *Tel. 787/791-4155.*

City buses in the San Juan area are frequent and good. Bus stops are marked by orange, white and magenta signs reading Parada, with yellow and white lines marking bus stops on main highways. Bus terminals are in the Covadonga parking lot in Old San Juan. For information, call the **Metropolitan Bus Authority**, *Tel. 787/767-7979.* Each time you board, you must pay 25 or 50 cents, depending on the route.

Parking space is at a premium almost everywhere, so consider carefully whether you really need a rental car. Hotels may charge $12 a day or more for parking if it's available at all. Restaurants, if they have parking at all, may require you to valet park. If you do rent a car, avoid cut-rate rental agencies that don't have satellite offices island-wide because you could be stranded if you break down out on the island. Major car rental companies also offer transportation from hotels or the airport to their lots, and their cars are equipped with anti-theft devices.

Rental car agencies include:
- **Avis**, *Tel. 800/874-3556 or 787/253-5933, www.avis.com*
- **Budget**, *Tel. 787/791-0600 or 800/468-5822, www.budget.com*
- **Dollar,** *Tel. 787/791-5500, www.dollar.com*
- **Hertz**, *Tel. 787/791-0840 or 800/654-3131, www.hertz.com;* locations are at the airport, Condado, and Isla Verde
- **L&M Car Rental**, *Tel. 800/666-0807 or 787/791-1160*
- **Leaseway of Puerto Rico**, *Tel. 800/468-2647 or 787/791-5900*

- **National,** Tel. *787/791-1805 or 800/568-3019, www.nationalcar.com*
- **Payless Car Rental,** Tel. *787/791-0040, www.paylesscarrental.com*
- **Target Car Rental,** Tel. *787/728-1447*
- **Thrifty,** Tel. *800/367-2277, www.thrifty.com;* locations are at Isla Verde, Fajardo, and Mayagüez
- **Tropical Car Rental,** Tel. *787/791-4120*

For **Wheelchair Getaways Rent-a-Car,** Tel. *787/383-0131 or 800/868-8028.* In Mayagüez or Ponce, try **Popular Leasing,** Tel. *787/265-4848, 787/259-4848 or 800/981-9282.*

Ferry Service

Ferries serve the islands of Vieques and Culebra from Fajardo. You must arrive one hour before departure time. Schedules can vary according to weather, and are different on weekends from weekdays, but ferries generally run about three round trips to Vieques daily and two round trips to Culebra. Fares are $2 per person to Vieques and $2.25 to Culebra. For information in Fajardo, Tel. *787/863-4560;* in Vieques, Tel. *787/741-4761;* and in Culebra, Tel. *787/742-3161.*

Where to Stay

The room tax in hotels that do not have a casino is nine percent; in hotels that have a casino it is 11 percent. Some hotels often charge 15 percent or more in lieu of tipping. Rates given are for a double room in high season. Unless stated otherwise, major credit cards are accepted.

Old San Juan

HOTEL EL CONVENTO, *100 Cristo Street, Old San Juan 00901. Tel. 787/723-9020, Fax 787/721-2877, toll-free 800/468-2779, www.elconvento.com. Rates, which include continental breakfast, are from $265 for a moderate room to $1200 for the Gloria Vanderbilt Suite. Ask about the many packages. It's a $6 cab ride from the pier and $16 from the airport.*

You're not just in the heart of history, you are part of history when you stay in a building that was built as a convent more than 400 years ago. Now lavishly restored, it's one of the city's most talked-about showplaces not just for overnighters but for locals who patronize the shops and meet in the smart restaurants such as El Picoteo, famed for its tapas menu, and Blue Agave Tequila Bar & Grill, a Mexican room where you can get superb gazpacho, totopos and mole poblano. An especially popular suite with families is Room 404 with two doubles in the bedroom and a convertible sofa in the living room. It's next to the pool terrace, radiant with great views. Ask about pre- and post-cruise packages.

Selected as one of my *Best Places to Stay* – see Chapter 13.

GALLERY INN AT GALERÍA SAN JUAN, *Calle Norzagaray #204-206, Old San Juan PR 00901. Tel. 787/787/722-1808, Fax 787/724-7360. Rates at this 22-room inn start at $95, suites at $200, Rates include continental breakfast. Cab fare from the airport is $16 and from the pier $6.*

Everything you've ever dreamed of in a bed and breakfast inn is found here in a romantic, 300-year-old building that rambles from the north wall of the old city through a warren of stony courtyards, balconies filled with flowers, and hidden rooms. It's so private, there isn't even a sign outside, so don't arrive without a reservation and directions. Most rooms have private bath and some have air conditioning, but each is so different, so eclectic, that most guests choose a favorite and book it year after year.

Built for a Spanish artillery captain, the home is now the studio of talented artists Jan D'Esopo and Manuco Gandia whose works are part of the decor and are also for sale in the gallery. Visitors can look on as a frenzy of creative activity produces paintings, sculptures, silkscreening, mold making, and bronze castings. In her spare time, Jan plays her Steinway concert grand or brings in talented conservatory students to play for her guests. This is the ideal *pied-a-terre* for exploring the old city on foot. Parking is very limited, so skip the rental car until you're ready to leave for the countryside.

WYNDHAM OLD SAN JUAN HOTEL & CASINO, *100 Brumbaugh Street, , Old San Juan. Tel. 787/721-5100 or 800/822-4200 U.S. and 800/631-4200 Canada. Rates are $100-$380. It's a $16 taxi ride from the airport.*

You can overlook the bustling harbor in this splendid city hotel. It's handy to exploring and shopping Old San Juan, and is only footsteps from cruise ship docks. The hotel is wheelchair accessible, business-friendly as well as a find for leisure travelers and cruisers, and it has a small, rooftop swimming pool. Dine outdoors on the street level or on the second floor patio, a popular spot for afternoon cocktails, or eat in air conditioned comfort in the surprisingly good restaurant, Darsena's. The breakfast buffet is an excellent value, or grab juice, coffee and pastry in the lobby.

The casino, just off the lobby, is a local hotspot for locals, cruisers, and drop-ins from other hotels. Standard rooms aren't oversize, but are furnished in classic woods and prints and upscale amenities. Armoirs hold a big-screen TV with cable, pay movies, and VCR. Each room has voice mail, hair dryer, iron, ironing board, and coffee maker. Premium rooms overlook the water and have a balcony

Greater San Juan – Expensive

CARIBE HILTON, *Fort San Geronimo, Puerto de Tierra, San Juan. Tel. 787/721-0303 or 800/HILTONS in the U.S. and Canada; www.caribehilton.com. Rates start at $375, suites at $680. The hotel, which was extensively renovated in 2000, has 645 rooms. Valet parking is $20 daily, self parking is*

$10 a day. On the concierge level, breakfast is included. Taxi fare from the airport is $12; from the pier, $6. The hotel can also be reached by the A7 bus.
The beach is a tiny jewel rarely found in the heart of the city, and the hotel offers classy accommodations for business or pleasure plus a 400-year-old fort to explore and photograph. Oceanview rooms gaze out over crashing surf and the ramparts of Fort San Jeronimo. Work out in the health club or book one of the rooms or suites that has its own Action Stepper fitness machine. There's a full spa, a freshwater pool, three tennis courts lit for night play, a playground for the children, nd five excellent restaurants as well as lounges and bars. The pool complex is one of the most spectacular on the island. The 12,000 square foot spa offers a long menu of massages, wraps, facials, hydrotherapy and other services.

Accommodations are spacious and posh, offering luxury touches for the leisure traveler plus the desk, telephones, and business center that a working visitor requires.

Camp Coco for children ages 4-12 operates during school vacations and holiday periods at a cost of $35 per child per day or $125 a week. Included are supplies, lunch, and two snacks daily. Kids tennis lessons can be added at special rates. Each day the camp also offers a family activity such as rafting, a limbo contest, dance lessons, bingo, hula hoops, or fish feeding. The resort has an on-site bird sanctuary. Staff are bilingual.

CONDADO PLAZA HOTEL & CASINO, *999 Ashford Avenue, Condado PR 00907. Tel. 787/721-1000 or 800/468-8588. Rates at this 590-room hotel start at $320. The hotel is a $12 cab ride from the airport.*

First-class service and accommodations mean a private balcony for every room, a choice of three swimming pools, a sandy beach, black tie gaming and dancing, and a spectrum of restaurants including Mandalay Oriental, Las Palmas poolside grill, elegant Molina's, the award-winning La Posada for Puerto Rican food, Tony Roma's for its famous ribs, and Max's Grill. Room service operates around the clock. It is managed by the same company as El San Juan Hotel & Casino, so guests in either, and at Cobia's Restaurant (tapas) can charge meals to one account.

DIAMOND PALACE HOTEL CASINO, *55 Condado Avenue., Santurce. Tel. 787/721- 0810 or 800/468-2014. Fax 787/725-7895. Rates at this high-rise hotel start at $160. It's 20 minutes from the airport, seven minutes from Old San Juan. Parking costs extra.*

Book an ocean view room here for a holiday or a business stay in the heart of metro San Juan. The hotel has two restaurants, a cocktail lounge, a swimming pool, a casino, and cable television, and it's near the famous Atlantic beaches. Rooms are done in blond woods and tropical prints.

RADISSON AMBASSADOR PLAZA HOTEL & CASINO, *1369 Ashford Avenue, Condado, San Juan PR 00907. Tel. 787/721-7300, U.S. 800/333-3333. Rates at this 233-room hotel start at $179. It's a $12 taxi ride, or 15 minutes, from the airport.*

You're in Condado's action-packed tourist strip, only ten minutes from Old San Juan, half a block from the beach, and surrounded by shops, restaurants, and bars. The hotel rises in two towers, one of 146 rooms and the other with two-room suites. Stay on the Ambassador Club floor with its own lounge, concierge, and prestige perks. Swim in the rooftop pool, which has its own whirlpool, work on in the fitness center, shop the boutique, choose from two restaurants, and stay late in the Cabaret Lounge to listen to live music. The hotel has its own beauty shop, game room, and travel desk and the casino is said to be one of the island's most user-friendly.

RITZ-CARLTON SAN JUAN HOTEL, SPA, AND CASINO, *6961 State Road 187, Isla Verde, Carolina PR 00979. Tel. 800/241-3333 or locally 787/ 253-1700, Fax 253-0700. Rates at this 419-room, 45-suite hotel start at $505; one-bedroom suites start at $1045. The hotel also has a club floor with rooms and suites. It's five minutes from the international airport and 15 minutes from Old San Juan. Through the hotel, get airport transfers for $8 each way.*

A bustling business hotel with a ballroom, meeting rooms and a business center, the Ritz is also ideal for the leisure traveler who wants unabashed luxury in rooms lavished with works by local artists. Each guest room has a stocked honor bar, personal safe, marble bath with hair dryer, scale, and telephone, individual heat and air conditioning control, plush terry robes, three telephones with dual lines and data port, and AM/FM radio with digital clock/alarm. Enjoy the 450-foot beach, a full-service spa, and a city location handy to the airport, financial district, Old San Juan, and shopping at Plaza Las Americas. Nightlife and dining at Condado are ten minutes away. Dine in the Vineyard Room, the hotel's signature restaurant serving California and continental cuisine or in more informal restaurants indoors and out. Room service answers 24 hours a day.

Swim in the supersize, 7,200-square foot pool, soak in the whirlpools, play tennis on the hotel's courts, and gamble late and luxuriously in the 17,000 square foot Monte Carlo by the Sea Casino. The hotel's 12,000 square foot spa is created by the Sonoma Mission Inn and Spa, featuring life-enhancing Sonomotherapy treatments. Hotel guests have golf privileges at nearby courses. The Fitness Center offers aerobics, exercise equipment and free weights. Three fishing clubs are nearby; horse racing is 20 minutes away. View are of the sea or of El Yunque rainforest.

On the Club floor with its private lounge and personal concierge staff, guests get complimentary continental breakfast, light lunch, afternoon tea, hors d'oeuvres, and a variety of beverages throughout the day and evening. New in 1998, the hotel is surely destined for five-star status with its twice daily maid service, 24-hour room service and valet parking, child care, and much more.

Selected as one of my *Best Places to Stay* – see Chapter 13.

INTER-CONTINENTAL SAN JUAN RESORT & CASINO, *5961 Isla Verde, Isla Verde PR 00913. Tel. 787/791-6100, Fax 791-8525; U.S. 800/443-2009; www.sjgrand.com. Rates at this 400-unit hotel start at $235; suites at $270. It's an $8 cab ride from the airport. Parking is $5 per day; valet parking, $10.*

The gambling glitter of the Sands Hotel in Atlantic City is cloned here. On the beach and surrounded by lush, flowery tropical plants, the hotel does a brisk tour and group business. Dine in Ruth's Chris Steak House, Guiseppe for northern Italian cuisine, Momo Yama for Japanese classics, or the informal cafe. For the ultimate luxury, stay in the Plaza Club, the resort's five-star prestige section.

WYNDHAM EL SAN JUAN HOTEL & CASINO, *6063 Isla Verde Avenue, PR 00979. Tel. 787/791-1000, Fax 787/791-6985; toll-free in the U.S., Canada, and U.S. Virgin Islands, 800/223-6800, www.wyndham. Rates at this 304-room, 49-suite resort start at $420. Premier garden suites are from $635; premier ocean suites from $775 and the duplex Monarch suite, which has a baby grand piano, is $3,500 nightly.*

For luxury leisure travelers and business travelers too, this hotel offers the best of both: 15 acres on the beach, grounds landscaped with palms and flowering shrubs, as well as meeting rooms and a business center. Rooms are air conditioned; some have a Jacuzzi or sunken tub; many have a private terrace or balcony. Lose yourself in the gardens, or savor all the bustle of a big hotel: six restaurants, 24-hour room service, tennis courts that are lit for night play, a state-of-the-art fitness center, the fantasy pool with bar and underwater seats, the massage center, five acres of botanical gardens, and an extensive watersports center with board sailing, deep sea fishing, and parasailing. Ask about the optional meal plan.

Have dinner in The Ranch at El San Juan restaurant to try the rattlesnake sausage, chunky chili, country-fried steak, barbecue chicken or ribs, and sarsaparilla. After dinner, ride the bucking bronco or play horseshoes. The 203-seat restaurant is western to the max, complete with a bar straight from an 1890 saloon and servers in cowboy get-up.

Greater San Juan – Moderate

CARIBE MOUNTAIN VILLAS, *Road 857, Kilometer 6.0, Canovanillas Sector, Carolina. Tel. 787/769-0860. Rates start at $100 for a studio apartment.*

Settle down in your own housekeeping unit in this popular residential and tourism area east of San Juan. The place has tennis courts and a swimming pool and plenty of restaurants are nearby.

THE WATER CLUB, *2 Tartak Street, Isla Verde PR 00979, Tel. 787/728-3666, 888/265-6699. or 800/337-4685, Rates at this 84-unit hotel are $199-$825. It's on a private, gated street five minutes from the airport and 15 minutes from the cruise ship docks.*

San Juan's only boutique hotel on the beach is hip and contemporary, with the sound of ocean waves playing softly in the corridors and sexy, custom-designed beds facing the ocean. The pool and fitness center are outdoors, high above the sea. The main bar, Liquid, is a popular hangout for smart locals but if you want a more exclusive room, Moist is a private club reserved for guests and VIPs and there's also the aptly-named Wet Bar. Dine on Pacific Rim cuisine overlooking the ocean in Tangerine, or order from room service around the clock. Everywhere the look is *moderne,* with plenty of glass and flowing waters. The roof-top bar has zebra wood bar stools, a fireplace, and walls covered with Indonesian carvings. Rooms, all of them with an ocean view, are furnished with a king- or double-size bed, down comforters and pillows, cable television, CD player, wireless Internet access, cordless phone with two lines, iron and ironing board, minibar, and safe. Balcony rooms and one-bedroom suites are also available.

EMBASSY SUITES HOTEL & CASINO, *8000 Tartak, Isla Verde PR 00902. Tel. 787/791-0505; U.S. 800/362-2779; www.embassy-suites.com. Rates at this 300-suite hotel start at $175 including breakfast cooked to order and evening cocktails. The hotel is an $8 cab ride, five minutes from the airport.*

Any time we can get a homey, one-bedroom suite with two televisions, microwave, refrigerator, and coffee maker for this price, with a full breakfast on the house, we are sold. The hotel has an Outback Steakhouse, casual dining in the Atrium Cafe, a swimming pool with pool bar, and a casino. It's handy to Old San Juan, the beach, shopping, restaurants, and expressways, and it's wheelchair accessible. Don't confuse this address with the Embassy guest house in Condado.

HAMPTON INN, *6530 Isla Verde Avenue, Isla Verde. Tel. 787/791-8777. Rates are from $145 including continental breakfast. Parking is additional.*

Isla Verde has a public beach, 24-hour supermarket, and it's handy to the airport and Old San Juan. Stay in this familiar chain hotel and get a generous, continental breakfast. The inn has a whirlpool and a big swimming pool with a swim-up bar.

HOTEL EL PORTAL, *76 Condado Avenue. Tel. 787/721-9010, e-mail reservation@hotelelportal.com Fax 787/724-3714. Rates at this seven-story hotel are from $115.*

Located in the heart of Condado, this seven-story hotel is within walking distance of the beach, discos, shopping, and restaurants ranging from fast food to gourmet.

NUMERO 1 GUEST HOUSE ON THE BEACH, *1 Santa Ana Street, Ocean Park (between Condado and Isla Verde). Tel. 787/726-5010. Rates are from $105. It's about 10 minutes from the airport.*

Friendly, small and on the Atlantic beach is this pleasant guest house with its own restaurant, Pamela's Caribbean Cuisine. Swim in the sea or the swimming pool.

RAMADA SAN JUAN, *1045 Ashford Avenue, Condado. Tel. 787/724-5657, www.ramadasanjuan.com. Rates start at $150. Valet parking is available.*

Spacious, comfortable, airy rooms are a homey spot to be near the beach as well as all the city events, shopping, restaurants and commercial centers. The hotel has a swimming pool, fitness center, and restaurant.

PARK PLAZA NORMANDIE HOTEL, *Avenida Muñoz Rivera, Puerto de Tierra, San Juan PR 00902 (on the corner of Los Rosales Street). Tel. 787/729-2940, Fax 787/729-3083 or 725-1931; U.S. 800/333-3333. Rates at this 177-room hotel start at $165, suites at $280. Rates include breakfast.*

A nostalgic favorite, this ship-shaped hotel was built before World War II and named for the French cruise liner *Normandie*. Long a choice for honeymoons in the sunshine and still a great location for vacationing and business, the hotel is refurbished time and again to its original, art deco splendor. The hotel has an excellent restaurant, a lounge, a swimming pool with pool bar, a fitness center and spa, room service and a beauty salon.

SAN JUAN MARRIOTT RESORT & STELLA SOLARIS CASINO, *1309 Ashford Avenue, San Juan 00907. Tel. 787/722-7000 or 800/981-8546. Rates at this 525-room resort start at $199, suites at $210. Located on the beach in Condado, it's a $12 taxi ride from the airport.*

High-rise hotels along San Juan's hotel "strip" can be seen from miles out to sea, and this 21-story beauty tops them all. Entering the lobby, you immediately grasp the sense of luxury and ease that marks a first class, modern hotel with advanced voice mail systems, 24-hour room service, in-room VCRs, and a full range of services including concierge, car rental, tour desk, a shopping arcade, and beauty shop. Live music plays in the lobby during cocktail hour, so it's a good place to meet friends. Dine in Ristorante Tuscany for northern Italian cuisine, the poolside grill, or La Vista which features a theme buffet every evening and, at breakfast and lunch, menu or buffet service. Calypso music plays on Saturday and Sunday afternoons poolside and there's merengue dancing in the lounge Thursday through Sunday from 9pm until almost dawn. The massive pool is a stunner.

Greater San Juan – Budget

BUDGET HOST HOTEL DEL CENTRO, *4th Floor, Rio Piedras Medical Center, corner of Ferre Expressway and Avenida Americo Miranda. Tel. 787/751-1335 or 800/BUD-HOST, www.budgethost.com, E-mail: mail@budgethost.com or* *titoalva@coqui.net. Rates at this 29-unit hotel start at $85. Seniors get a 10% discount. The hotel is 10 minutes from downtown San Juan, Isla Verde, or Condado. Parking is available at extra cost.*

This reliable chain hotel, well known to mainlanders who travel on a budget, offers queen- or twin-size rooms with cable television, the movie channel, and a coffee shop. It's near the beach, restaurants and bars in a quiet location handy to medical care in a center that specializes in cardiovascular care. Roll-away beds are available for extra persons at added cost. No-smoking rooms and kitchenette units are available.

HOWARD JOHNSON, *4820 Isla Verde Avenue, Isla Verde, Tel. 787/728-1300 or 800/446-4656, www.hojo.com. Rates are $120-$150. Can fare from the airport is about $8.*

Stay in a full-service hotel that has two fine restaurants and lounges. It's only one block back from one of the best beaches in greater San Juan. Spacious rooms, which are popular with both business and leisure travelers, have cable television, microwave, refrigerator, and coffee maker.

CASA DEL CARIBE, *57 Calle Caribe, Condado, San Juan PR 00907. Tel. 787/722-7139. Rates at this 7-room guest house start at $55 including continental breakfast. Cab fare from the airport is $12.*

You're near the beach in a delightful little inn favored by Puerto Ricans and savvy visitors who like the garden setting, breezy porch, and comfortable, clean rooms that have air conditioning and a ceiling fan.

CASA DE PLAYA BEACH HOTEL, *86 Isla Verde, Isla Verde PR 00979. Tel. 787/728-9779. Rates at this 22-room hotel start at $80, including parking. From the airport it's an $8 taxi ride.*

Handy to town, the airport, and near the beach is this unassuming hotel with its own restaurant, lounge, and beach bar.

DAYS INN CONDADO LAGOON, *6 Clemenceau Avenue, Condado PR 00907. Tel. 787/721-0170 or 800/858-7407, www.daysinn.com. Rates at this 44-room hotel start at $$99, including continental breakfast. Cab fare from the airport is $12.*

The location is ideal for business travel or as a home port while you're exploring Old San Juan, the shopping and dining of "hotel row" and the attractions of the north side of the island. The hotel is a typical, price-appeal Days Inn with a restaurant and a swimming pool.

EL CANARIO BY THE LAGOON, *4 Clemenceau Street, Condado, San Juan PR 00907. Tel. 787/722-5058. Rates at this 40-room hotel start at $80 including breakfast.*

Back from the beach one block and on a quiet street, this small hotel has the homey look and feel of a European inn. Most of the rooms have a balcony and there is a laundry for guest use. The hosts will be glad to arrange tours and to steer you to nearby restaurants and entertainment.

EL PRADO INN, *1350 Calle Luchetti, Condado. Tel. 787/728-5925 or 800/468-4521. Fax 787/725-6978. Rates are $89-$139 including breakfast. Apartments are available.*

The look is that of an intimate Spanish inn in the heart of smart Condado. The beach is a three-minute walk away, or just stay by the pool in a sunny or shaded spot on the patio. Rooms have both air conditioning and ceiling fan. Casinos, restaurants and shopping are only footsteps away.

GREEN ISLE INN, *6 Calle Uno, Isla Verde PR 00979. Tel. 787/726-4330 or 787/726-8662, Fax 787/268-2415. Rates start at $42 to $74. The hotel is an $8 taxi ride from the airport and $16 from the pier.*

It's in the heart of the luxury hotels yet it's pittance-priced. Walk to beaches, casinos, dining, and shopping. The hotel offers courtesy coffee, furnished kitchenettes, and two big swimming pools.

HOTEL OLIMPO COURT, *603 Avenida Miramar, Miramar. Tel. 787/724-0600. Rates at this 45-room hotel start at $67. Cab fare from the airport is $8.*

Don't expect mints on your pillow at this price, but it's hard to beat the location for the traveler who wants to sleep near the airport. The hotel has its own restaurant, Chayote, *Tel. 722-9385.*

TRES PALMAS INN, *2212 Park Boulevard, San Juan. Tel. 787/727-4617, www.trespalmasinn.com, e-mail trespalm@coqui.net. Rates are from $64 including continental breakfast. It's ten minutes from the airport or Old San Juan.*

This modern inn is located on the beach, and features electronic safes, air conditioning, cable television, swimming pool, and a sun deck with whirlpool. Suites with kitchenette are available.

Southeast of San Juan

CANDELERO RESORT AT PALMAS DEL MAR, *170 Candelero Drive; mail address: Box 2020, Humacao, Puerto Rico 00791-2020. Tel. 787/852-6000 or U.S. 800/725-6273. Found at Kilometer 84.6 on Road #3, Route 906, Humacao. A 45-minute drive from the San Juan airport, the resort has 250 rooms and suites. Rates start at $194. Villas with up to three bedrooms are available. Ask about packages.*

Your domain includes a Gary Player-designed, 18-hole golf course said to have more scenic holes than any other course in the world, and a tennis center managed by Peter Burwash International. Snorkel right off the beach; take a horse from the Equestrian Center and cantor off through the surf. Scuba dive with the resort's own dive masters, the only on-site dive operation on the island.

Put yourself in a spacious hotel room with a private balcony or in a villa to house the entire family. Furnishings are tropical and bright; accessories are drawn from Puerto Rican folk art. The Adventure Club gives children, ages 3 to 13, the time of their lives while adults sun, read, or play golf or tennis.

Developed in the 1960s by Charles Fraser, known for his ecologically-sensitive developments, the resort is a complete community with branch banks, churches, school, shops, casino, beauty services, restaurants, lounges, and permanent residents living in homes costing $225,000 to $1 million. Once registered, you can charge everything in "town" to your account.

Choose from an ever-changing list of planned activities, a dozen restaurants, workout facilities, scuba, deep sea fishing, sailing, swimming pools galore, bicycling, and camaraderie without crowding. The grounds, graced with 3,000 coconut palms, cover 2,750 acres.

Hotel rooms are done in tropical pastels. Each has a small refrigerator, electronic door lock, in-room safe, and a private patio or balcony. The hotel, which faces the golf courses, has thousands of square feet of tempting shops. If you like a big resort offering everything you need in a vacation without having to traipse all over the island, this is the place.

If you like a big resort with all the bells and whistles and enough to do for weeks without having to traipse all over the island, this is the place.

Selected as one of my *Best Places to Stay* – see Chapter 13.

East of San Juan – Expensive
HOSTAL BAHIA MARINA, *Fulladosa Cove, Culebra, mailing address P.O. Box 41292, Minillas Station, Santurce PR. Tel. 787/717-1855, 763-5289, or 742-0366, Fax 787/754-8409. Rates are $325 nightly for two and $550 nightly for four including meals and taxes.*

The opening of this 16-unit, European style inn on the island of Culebra is exciting news for locals as well as for visitors in search of a fantasy island. High above the cove overlooking Great Harbor, you can see St. Thomas on most days. Fully-equipped units have air conditioning and kitchen with microwave oven. Watersports equipment is available in the cove; swimming and snorkeling are behind the barrier reef in Dakity Cove. The hostel operates a high-speed catamaran to Culebrita Island and whale watching outings. A minimum three-night booking is required.

WESTIN RIO MAR BEACH & COUNTRY CLUB, *6000 Rio Mar Boulevard, Rio Grande PR 00745. Tel. 787/888-6000, Fax 787/888-6600. U.S. and Canada call 800/WESTIN-1 or 800/4 RIO-MAR. Rates start at $395 double; MAP and FAP are available. The 59-villa Ocean Villas section offers units with one, two, or three bedrooms. They each have a full kitchen, separate living room, and balcony and their own beach-side pool, concierge, and gourmet provisions shop. Children under age 18 sleep free in their parents' room. It's between Rio Grande and Fajardo off Route 3 on Highway 968, Kilometer 1.4, 19 miles east of San Juan and about $65 by taxi from the airport. Parking is $12 daily.*

This 481-acre playground is bordered by the Atlantic, the Mamayes River, and El Yunque Caribbean National Forest. There are 13 tennis courts and two championship golf courses, one a 6,800-yard course designed by George and Tom Fazio and the other a 7,000-yard course created by Greg Norman. The hotel has a complete dive shop offering dives, gear, certification, snorkel trips, and scuba "discovery" courses.

The hotel is done in Mediterranean modern, with classic pieces accented by whimsical shapes and colors. Rooms have balconies overlooking the garden or beach, hair dryer, telephones at desk and bedside, signature toiletries, and a safe with key.

Work out in the fitness center and health studio, then choose from a long menu of spa services and treatments including body toning, anti-stress treatment, body wraps, salt glo, deep tissue massage, and jet-leg massage. If you like gambling, seek out the Las Vegas-style casino. It has its own concierge, a player's lounge with drinks and appetizers (under Puerto Rican Law, drinks cannot be served at the gaming tables) five ATM machines including three in the pit area, and free limousine pick-up at the airport for high rollers. Play Caribbean Stud Poker, Let It Ride, Pai Gaw Poker and a Big Six wheel. In addition you can play blackjack (classes for resort guests are free) and 224 slot machines.

Choose among ten places to drink and dine, including the outstanding Palio, the hotel's signature restaurant and a clone of the original in the Swan at Walt Disney World. Nightly theme buffets at Marbella (mar BAY ya) are a buy; for Puerto Rican food try Cafe Carnival or La Estancia. The Grille at the golf club is known for its steaks; Bolero in the hotel is for tapas before dinner and cigars and brandy after. Sample Asian specialties at the bistro-sushi bar.

The children's center is staffed all year; day care costs $35 including lunch, craft supplies and a tee shirt. Babysitting is available at $5 an hour. The hotel has three pools: a quiet pool for adults, a wading pool with sandy play area for tots, and a busier pool with waterfall and water slide for all ages. The hotel has shops and a beauty salon, valet parking, and a free shuttle serving the hotel, tennis center, and golf club.

Selected as one of my *Best Places to Stay* – see Chapter 13.

WYNDHAM EL CONQUISTADOR RESORT & COUNTRY CLUB, *1000 El Conquistador Avenue, Carretera 987, kilometer 3.4, Las Croabas. Tel. 787/863-1000, Fax 787/863-3280; in the U.S., Canada, and U.S. Virgin Islands, call 800/441-0418 or 800/WYNDHAM, www.williamshosp.com. Rates are $295-$2,290 for a three-night stay in high season, including breakfast and dinner daily, oceanview room, unlimited golf, tennis and non-motorized watersports, tax, and airport transfers. Ask about other packages. Off-season rates are in effect early May to mid-December and are deeply discounted. Casitas with one or two bedrooms are available. From the San Juan airport, it is 31 miles east to the hotel, which is northeast of Fajardo.*

Splayed around and carved into an imposing bluff overlooking the ocean, this dazzling resort sprawls on for 500 lush acres in the colorful fishing hamlet of Las Croabas. In addition to the hotel there are clusters of accommodations, each a village itself with its own style. Stay in the AAA Five Diamond Las Casitas Village for away-from-it-all privacy in a two- or three-bedroom suite. You'll have a personal butler, 24-hour concierge, private check-in, around-the-clock room service, and nightly turndown with an orchid left on your bed. Stay in Las Olas for panoramic views of the Caribbean; La Marina is harborside and has a salty ambience.

The Grand Hotel is the heart of the resort, for guests who prefer a hotel setting. You're surrounded by shops, swimming pools, Jacuzzis, a casino, full-service Golden Door spa, tennis courts and restaurants. Watersports center around private Palomino Island. There's also a marina, 18-hole championship golf course, and fitness center. For the children, Camp Coqui promises all-day, supervised fun in two age groups, for $40 per child per day including lunch.

This is a sprawling resort that does an enormous business in meetings and large conferences, so expect to encounter long lines for check-in, buffets, and other services. We waited 35 minutes in the check-in line and 50 minutes for Room Service to bring a breakfast of cold cereal, a green banana that was not ready to eat until three days later, coffee and juice. The next morning, to be sure of getting breakfast before an appointment, we went to the buffet and helped ourselves. However, we were never offered coffee or a greeting of any kind–including a bill. It's hoped that staffing shortages have been solved by now. Check-out can be handled by video.

The many restaurants are stellar, each in its own style, and the pricier ones have swift, efficient service. (Lines at the fast food spots are long and slow moving.) Unless you have a rental car, you have to dine on property, so be sure to make reservations in the restaurant of your choice early in the day or before. Take-out in disposable dishes is available from Blossoms, which features Asian specialties. Transportation to the airport is available; book yours for three hours before the flight. As you near San Juan, traffic tie-ups can be a problem.

East of San Juan – Budget
ANCHOR'S INN, *Route 987, Kilometer 2.7, Fajardo. Tel. 787/863-7200. Rates at this seven-room guest house start at $55 including breakfast.*

Share the same dazzling cape as the exclusive El Conquistador at less than half the price. This inn is near the beach, it is wheelchair accessible, and credit cards are accepted. The inn's restaurant is popular for its local seafood and prime meats. Try its coffee pub too.

CEIBA COUNTRY INN, *Route 977, Kilometer 1.2, Ceiba. Tel. 787/885-0471. Rooms at this nine-room guest house start at $70 including continental breakfast.*

Wheelchair accessible and handy to marinas, the beach, El Yunque, and the U.S. Naval Station, this is an affordable address for travelers who have a car for sightseeing and restaurants.

Northwest Puerto Rico – Expensive
HYATT DORADO BEACH HOTEL, *Dorado PR 00646. Tel. 787/796-1234 or 800/233-1234, www.hyatt.com. Rates are from $195. Casitas are available to $1,300. Ask about golf, packages, and meal plans. The hotel is 22 miles west of San Juan; ask about airport transportation, which is available at additional cost.*

The two Hyatts in Dorado, linked by free shuttle buses, are a vacation powerhouse, offering four golf courses between them plus a $6 million clubhouse, a pro shop, restaurants galore, and a restaurant and lounge that overlooks the 18-hole East Golf Course. Add in a shining crescent of toasty beaches, plenty of tennis courts (some lit for night play), and 1,000 acres of gardened grounds.

Rooms, which have marble baths and terra cotta tile floors, are furnished South Seas style in wicker, rattan and bamboo, accented in ice cream pastels. Your room will have a mini-safe, patio or balcony, air conditioning and ceiling fan, hair dryer, direct dial telephone, mini-bar refrigerator, and cable television. Casita rooms, which are the premium, split-level suites, have skylights. Bathrobes are provided for guest use. Su Casa, the original estate house, serves as the signature restaurant offering gourmet dining in a candlelit, open-air room shrouded in fragrant foliage. Meals are also available in the equally dressy Surf Room and in the more informal Ocean Terrace.

Camp Hyatt for the kids is one of the best children's programs on the island and it operates year 'round. Miles of pathways make the resort perfect for bicycling.

HYATT REGENCY CERROMAR BEACH RESORT & CASINO, *Highway 693 Dorado PR 00646. Tel. 787/796-1234; U.S. 800/233-1234, www.hyatt.com. Rates at this 506-room resort start at $310; suites at $750. Add $65 daily for breakfast and dinner (MAP). The hotel is 22 miles west of San Juan; airport shuttles for the 45-minute ride charge $15.*

One of a Hyatt double play that offers all the restaurants and facilities of two luxury landmark Hyatt Regency resorts, the venerable Cerromar has one of the most eye-popping swimming pools in the world. A 1,776-foot river flows on past waterfalls and grottos from one pool to another. If that is too tame for you, take a chute down the three-story-high water slide. Going with the flow, it takes a delicious half hour just to float the course. The hotel has a full spa, workout facilities, a year-round children's program, 24-hour room service, and 21 tennis courts. Dine indoors or out in a choice of restaurants here and at the neighboring Hyatt.

Room features include a mini-bar, air conditioning, hair dryer, private safe, and tropical decor rich in sea and earth tones. Most have a private balcony. At the same complex, the **Hyatt Hacienda del Mar Resort,** *Tel. 787/796-3000,* is a time-share complex with apartments and villas, its own swimming pool, and access to all the features of the two resorts. Rates are from $725.

Northwest Puerto Rico – Moderate

COSTA DORADA BEACH, *900 Emilio Gonzalez Street, Route 466, Kilometer 0.1, Isabela. Tel. 787/872-7255. Rates at this 53-room hotel start at $122. It's a two-hour drive from San Juan, between Arecibo and Aguadilla.* Don't confuse this with the Hyatt Dorado Beach, which is a far grander, most expensive resort an hour east of here. There is a beach, though, and the hotel has a restaurant, swimming pool, and tennis courts. It's wheelchair accessible, and is a good stopping point on the Atlantic north of the main highway from Arecibo to Aguadilla.

Northwest Puerto Rico – Budget

HOTEL OCEAN FRONT, *Road 4466, Kilometer 0.1, Isabela, Jobos Beach Sector, Bajuras Area. Tel. 787/872-0444 or 872-3339. Rates are from $65.* This attractively priced in is on world-famous Jobos Beach and has a small, but unique restaurant.

West & Southeast Puerto Rico – Expensive

HORNED DORSET PRIMAVERA HOTEL, *Route 429, Kilometer 3.0, Rincón. Tel. 787/823-4030, www.horneddorset.com. Rates at this 31-room hotel start at $280. Units at the 22-unit condo complex are $800. The hotel is 15 minutes north of the airport at Mayagüez or 2 1/2 hours from San Juan via the northern route through Arecibo then south through Aguadilla.*

Rincón, known as a world capital of surfing, is on a windswept cape overlooking the Mona Passage on Puerto Rico's west coat. Known familiarly as the Primavera, the hotel is a sprawling collection of dashing suites and villas obviously designed for discerning travelers who shun the beaten path. Of all the U.S. inns and B&Bs nationwide cited in one Zagat Survey, this one was rated 13th. Handmade mahogany furniture, including the stately four-poster beds, was made on the island. Marble and red clay tiles are set off by louvered wood doors that open to balconies overlooking the sea, and rich tapestry-type draperies and upholstery. Bathrooms are lavishly furnished with bidet, footed bathtub, and glowing brass trim.

The main building houses the restaurants. The hotel has a freshwater pool, library, and bar. Rooms have ceiling fan but no radio or television, room service (except breakfast) and no accommodations for children under age 12. Dining is in the open air for breakfast and lunch; dinner in the main dining room offers a choice of open air or air conditioning.

West & Southwest Puerto Rico – Moderate

MAYAGÜEZ RESORT & CASINO, *Route 104, Kilometer 0.3, Mayagüez PR 00680. Tel. 787/832-3030, www.mayaguezresort.com. Rates are $155-$285. Ask about packages.* A booming business hotel as well as a family resort, this affordable hotel has a restaurant, lounge, swimming pool, a casino, and tennis courts and it is wheelchair accessible. Valet parking is available. Expect good, no-frills value. **HOLIDAY INN AND TROPICAL CASINO MAYAGÜEZ,** *Route 2, Kilometer 149.9. Tel. 787/833-1100 or 800/HOLIDAY. Rates at this 154-room hotel start at $121. The hotel is two miles north of the city, ten minutes south of the airport.*

Although it's not on the beach, this impressively modern hotel is set on steeply dramatic grounds filled with forestry and flowers. There's a big swimming pool, a casino, a restaurant and a lounge.

VILLA COFRESI HOTEL & RESTAURANT, *Route 115, Kilometer 12.3, Rincón. Tel. 787/823-2450, Fax 787/823-1770, E-mail: info@villacofresi.com. Rates at this 80-room hotel are $105-$155. Ask about packages.*

Right on the beach is this modern, motel-style hotel with a big swimming pool, restaurant, bar and souvenir shop. Air-conditioned rooms have cable television. Ask your hosts how the hotel got its name. (Hint: Confresi was a pirate.)

West & Southwest Puerto Rico – Budget
ANDINO'S CHALET AND GUEST HOUSE, *133 Eighth Street, La Parguera Sector, Lajas. Tel. 787/899-0000. Rates start at $45.*

Off the beat path between in the southwestern corner of the island is this pleasant inn. Drive to the beach, restaurants, sightseeing.

Central Mountain Range
GUTIÉRREZ GUEST HOUSE, *Road 119, Kilometer 26, El Llano Sector, Maravilla Norte Area, Las Mariás. Tel. 827-2087 or 827-3453. Rates at this 12-room guest house start at $47. Credit cards aren't accepted. It's an hour east of Mayagüez in the mountains.*

If all you want is a humble mountain getaway in a pleasant inn with a swimming pool, meeting room and bar, this is the overnight for you.

LA CASA GRANDE, *Road 612, Kilometer 0.3, Caonillas Abajo Sector, Utuado. The hotel is ten miles northeast of Utuado on Route 612 near the intersection of Route 140. Tel. 787/894- 3939, 894-3600, or 888/343-CASA, www.hotelcasagrande.com. Rates at this 20-room inn are from $75.*

This is the place to get away from it all in a secluded, mountain retreat where units are scattered in the hills. Each room has its own balcony, hammock, and private bath. Eat in Jungle Jane's, take side trips to the Acrecibo Observatory, Rio Camuy and Caguana Indian Ceremonial Park, and hike the Toro Negro Forest. Start the day with yoga meditation, then go kayaking on Dos Bocas Lake. The resort has a freshwater swimming pool.

South Coast

COPAMARINA BEACH RESORT, *Route 333, Kilometer 6.5, Guánica (near Ponce), mail address P.O. Box 805. Tel. 787/821-0505 or 800/468-4553, Website: www.copamarina.com. Rates at this 107-room, deluxe resort are from $165; mini-suites from $230. It's about 30 minutes from the Ponce airport.*

A favorite with divers and snorkelers, this beautiful 18-acre resort is a UNESCO-designated biosphere adjacent to the Guánica dry forest at the edge of a sea filled with colorful fish, shells and sea gardens. Swim and dive in crystal-clear waters. Hike and birdwatch in the forest reserve, which is said to have even more bird species than El Yunque. Dine in your choice of two restaurants; enjoy the lounges, swimming pool, lap pool, Jacuzzi, tennis course, and live entertainers on some nights.

HOTEL MELIÁ, *75 Christina Street, Ponce. Tel. 787/842-0260, http://home.coqui.net/melia. Rates are from $85 plus parking.*

Stay in the heart of this captivating city while you explore the city and countryside. Rooms are air conditioned and have telephone and cable television. Mark's at the Meliá, the hotel's restaurant, is a local favorite. Try the seared tuna with soy wasabi dip, the homemade duck sausage, shrimp mofongo, or the rack of lamb roasted in a crust of goat cheese. It's open for lunch Wednesday through Sunday and for dinner nightly. *Tel. 284-6275.*

HOLIDAY INN PONCE & EL TROPICAL CASINO, *3315 Ponce By-Pass Road. Tel. 787/844-1200, www.holiday-inn.com. Rates are from $125.*

Have the predictable, reliable comforts of a Holiday Inn plus a lively casino in a hotel that offers a swimming pool, restaurant, lounge with entertainment, and ample parking.

PONCE HILTON & CASINO, *1150 Caribe Avenue, Ponce. Tel. 787/259-7676, Fax 787/259-7674, or 800/HILTONS, www.hilton.com. Rates at this 156-room hotel start at $260 plus $10 daily for valet parking and $4.50 daily for self parking. Ask about packages. The hotel is seven minutes from the city.*

Ponce is coming into the spotlight as a tourism center and this exclusive Hilton meets the challenge by offering luxury surroundings, two restaurants, three bars, a swimming pool, tennis courts, a fitness center and a casino that jingles from noon to 4am. The cove-shaped swimming pool with its splashy waterfalls is surrounded by tropical landscaping that sets off the striking turquoise and white of the hotel.

For children there's a playground and a kids' camp in summer; for working travelers there's a well-equipped business center. Rent a boat or watersports equipment, ride a bicycle, swim off the beach, and let the concierge arrange sightseeing excursions to nearby attractions. The hotel is wheelchair accessible.

East of San Juan & Offshore Islands
The islands of **Culebra** and **Vieques** are reached from Fajardo by ferry. (See *Getting Around Puerto Rico* earlier in this chapter).
POSADA LA HAMACA, *68 Castelar Street, Culebra. Tel. 787/742-3516. Rates at this guest house are from $60.*
It's fun to take the ferry to this island off Fajardo, and live the Robinson Crusoe life in this friendly guesthouse by the sea.
AMAPOLA INN & TAVERN, *144 Flamboyan Street, Esperanza Sector, Vieques. Tel. 787/741-1382. Rates are from $65.*
Kick back in an end-of-the-world guesthouse near the beach. The inn has its own restaurant.
CROW'S NEST GUEST HOUSE, *Box 1521, Road 201, Kilometer 1.6, Florida Sector, Vieques PR 00765. Tel. 787/741-0033; Fax 787/741-1294. Rates at this 16-room hotel start at $80. Town and the beach are six minutes away.*
The name describes the setting, high atop a hill overlooking rolling green hills in the middle of the island. It's not in town nor on the beach, but the breezes and lofty loneliness of the hills have an appeal all their own. Rooms have a living area and facilities for light cooking. Make your own breakfast and lunch; dine in the oceanview restaurant, one of the best on the island for both food and caring service. Don't miss the weekly Tuesday Happy Hour for bargain drinks and great camaraderie. Hang out in the poolside gazebo or sign up for diving, snorkeling, riding, or an excursion to Phosphorescent Bay.
LA CASA DEL FRANCÉS, *Route 996, Box 458, Esperanza, Vieques PR 00765. Tel. 787/741-3751; Fax 787/741-2330. Rates at this 18-room guesthouse start at $75.*
A turn-of-the-century plantation mansion and designated historic landmark is your home. Swim in the pool, go horseback riding, explore the palm-fringed beach nearby, walk the verdant grounds, and dine each evening on fresh fish or lobster.
HACIENDA TAMARINDO, *Box 1569, Route 996, Kilometer 4.5, Vieques PR 00765. Tel. 787/741-8525; Fax 787/741-3215. Rates at this 16-room guesthouse are from $135 including full, American breakfast.*
Owner Linda Vail decorated each room with a special touch of art, antiques or some of her collectibles. The central atrium, split by a three-story-high tamarind tree, is stunning. Half the rooms have an ocean view; others look out over the green countryside. Swim in the pool or walk to the nearby beach. The hotel has no restaurant except for breakfast.
INN ON THE BLUE HORIZON, *Vieques PR 00765. Tel. 787/741-3318; Fax 787/741-0522. Rates at this 15-unit inn are from $175, including breakfast. When booking arrange for pick-up at the airport or ferry dock.*
This hotel offers not only the best digs on the island but also the finest dining. Have breakfast in the terrace restaurant and return for dinner of

blackened fish, a hearty creole soup, or an exotic game dish. Go fishing or sailing, or just lounge by the magnificent pool overlooking the sea and outlying cays.

East of San Juan – Moderate

FAJARDO INN, Road 195, Parcelas Beltrán Sector, Puerto Real area, Fajardo. Tel. 787/863-5195. Rates at this 115-room inn are from $85.

Relax in a country inn setting in a pleasant little *parador* with a swimming pool and restaurant.

RIO GRANDE PLANTATION ECO RESORT, Route 956, Kilometer 4.2, Guzman Abajo Sector, Rio Grande. Rates are from $125. Tel. 787/887-2779, www.riograndeplantation.com.

This resort does a lot of group and team-building business. The 40-acre resort has a small lake, an impressive swimming pool, and lavish gardens in the shadow of El Yunque, the rain forest. Walk boardwalks through the splendor of the Rio Grande valley.

East of San Juan – Budget

HOTEL DELICIAS, 499 Union Street, Puerto Real Area, Fajardo. Tel. 787/863-1818. Rates start at $60.

Puerto Ricans frequent this modest establishment, which has a restaurant and is near the beach.

HOTEL LA FAMILIA, Road 987, Kilometer 4,1, Las Croabas Sector, Fajardo. Tel. 787/863-1193, www.hotellafamilia.com. Rates are from $79. Up to two children can stay free in parents' room.

A windswept setting and attractive rates make this a good buy. The hotel has a swimming pool with sun deck, and, like almost all accommodations in Puerto Rico, is handicap accessible. It's a short walk from the beach and is near golf, tennis, casinos and water sports. The hotel's Tropical Paradise Restaurant is open breakfast through dinner, serving native as well as international dishes.

LUQUILLO BEACH INN, 701 Calle Ocean Drive, Luquillo. Tel. 787/889-3333, www.luquillobeachinn.com. Rates start at $126 for an apartment that sleeps up to four. Two-bedroom apartments that sleep up to six are from $115. Ask about special weekday rates. It's between San Juan and Fajardo, about an hour from the airport.

Settle into your own housekeeping unit near the famous beach at Luquillo and not far from El Yunque, the rain forest. The inn has a swimming pool and whirlpool; units have television with cable and VCR.

Country Inns (Paradores) Throughout Puerto Rico

The *parador* network of country inns is sponsored by the Puerto Rican Tourism Company to provide budget lodgings in less-traveled parts of the island. Most sites are chosen for their outstanding natural beauty. Unless stated otherwise, all paradores listed below offer double rooms for less than $76 nightly. All are booked individually. For more information, *Tel. 800/866-7827, www.gotopuertorico.com*. Accommodations are basic and not all have room telephones, but all take credit cards.

BAHIA SALINAS, *at the end of Road 301 at El Faro, Cabo Rojo in Puerto Rico's southwest corner. Tel. 787/254-1212. Fax 787/254-1215. Rates are $90-$125.*

This 24-room inn on the beach has a swimming pool, authentic Puerto Rican cuisine, and air conditioning. It's handy to Phosphorescent Bay.

PARADOR BOQUEMAR, *Box 133, Boquerón PR 00622. Tel. 787/851-2158, Fax 787/851-7600. Overlook Boquerón Bay near Cabo Rojo. It's at the end of Highway 100 at Road 101.*

A nature refuge and other attractions of southwestern Puerto Rico are nearby. The 75 rooms have refrigerators and air conditioning and some overlook the bay. The hotel has a bar, restaurant, and swimming pool.

PARADOR BORINQUEN, *Route 467, Kilometer 2, Borinquen, Aguadilla. Tel. 787/891-0451, Fax 787/882-8008.*

A good home base for exploring northwest Puerto Rico, this 32-room parador has parking food service and a bar, a swimming pool, air conditioning and television. It is wheelchair accessible.

PARADOR EL BUEN CAFÉ, *381 Route 2, Kilometer 84, Hatillo, Tel. 787/898-1000, Fax 787/898-7738.*

West of San Juan, this 20-room parador is handy to north coast beaches, Arecibo Observatory, Rio Abajo Forest, and the caves at Rio Camuy. It is air conditioned, has parking for guests, and offers native meals at native prices.

HOTEL PARADOR EL FARO, *Route 107, Kilometer 2.1, mailing address Box 5148, Aguadilla PR 00605. Tel. 787/882-8000, Fax 787/is 891-3110.*

This 75-room parador has air conditioning, telephone, television, a restaurant and bar, tennis courts, and a swimming pool. El Faro is wheelchair-accessible.

FAJARDO INN, *Road 195, Parcelas Beltrán 52, Fajardo. Tel. 787/860-6000. Fax 787/860- 5063. This inn is an hour east of the San Juan airport and has 75 rooms.*

Handy to the ports where boats leave for Vieques, Culebra, and the U.S. Virgin Islands is this pleasant inn with a restaurant, swimming pool, air conditioning, room phones, and wheelchair access.

HOTEL PARADOR HACIENDA GRIPIÑAS, *Route 527, Kilometer 2.5, mailing address Box 387, Jayuya PR 00664. Tel. 787/828-1717, Fax 787/828-1719.*

Near the village of Jayuya, known for its crafts and Taino Indian history, this 19-room parador is near one of the island's highest peaks. The old estate house once anchored a coffee plantation and it's surrounded by flowers and shrubbery. Its restaurant specializes in traditional foods.

HIGHWAY INN, *Road 100, Kilometer 8.0, Cabo Rojo. Tel. and Fax 787/851-1839. This 17-room inn is at the southwest corner of Puerto Rico.*
The Inn has a restaurant and bar, room service, satellite television, beauty salon, and private parking for guests.

PARADOR J.B. HIDDEN VILLAGE, *Road 2 at Route 4416. It's in northwest Puerto Rico between Aguadilla and Rincón. Box 937, Aguada PR 00602. Tel. 787/868-8686, Fax 787/868-8701.*
On a country road near the historic hamlet of Aguada, this 43-room parador has a restaurant that has been named a Méson Gastronomico, indicating exceptional value in good, local cuisine. Your balcony will overlook the swimming pool; nearby are ocean sports, bowling, and roller skating. Rooms are air conditioned, wheelchair accessible, and have cable television.

PARADOR EL GUAJATACA, *Route 2, Kilometer 103.8, mailing address Box 1558, Quebradillas PR 00678. Tel. 787/895-3070, Fax 787/895-3589; toll-free 800/964-3065.*
A dramatic seashore where the Guajataca River pours into the sea is the setting for this 38-room parador. Rates here are in the $70-$90 category, more than the other paradores, but you'll have volleyball courts, a swimming pool, restaurant and bar, air conditioning, telephone, cable television, and a million dollar location.

HOTEL PARADOR EL SOL, *9 East Santiago R. Palmer, mailing address Box 1194, Mayaguez PR 00681. Tel. 787/834-0303, Fax 787/265-7567.*
Lower floors of this 52-room parador, which is in downtown Mayagüez, wrap around a tiled swimming pool. Rates include a continental breakfast and the staff are glad to help you find your way around the attractions of the west coast. Rooms have refrigerator, hair dryer, air conditioning, telephone and cable television. The parador has a restaurant.

HOTEL PARADOR JOYUDA BEACH, *Route 102, Kilometer 11.7, mailing address Box 1660, Cabo Rojo PR 00681. Tel. 787/851-5650, Fax 787/255-3750.*
This 41-room hotel is on a beach famous for its seafood restaurants, sunsets, and fishing charters. Play volleyball on the beach and swim in the sea. Rooms have air conditioning, television, and telephone, and there's a restaurant and bar.

PARADOR LA HACIENDA JUANITA, *Route 105, Kilometer 23,5, mailing address: HC 01 Box 8200, Maricao PR 00606. Tel. 787/838-2550, Fax 787/838-2551, toll-free 800/443-0266.*
Once the greathouse of a 19th century coffee plantation, this 21-room parador is family operated and has a restaurant and bar. Swim or play tennis, then explore the surrounding mountains and rainforest. Rooms have four-poster beds; the lobby is decorated with antique coffee-making equipment.

PARADOR MARTORELL, *6A Ocean Drive, mailing address Box 384, Luquillo PR 00773. Tel. 787/889-2710, Fax 787/889-4520.*
This 10-room, family-run parador is next to famous Luquillo Beach with its colorful vendors, shapely palm trees, and acres of pristine sand. Rooms are air conditioned and havė cable television; restaurants are nearby. Rates include a full breakfast.

PALMAS DE LUCÍA, *Panoramic Road 901 at 911, Camino Nuevo, Playa Lucia, Yabucoa. Tel. 787/893-4423. Fax 787/893-0291.*
Located on a remote Caribbean beach off the tourist path in Puerto Rico's southeast corner, this 21-room inn has a restaurant, air conditioning, a swimming pool, room phones and a swimming pool.

PARADOR PERICHI'S, *Route 102, Kilometer 14.3, Cabo Rojo, Tel. 787/ 851-3131, Fax 787/851-0560.*
Facing Rones Island is this 41-room hotel. It's near the beach and has parking, restaurant and bar, volleyball, air conditioning, telephones, and television. Many of the rooms have balconies. The location is ideal for exploring the beaches and playgrounds of Puerto Rico's southwest corner. By January 2001, an additional 22 rooms will be open.

PICHI'S, *Road 132, Kilometer 204.6, Guayanilla. Tel. 787/835-3335, fax 835-3272.*
This air-conditioned inn has good local cookery, a swimming pool, and room phones. It's located along the Paso Fino Horse route and is handy to Guánica Dry Forest, south coast beaches, and seafood restaurants along the south coast.

PARADOR POSADA PORLAMAR, *Kilometer 3.3, mail address P.O. Box 3113, La Parguera, Lajas PR 00667. Tel. 787/899-4015.*
Right on the water in a resort village, this 18-room parador is wheelchair accessible and air conditioned. All around are places to dine and have fun. Boats leave from its dock for the area's outstanding dive sites.

PARADOR VILLA ANTONIO, *Route 115, Kilometer 12.3, Rincón PR. Tel. 787/823-2645, Fax 787/823-3380.*
Cottages and apartments on the beachfront are handy to Rincon and west coast attractions. Enjoy the swimming pool, playground, and tennis courts and use the barbecue. Rates at this 61-room parador are in the $90-$144 range. Rooms are air conditioned and have cable TV.

VILLAS DEL MAR HAU, *Road 466, Kilometer 8.3, Isabela. Tel. 787/872-2627, Fax 787/872-2045, www.villadelmar.net. This parador has 37 rooms.*
Headquarter at this handy address in the heart of in increasingly touristy area on the inn's private beach along Puerto Rico's northern coast west of San Juan. There's a restaurant serving local specialties, tennis, a swimming pool, horseback riding, and air conditioning. Every cottage has a kitchenette, but planned meals are available.

VILLA DEL MAR, *Road 304, Albizu Campos Street, La Parguera, Lajas. Tel. 787/899- 4265. Fax 787/899-4832.*

Make this 25-room inn your headquarters for exploring Puerto Rico's southwest region. Rooms are air conditioned and have telephones, and there is a swimming pool. Wheelchair access is available but the inn does not have its own restaurant.

PARADOR VILLA PARGUERA, *Road 304, La Parguera, Lajas. The inn is west of Ponce and south of Mayagüez. La Parguera, mailing address Box 273, Lajas PR 00667. Tel. 787/899-7777, Fax 787/899-6080, toll-free 800/288-3975. Rates at this 70-room parador are from $90-$112.*

Rooms have two double beds, a balcony, air conditioning and telephone and there's a restaurant and bar. Take a night cruise to Phosphorescent Bay, swim in the saltwater pool, and enjoy the Saturday night dancing and show.

PARADOR VISTAMAR, *6205 Route 113, Kilometer 102.8, Quebradillas PR 00678. Tel. 787/895-2065, Fax 787/895-2294.*

When you stay in this 55-room parador you're in the heart of one of Puerto Ricans' favorite vacation regions on a hilltop overlooking the rugged Guajataca coast. There are swimming pools, a basketball court, tennis courts, a laundry, garden pathways, dancing and live music on weekends, and a gift shop. Nearby are the Rio Camuy caves and other points of interest. Rooms have air conditioning, telephone, and cable television and are wheelchair accessible.

Where to Eat

Here is great news for less-than-adventurous foodies! Throughout Puerto Rico, you'll see familiar mainland fast food outlets – not just McDonald's, Subway, Taco Bell, Pizza Hut, and KFC, but more upscale chains such as Chili's, Pizzeria Uno, and specialty chains such as Baskin Robbins and Orange Julius. Even the popular Ruth's Chris Steakhouse is part of a chain, and Palio at the Westin Rio Mar is a clone of the one at the Swan in Walt Disney World.

The locally popular **Pollo Tropical** chain features fruity roast chicken, rice, beans, and plantains. Fast food or gourmet fare, Puerto Rico offers the widest range of Caribbean, Latin, and American foods in the islands. Unless stated otherwise, these restaurants accept credit cards.

One of the most exciting dining options in the Caribbean is Puerto Rico's **Dine Around Program**. Pay one set price of $49 per day, which buys breakfast at your hotel and dinner at any of 12 other restaurants in the San Juan area. Ask your travel agent, or inquire when you arrive at your hotel whether it's available. The program does not apply in peak seasons.

Foods of Puerto Rico

Puerto Rico's version of bon appetit is **buen provecho**, a lip-smacking way of starting meals featuring the island's unique blend of old and new, Spanish and Caribbean. **"Cocina criolla"** or creole cuisine, started with the Tainos, Amerindians who grew cassava, corn, yams, and taro that are still island staples. Yuca flour is the basis for a flat bread that is still an everyday favorite. Introduced by the Spanish were wheat flour, garbanzo beans, cilantro, coconut, garlic, rum, and a cornucopia of vegetables including tomatoes, eggplant, and onions. With African slaves came gandules (pigeon peas), plantains, and okra.

Island favorites include fried **green plantains**, or tostones, which are seen commonly on a plate that includes meat, rice , and beans. Fast-food stands offer **alcapurrias**, a dough of grated taro root and green bananas stuffed with meat, crab, or chicken. **Empanadillas** are deep-fried turnovers filled with cheese, meat or chicken. Try **bacalaitos**, fritters made from salt cod, or **surrullitos**, which are cigar-shaped cornmeal fritters dipped in a sauce made from mayonnaise and ketchup. **Rellenos de papa** are deep-fried mashed potato balls with a filling of meat, chicken, or cheese. **Amarillos** are yellow plaintains cooked in butter or oil.

Your criollo meal will probably consist of meat, fish or chicken plus a side dish of **arroz blanco**, or white rice, and **habichuelas**, or beans cooked in a pungent sofrito sauce. Try **mofongo**, a popular side dish of mashed fried green plaintains seasoned with garlic and pork. The national celebration dish is roast suckling pig but Puerto Ricans also love their seafood, often served escabeche-style, which means marinated.

For dessert, flan is a favorite that is usually a vanilla custard but is sometimes flavored with coconut, mashed pumpkin, or breadfruit.

The local bread pudding, **tembleque**, will be familiar to mainland taste buds. So will rice pudding, called **arroz con dulce**. Try one of the tropical versions flavored with tamarind, coconut or soursop. Guava shells served with crackers and cream cheese are a typical dessert. The meal ends with Puerto Rican coffee, drunk black or with whipped, boiled milk.

Old San Juan – Expensive

CHEF MARISOLL CONTEMPORARY CUISINE, *202 Cristo Street. Tel. 787/725-7454. Park free for two hours at La Cochera. Open for dinner only. Closed Monday. Main dishes are priced $20 and higher. Reservations are essential.*

Dine in a romantic courtyard on the creations of Marisoll Hernandez who learned her art at Hilton hotels abroad. Make reservations well ahead and prepare yourself for an unusual feast according to the best of today's marketplace. There will be a couple of wonderful soups and perhaps pheasant, a curry, a roast, and always the catch of the day. The menu is brilliant and innovative but is also limited and very esoteric, so this isn't the place for fussy eaters who always look for the burger and fries while others order the chef's special of the day.

CHERRY BLOSSOM, *in the San Juan Marriott Resort, 1309 Ashford Avenue, Condado. Tel. 787/723-7300. Open daily for lunch and dinner. Plan to spend $35 per person. Live music sometimes serenades diners. Reservations are suggested.*

Dote on the finest Asian dishes in this pleasant room. Plenty of vegetarian dishes are available, or order any of the classic beef, pork, duck, chicken or seafood dishes with just the right amount of heat–or none at all if you say so.

LA CHAUMIÈRE, *367 Tetuan Street, Old San Juan behind the Tapia Theater. Tel. 787/722-3330. Reservations are urged. Main dishes are priced $20 to $40. Hours are 6pm to midnight nightly except Sunday. Use the valet parking.*

Dine on classic French cuisine in a rustic, heavily beamed room that takes you to the French countryside. Start with one of the patés, oysters Rockefeller, or a soup followed by roast lamb, the chateaubriand with vegetables served for two, veal Oscar, bouillabaisse, or *coq au vin.* Live music is often on the menu.

DÁRSENA, *in the Wyndham Old San Juan Hotel, second floor, 100 Brumbaugh Street. Tel. 787/721-5100. Open daily for breakfast, lunch and dinner, it's an easy walk from the cruise terminal and other points in Old San Juan. Parking is hard to find; use the valet parking. Expect to pay $25 for lunch and $45-50 for a three-course dinner.*

Tourist hordes have overlooked this delightful room, so it's the perfect hideaway except during periods when something is going on in the harbor. Then it's busy with in-the-know diners who fill tables on the outdoor terraces, one on the ground floor and another off the restaurant on the second floor. The breakfast buffet is an excellent value, with two price tiers–one for cold foods only and the other including made-to-order omelets and an array of other hot dishes. Escape here on a hot day to lunch in quiet, air-conditioned bliss far from the streetside din. There's a good choice of salads, sandwiches and main dishes. Dinner is elegantly prepared and presented, on a par with

Coqui

Here's how to make this popular Puerto Rican dessert/drink:

• 1 cup coconut cream, 3/4 cup half and half or light cream, 1 teaspoon vanilla extract, 1 cup dark rum, 1 cup medium rum, 2 tablespoons orange-flavored liqueur, nutmeg.

• Shake everything except the nutmeg together in a one-quarter bottle and chill several hours or overnight. Shake and pour into parfait glasses. Sprinkle lightly with nutmeg, and serve as a dessert or after-dinner drink.

any of the better-known restaurants we have tried in Old San Juan. Try one of the seafood inventions, a fork-tender steak, or one of the flavorful chicken recipes. Desserts are irresistibly eye-appealing.

MARISQUERÍA RESTAURANT CASA ESPAÑA, *on the second floor of the Casa de España, 1066 Ponce de León Avenue, Puerta de Tierra. Tel. 787/722-7080. Hours are noon to 3pm and 6-10:30pm Tuesday through Friday, 4-10pm Saturday and noon to 7pm Sunday. Self- or valet park. Plan to spend $30 per person for dinner.*

Many people overlook this delightful room, thinking it isn't open to the public, but call for reservations and prepare yourself for a treat. Chef José Abrue, who is also executive chef at José José in Condado, will create a Spanish or Creole meal you won't forget. Lobster and fresh fish are always a good bet, and Jose prides himself on his seafood presentations. You can also have one of the chicken dishes, steak, or pork. Although jackets aren't required, do dress well for the evening. Patrons are locals, who come here for special occasions, business dining, and special dates.

THE PARROT CLUB, *363 Fortaleza Street. Tel. 787/725-7370. Hours vary seasonally but it's open for lunch and dinner. Call for hours and reservations. Dine for $30 per person; children order from the kids' menu for $10 or less. Parking is difficult and no valet is available, so walk or take a cab.*

Live music rings from this hotspot into the surrounding street. It's noisy, crowded and just the place to have a roaring good time with tourists and friendly locals. You might come here just for a drink before or after dinner, but the food is excellent too. Have one of the mofongos, fresh seafood, or steak served Caribbean style.

IL PERUGINO, *105 Cristo Street. Tel. 787/722-5481. Open for dinner nightly 6:30 to 11pm, the restaurant requires reservations after 4pm. Main dishes are priced $20 to $30.*

It calls itself San Juan's best Italian restaurant and displays the awards that seem to prove it. Owner-chef Franco Seccarelli is on hand nightly to make sure guests receive the kindest welcome, superb dining, and one of the most comprehensive wine lists in the city. Try the pastas, polenta with shrimp, carpaccios, rack of lamb, or marinated salmon. The building, a restored, 200-year-old townhouse, is named for Perugia, Franco's home town.

TROIS CENT ONZE, *311 Fortaleza Street. Tel. 787/725-7959. Expect to pay $100 for dinner for two. It's open for dinner daily except Monday. Reservations are strongly recommended.*

The name (say TWAH-SAWNT-OHNZE) simply states the street address of this deliciously Parisian restaurant. Rejoice in fine wines and fragrant French specialties such as coq au vin, seafood in puff pastry, velvety soups, roasts wreathed in just the right touch of fresh herbs, buttery vegetables steamed to perfection, and delicately sauced fresh fish, scallops or lobster. Service is precise without being stuffy, and you're forgiven if your French has a Spanish accent.

YUKIYÚ, *311 Recinto Sur, Old San Juan. Tel. 787/722-1423. Expect to pay $45-$50 for dinner. Hours are noon to 2:30pm and 5-11pm. Reservations are suggested; parking is by valet.*

You may not get beyond the sushi bar, a rare find in Puerto Rico. Choose from a long list of sushis then move on to the grilled lamb with polenta, fresh salmon with udon noodles, lobster tail in a creamy sauce, fresh cod in basil butter, or hibachi chicken. If you prefer, your favorite stir-fry combinations will be made for you tableside in a frenzy of fiery theatrics.

Old San Juan – Moderate

AL DENTE, *309 Recinto Sur, Old San Juan. Tel. 787/723-7303. Reservations are recommended. The restaurant is open Saturday noon to 10:30pm. Expect to pay $25 for dinner.*

The style is casual Italian and the food a fusion of continental flavors and fresh Puerto Rican harvests. Start with the spinach stuffed with rice and cheese, then try the specialty of the house, fettuccine with shrimp and red and green sweet peppers. Veal is served in a variety of ways including a delectable, veal-stuffed tortellini; chicken comes in a sassy sauce of white wine, black olives, mushrooms, capers and tomatoes.

AMADEUS, *106 San Sebastian Street, Plaza San José. Tel. 787/722-8635 for reservations. Hours are Tuesday through Sunday noon to 2am but last orders are taken at midnight. Entrees are $10-$24.*

This old stone building has stood since the 1700s, when it was built for a wealthy merchant. You can dine economically on pizza or a sandwich (the Amadeusburger weighs 10 ounces and sells for $10.25 with sweet potato chips and salad). Or spend more freely for the fresh fish of the day, shrimp in garlic sauce, fresh salmon risotto, grilled tenderloin mignonettes in grainy mustard sauce, pork scallopini, or baked chicken breast stuffed with escargot and mushrooms. Pastas are priced in the $15-$17 range. The choice of appetizers is impressive. There's always a soup of the day, fritters, rice balls filled with Parmesan, dumplings, codfish croquettes, and Buffalo wings. We like the ripe plantain mousse or the fried plantains with caviar. For dessert, have the chocolate tart, flan, guava cheesecake, or guava and mango mousse. Afterwards, linger over espresso, tea, or–and this is a nice touch–hot chocolate. Cigar smoking is permitted at the bar.

EL PATIO DE SAM, *Calle San Sebastian 102, Plaza San Jose, Old San Juan Tel. 787/723-1149 or 723-8802. The kitchen is open Friday-Saturday to midnight, Monday-Thursday to 11pm, Sunday to 10pm. Main dishes are $10 to $35. Reservations aren't required. Park at Ballaja and your ticket will be validated.*

Lavish use of plants and potted trees turns this air conditioned indoor restaurant into an outdoor patio known among Americans for its juicy burgers. For something different try the seafood-stuffed sole, breaded cheese stuffed shrimp, or rabbit in garlic sauce. Standards such as homemade lasagna, barbecued ribs, and beef *en brochette* are popular with homesick gringos. For dessert there's flan or Hungarian chocolate torte.

LA BELLA PIAZZA, *355 San Francisco Street. Tel. 787/721-0396. Reservations are suggested. Dine for $25 or less. It's open for lunch noon-2:30pm and dinner 6:30-10:30pm. Dress is elegant casual.*

Authentic Italian dishes are celebrated in this pleasantly, old-world setting in the heart of the old city. Have one of the soups, a zesty Caesar salad, the pasta of the day or one of the seafood dishes.

LA MALLORQUINA, *207 San Justo Street, Old San Juan. Tel. 787/722-3261. Hours are Monday through Saturday, 11:30am to 10pm. Main dishes are priced $14 to $30. Reservations are recommended for dinner but are not accepted for lunch. Open Sundays except in September.*

Opened in 1848 and set among the arches and courtyards of a colonial-era building filled with antiques, this is a local icon packed at lunch time with visitors. If you want to try traditional Puerto Rican dishes in an old-island setting, this is the place to order asopao (gumbo), arroz con pollo (chicken with rice), garlic soup, corn sticks, and homemade flan.

PANORAMA, *in the Hotel Milano, 307 Fortaleza Street. Tel. 787/729-9050. Dine for $20-$25. It's open daily for lunch and dinner.*

Order from an international menu with Creole specialties as you gaze out over the harbor from the terrace. Live music plays at peak times.There's a special menu for kids.

Old San Juan – Budget

BUTTERFLY PEOPLE CAFE, *Calle Fortaleza 152, Old San Juan. Tel. 787/723-2432. Light dishes are priced $5 to $10 but steaks are also available. It's open for lunch only, daily except Sunday.*

This is a witty, whimsical operation that we were delighted to find still thriving under the care of the "butterfly people" we met a few years back. They're a real family who love butterflies and have a real sense of what has lasting appeal to travelers and locals alike. Shop the gallery for butterflies in a variety of art forms. Then lunch on a cold soup, a creamy fruit drink, a steak, or quiche.

CYBERNET CAFÉ, *5575 Isla Verde Avenue, Tel. 787/791-3138, E-mail: cybernetcafepr@hotmail.com. Hours are 10am-10pm daily except Sunday, when it's open 11am-9pm.*

Check your e- mail or have a chat. The cafe serves snacks and coffee. Also available here are faxing, copies, printing, scanning, and other computer services. After dark, come here for the reggae and salsa.

HARD ROCK CAFE, *253 Recinto Sur, Old San Juan. Tel. 787/724-7625. Prices are $4.50 to $17. Reservations aren't required but call for news of special events involving live music or happy hours. Hours are Monday-Friday 11:30am to 11 pm and Saturdays and Sundays 11am-11pm. The shop opens at 10:30am.*

If you "collect" Hard Rock Cafes, this busy, din-filled cafe is one to add to your list. Chicken or beef is served with pico de gallo, guacamole and sour cream. Eat inexpensively on red-hot chili or a sandwich, or splurge on a steak. The sizzling fajitas are a favorite and the classic H.R.C. hamburger is a juicy treat. Rock memorabilia on display includes items that belonged to John Lennon, Pink Floyd, and Phil Collins.

EL PICOTEO, *in the El Convento Hotel, 100 Cristo Street. Tel. 787/643-1597 or 723-9020. It's open daily except Monday for lunch and dinner. Reservations are required. Main dishes are under $10. In the hotel's Patio del Nispero, a three-course, fixed price lunch is $25.*

Don't miss the chance to visit this historic setting in a former convent. Dine in the courtyard, lushly transformed with potted plants and surrounded by boutiques you'll want to shop after lunch. Order a Caesar salad plain or with fish or blackened chicken, chicken sauteed with chestnuts, or a supersize burger. For dessert, try the guava cheesecake.

LUPI'S MEXICAN GRILL & SPORTS CANTINA, *313 Recinto Sur Street. Tel. 787/722- 1874. Eat for $10-$15. It's open daily for lunch and dinner. Lupi's is also found at Kilometer 1.3 on Highway 187, Isla Verde Avenue. Tel. 253-2198 or 253-1664.*

Let the good times roll when you tune into the game, pour from a pitcher of cold beer, and tank up on fajitas, tortillas, towering taco salads, or a juicy burger with salsa.

MARIÁ'S, *204 Cristo's Street. No telephone, no reservations. Open daily 10:30am to 3am. Eat for $10 or less.*

Order a tall, icy pitcher of sangria and a plate of nachos, rice and beans, quesadillas, or tacos. Spend the afternoon here sipping such tropical drinks as orange frost, lime freeze, papaya frost, coconut blossom or café tropical. The tee shirt outlet closes at 6pm but the drinking and Mexican dining go on into the wee hours.

Greater San Juan – Expensive
ALLEGRO RISTORANTE, *1350 F.D. Roosevelt Avenue, Puerto Nuevo. Tel. 787/273-9055 or 793-0190. It's open Tuesday-Friday for lunch and dinner, Saturday for dinner only, Sunday noon-6pm. Reservations are advised. Use the valet parking. Plan to spend $90 for dinner for two. Entrees are priced $12.95 to $32.95.*

Put on your best bib and tucker for a dining experience surrounded by doting, sensitive servers, gleaming crystal and silver, and crisp linens. Italian gourmet cuisine is featured, but you'll also find a good choice of French, California, and Caribbean dishes. You can't go wrong with one of the veal dishes or the fresh seafood. The wine list is comprehensive and international.

CHAYOTE, *603 Miramar Avenue, Miramar, in the Olimpo Court Hotel. Tel. 787/722-9385. It's open for lunch and dinner except Sunday and Monday. Use the valet parking. Main dishes are priced $10-$20. Reservations are advised.*

Sample superb Puerto Rican cuisine at this locally popular restaurant. Start with a cream of yautia soup, the prosciutto-stuffed chayote (this bland vegetable is called christophene in the French islands), or battered and deep-fried vegetables. There is a good choice of fresh fish dishes. Try the pan-seared tuna with ginger, coconut shrimp, or the juicy grouper, a filet of beef or roasted lamb. For dessert, have the almond-scented custard.

COMPOSTELA, *106 Avenida Condado, Santurce. Tel. 787/724-6088. Dinner for two without wine costs about $90. Reservations are suggested. The restaurant is open for dinner daily.*

Owner-chef José Manuel Rey prizes himself on adapting peasant dishes for modern tastes. He sprinkles fresh halibut with the juice of freshly roasted pepper and olive oil infused with coriander. His scallops are done with caramelized sweet onions and sautéed foie gras; his duck is roasted with an exotic coffee glaze. The wine cellar boasts 300 labels. White-clothed tables sit among chrome columns and lots of greenery, creating an ambience popular with up-market locals as well as visitors.

EL ZIPPERLE, *352 Roosevelt Avenue, Hato Rey. Tel. 787/763-1636 or 751-4335. Call for hours and reservations. Main dishes start at $20.*

Dine in a darkly splendid room surrounded by wine vaults filled with one of the finest wine lists in Puerto Rico. The paella Valenciana is a specialty. The family who have operated the restaurant since 1953 also offer such continental choices as wiener schnitzel, roasts, and fresh seafood in delicate sauces. Save room for a Viennese dessert.

GIUSEPPE'S, *in the San Juan Grand Beach Resort, Road 187, Isla Verde Avenue, Isla Verde. Tel. 787/791-1111. Reservations are recommended by owner-chef Giuseppe Acosa. Pastas start at $15; entrees at $20. It's open daily for lunch and dinner. Use the valet parking.*

Tables are clustered around a banquette that forms a gazebo for a mountain of flowers. A pink and white decor is anchored by a garnet carpet; paintings ring the room. Giuseppe recommends his trio of three pastas in different sauces. Italian classics on the menu include veal scaloppini in white wine, a meltingly tender osso bucco, steaks, filet, jumbo shrimp in garlic butter and a memorable linguine fruita d'mare.

LA SCALA, *in the Radisson Ambassador Plaza Hotel, 1369 Ashford Avenue. Tel. 787/725-7470. Main dishes are priced $20 to $30. Use the valet parking; two hours of free parking is provided for La Scala diners. It's open for dinner nightly 5:30 to 11pm.*

Chef Guilio is known for his northern Italian cuisine, velvety sauces, perfectly seasoned pasta dishes, fresh seafood combinations to smother linguine *al dente*, tender steaks, and sumptuous veal creations. After dinner, retreat to the casino or hit the dance floor in the Cabaret Lounge until 2am.

MANGE'RE, *311 De Diego Avenue, Puerto Nuevo. Tel. 787/792-6748. Hours are noon to 3pm and 6-10pm Monday-Thursday, to 11 pm Friday. On Sunday the kitchen closes at 9pm. Open Saturday noon to 11pm. Plan to spend $80 for dinner for two. Valet parking is available. There is also a Mange're in Dorado on Highway 693, Kilometer 8.5. Tel. 796-4444.*

You'll see a loyal local following here as well as in-the-know visitors who savor chef Gerard Cribbin's wizardry with Italian classics. Try the shrimp diavola with linguine, saltimboca, the prosciuto-stuffed jumbo veal chop, the shrimp primavera swimming in calamari ink, or the Salmone Cardinale, topped with lobster and asparagus. For starters, have one of the soups or the seafood-stuffed jumbo mushroom caps, followed by the signature Caprese salad. Pastas are made to order, al dente, and topped with your choice of half a dozen sauces. The wine list is commendable. Have the tiramisú or the white chocolate/dark chocolate cake for dessert.

MARTINO RISTORANTE ITALIANO, *in the Diamond Palace Hotel & Casino, 55 Condado Avenue, Santurce. Tel. 787/722-5256, 722-5264, or 721-0810. Plan to spend $50 per person for dinner. Call for hours and reservations. Use the hotel's valet parking.*

One of the smartest restaurants in Greater San Juan is this penthouse garden, with its mellow wood chairs and snappy white linens. Choose from an impressive wine list and a long menu of antipastos, soups, salad, and Italian favorites including a range of pastas, cooked and sauced to order. The choice of beef, veal, chicken and fresh seafood allows you to put together just the right meal with the right wine for a memorable dinner before an evening of gaming at the hotel's casino or dancing in the lounge.

MIRO MARISQUERIA CATALANA, *78 Condado Avenue, Condado. Tel. 787/723-9593. Main courses are priced $10 to $25. Use the valet parking. Hours are Tuesday through Sunday, lunch and dinner from 11:30am.*

Pungent Catalonian dishes prepared with the freshest seafood make for a special evening hosted by owner-chef José Lavilla. Start with marinated salt cod with onions and peppers or the calamari, then the superb paella cooked for two or more. Other choices include cod in cream sauce, grilled tuna with peppercorns and roast peppers, baked halibut with fresh herbs or, for parties of six or more, roast suckling pig. If you love to make a meal out of tapas alone, this is the place to choose from a long list that includes salads, fried cheese with tomato marmalade, and homemade Catalan style tomato bread.

NORMANDIE RESTAURANT *in the Normandie, Avenida Munoz Rivera, Puerto de Tierra, corner of Calle Los Rosales. Tel. 787/729-2942. Hours are 6-10pm daily. Entrees are priced $18 to $35 per person. Parking is $3.*

Located in a showy atrium in a distinctive art deco-era hotel, this restaurant is worth the trip just to see the architecture. Order from the menu of specialties that are cooked tableside, or let the waiter suggest something from tonight's specials. Ask to see the extensive wine list.

RAMIRO'S RESTAURANT, *1106 Magdalena Avenue, Condado. Tel. 7 787/21-9049. Plan to spend $50 per person for dinner. Reservations and valet parking are essential. Hours are daily noon to 3pm and 6:30 to 11pm.*

You'll remember an evening at Luis Ramiro's as a culinary highlight of a lifetime. Original, deftly created dishes include steamed cuttlefish with herbs, smoked lobster in light lemon sauce, cold avocado cream with smoked salmon, lamb pie with port wine and raisins, lentil and chickpea soup, and artichoke hearts foie gras – and that's just the starters. Main courses include a succulent roast duckling with guava and an unforgettable venison with pear in a sauce of wine, blackberries, and Armagnac or fish mousse served in sweet peppers shaped like flowers. The wine cellar boasts 25,000 bottles bearing 400 labels from wineries around the world. Dress for an upscale neighborhood.

RESTAURANTE CALIENTÍSIMO, *164 F.D. Roosevelt Avenue, Hato Rey. Tel. 787/738-3105. Most main dishes are priced $30 and up. It's open for lunch and dinner Tuesday through Saturday. Reservations are advised. Use the valet parking.*

There is a children's menu, but this is a sophisticated restaurant where you can take a business client and dine in style. Try inventive Caribbean dishes and experimental international cuisine built around local produce, fruits of the southern seas, and the finest imported meats and poultry. Don't miss the dessert list. After dinner, linger in the elegant, bohemian atmosphere for music until 1am.

RUTH'S CHRIS STEAK HOUSE, *on Isla Verde Avenue. Tel. 787/253-1717 or 791-6100. It's open nightly for dinner; valet parking is complimentary. Plan to spend $100 for dinner for two.*

Revered for its butter-tender, corn-fed prime beef, Ruth's blasts its steaks to seared perfection in an 1800-degree broiler designed by Ruth Fortel herself. After dinner, take in a show at the hotel's own night club.

THE VINEYARD, *in the Ritz-Carlton San Juan Hotel, 6961 Los Gobernadores Avenue. Tel. 787/253-1700. Plan to spend $100 for dinner for two. It's open daily for lunch and dinner. Use the hotel's valet parking. Reservations are recommended.*

Ritz-Carlton provides a regal setting for gourmet American and Mediterranean cuisine. Seafood is always a good choice in the hands of these talented chefs, but there is also a good choice of roasted beef and chicken, succulent pork dishes, lamb, and colorful vegetarian plates straight out of a picture book. The wine list is commendable and the desserts are irresistible.

PIKAYO, *Avenida de Diego 299, Santurce. Tel. 787/721-6194. It's open Tuesday through Friday for lunch and dinner, Sunday for lunch and Saturday for dinner. Expect to pay $150 for dinner for two plus $10 for valet parking and $2 per person for water. Tasting menus are priced $55 and $85. Reservations are a must, and should be made as far in advance as possible.*

Dinner here is an Occasion, whether or not you combine it with a visit to the Museum of Art, in which it is located. Museum admission isn't required but it makes for a dynamite day to browse this superb museum, then dine in a setting where you're surrounded by fine art showcased by subtly colored lighting that keeps changing. Although there's a good offering of international dishes made from imported foods, it's the local foods where Pikayo shines brightest: grilled shrimp in soursop sauce, roasted pork enhanced with spicy chorizo sausage, and always a heavenly mofongo.

The wine list is noteworthy, with an especially nice selection of Spanish and Portuguese labels. For dessert, have something sauced with the traditional dulce de leche. This is a non-smoking restaurant except for a small balcony.

Greater San Juan – Moderate

AJILI MOJILI, *1052 Ashford Avenue Tel. 787/725-9195, www.icepr.com/ ajili-mojili. Hours are Monday-Friday 11:45am to 3pm, Monday-Thursday 6-10pm and Friday and Saturday 6-11pom. Sunday 12:30-6pm and 6-10pm. Dinner main dishes are priced $15-$25.*

Pronounce it "ah-HILL-ee moh-HILL-ee." Dining here is like going home to Mom, if your mother happens to be Puerto Rican. The air conditioning adds to the comfort of an unpretentious room where the focus is on good food and fellowship. Regional dishes from around the island are featured on a menu that changes twice a month, but there's always arroz con pollo plus pumpkin fritters, a guinea hen of the day, and a selection of mofongos and inexpensive rice dishes. Most of the meats, seafood and produce come from local farms. We loved the steak marinated in rum and served with fresh mushroom sauce, although it could have done with less salt. Try the Tembleque, a quivering, coconut custard. Desserts come on a trolley. Take your pick.

The room can be noisy, especially when diners are trying to out-shout the live music, so come here for a lively evening with friends and not for whispering sweet nothings. The dress code is resort chic. Don't wear shorts or a shirt without a collar.

TANGERINE, in the Water Club, 2 Tartak Street, Isla Verde. Tel. 787/728-3666. Appetizers are priced $7 to $11; main dishes $17 to $27 and desserts $6-$7. It's open Wednesday-Sunday from 6:30pm. Don't miss the Club's other dining too. Liquid is the main bar and lounge, open for breakfast 7-11am and from 6pm onward. Specialty drinks are in the $12 range and finger foods are priced $6.50-$16.50.

In keeping with the chic, switch-on ambience of the Water Club, this restaurant calls its appetizers Foreplay, its main dishes Loss of Innocence, and its desserts Sensuous Pleasures. The room is dashingly contemporary, overlooking the main lobby from the second floor, and providing a smoker's dining area overlooking the beach. Start with sweet carrot soup, tempura frogs legs or Muscovy duck salad. Main courses include a heady cinnamon-based breast of chicken with garlic mashed potatoes and coconut-peanut sauce; salt-baked whole shrimp, grilled salmon, crisply pan-seared sea bass and tender steaks and chops.

Dessert can be a simple sorbet or ice cream, or the banana chocolate cheese cake, dripping with fudge sauce. End the meal with espresso or cappuccino followed by a fine port.

BACK STREET HONG KONG, in the Wyndham El San Juan Hotel, 6063 Isla Verde Avenu. Tel. 787/791-1224. Reservations are recommended. Hours are 6pm to midnight nightly except Sunday, when it's open for lunch only. Entrees are priced $18 to about $30. Valet parking is available.

The illusion is that of a gracious private home owned by people who have traveled and collected in the Far East. Built for the 1964 World's Fair, the restaurant was shipped here and re-assembled. Entering, it's easy to forget you're in a hotel as you are transported to a Hong Kong street. With attentive service and crisp pink table linens, the restaurant features its orange sauce served with your choice of sautéed lobster, jumbo scallops, diced chicken sliced beef, or jumbo shrimp. Live Maine lobster is almost always on the menu at today's market price. The menu has an impressive selection of Chinese poultry, seafood, and beef specialties, all expertly sauced and presented.

CASA DANTE, Avenida Isla Verde 39, Isla Verde. Tel. 787/726-7310. Open every day. Main dishes are $7.95 to $28.95 for a 12-24-ounce lobster tail. Valet parking is available.

Dante and Milly personally welcome guests to this relaxed, family, Puerto Rican restaurant. The house specialty is crushed plantain with your choice of pork, steak, shrimp, lobster, chicken, veal, or fish in a variety of presentations.

CHE'S RESTAURANTE ARGENTINO, *35 Caoba Street, Punta Las Marias. Tel. 787/726- 7202. Valet parking is available and there's also a children's menu. It's open daily for lunch and dinner.*

Come here for the giant, juicy steaks and man-size hamburgers with crisp, gleaming French fries and a nice choice of South American wines. Sweetbreads and lemon chicken and also specialties of the house.

EL CAIRO RESTAURANT, *Avenida Roosevelt (Route 23) Ensenada #352, Caparra Heights (next to Borinquen Towers). Tel. 787/273-7140 or 774-0095. It's open Tuesday-Sunday noon to 10pm. Main dishes start at $12. Valet parking is available.*

It's fun and different to try this Arabian-Lebanese restaurant and to shop its gift counter for Arabian items and take-out pastries. Belly dancers perform Friday and Saturdays, yet it's all G-rated and families are invited. Start with hummus or falafel, then choose from a host of Middle Eastern classics: shish kebob, steak tartare, curried chicken with Arabian rice, curried lamb, or a plentiful sampler platter filled with all the above and then some.

GREENHOUSE RESTAURANT & LOUNGE, *1200 Ashford Avenue, Condado. Tel. 787/725-4036. It's open for breakfast, lunch and dinner; call ahead for hours and reservations. A wide range of prices allows you to dine on beans and rice, a drink and bread for under $10, or splurge on the lobster for $39.95 plus appetizer, drinks, and dessert.*

We are reminded of a big, bustling, Broadway restaurant. Menu choices range from the very modest to the most spendthrift. It's all hearty, nononsense, American cuisine with a Puerto Rican touch. Charbroiled steaks and chops, can be ordered a *caballo* (with two eggs) for $2 extra. For breakfast, have a platter-size omelet or eggs Benedict. Later, the chicken crepe at $12.95 is a creamy, luscious lunch or dinner. The black bean soup topped with rice, chopped onion and egg, is a great buy at $4.95. (Bread and butter cost $2 extra except with full meals.) Appetizers include escargot or hearts of palm. Have the Greenhouse Salad, or make a meal of the mammoth chef salad. Main dishes include shrimp, lobster, chicken, pork chops, and steaks. For lighter dining, have a gourmet burger, cold platter, or a sandwich. Homemade cakes are offered for dessert. Like the menu, the wine list starts in the bargain basement with sangria by the pitcher, and escalates to top-floor vintages by the bottle.

HAVANA'S CAFE, *409 Calle del Parque, Stop 23, Santurce. Tel. 787/725-0888. Main dishes are priced $5 to $20. Hours are noon to 10pm Monday through Friday and 11:30am to 10pm Saturday and Sunday. Reservations are recommended for dinner Friday and Saturday. Drinks and wine could boost this into the Expensive category.*

Enjoy authentic Cuban dishes in a casually elegant room reminiscent of Havana in the 1950s. Try mofongo stuffed with shredded beef or shrimp, fresh codfish, or lobster timbales. Tuesday is cigar night.

INDIANA JOHN'S RESTAURANT, *in the Atlantic Beach Hotel, 1 Vendig Street, Condado. Tel. 787/721-6900, extension 111. Dishes are priced under $20. Open daily except Wednesday for breakfast, lunch, and dinner. A children's menu is available.*

If you're longing for yanqui cuisine in a deli setting, come here for towering sandwiches, hearty soups, eggs or pancakes cooked to order, and unpretentious, comfort food dinners.

LOS CHAVALES RESTAURANT, *Avenida F.D. Roosevelt #253, Hato Rey. Tel. 787/767-5017. Valet parking is available; major credit cards are honored noon to midnight, Monday through Saturday. Main dishes start at $20; chateaubriand for two is just under $50.*

Relaxed enough for family dining, but elegant enough for business or romance, this white tablecloth restaurant with its scenic, trompe l'oiel murals has a fine selection of California, French, Spanish and Portuguese wines to complement Spanish and international dishes. Among five menu offerings that serve two or more is a grilled seafood platter, rack of lamb, double sirloin, and a paella like mamacita used to make. Desserts for two include crepes Suzette at $13.95 and baked Alaska at $12.95.

LUPI'S MEXICAN GRILL & SPORTS CANTINA, *Isla Verde Road, Kilometer 1.3, Isla Verde. Tel. 787/253-2198 or 253-1664. Open daily 11am to 5am. Lupi's doesn't require reservations. Main dishes are $10 to $20.*

A rollicking sports bar with live music nightly after 11pm, this is the place to tank up on zesty Tex-Mex dishes such as fajitas and nachos before an evening of cheering the team and line dancing into a wee hours. Lupi's is also found at 313 Recinto Sur in Old San Juan, Tel. 722-1874, with the same hours and live jazz.

ST. MORITZ, *Avenida Ashford 1005 in the Hotel Regency, Condado. Tel. 787/721-0999. Reservations are recommended; all major credit cards are honored. Main dishes start at under $20; the lamb provençale for two is $49.*

The name promises a Swiss touch in this ocean-view dining room. Start with Swiss cheese croquettes and, if you're still in a yodeling mood, have the minced veal with roesti potatoes, or the veal schnitzel cordon bleu. The rack of lamb provençale for two is served with English mustard, a feast of vegetables, and baked potatoes. The dessert cart is laden with choices from flan to fruit tarts.

ZABÓ CREATIVE CUISINE, *14 Candina Street, Condado. Tel. 787/725-9494. The parking entrance is on Ashford across from Citibank. It's open for lunch and dinner, Tuesday through Saturday. Main dishes are $18 to $25.*

Have a drink in the cozy bar, then relax in this restored, 1910 country house while dining on conch fritters in mango and sesame sauce, rack of lamb in tamarind and ginger sauce, or salmon in parchment with black bean sauce. Eat indoors in air conditioning or on the balcony outdoors. This is a popular grazing bar. Many guests come only for tapas or only for dessert. The over-35 crowd gathers here after dinner for ballads, rock and disco.

CASITA BLANCA *Calle Tapia 351, Villa Palmera, Santurce. Tel. 787/726-0551. Hours are Monday-Thursday 11:30am to 7 pm, Friday and Saturday to 10pm Sunday noon to 5pm for buffet only. Only on-street parking is available. Two can dine for $40 to $50; the Sunday buffet is $12.*

Handy to the airport and about ten minutes from downtown is this locally-popular, family restaurant house in a *casita blanca*, or little white house. Dote on native food such as bacalaitos, the traditional codfish cakes, or a rice dish with seafood, pork, or chicken. A side dish of beans and greens, fragrant with garlic and cilantro, is served with all the rice dishes and it's superb. Roasted pork is served with rice, the bean side dish, and mashed plantains. There's beer and wine, and flan for dessert.

EL MESÓN DE MELQUIADES, *Carretera 15, Ramal 738, Kilometer 0.5, Cayey, in Barrio Culebra Alto. Expect to pay at least $40 for a meal for two, to $80 if you splurge. It's open only Friday through Sunday and no reservations are accepted. If you have to wait, take a number.*

The drive to the scenic hills lying less than an hour from San Juan can be part of the fun if you get directions at your hotel, or have a good map, or both. Start with one of the famous alcapurias, deep-fried dough stuffed with beef. Relax overlooking the hills while you dine on ham croquettes, one of the rice dishes, or the rack of lamb. Your fellow diners will be in-the-know locals. There's a nice wine list, but don't forget that the road home is hilly and twisty. Speaking of hills, you'll self-park off the road on a steep incline.

Greater San Juan – Budget

CAFÉ MEZZANINE, *in the Radisson Ambassador Plaza Hotel. Tel. 787/721-7300. Dishes are priced $10 and less. It's open for breakfast, lunch and dinner daily.*

The good thing about hotel coffee shops like this one is that they are almost always open, offering reliable food at reliable prices. Order American classics such as the BLT, pastas, burgers with fries, soups and stews, omelets, or a chop. Cooks promise the snappiest breakfast in town.

CHARDÓN BISTRO DELI RESTAURANT, *205 Chardón Avenue, Plaza Chardón, Hato Rey. Tel. 787/756-5248. Dishes are priced under $10. It's open for breakfast, lunch, and dinner daily.*

Dine simply on an American breakfast, Puerto Rican pastries, generous sandwiches, soups, salads, pastas and stews. There is a full bar.

CHEEZSTEAK GRILL, *Route 187, Isla Verde Avenue in the Isla Verde Mall, site 107-A. Tel. 787/791-4146. Dishes are priced under $10. It's open for breakfast, lunch and dinner daily. Children's dishes are available.*

This is the essential American fast food establishment, clean and uncomplicated, a place to take on fuel before you hit the mall. Please the whole family

with hot sandwiches, burgers, fries, or a salad, with a good choice of frosty drinks.
DENNY'S, *in the Isla Verde Mall, Isla Verde. Tel. 787/253-3080, is open 24 hours. Most main dishes are $10 or less.*
Although this is a member of the popular chain known for its inexpensive meals and Grand Slam breakfasts, it also offers local foods through its Sabroso Criollo menu. Other Denny's are around the city and in major cities island-wide.
JERUSALEM RESTAURANT, *Calle O'Neill G-1, Hato Rey. Tel. 787/281-8232. Dine for under $20; valet parking is available.*
Make an economical meal just from the appetizers if you like. They include Middle Eastern musts: baba ganoush, hummus, falafel, or taboulleh. Main dishes focus on fish or lamb, cooked and served in the Arabic manner. The sampler platter is the best buy; for dessert there's baklava. When you call for reservations, ask the best time to arrive for the belly dancer show. It's family oriented, exotic, and straight out of a 1950s movie.
LA PATISSERIE DE FRANCE, *1504 Ashford Avenue, Condado. Tel. 787/728-5508. It's open for breakfast, lunch, and dinner. Valet parking is available. Dishes are priced $10 or less.*
It's best at breakfast time if you love freshly baked French breads and sweet breads, but it's also a pleasant, economical spot to grab a croissant sandwich for lunch, a salad, coffee and pastry, or a light supper of quiche or soup.
SUNNY'S OCEAN VIEW TERRACE, *in the Empress Hotel at 2 Amapola Street, Isla Verde. Tel. 787/791-3083. Eat for $15-$20. It's open for breakfast, lunch, and dinner.*
Dine casually or grab something from the snack bar. Puerto Rican dishes are a popular choice here, where locals vacation, or have a Caribbean favorite. International dishes include pastas, stews, steaks and seafood.
ZUCCHINI HEALTH BAR, *1054 Ashford Avenue, Condado. Tel. 787/725-6986. Open weekdays for breakfast, lunch and dinner. Closed weekends. Valet parking is available. Eat for $10-$15.*
Dine on healthful, colorful, vegetarian cuisine and wholesome grains in this sunny, scrubbed setting. Or, drink your meal in a zesty smoothie made from local fruits or vegetables.

East of San Juan to Fajardo – Expensive

PALIO, *in the Westin Rio Mar Beach Resort, 6000 Rio Mar Boulevard, Rio Grande, 19 miles west of San Juan. Tel. 787/888-6000, extension 4808. Reservations are essential. The restaurant is open nightly for dinner; take a taxi ($20 from Fajardo) or drive in and valet park for $6. No self-parking is available. Plan to spend $50-$60 for a three-course dinner without wine.*
A woody, Mediterranean room welcomes diners who are first served a tiny pitcher of red wine in a 2,000-year-old tradition of Roman welcome. The

food here is northern Italian in a grand sweep of choices. Start with the grilled vegetable terrine, roasted portobello mushrooms with sun-dried tomato dressing, or fried calamari rings served with spicy tomato sauce and roasted pepper aioli. Tuscan white bean soup or Caesar salad precede a meal of inspired pastas or meltingly tender meats such as the 12- ounce filet of Black Angus beef with flamed morels or the rosemary chicken with braised savoy cabbage. Many dishes are accompanied by satiny risottos, which aren't to be missed. Let the sommelier suggest a wine from more than 200 selections; let the server suggest a dessert from tonight's list of sweets.

PARADISE SEAFOOD,, *Route 3, Kilometer 75.0, Principal Street, Punta Santiago Sector, Humacao. Tel. 787/852-1180. Dishes are priced $20-$30. Open daily except Monday for lunch and dinner. Reservations are suggested.*

Choose from a generous selection of fresh fish, shrimp, scallops, Caribbean lobster, chowder and seafood combination specialties served with plantains or French fries, and rafts of colorful garnishes. Start with one of the crusty, flavorful appetizers, then have a leafy salad. Children can order from their own menu.

East of San Juan to Fajardo – Moderate

A LA BANDA WATERFRONT RESTAURANT, *Highway 3, Kilometer 51.4, in the Puerto del Rey Marina, Fajardo. Tel. 787/860-9162. Main dishes are priced $10-$20. It's open daily for lunch and dinner.*

Things can get crowded at this popular marina during vacations and holidays, when the great seafood brings 'em in and brings 'em back. Order fresh fish done Puerto Rican style, live Caribbean lobster, a steak, chicken, a hearty salad, or a sandwich. Children get their own menu. Dine indoors with air conditioning of outside in the marina setting.

ANCHOR'S INN, *Route 987, Kilometer 2.5, Sardinera Sector, Fajardo. Tel. 787/863-7200. Open daily except Tuesday for lunch and dinner. Main dishes are priced $10-$20. There's a children's menu.*

A delightful find in the Farajdo area is this treasure with its moderately-priced fresh seafood and imported beef dishes. End the meal with a cup of the wonderful Puerto Rican coffee.

MARBELLA, *in the Westin Rio Mar Beach Resort, 6000 Rio Mar Boulevard, Rio Grande, 19 miles west of San Juan. Tel. 787/888-6000, extension 4812. Reservations are recommended. Buffet breakfast is $13.50; lunch $15.95 and dinner $23.95. Only valet parking is available.*

The dramatic decor in a bright, three-story-high room overlooking the sea sets the mood for a riot of great eating from buffets laden with fresh fruits, hot and cold dishes, bushels of breadrolls, and some of the best pastries on the island. Each night celebrates a different theme such as Italian, Caribbean, Puerto Rican, Asian, or Greek, so call ahead to see what's on for tonight. Menu service is also available for those who can resist the buffet. The hotel's other moderately priced restaurant, **La Estancia**, is in the tennis club and is open for lunch and dinner. Valet park, then take the free shuttle. Pan-seared red snapper is served in orange ginger sauce, Cornish game hem is stuffed with yuca and topped with Spanish sofrito sauce, and there's a mofongo of on the day.

Also in the resort are Club Coqui and Cobitos, both delis in the moderate price range, and The Grille Room for Caribbean and international food and Shimas for Asian food, including a sushi bar, both in the expensive range.

MARIE'S, *Route 3, Kilometer 70.3, Principal Street, Humacao in the Punta Santiago Sector. Tel. 787/852-5471, Dishes are priced $10 to $20. It's open daily except Tuesday for lunch and dinner.*

Fresh seafood is the specialty of the day. Have the grouper fried or broiled, dorado done Puerto Rican style, swordfish, shrimp, scallops, or a steak or burger grilled to order. Children can order from their own menu. Dress is resort casual.

PORTO FINO FINE PIZZA & GRILL, *Highway 3, Kilometer 51.4, Puerto del Rey Marina, Fajardo. Tel. 787/860-9162. It's open daily for lunch and dinner. Main dishes are priced $10-$20; children get their own menu.*

This is a vacation hotspot for Puerto Ricans, so it can get crowded on weekends and holidays. Everyone loves the pizza but you can also choose from a menu rich in Italian classics, American favorites, and Caribbean staples.

VICTOR'S PLACE SEAFOOD, *2 Jesús T. Piñero Avenue, Luquillo. Tel. 787/889-5702. Dishes are priced $10-$20. It's open daily except Monday for lunch and dinner.*

Victor knows his seafood, and locals flock to this casual, unpretentious place for the mahi- mahi, swordfish, scallops, salmon, grouper and shrimp, all served with plenty of salad and fries. There's chicken and beef for those who don't eat seafood.

Ponce Area & the South Coast

EL BODEGÓN DE TALAVERA, *Calle Lena 4474, downtown Ponce. Tel. 787/843-5271. Main dishes are priced $10 to $24. Salads are $3.25 to $5.50. Call for reservations and hours.*

Our guess is that this superb, small restaurant on a back street near the square sees very few gringos. Only a few of the staff speak English, but they all speak Hospitality with a capital H and the chef is a genius. Start with a platter of tapas such as fritters filled with conch or plantain, chicken bites, steamed shrimp as big as robins, or smoked salmon with all the trimmings. The grouper presentation is a golden fillet surrounded by sliver-thin fried plantains and creamy mashed potatoes. There are lots of chicken and beef choices but it's hard to resist the fresh seafood. Order calamari, shrimp en brochette, grouper in red sauce made with garlic and wine, fresh mahi-mahi surrounded by a medley of vegetables, swordfish grilled to perfection, or the seafood stew with pasta. There's a choice of homemade desserts including flan, but we didn't get that far.

EL MOLINITO, *Route 54, Kilometer 0.5, Guayama, one hour east of Ponce. Tel. 787/866- 1515. Open daily for lunch and dinner. Main dishes are priced $10 to $20. There's a kids' menu.*

Dine in style in his resorty spot, where Puerto Rican and Caribbean dishes are a good choice and you'll find some international dishes, such as pastas, on the menu.

EL PUERTO, *Highway 3 at the end in the Pozuelo Sector, Guayama, one hour east of Ponce. Tel. 787/866-2664. Dishes are priced $20 to $30 except for the children's menu. Except for Monday, it's open for lunch and dinner. Reservations are advised.*

Order steak or fresh seafood, prepared with a Puerto Rican twist, in this untouristy, local spot off the beaten path.

LA CAVA DE LA HACIENDA, *in the Ponce Hilton, Avenida Santiago Caballeros 14, Ponce. Tel. 787/259-7676. Reservations are urged. Hours are 6:30pm to 10:30pm daily. Plan to spend $35 per person for dinner.*

As the name suggests, La Cava looks like a wine cellar, intimate and darkly cool. It's part of a brighter restaurant, La Hacienda. The two, rambling from one room to the next, offer elegant dining on an inspired menu that changes often. Always excellent are the fish and lobster dishes, fresh vegetables, toothsome breads and rolls, and luscious desserts.

LA TERRAZA, *in the Ponce Hilton, Avenida Santiago Caballeros 14, Ponce. Tel. 787/259-7676. Call ahead for hours and reservations. Plan to spend $25 for dinner. Use the valet parking.*

Dine outdoors for breakfast, lunch, and dinner, especially at dinner time when such themes as Steak Night or Lobster Night are held. Before dinner, have a margarita at Los Balcones in the hotel and have an after-dinner drink while listening to live Latin sounds in La Bohemia lounge.

PITO'S SEA FOOD CAFE, *Route 2, Kilometer 252, Las Cucharas, a mile southwest of Ponce. Tel. 787/841-4977. Main courses are $10 to $20. Hours are 11am to midnight daily. Reservations aren't required.*

Sit outdoors overlooking Cucharas Point or indoors in the air conditioning while you dine on chicken steak or fresh fish from the seas off Ponce.

RESTAURANT EL ANCLA, *805 Avenue Hostos, Playa Ponce, Ponce. Tel. 787/840-2450. Reservations are accepted but not required. Main dishes are priced $15 to $45. It's open for lunch and dinner daily.*

You'll be at sea, literally, in a family-run restaurant built on a pier over the water. Start with a half dozen crispy tostones, followed by a paella prepared for two, filet mignon with French fries, or the red snapper in lobster and shrimp sauce.

TANAMÁ RESTAURANT, *in the Holiday Inn & Tropical Casino, Route 2, El Tuque, Ponce. Tel. 787/844-1200. Two can dine for about $50. Hours are 6am to 10pm Sunday through Thursday, and Friday and Saturday until midnight. Reservations aren't required.*

It's always a nice surprise to find fine local cuisine in a chain hotel. We also like the family-friendly ambience and the sea views. After dinner, there's gaming in the casino or listening in the lounge.

West & Southwest Puerto Rico – Expensive

AGUA AL CUELLO, *Route 301, Kilometer 11.5, El Faro Sector, Boquerón area, Cabo Rojo. Tel. 254-1212. Open for breakfast, lunch and dinner daily except Monday and Tuesday. Dinner dishes are priced $20-$30. A children's menu is offered.*

One of the "gastronomic inns" of Puerto Rico's countryside, this restaurant in a popular tourist area is famed for its fresh fish and lobster and its down-home, Puerto Rican specialties featuring fluffy rice, beans flavored to perfection, crisply fried plantains, scrumptious mofongos, fresh produce, and spicy seafood combinations.

EL RAFAEL, *Route 115, Kilometer 6.6, Caguabo Sector, Añasco, between Aguadilla and Mayagüez. Tel. 787/826-5023. Dinner main dishes are priced $20-$30. It's open daily for lunch and dinner.*

Stop here for a leisurely lunch while you're traveling the west side of the island, or make it a point to be here for a special dinner. Fork-tender steaks are cooked to order, or revel in the broiled langouste, deftly fried grouper, broiled swordfish, chicken, or a seafood stew. The setting is sophisticated casual. Children get their own menu.

HORNED DORSET PRIMAVERA, *Route 429, Kilometer 3, south of Rincón Tel. 823-4030. Reservations are essential for dinner and recommended for lunch. Hours are noon to 2:30 daily and dinner seatings at 7pm, 8pm, and 9pm. Main dishes are priced $25 to $30 and a fixed price meal is available for $68 without wine.*

Worth a special trip, this devotedly French restaurant keeps its standards to that of its parent, the Horned Dorset in upstate New York. Accustomed to a sophisticated, international clientele, the chef always has fresh seafood ready for the broiler to serve with an inspired sauce. Also on the menu are Long Island duckling, the finest meats, and delicately steamed vegetables.

MÉSON ESPAÑOL, *525 José González Clemente Avenue, Suite 3, Mayagüez. Tel. 833- 5445. Main dishes are priced from $13. It's open for lunch and dinner except Monday and Tuesday. Reservations are urged.*

Dine in splendor at one of the finest restaurants in this corner of Puerto Rico. The fare is Spanish, with Caribbean and California flair and a knowing, Puerto Rican hand. Start with one of the tapas, or make an entire meal of a half dozen plates of appetizers. Have the saucy chicken, fresh dorado in a

Mediterranean-inspired sauce, a succulent steak, or a roast, all presented with a suitable surrounding of seasonal vegetables. Try the Spanish desserts.

SU CASA RESTAURANTE, *in the Hyatt Dorado Beach Resort, Route 693, Kilometer 12.8, Dorado. Tel. 796-1234. Main dishes are priced $20 to $30. Reservations are required. Dinner served daily 6:30-10pm. Dress is elegant casual; shorts are not allowed.*

A visit here captures the essence of old Puerto Rico, in the original, oceanfront hacienda that was here before the resort was built. Dine on the veranda or in one of the Spanish-style rooms on menus from Old Spain melded with modern, Caribbean touches. Strolling musicians and candleglow add to the romance here, although there is a children's menu and older children will appreciate the magic spell cast by this graceful house.

TONY'S RESTAURANT, *Route 102, Kilometer 10.9, Joyuda Beach between Mayagüez and Cabo Rojo. Tel. 851-2500. Open daily for lunch and dinner. Main dishes are priced $8.95 to $23 except for the children's menu.*

Dining is part of the fun of visiting this beach area. Order one of the pasta dishes, fresh fish cooked to order, grilled lobster tail, or a steak. Lunch features hearty fare and lighter choices including salads, sandwiches, and burger platters. Children can order from their own menu.

ZEN GARDEN, *in the Hyatt Regency Cerromar Resort, Route 693, Kilometer 12.9, Dorado. Tel. 796-1173 or 796-1603. Reservations are required. It's open daily for dinner, 6-11pm but the sushi bar isn't open on Monday. Use the valet parking and dress in your smartest resort wear. Main dishes are priced $20-$30.*

When you have a yen for the finest in Asian cuisine, come here for a special evening of fine dining on the freshest fish, shrimp, or lobster. Or, order duckling, chicken, beef, and pork dishes galore. We could live on the sushi alone. There is seating for smokers on the outdoor terrace. Arrive early and have a sundowner overlooking the sea at the Flamingo Bar and end your evening in the casino.

West & Southwest Puerto Rico – Moderate

HOLLY'S RESTAURANT, *in the Holiday Inn, Highway 2, Kilometer 149.9, Mayaguez. Tel. 833-1100. Plan to spend $50 for dinner for two.*

Sample Puerto Rican food, fresh fish, an abundance of island vegetables, and a nice choice of sweets in this quietly elegant spot before an evening of gaming in the casino or listening to salsa sounds in Holly's Lounge.

North & Northwest Puerto Rico – Moderate

DEL MAR BAR & RESTAURANT, *13 Carro Street, San Germán. Tel. 636-4265 or 264- 2715. Open daily except Monday noon to 11pm. Main dishes are priced $10 to $20.*

The specialty of the house is Spanish paella but there is also a good choice of seafood, beef, pork and chicken dishes as well as a full bar. Make a day of it in this historic hamlet in the southwest mountains and have a meal at Del Mar.

EL OBSERVATORIO, *Route 625, Kilometer 1.1, San Rafael Sector, La Esperanza Area, Arecibo. Tel. 880-3813. It's open for lunch Wednesday through Sunday. Dine for $20 or less. Children's dishes are available.*

This is the place to stop when you're visiting the observatory at Arecibo. Native specialties include fresh fish, mofongo with chicken or shrimp, fritters, plump patties, chicken with rice, escabeche, beans and rice, and sweet rice pudding for dessert.

MANGE'RE, *Route 693, Kilometer 8.5, Dorado. Tel. 796-4444. It's open daily for lunch and dinner. Main dishes are priced $20-$30. Valet parking is available. Dress is resort casual.*

This clone of the popular restaurant at Puerto Nuevo also serves its chef's popular salmon dishes, signature salad, pastas cooked and sauced to order, and famous tiramisú dessert.

MORGAN'S, *94 Las Nereidas Avenue, next to the New Government Center in Cataño just west of San Juan. Tel. 275-0850. Open daily, noon to 11pm. Main dishes are priced $10-$20. Valet parking is available.*

Gaze out over the bay and a view of San Juan while you dine on authentic Puerto Rican specialties. Stuffed mofongo is a specialty, and there's a good choice of steaks, seafood and chicken dishes. The pub features Happy Hour prices, 5-7pm and live music plays on Friday evenings.

NEW GOLDEN CROWN, *Route 110, Kilometer 9.2, in the La Cima Hotel, Aguadilla. Tel. 890-5077. It's open daily for lunch and dinner. Dine for $20 or less.*

Choose from a big menu of Asian classics including sweet and sour pork, chicken with vegetables, soups, noodles, moo shu, beef with broccoli, or shrimp, all served as spicy or mild as you like, with a mountain of snowy, steamed rice. There's a full bar.

Chili's Grill & Bar

Puerto Rico is a fast foodie's dream, with McDonald's, Burger King, and KFC's aplenty. One of the chains that has caught on here bigtime is **Chili's**, where main dishes are priced $10-$20 and you can count on generous portions of sizzling fajitas, fries, ribs, family favorites including pastas, and desserts, washed down with their famous margaritas. Find Chili's at 1004 Ashford Avenue, Condado, Plaza Plama Real in Humacao, Plaza del Norte in Hatillo, Plaza del Sol, Bayamón, Los Colobos in Carolina, in the Mayagüez Mall, in Ponce and in other locations.

THE STEAK COMPANY, *in the Hyatt Regency Cerromar Resort, Route 693, Kilometer 12.9, Dorado. Tel. 796-1234, extension 3240. Reservations are required. It's open for dinner daily, 6:30-9:30pm. Dress shorts are allowed, but wear closed shoes and a shirt with a collar. Dress is elegant casual. Main dishes are priced $10 to $20.*

If you love a classic American steak house, this is the place for generous cuts of prime beef, prepared precisely to order. Meat-and-potatoes diners love the big, baked potatoes or mountains of fries, completing the meal with a salad, but you'll also find side dishes of vegetables, appetizers, soup, and a fine line of desserts with a Caribbean accent. Dine early, then make an evening out of it at Bacchus, a high-tech, Las Vegas-style night club.

OCEAN FRONT RESTAURANT, *Route 4466, Kilometer 0.1, Jobos Beach, Bajuras Sector, Isabela. Tel. 872-3339. Main dishes are priced $10 to $20. It's open for lunch and dinner except Monday and Tuesday. Open every day from May to September.*

Stop at this delightful north coast location for seafood or steak with a Caribbean accent. Children get their own menu. At lunch, sandwiches, salads and soups are also on the menu.

GASTRONOMIC INNS – MESÓN GASTRONÓMICO

The best of traditional Puerto Rican cuisine is served in these roadside restaurants, many of them in paradores and all of them near attractions that are of interest to local and visiting travelers. To get the coveted **Mesón Gastronómico** symbol, which appears as a green sign showing knife, fork and spoon, restaurants must meet government-set standards and must provide local fare at reasonable prices. It would be repetitious to talk about menus because you'll find here the kinds of soups, mofongos, seafoods, baked goods, salads and desserts that are local classics. Expect to pay under $20 for a three-course lunch and less than $30 for a three-course dinner (excluding lobster).

Hours vary but many of the *mesones* are open every day and many, especially those that are in paradores, serve breakfast, lunch, and dinner. All those we have visited have bar service, offer a children's menu (or are very accommodating about children's needs), and are wheelchair accessible, and we have not encountered one that did not accept major credit cards. It's always wise, however, to call ahead about features that are important to you.

North Coast

Casabi, *Road 2, Kilometer 103.8, Terranova Sector, Quebradillas. Tel. 895-3070.*

El Buen Café, *Road 381, Kilometer 84, Carrizales Sector, Hatillo. Tel. 898-3494.* Prices are a bit higher than the average mesón gastronómico if you order steaks and fresh seafood.

El Fogón de Abuela, *Road 485, Kilometer 3.1, Peñon Amador Sector, Camuy. Tel. 262- 0781*
El Ladrillo, *334 Méndez Vigo Street, Dorado. Tel. 796-2120*
Vistamar, *Road 2, Kilometer 7.9, in the Parador Vistamar, Quebradillas. Tel. 895-2065*

South Coast
Agua al Cuello, *Road 301, Kilometer 11.5, El Faro Sector, Boquerón area. Cabo Rojo. Tel. 787/254-1212. It's closed Monday and Tuesday.*
Canda's Restaurant, *12 Alfonso Street at the corner of Bonaire Street, Ponce Beach. Tel. 843-9223*
El Ancla, *9 Hostas Avenue, Ponce Beach. Tel. 840-2450*
Pichi's Steak House & Seafood, *Road 132, Kilometer 204.6, Guayanilla. Tel. 835-4140.* It's closed Monday and Tuesday.
Pito's Seafood, *Highway 2, Kilometer 2.18, Las Cucharas Sector, Ponce. Tel. 841-4977*

Central Mountains
Criollo Buffet & Salad Bar, *Road 129, Kilometer 19.6, Callejones Sector, Lares. Tel. 897- 6463.* It's closed Monday.
Don Pedro, *Road 527, Kilometer 2.5, Veguita Sama Sector, in the Parador Hacienda Gripiñas, Jayuya. Tel. 828-1717.* Prices are lower than the average mesón.
El Dujo, *Road 140, Kilometer 7.8, Jayuya. Tel. 828-1143.* Priced a little higher than other inns, this one is closed Monday.
El Mesón de Jorge, *Road 14, Kilometer 57, Montellano Sector, Cayey. Tel. 263-2800.* It's closed Monday.
El Paraiso, *Road 1, Kilometer 29.1, Cañas Sector. Caguas. Tel. 747-2012*
La Casona de Juanita, *Road 105, Kilometer 23.5, Montoso Sector, Maricao. Tel. 838-2550*
La Piedra, *Road 7718, Kilometer 0.8, Panoramic Route, La Torre Sector, Aibonito. Tel. 735-1034.* It's open only for lunch and dinner.
Marcos' Restaurant, *3 Muños Rivera Street, Caguas. Tel. 743-2306.* It's on the second floor and is priced a notch above the average gastronomic inn.

East Coast
Anchor's Inn, *Road 987, Kilometer 2.5, Sardinera Sector, Fajardo. Tel. 863-7200.* It's closed Tuesday.
Daniel Seafood, *Highway 3, 7 Marina Street, Humacao. Tel. 852-1784.* Prices are a little higher than the average inn. It's closed Tuesday.
El Tenedor, *1 Emilia Principe Street, Madrid Sector, Juncos. Tel. 734-6573*

Las Vegas, *Road 191, Kilometer 2, Palmer Sector, Rio Grande. Tel. 887-2526.* It's closed Monday and Tuesday.

Rosa's Seafood, *Road 195, 536 Tablasco Street, Puerto Real Beach, Fajardo. Tel. 863- 0213.* It's closed Wednesday.

Tulio's Seafood, *Highway 3, Kilometer 76.6, Isidro Andreu Street, Punta Santiago Sector, Humacao. Tel. 850-1840.* It's closed Monday.

West Coast

Dário's Gourmet, *Highway 110, Kilometer 8.8, Aguacate Sector, Aguadilla. Tel. 890-6143.* It's closed Monday and Tuesday.

La Cascada, *Road 101 on the corner of Gill Buyé Street, Boquerón Village, Cabo Rojo. Tel. 851-2158, extension 185.* It's closed Wednesday.

La Concha, *C4 Principal Street, Ensenada Sector, Playa Santa Area, Guánica. Tel. 821- 5522.* Prices are a little higher than those of the average mesón gastronómico.

Las Colinas, *Road 4416, Kilometer 1.3, Villa Rubia Sector, Peidras Blancas Area, Aguada. Tel. 868-8686*

Perichi's, *Road 102, Kilometer 13.6, Joyuda Beach, Cabo Rojo. Tel. 851-3131*

Tino's, *Road 102, Kilometer 13.6, Joyuda Beach, Cabo Rojo. Tel. 851-2976.* It's closed Tuesday.

Tres Amigos, *Highway 107, Kilometer 2.1, Borinquen Sector in the Parador El Faro, Aguadilla. Tel. 882-8000*

Villa Parguera, *Road 304, Kilometer 3.3, La Parguera Sector, Lajas. Tel. 899-7777.*

Seeing the Sights

San Juan

If you love old stones, it's a thrill just to stroll the slit-sized lanes of **Old San Juan** to soak up the delicious oldness of it all. Many streets have changed so little that you can imagine yourself in the days of swaggering Conquistadores, shy señoritas batting eyelashes behind their fans, and good friars gliding through the crowds. Then suddenly you see a Sony sign or a carelessly dropped gum wrapper and the 20th century comes rushing back.

Don't drive into the old city, where on-street parking is next to impossible. Instead, ride the two **free trolley tours** that cover two routes in the heart of Old San Juan. They operate every day, 16 hours a day plus evenings during **Gallery Nights** (Noches de Galerias), which are the first Tuesday of the month February through May and September through December, *Tel. 723-6286*, and they are all wheelchair accessible.

If you have a car, park it at the Covadonga lot, where trolley service begins and ends. It's one of a handful of parking areas in the old city. Others are below El Morro, at La Puntilla near El Arsenal, and Felisa Rincón near the Marina. Get off and on as you please, spending a few minutes here and a few hours there. To "do" the city right, with enough time at museums and the forts plus time out for the many shops and fine restaurants, will take several days of trolleying. For more information about Gallery Nights, Tel. 723-7080.

On Sundays from 5:30-7pm, watch the sunset from the **Paseo La Princesa** in Old San Juan while you're serenaded by local musicians. It's one of the old city's most romantic entertainments, and it's free. On Saturdays at the Plaza de la Darsena adjacent to Pier 1, local musicians, artists and sculptors display their work 6-8pm at **La Casita Tourist Information Center**. For information, Tel. 722-1709.

La Princesa, Tel. 721-2400. Puerto Rican Art Collection features the works of contemporary island artists outside the city walls along the Paseo de la Princesa in front of La Puntilla parking lot. Featured are about 200 art works including pieces from the Puerto Rican School of the '50s and '60s, the Abstractionist Movement, the Integrationist Generation, and the Puerto Rican Plastic Arts that emerged in the 1980s. The gallery is open weekdays 9am to noon and 1-4pm. Admission is free. The promenade along the bay here is a popular spot for strolling and jogging.

El Morro Castle, Tel. 729-6777, is a must, the oldest fortress still extant in the Americas. It was begun early in the 1500s and fell only once, and that briefly, to the English enemy. It saw service as late as World War II. Now managed by the U.S. Park Service, it has a souvenir shop, museums, bookstores, and miles of dungeons and ramparts to explore. Guided tours are given in English at 10am and 2pm and in Spanish at 11am and 3pm.

Also managed by the U.S. Park Service is **San Cristobál** on Norzagaray Street, Tel. 729-6777. Connected by moats and tunnels, this fort defended the city against attacks from the land side while El Morro stood sentinel against sea raiders.

Early Spanish planners built the city around grand plazas. A new one is **Quincentennial Plaza** on the city's highest point. It adjoins San José Plaza where you'll find **San José Church**, the second oldest in the Americas, and the ancient Dominican Convent. The church is open daily from 7am to 3pm and offers services on Sundays at noon and 1pm. The convent is the home of a bookshop that sells Puerto Rican literature, posters, and folk art.

The trolley guide will explain that **Casa Blanca**, Tel. 725-1454, was the home of **Juan Ponce de León**. See its fountain-filled gardens and its superb museum of artifacts from the 1500s and 1600s. It's open Tuesday through Saturday, 9am to noon and 1pm to 4:30pm. At the end of Cristo Street, **Casa del Libro**, Tel. 723-0354, is a printing museum housing one of the New World's most important 15th century collections of volumes published in Spain. It's open Thursday through Saturday, 11am to 4:30pm. Next door, the **National Crafts Center** displays local arts and crafts and nearby, the Banco Popular has a gallery featuring local arts.

In the **Plaza de la Rogativa**, see a sculpture of women bearing torches, commemorating an event during a British siege in which the women, who were merely staging a religious procession, fooled the English into thinking that reinforcements had arrived.

San Juan Cathedral is a Gothic masterpiece built in 1540 on the ruins of an early cathedral that was destroyed in a hurricane. It's here that the body of Ponce de León, seeker of the Fountain of Youth and Puerto Rico's first governor, lies in a marble vault. The cathedral is open to the public daily 8:30am to 4pm and for mass weekdays at 12:15pm, Saturday at 7pm and Sunday at 9am and 11am. A Healing Mass is held at 11am on the fourth Sunday of each month. *Tel. 722-1709* for tourist information and *Tel. 722-0861* for information on religious activities.

Next comes the **Capilla del Cristo** with its silver altar. It was built in gratitude to the Christ of Miracles by a man who had lost control of his horse and would have plunged over the edge of the cliff if a miracle hadn't brought the horse to a stop. The tiny chapel can be seen through the gate but if you want to go inside, it's open Tuesdays 10am to 3:30pm. A special mass is celebrated at the chapel on the first Sunday of August. Special masses are held during Holy Week. *Tel. 722-1709* for tourist information and *Tel. 722-0861* for information on religious activities.

A **Children's Museum** at 150 Cristo is entered through the legs of a wood giant. Inside, children can frolic through a village of playhouses, play dentist, and learn about cars and airplanes. Hours are Tuesday to Thursday, 9:30am to 3:30pm and weekends 11am to 4pm.

La Fortaleza, *Tel. 721-7000, extension 2211,* a grand ramble of archways and courtyards, is the oldest executive mansion in continuous use in the New World, dating to 1533. Guided tours are offered Monday through Friday, 9am to 4pm.

Seen from the trolley at Fortaleza and San Jose streets is the **Plaza de Armas**, surrounded by Spanish Colonial buildings as ornate as wedding cakes. On the Plaza Colon is the **Tapia Theater**, which is being renovated, and the 18th century Government Reception Center. Walk the Paseo de la Princessa, a boulevard that surrounds the old city walls, to San Juan Gate, the last survivor of the gates that were once the only passages through the mighty city wall.

South of the Plaza de Hostos is the **Arsenal de la Marina**, built in 1800 as a marina for small boats that patrolled the shallow waters around the city. At **La Casita**, home of a tourism information office, stop for information on the following museums, a cold drink and a rest on a park bench.

The **San Juan Museum of Art and History** was once the city's marketplace. Now it's filled with fine arts and changing displays. **The Museum of the Americas**, *Tel. 724-5052*, displays one of the most comprehensive and extensive exhibits of Puerto Rican and Hispanic folk art in the Caribbean in a magnificent 19th century military hospital. It's open Wednesday through Sunday, 9am to 4:30pm. On the Plaza San Jose, small museums include one devoted to Pablo Casals, the renowned cellist who moved from Spain to Puerto Rico in 1956 to protest the Franco government. The **Casa de los Contrafuentes**, an 18th century home, now houses a **Pharmacy Museum** and the **Latin American Graphic Arts Museum and Gallery**. Also in the Casa de los Contrafuentes on the Plaza San José is the **Museum of Our African Roots**, which focuses on Puerto Rico's African heritage with exhibits, masks, sculptures and historic documents. *Tel. 724-4294 or 4184*. Hours are Tuesday-Saturday 8:30am to 4pm.

The **Puerto Rico Museum of Art** (Museo de Arte de Puerto Rico), 300 De Diego Avenue, Santurce, *Tel. 977-6277*, opened in 2000 and is truly a showplace, worth a special visit even if you are not an art buff. Works in the 18 galleries are by Puerto Rican artists since the early days of European presence into modern times. The building itself is of interest because it was built as a hospital in the 1920s. It stood derelict for years before authorities realized its former wards were perfectly arranged to create dazzling art galleries. The size was doubled, using native marble and stone. While you're here, something may be playing in the 400-seat theater with its ingenious curtain based on Puerto Rico's famous mundillo lace, and its 78-foot mural. A massive, stained glass wall was created for the museum by artist Eric Tabales, who titled it *Taino Sunrise*.

Eat in the cafeteria at reasonable prices, or make an evening of it by reserving a table at **Pikayo**, *Tel. 721-6194*, the famous restaurant that moved here from Condado to be a part of this exciting effort. Meals are in the expensive category. If you want to come just for dinner, museum admission is not required. Use the restaurant's own valet parking. Parking for the museum itself is in a 600-space underground garage. See separate listing under *Where to Eat* above.

Plan an entire day to do the museum properly, with lunch, dinner, shopping the gift gallery, exploring the five-acre garden of sculpture and native flora, perhaps a program in the theater, and a long, leisurely examination of all the works of art.

Admission is $5 adults and $3 children. Hours are 10am to 5pm daily except Monday, when it is closed, and Wednesday when it's open until 8pm. Special packages that include lunch can be arranged for cruise passengers, who often arrive too early for hotel or ship check-in, or who must check out hours before their flight. Ask about it when booking a cruise.

The Ramon Power Y Giralt House, headquarters of the Conservation Trust, was the birthplace of Don Ramón Power y Giralt in 1775. He became a lieutenant in the Spanish Navy, fought against Napoleon, and participated in warms against the French in Hispaniola. The restored home is at 155 Tetuán Street, two blocks north of the Plaza de Armas, *Tel. 722-5834*, *www.fideicomiso.org.* Hours are Tuesday-Saturday 10am to 4pm. Admission is free.

Side Trips In & Near San Juan

At the **University of Puerto Rico** on the Avenida Ponce de León in Rio Piedras, *Tel. 764-0000,* browse the museum with its collection of artifacts from the pre-Columbian Taino Indians, and botanical gardens filled with tropical trees, flowering shrubs, bamboo, ponds, palms, and shaded pathways. Hours vary, so call for information.

El Yunque, whose official name is the **Caribbean National Forest**, is found 16 miles east of San Juan. The only tropical rainforest in the U.S. National Forest System, it is laced with roads and hiking paths that take you through sun-dappled trees and flowers deep into gullies wet with waterfalls. It's the home of the rare Puerto Rican parrot, which one ranger who has been here 20 years says he has heard but never seen.

It is a chilly climb to its fog-shrouded peaks and a long, hot walk to depths where waterfalls dash into clear, cold pools. The walk to **El Yunque Peak**, with its awesome view, takes about 45 minutes from the Mount Britton Lookout Tower and two hours each way on the path that leads from the Palo Colorado Visitor Information Center.

The 30-minute hike to **La Mina Falls** takes you through a fern gully filled with shy wildflowers and towering trees, ending at a wispy waterfall. Climb **Yokahu Tower** for panoramic view and stop at the many observation points, visitor information points, and picnic areas for a closer look. The visitor center at **El Portal** has a gift shop with a good selection of nature guides, maps for camping and hiking the 28,000-acre forest, cold drinks, and rest rooms. Whatever your route, it's either hot and wet or cold and wet, so it's wise to take a sun hat and poncho. There are no predatory animals, we were told, and we saw few mosquitoes.

The **Bacardi Rum Plant** is at Kilometer 2.6, Int. 888, on Route 165 in Cataño, on the northwest side of Greater San Juan, *Tel. 788-1500.* Free guided tours are conducted daily except Sunday, 8:30am to 4:30 pm. Ride the tram through tropical gardens, have a fine view of the bay and shop for souvenirs.

Take half a day to seek put the colorful marketplaces in **Rio Piedras** near the plaza and off Canal Street in **Santurce**. Open daily, the outdoor vendors display fresh island produce by locals for locals. Also in Rio Piedras is **The Botanical Garden**, where you'll see a fortune in orchids as well as hundreds of species of tropical and subtropic trees, flowers, blooming shrubs, palms, and water lilies. Bring a picnic (no alcohol is allowed) and enjoy it under a nutmeg tree. There's also a sculpture garden, herbarium, and a chapel that's popular for weddings. On the south side of the intersections of Highway 1 and Road 847, Rio Piedras. *Tel. 250-0000, extension 6580, 767-1710 or 763-4408; extension 6579 for Botanical Garden.* Admission is free. Wheelchair access is limited. Hours are 8am to 4:30pm daily except holidays. On San Juan's west side, in Bayamón. **Luis A. Ferré Science Park** is a 42-acre complex that incorporates a Transportation Museum (old cars and the oldest bicycle in Puerto Rico), an Archaeology Museum with artifacts dating to 350 BC, a lake with pedal boats for rent, a planetarium, Electric Energy Historic Museum, NASA rockets, a telephone museum, natural sciences museum with stuffed animals, and a museum of marine ecosystems and an Aerospace Museum with exhibits on space exploration, a rock collection, and an Art Museum. The Health Education Pavilion was the first of its kind in the Caribbean. It's on Route 167 south of De Diego Expressway (Highway 22). *Tel. 740-6868, 740-6878 or 740-6871.* Admission is $3 children ages 2-12, seniors, and people who are handicapped, and adults $5, plus $1 for the trolley, $3 for the planetarium movie and $2 for the simulator. Hours are Wednesday-Friday 9am-4pm, and Saturday, Sunday and holidays 10am-6pm. The box office closes 90 minutes before closing.

Out on the 'Island South'

Heading south from San Juan across the mountains, you'll pass the **Carite Forest Reserve** north of Guayama along Route 184. Stop at **Lake Carite**, stopping for snacks at a long line of folksy food stands selling pit-roasted pork, blood sausage, tripe, tropical fruits, and queso blanco (white cheese). In Guayama, the **Casa Cautino Museum** is housed in an 1887 mansion furnished with the belongings of the original family that lived here a century ago, *Tel. 864-9083.* Take the trolley tour of historic **Arroyo**, *Tel. 866-1609.*

Coamo, a city northeast of Ponce, is known for its hot springs. Founded in 1778, the town was a battle site in the Spanish-American War. Visit the historic church and the old city and take a dip in the healing springs. For tourism information, *Tel. 825-4423.* A delightful native restaurant is found at the baths.

Ponce is Puerto Rico's second city, known as the Pearl of the South. Its gas-lit streets are a movie set of neo-colonial buildings in the style known as Ponce Creole, built with riches gained from sugar and shipping. Stop at the tourist office in the Citibank on the Plaza de las Delicias, or call *841-8044, 284-4913, 843-0460 or 841-0445* for information on any Ponce sightseeing. **La Perla Theater** has been a cultural center since 1864, when it opened with a dramatic Catalonian production.

Other must-see sites in Ponce include the **Ponce History Museum**, *Tel. 844-7071 or 7042,* housed in two buildings dating to 1911 and the Plaza Las Delicias with its **Cathedral of Our Lady of Guadeloupe**. She's the city's patron saint and her feast day in February prompts one of the island's most colorful fiestas. The plaza is a place for musing and people watching, and its side streets lead past more restored 19th century treasures.

The **Parque de Bombas** (firehouse) was built in 1883 as an exhibition hall and now it is a general museum with Fire Brigade memorabilia. Two restored historic homes are the **Castillo Serralles**, *Tel. 259-1774 or 259-1775*, the mansion built by the Don Q rum fortune, and **Casa Paoli**, now a folk center, built as a home for opera star Antonio Paoli at the turn of the century. The crown jewel of Ponce's sightseeing is the **Ponce Museum of Art**, *Tel. 848-0505*, housing more than 1,000 paintings and 400 sculptures. Its contemporary collections, Italian Baroque pieces, and 19th century pre-Raphaelite paintings are outstanding.

Tibes Indian Ceremonial Center is built on the site of the oldest burial site yet found in the Antilles. A Taino village has been re-created complete with ceremonial ball court, homes, and dance ground. The complex has a museum, exhibits, an orientation movie, and a cafeteria. It's on Route 503, Kilometer 2.7. *Tel. 840-2255*. Admission is $2 adults and $1 children and seniors. Hours are Tuesday-Sunday 9am to 4pm. It's closed Mondays except holidays. English-speaking guides are on site at all times. Visitors are not permitted to wander the grounds alone and you'll miss a lot if you don't understand the Spanish-speaking guides.

Stop at the **Hacienda Buena Vista**, just north of Ponce on Road 10, and park in the lot at kilometer 16.8. Set in a subtropic forest along the Canas River, this working plantation has exhibits on coffee and maize growing. See historic exhibits showing how plantation crops were grown until the 1950s. *Tel. 722-5882;* weekends, *284-7020*. Admission is $5 adults and $2 children. Call ahead for hours. Reservations are required, and tours are given in Spanish and English and different times. Wheelchair access is limited.

If you continue west from Ponce along a route known for its fine seafood restaurants, you'll reach Guanica and the **Dry Forest Reserve** off Route 333. One of the finest examples of tropical dry forest in the world, it's the home of more than 700 varieties of plants, 1,000 types of insects, and more than 100 bird species both migratory and resident. Walk its trails under lignum vitae trees, stopping at picnic areas and Spanish ruins. Between Guanica and La Parquera is the famous **Phosphorescent Bay** (Bahia de Fosforescente). Sightseeing cruises in the area sail at night to view the natural luminescence in the water. Offshore, dive the continental shelf.

If you follow an inland route west from Ponce towards Mayagüez, it rewards you with a visit to San Germán, the second city founded by the Spanish. Its **Porta Coeli Church** dates to 1606 and it streets and plazas still retain the sleepy, sun-baked look of a 17th century colonial village. Leaving on the road to Lajas, you'll pass the **Alfred Ramirez de Arellano y Rosell Art Museum**, *Tel. 892-8870*. Shown are 19th century furniture and a small art collection. It's open Wednesday through Sunday, 10am to noon and 1 to 3pm.

East of San Juan

Route 3 leading east from San Juan is filled with commuters and commerce as well as tourists rushing to **El Yunque** and the famous beach at **Luquillo**. Almost anywhere along the highway you'll find simple restaurants serving authentic local food at modest prices, as well as roadside stands selling fried foods, fresh produce, and a native drink called mavi. Made from tree bark, it's mildly fermented.

The new (summer 2000) **Eastern Center for Art and Culture**, *Tel 447-5233 or 633-1096,* shows regional and international arts and handicrafts and also offers professional theater indoors and in an outdoor amphitheater. The permanent collection includes works of artist and sculptor Tomás Batista. It's on Highway 3 at the entrance to Luquillo.

Fajardo and the surrounding area are one of the island's seagoing centers, with massive marinas offering watersports of all kinds. At the island's eastern corner, **Las Cabezas de San Juan Nature Reserve**, locally called El Faro after its 1882 lighthouse, has hiking trails and boardwalks ending at the lighthouse with a spectacular view. It's north of Fajardo on Road 987 near Croabas. The reserve is open Friday through Sunday except major holidays; reservations are required. Tours in Spanish are given at 9:30am, 10am and 2pm. English language tours are offered at 2pm only. Admission is $5 adults and $3 children. Wheelchair access is limited. *Tel. 722-5882* on weekdays and *860-2560* weekends, *www.fideicomiso.org.*

From Puerto Real, catch a ferry to **Vieques** where the tiny fishing village of Esperanza has end-of-the-world restaurants and inns. **Mosquito Bay** here is phosphorescent (another bioluminous cove is on the southeast coast). The island offers three museums including a lighthouse, a fort and an old sugar mill. Farther out to sea lies **Culebra**, largely a wildlife refuge, with some first class beaches.

Continuing south from **Fajardo** brings you to Palmas de Mar Resort, a city in itself. In downtown Humacao, see **Casa Roig**, *Tel. 852-8380,* a home built in the 1920s by architect Antonin Nechodoma and now a museum devoted to contemporary art and architecture.

Northwest

Beaches along the Atlantic coast can be rough, but for surfers that means great waves at such places as **Jobos Beach** near Quebradillas. For calmer waters try the area near Isabela known as **The Shacks**. South of Quebradillas, **Lake Guajataca Wildlife Refuge** has miles of hiking paths through lush forests filled with sinkholes.

One of the island's blockbuster attractions is the **Arecibo Observatory**, *Tel. 878-2612,* which holds endless fascination for space groupies. Cornell University has erected mammoth equipment over a giant sinkhole to listen for radio signals from distance galaxies. Admission is $3.50 adults and $1.50

children and seniors. Hours are Wednesday-Friday noon to 4pm and Saturday, Sunday, and holidays 9am to 4pm. Bilingual interactive exhibits and video presentations introduce visitors to the world of astronomy.

Morovis, the artisan capital of Puerto Rico and a historic community dating to 1815, is worth an all-day trip. From San Juan take the De Diego Expressway west to Arecibo and continue on Highway 52 to the Trio Vegabajeño exit, then take Exit 41 (Vega Baja and Morovis) to Expressway 137 or Road 155. In the central plaza, which dates to 1834, you'll see **Our Lady of Carmen Catholic Church**, founded in 1823 and the Panaderia La Patria, one of the oldest bakeries in Puerto Rico. Try its famous breads. More than 18 of the island's best artisans live and work here and you can get a list from the city's public relations department, *Tel. 862-2155 or 862-3610.* Then seek out the workshops you want to visit to buy embroidery, stringed instruments made from native woods, santos and nativity figures, silk flowers, carved wooden birds, hand-made furniture, porcelains, baby clothes, and so on. The hamlet is especially colorful during festivals in June and July and on Sundays, when Horse Fairs are held.

South of Arecibo on Route 111 west of Utuado, **Caguana Indian Ceremonial Park**, *Tel. 894-7325,* was built 800 years ago by the Taino Indians as a ceremonial and religious site. Its stone walkways and ball courts have been unearthed, and a small museum built. The park is open Wednesday through Sunday 9am to 4:30pm.

East of Arecibo on Punta Morillo, a 19th century **lighthouse** has been restored and outfitted as a museum. Arecibo Lighthouse and Historical Park is open Tuesday-Thursday 9am to 6pm, Friday-Sunday 9am-9pm. Closed Mondays except holidays. Admission is $5. Just south of Arecibo on Route 10, **Rio Abajo Forest**, *Tel. 724-3724,* offers boat rides on a verdant valley lake. Just as in many national forests, camping is allowed by permit.

Rio Camuy Cave Park, *Tel. 763-0568 or 898-3100,* with its caverns and underwater rivers is as ancient and wildly natural as Arecibo is modern and manmade. Near the town of Lares, the Camuy River disappears into a giant labyrinth of caves carved out by the water. Trams carry passengers deep into a sinkhole and cave where impatiens bloom in tiny patches of light admitted by holes in the limestone high above. Truly one of the National Park Service's most exciting rides, the tram can accommodate only limited crowds. The park has picnic areas, rest rooms, a gift shop, and food service, a mine where you can look for gemstones, and a wild caving tour through Cathedral Cave, where you'll see ancient pictographs thought to be done by the Taino Indians. Hours are Wednesday-Sunday 8:30am until the park reaches its capacity. Call ahead to ask about availability, then arrive early. The last tours depart at 4:15pm to one area and 2pm to three other areas. Wear comfortable shoes and clothing and expect to walk.

West & Southwest

Cabo Rojo and the picture-postcard fishing village of **Boquerón** surround a long bay that probes three miles inland, spreading one of the island's largest and finest balnearios, or public beaches. **Buyé Beach** north of Boquerón is another beaut; so is **Joyuda Beach** with its long string of seafood restaurants. **Cabo Rojo Wildlife Refuge**, Route 301, Kilometer 5.1, *Tel. 851-7258*, has informative displays and nature trails. The bird watching is particularly good.

Although it's a commercial city known for its tuna processing plants, Mayagüez has some appealing attractions. At the city center, the plaza has an imposing statute of **Christopher Columbus** and is surrounded by historic buildings including the **Yaguez Theater**, a National Historic Monument that has been caringly restored. It is used to stage Spanish language plays and concerts. There's a small zoo with a children's playground, and the U.S. Department of Agriculture's Tropical Agricultural Research Station has rambling gardens that invite self-guided tours through acres of exotic plants.

Mona Island, 50 miles off Mayagüez, is managed by the Puerto Rico Department of Natural Resources and can be reached only by chartered boats. The passage can be a frisky one, so consult your doctor about seasick medication. The island is the perfect place for primitive camping at the edge of the world. The best place to find a boat and skipper is in Puerto Real, Cabo Rojo.

Driving north from Mayagüez brings you to **Rincón**, a surf-washed shore in the foothills of La Cadena Mountains. A favorite of eco-tourists, it's a place to catch a whale watching cruise or to hole up in a small country hotel. The **Rincón Maritime Museum** is on Route 413, Kilometer 2.5 and it's open weekdays noon to 4pm.

It's thought that Columbus' exploration of Puerto Rico began somewhere along the northwest coast in 1493. The **Aguadilla** area is locally renowned for its crafts shops and for its coconut palm-fringed beaches. One of the best and calmest is **Crash Boat Beach** north of Aguadilla. **Ramey Air Force Base** is now a civilian area gradually turning to tourism.

At La Parguera between Mayagüez and Ponce, **Phosphorescent Bay** comes alive at night with the sparkle of the "fireflies of the sea", actually living dinoflagellates that shine with bioluminescence. Take Highway 2 to Road 101 and Road 116 to La Parguera, where boats leave every half hour from just after dusk until about 10:30pm to cruise the bay. Fare is $4 per person. Private boats are also available for charter. By day, swim and snorkel at **Plaza Rosada**, a beach east of town or visit Mata de la Gata Island, two miles from shore.

Nightlife & Entertainment

Puerto Rico is sufficiently Americanized that most shops stay open through the siesta hours, but also Latin enough to love music, dancing, and socializing long after midnight. Casinos, which usually have adjacent bars,

often have live music and dancing and are always a good bet for night owls
because they stay open until as late as 4am.

Dancing

Lazer, on Calle Cruz, Old San Juan, *Tel. 721-4479* is open every night,
offering different themes and age limits. For a very dressy night out, dance at
the **Chico Bar** in the Wyndham El San Juan, *Tel. 791-1000*, until 1am week
nights and 3am Friday and Saturday. **Liquid**, in the Water Club is a bright,
beach overlook by day but is softly shadowed at night for romance. It's open
late and serves drinks and finger foods. In the same hotel, another bar hotspot
is **Wet**, *Tel. 728-3666*.

Dance music plays live in the **Lobby Lounge** at the Marriott Hotel, *Tel.
722-7000*, from 7pm to 1am Sunday through Wednesday and 6pm to 3:30am
Thursday through Sunday. If you need dance lessons, ask the concierge or
front desk. If you're over 40 and love Latin dancing, try **La Fiesta Lounge** in
the Condado Plaza, *Tel. 721-1000*. Dancing is 5pm to 2am Monday through
Thursday, until 3am Friday and Saturday, and until 1am Sunday.

For romance, locals and visitors simply take to the streets and plazas for
strolling, having a drink at a sidewalk café or listening to strolling musicians.
To find a horse-drawn carriage, look around the waterfront in San Juan just
off Pier 1. Or, just follow the sound of music and pop into whatever pubs are
playing your song.

In the Palmas Del Mar resort at Humacao, drink and dance at the **Palm
Terrace Restaurant & Lounge**, *Tel. 852-6000*, until 2am.

Listening posts in Old San include **Amadeus** for Latin, American, and
classical music. It's at 106 San Sebastián Street, *Tel. 722-8635* and also has a
cigar bar. Blues and Brazilian play at the **Café Bohemio**, 100 Cristo Street in
the El Convento Hotel, *Tel. 723-9200*. You must have ID proving that you're
over 21; the crowd tends to be 25-35. The bar is open until 2am. For Brazilian
music, salsa and Latin jazz, visit **The Parrot Club**, 363 Fortaleza Street, *Tel.
725- 7370*. You'll be carded. Most of the crowd are 25-35. **Stargate**, 1 R.H.

Cigar Mania

Smoke stogies with fellow smokers at the Cigar Bar at the El San
Juan Hotel & Casino in Isla Verde, Bolero's in Westin Rio Mar Beach in
Palmer, Ruth's Chris Steak House in the Sands Hotel, the smoking
balcony at the Hard Rock Cafe, The Bar at the Ritz-Carlton, and Isla
Verde. The Wyndham El Conquistador, Fajardo, has a cigar and martini
bar with pool table. It's important to call ahead for hours of cigar
evenings because not all cigar-friendly places allow smoking all the time.

Folklore & Flamenco

LeLoLai is a program that gives visitors a week-long choice of cultural shows, music and dancing, museum and dining discounts, and tours. For information on the $10 LeLoLei card, *Tel. 787/723-3135 weekdays or Tel. 791-1014 weekends and evenings*. Hotels that participate by offering folkloric music and dance programs include the **Caribe Hilton** and **Sands Hotel**. Programs are also held at the **Condado Convention Center**.

Todd Avenue, is the happening place for generation X-ers, starting at 9:30pm. *Tel. 725-4664*. Bring ID.

Out on the Island

For nightlife in Aguadilla, try **La Cabaña** on Route 110 South. In Lajas, try the **Blues Café** in the El Muelle Shopping Center, *Tel. 899-4742*. Nightclubs in Mayagüez include **Don Pepe Bar & Restaurant**, 56 Mendez Vigo Street East. **La Casita** at 36 Pearl Street, **Neno's** at 66 Diego Street, and the **Red Baron Pub** at 73 Post Street.

In Rincón, party at **The Landing** on Route 413, Kilometer 4.7 in Barrio Puntas, *Tel. 823-3112* or the **Tropical Jazz Bar** at the entrance to Córcega Beach, *Tel. 823-4922*. For nightlife in San Germán, try the **Red Baron** on Manzanares Street. In Fajardo, try the **Wyndham El Conquistador**, which has a number of venues for dancing, dining and listening. *Tel. 863-1000*. At the **Hyatt Regency Cerromar,** Bacchus is a high-energy, Las Vegas-style night club, *Tel. 787/796-1234*.

Casinos

Casinos, which are open to hotel guests and non-guests alike, open at noon and close as late as 4am. Dress is casual. Puerto Rican law doesn't permit the serving of drinks at gaming tables, so casinos have lively bars where drinks and snacks are served. If gaming is an important ingredient in your vacation, it's more convenient to stay at a casino hotel.

Hotels with casinos include:
- **Condado Plaza Hotel & Casino**, *Tel. 787/721-1000*
- **Wyndham El Conquistador**, *Tel. 787/863-1000*
- **Wyndham El San Juan Hotel & Casino**, *Tel. 787/791-1000*
- **Diamond Palace Hotel & Casino**, *Tel. 787/721-0810*
- **Radisson Ambassador**, *Tel. 787/721-7300*
- **Embassy Suites**, *Tel. 787/791-0505*
- **San Juan Marriott Resort and Stella Solaris Casino**, *Tel. 787/722-7000*

- **Inter-Continental San Juan Resort and Casino**, *Tel. 787/791-6100*
- **Wyndham Old San Juan Hotel & Casino**, *Tel. 787/721-5100*
- **Ritz-Carlton San Juan Hotel, Spa & Casino**, *Tel. 787/253-1700*

Out on the island, casinos are found at:
- **Holiday Inn Tropical Casino** *in Ponce, Tel. 800/981-2398 or Tel. 855-1200*
- **Holiday In Mayagüez**, *Tel. 800/981-8984 or 833-1100*
- **Hyatt Regency Cerromar Beach & Hyatt Dorado**, *Tel. 787/796-1234 or 800/981-9066*
- **Mayagüez Resort and Casino**, *Tel. 787/831-7575 or 724-0161*
- **The Doral at Palmas del Mar**, *Tel. 787/852-6000*
- **Ponce Hilton**, *Tel. 787/259-7676*
- **Westin Rio Mar Beach**, *Tel. 787/888-6000*
- **Mayagüez Resort & Casino**, *Tel. 787/832-3030*

Sports & Recreation
Beaches
Luquillo, off Route 3 an hour east of San Juan, is one of the most beautiful beaches in the world and has many quiet areas but, if you prefer a more festive beach, it also has vendors and food stands. It's impossible to list all the beaches of Puerto Rico and its satellite islands because they go on for mile after glorious mile. Simply drive any coast road, and drop off the highway when you see a likely spot (taking all precautions, of course, in areas where there is no lifeguard).

Balnearios, or government-run public beaches have dressing rooms, lifeguards, and parking, and are open daily except Monday. For information, *Tel. 622-5229 or 622-5228.* They include **Luquillo** listed above and **Seven Seas** in Fajardo. West of San Juan, try **Punta Salinas Beach**. Also handy to the city are **Carolina Beach** in Isla Verde and **Escambron** in Puerta de Tierra.

East of Humacao is the public beach at **Punta Santiago**. Swim on the south coast at **Punta Guilarte** east of Guayana, **Cana Gorda** west of Ponce, at **Boquerón** south of Mayagüez or at **Anasco** north of Mayagüez. Along the north coast between Arecibo and San Juan are **Cerro Gordo** and the beach at **Dorado**. **Vieques** has a public beach, **Sombé**, along its southwest shore.

Take Three Giant Steps Backward!
In San Juan, it is tradition to go to the beaches at midnight on June 23 and walk three times into the sea backwards to insure good luck in the coming year. It's the feast day of San Juan Bautista, patron saint of the city.

Bicycling & Horseback Riding
Ride bicycles with **AdvenTours**, *Tel. 787/530-8311*. Or, rise horseback on one of Puerto Rico's famous *paso fino* horses on a pristine white beach and through tropical forests with **Tropical Trail Rides**. From San Juan, take High 22 west to Highway 2. After about 23 miles, turn right on Highway 110, following signs to Rafael Hernandez Airport. After about 4 miles, turn right on Road 4466 and take the first left, following signs to the rides. Rides are available for beginning, intermediate, and experience riders every day, 9am and 4pm. For reservations, *Tel. 787/872-9256, E-mail: barker@coqui.net.*

Horseback riding is also available through **Tropical Paradise Horseback Riding** in Guaynabo, *Tel. 787/720-5454;* **Doral Palmas del Mar**, *Tel. 852-6000;* **Hacienda Carabali** ne near Luquillo, *Tel. 787/889-5820;* and **Hacienda Camp Alegre**, Yauco, *Tel. 787/856-2609.*

Camping
Many campsites are available in Puerto Rico's national parks, national forests, forest reserves and in El Yunque. Permits, which cost 50 cents per person per night, are required. For El Yunque information: *Tel. 787/721-5495 or 722-1373*. For others, contact the **Puerto Rico National Resources Department**, *Tel. 787/880-6557.*

Fishing
Deep sea and sport fishing trips can be booked through your hotel or through **Club Nautico de San Juan**, Miramar, *Tel. 787/722-0177*. Club Nautico is also found in Fajardo, *Tel. 860-2400,* Arecibo, *Tel. 878-8465,* and Boquerón, *Tel. 787/851-1336* – or reserve from the U.S., *Tel. 800/628-8426.*

At La Parguera on the southwest coast, fish with **Captain Mickey Amador**, who holds a master's degree in marine science. Fish the reefs, mangroves or deep sea by the day or half day aboard a sporty, 31-foot, twin diesel Bertram sportfish. Reservations are essential. *Tel. 787/382- 4698, E-mail: mareja@aol.com.* Also in the southwest part of the island, **Tour Marine** offers fishing charters out of Cabo Rojo, *Tel. 787/851-9259*. So does **Western Tourist Services**, *Tel. 787/265- 3214.*

Out of the Club Nautico at Santurce, fish with **Mike Benitez Fishing Charters**, *Tel. 787/723-2292.* Also at Santurce in the San Juan Bay Marina are Captain Mike's Sport Fishing Center, *Tel. 787/721- 7335* and the **Dorado Marine Center**, *Tel. 796-4645*. Also sailing out of Dorado is **Great Lady**, *Tel. 787/370-1104*. **Shiraz Fishing Charter** operates out of the Doral Resort at Palmas del Mar, Humacao, *Tel. 787/285-5718.*

Golf
Often the scene of internationally televised golf tournaments, Puerto Rico is one of the Caribbean's best choices for a golf vacation. At the **Westin Rio**

Mar Beach Resort, *Tel. 787/888-6000,* Greg Norman designed the River Course, which is surrounded by wetlands filled with bird life, and George Fazio designed the Ocean Course. Both are between the ocean and El Yunque rainforest. The twin **Hyatts** at Dorado have four golf courses designed by Robert Trent Jones, Sr., *Tel. 796-8961 or 796-1234, extension 3213.*
Wyndham El Conquistador Resort and Country Club, *Tel. 863-6784,* is one of the Caribbean's premier golf resorts. It's in Fajardo, 31 miles east of San Juan. Gary Player designed the par-72, 6,690-yard course at **Palmas Del Mar** in Humacao, *Tel. 285-2256.*
The closest public golf course to San Juan hotels is **Bahia Beach Plantation** in Rio Grande, *Tel. 256-5600,* which covers 75 acres of beach and lakes. **Berwind Country Club** in Rio Grande, *Tel. 876-3056,* is a private club that is open to the public four days a week. At **Aguirre**, *Tel. 853-4052,* the nine-hole golf course is set in an old sugar plantation. The nine-hole **Club Deportivo De Oeste** course runs up and down hills near Mayagüez, *Tel. 851-8880.* In western Puerto Rico near Ramey, the **Punta Borinquen Golf Club**, *Tel. 890-2987,* is a par-72, 18-hole course known for its windy fairways.
The **Dorado del Mar Golf Club** in Dorado is open to the public. *Tel. 787/ 796-3070.* So is the **Coamo Springs Golf and Tennis Club**, Coamo, *Tel. 787/ 825-1370.*

Kayaking

Kayaks can be rented from **EcoXcursion Aquatica** in Rio Grande, *Tel. 888-2887.*

Scuba Diving

Dive with:
- **Caribe Aquatic Adventures**, *Tel. 787/765-7444 or 787/724-1882*
- **Caribbean School of Aquatics**, *Tel. 787/728-6606*
- **Castillo Watersports**, *Tel. 787/791-6195 or 787/728-1068*
- **Coral Head Divers** in Palmas del Mar Resort, *Tel. 787/852-6000*
- **Dive Copmarina** in Guanica, *Tel. 787/821-0505, extension 729*
- **Dorado Marine Center**, *Tel. 787/796-4645*
- **Parguera Divers Trailing Center** in Lajas, *Tel. 787/899-4171*
- **Scuba Centro**, San Juan, *Tel. 787/781-8086*
- **Sea Ventures Pro Dive Center**, Fajardo, *Tel. 787/863-3483 or 800/739-3483*

Tennis

The best bet is to stay at a hotel that has tennis courts. Public play can be found at the **Isla Verde Tennis Club**, which has four lighted courts in Villamar, *Tel. 787/727-6490.* **San Juan Central Park** at the Cerra Street exit on Route 2, Santurce, has 17 courts with lights, *Tel. 722-1646.*

In Hato Rey, play the **Baldrich Tennis Courts,** *Tel. 787/763-1014.* In, Carolina, play is available at **Caribbean Mountain Villas Tennis Court,** *Tel. 787/769-0860.*

Whale Watching
January through April, whale watch with **Vikings of Puerto Rico,** *Tel. 787/823-7010.*

Shopping

Puerto Rico has a special program that arranges your visits to the shops and studios of local artisans. You'll follow a network of roads called the Rutas Artesanales to meet crafters in person and see their works in progress. For information on the **Fomento Arts Program,** *Tel. 787/758-4747, extension 2291;* the **Puerto Rico Tourism Company** artisan office, *Tel. 787/721-2400,* or the **Institute of Puerto Rican Culture Popular Arts Center,** *Tel. 787/722-0621.*

Of special interest to shoppers in search of local crafts are:
• **Aguadilla de San Juan**, 205 Old San Juan, no telephone
• **Artesanias**, Castor Ayala, Rote 187, Kilometer 6.6, Loiza, *Tel. 787/876-1130*
• **Artesanos La Casita** at the La Casita Information Center, Old San Juan, *Tel. 7 787/22-1709*
• **Centro de Artes Populares**, 253 Cristo, Old San Juan, *Tel. 787/722-0621*
• **Hacienda Juanita**, Route 105, Kilometer 23.5, Maricao, *Tel. 787/838-2550*
• **Kiosko Cultural**, El Area de la Feria, Plaza Las Americas, Hato Rey, no telephone
• **Mercado de Artesanias**, Plaza de Hostas, Recinto Sur, Old San Juan (no telephone; it's open Friday evenings and weekends)
• **Plaza las Delicias**, Ponce (no telephone, open weekends only)
• **Puerto Rican Arts and Crafts**, 204 Fortaleza, Old San Juan, *Tel. 787/July 18, 2002725-5596.* It's open daily 9am to 6pm, 5pm on Sunday. We are drawn back to this shop time and again for its authentic arts, crafts and collectibles from the hands of Puerto Rico's finest artisans.

Gallery Night (Noches de Galerías) in Old San Juan is where more than 30 art galleries stay open from 6pm to 10pm. Browse from shop to shop. Gallery Night is held the first Tuesday of each month February through May and September through December.

If you're looking for native crafts, s*antos* (hand-carved religious figures) are a popular collectable. Puerto Ricans also do basketry, leather work, papier-maché sculpture, and fine arts. Shop for antiques in buildings that are as old or older than the treasures themselves along Calle del Cristo. **Butterfly People**, Calle Fortaleza 152 in Old San Juan, is a wonderland of butterflies from all over the world, framed and frozen in time to display in your home in every size from miniature to mural. Purchases will be packed and shipped to your home if you like.

Barrachina Center at 104 Fortaleza Street, Old San Juan, claims to be the largest jewelry shop in the Caribbean and offers free samples of pina colada, which they say was invented here. Shop for custom jewelry, liquor, leather goods and sunglasses. It's open Monday through Saturday 9am to 6pm.

Now or Never, 405 Plaza Colon, Old San Juan, *Tel. 620-0123,* carries an exciting collection of local arts and imports including pottery, baubles, decorator pieces, crafts, lamps and accessories at very attractive prices. It's one of a chain found around the island. Hours are Monday-Saturday 10am-8om and Sunday 11am-5pm.

Casa Papyrus, upstairs at 357 Tetuan Street in Old San Juan, sells music and books and is also a coffee shop hangout for artists and writers. It is open daily 10:30am to 8pm. For handmade leather goods from a famous maker, shop **Dooney & Bourke's Factory Store**, 200 Cristo Street. **La Gran Discoteca**, 203 San Justo Street, is the largest record store in the Caribbean.

At **Malula**, 152 Fortaleza Street, shop for antiques and treasures from around the world. **Joseph Machini**, whose custom jewelry is also sold in Ketchikan, Alaska, has a shop at 101 Fortaleza Street. In the patio here is the **Frank Meisler Gallery** featuring whimsical sculptures and Judaica.

Puerto Rico's divinely aromatic **coffee** makes a meaningful souvenir and it is seen in gift shops and supermarkets throughout the island. One brand, Alto Grande, has been produced at the same hacienda since 1939. It's available in a variety of attractive gift packages. Locally-distilled rum is an excellent buy except at the airport, where it is priced higher than in supermarkets.

Arts & Crafts Fair

The annual **Arts and Crafts Fair** held in Old San Juan in late April is a shopper's nirvana, showcasing the works of woodworkers, basket weavers, jewelers, artists, leather workers, and makers of authentic musical instruments. The best artisans from all over the island bring their wares, so it's a good opportunity for one-stop shopping for island arts.

Of special interest are the motifs typical of Puerto Rico including santos, Three Kings, and Angel de la Guarda It's worth a special trip to be in San Juan for this event, which also features travel information from every corner of the island, plus music, food, and a festival air.

Excursions & Day Trips

The motor vessel *Caribe Cay* will speed you to St. Thomas, St. John or St. Croix to shop, snorkel or explore. Departures are at 8am Saturday and Sunday from Fajardo. From Fajardo, with Wal-mart on your right and McDonald's on your left, take the only lane to your left and pass four traffic lights. Turn left at the fourth, then right at Burger King to Fajardo Playa, the same place where ferries leave for Vieques and Culebra. Fares are $70 adults round trip and $50 one way. Children ages 204 pay $35 and ages 5-11 pay $55. U.S. citizens should carry proof of citizenship and photo I.D.; non-citizens need a passport. *Tel. 863-0582* or *860-8809, www.caribecay.com.*

For adventure and nature tours, **Copladet Nature and Adventure Travel**, *Tel. 787/765-8595,* will plan your trip on foot, horseback or vehicle to the rainforest, Luquillo Beach, the caves, Caja de Muertos Island, or San Cristobal Canyon. Sign up with **Colonial Adventure** for walking tours of Old San Juan, *Tel. 787/793-2992.*

Book an outdoor adventure with **Encanto Ecotours**, *Tel. 272-0005.* They'll take you to one of the islands or find a hiking, kayaking, or rafting adventure to your liking. Relaxation and wellness tours to the island's best nature spots are arranged by **Tropix Wellness Tours**, *Tel. 268-2173.* Nightlife and dining tours are offered by **Rico Suntours**, *Tel. 722-2080 or 800/844-2080.*

Fun Cat, *Tel. 787/728-6606,* is a 49-passenger sailing catamaran sailing out of Fajardo on two-and three-hour sunset cruises that include snacks and rum drinks for $69 per person, including bus transport to Fajardo from San Juan, snorkeling, lunch, and refreshments. The same skipper, *Tel. 383-5700,* also has a six-passenger sailboat that sails the bay for three or four hours for $495, including a sailing lesson if you like.

Animation Tours and Events offers two-hour voyages to El Morro on Wednesday from 6pm to 8pm and Friday, Saturday, and Sundays 7pm to 9pm. The $29.95 fare includes unlimited soft drinks or wine, hot and cold appetizers, disco and dancing. A cash bar serves other drinks. *Tel. 787/725-3500* or *725-3526.*

Plan an entire day for **Rio Camuy Cave National Park**, *Tel. 898-3100* or *898-2723,* a 300-acre network of sink holes, caves, and gullies formed by the Camuy River. Trams take visitors deep into the underground, visiting a couple of sinkholes including one so large it could hold El Morro. You can easily find the park on your own, 1 1/2-hours west of San Juan on Route 129, Kilometer 18.9, but most hotels also offer day trips by bus. The visitor center has a cafeteria and theater.

El Yunque National Forest deserves at least one entire day, and longer if you're a serious hiker or wildlife buff. If you drive in, it's difficult to find parking spaces but if you come on a group tour, there won't be enough time for anything more than brief hikes. The park is threaded with rest stops and kiosks where you can get souvenirs, drinks, and souvenirs. Find it 45 minutes east of San Juan on Route 3, then Route 191. Tours are offered by most hotels, or call *Tel. 787/888-1880.*

Leaving from La Parduera docks in Lajas are boats that sail **Phosphorescent Bay** by night, *Tel. 787/899-5891 or 899-2972.*

Practical Information

Area code: 787

ATM: more than 250 ATMs around the island accept MasterCard/Cirrus cards. They're found in settlements from Aguada to Yauco.

Crime: Keep your wits about you and always lock your room and car. Put values in your room safe or the hotel safe. Ask your hotel host about the best places to walk, drive, or park after dark. Security has been greatly reinforced in recent years, especially in tourist areas and in parking lots used by tourists. Tourist Zone Police in Condado are at *Tel. 787/726-7020* or *787/726-7015* and in Isla Verde, *Tel. 787/728-4770 or 787/726-2981.*

Customs & Immigration: an agricultural inspection looks for plants and products that are prohibited entry to the United States. Many fruits are allowed to be taken to the States including basketball-size pineapple that are packed and sold at the airport to take home in season. If you're unsure about agricultural products you want to take home, call the United States Department of Agriculture, *Tel. 787/253-4506.* Entry for citizens of other countries is the same as entering the United States.

Driving: holds few mysteries for the North American driver. Your driver's license is good here and most cars, equipment, and highway signs are familiar. An exception is the stop sign, which is red and six-sided but contains the word PARE. Also new to many Americans is use of kilometers in road markers. Speed limits are, however, posted in miles. Car theft is a problem; lock up and, if the rental agency provides a security device, use it.

Emergencies: much of Puerto Rico is on the 911 system, but check the telephone book in your hotel room so you will know for sure. For medical emergencies in San Juan, *Tel. 754-2222;* on the island, *Tel. 787/754-2550.* Travelers Aid at the airport is open weekdays 8am to 4pm, *Tel. 787/791-1054 or 791-1034.* For a dental emergency, 24-hour help can be found at *Tel. 754-0600.*

Government: Puerto Rico is a commonwealth of the United States.

Holidays: bank holidays include January 1, January 6, Eugenio Maria de Hostos Day (mid-January), Martin Luther King Day on January 20, George Washington's Birthday (February), Palm Sunday, Good Friday, Easter, Emancipation Day late March, Jose De Diego Day mid-April, Memorial Day (around May 26), July 4, Luis Muñoz Rivera Day mid-July, Constitution Day July 25, Jose Celso Barbosa's Birthday late July, Labor Day (early September), Columbus Day (mid-October), November 11, Thanksgiving day (third Thursday of November), December 25, December 31.

Tourist Information: Puerto Rico Tourism Company, 666 Fifth Avenue, 15th Floor, New York NY 10103, *Tel. 212/586-6262 or 800/223-6530, www.gotopuertorico.com*. In Miami, 901 Ponce de Leon Boulevard, Suite 101, Coral Gables FL 33134, *Tel. 305/445-9112 or 800/815-7391*. In Los Angeles, 3575 W. Cahuenga Boulevard, Suite 405, Los Angeles CA 90068, *Tel. 323/874-5991 or 800/874-1230*. In Canada, *Tel. 416/368-2680*. On the island, information centers are maintained at the Luis Muñoz Marin Airport, *Tel. 791-1014*; near Pier One in Old San Juan, *Tel. 722-1709*; at the airport in Aguadilla, *Tel. 890-3315*; on Route 100, Kilometer 13.7 in Cabo Rojo. *Tel. 851-7070*; and in Ponce at 291 Los Caobos Avenue, Vallas Torres Sector, Paseo del Sur Plaza, Suite 3, Merceditas, *Tel. 843-0465*. Towns that have their own tourism offices, usually open weekdays only, are Aguadilla, *Tel. 890-3315*; Ajuntas, *Tel. 829-3310, extension 247*; Anasco, *Tel. 826-3100, extension 223*; Bayamón, *Tel. 780-5552 or 798-1660*; Cabo Rojo, *Tel. 254-1922*; Camuy, *Tel. 820-4522* (this one, at Kilometer 4.8 on Route 119 is open daily); Culébra, *Tel. 742-3521*; Dorado, *Tel. 796-5740*, Fajardo, *Tel. 863-4013*; Guanica, *Tel. 821-2777*; Isla Verde, *Tel. 791-1014*; Jayuya, *Tel. 828-5010*; Luquillo, *Tel. 889-2225*; Naguabo, *Tel. 874-0389*; Old San Juan, *Tel. 722-1709*; Ponce, *Tel. 843-0465*; Rincón, *Tel. 823-5024*; San Juan, *Tel. 721-6363*; and Vieques, *Tel. 741-5000, extension 26*.

Weddings: at least ten days before you're going to be married, have a VDRL blood test from a federally certified laboratory, either in the U.S. or Puerto Rico. Have a doctor sign and certify the marriage certificate and blood test; take them to a Registro Demografico for a marriage license. A passport or other photo ID, plus copies of applicable divorce papers must be presented. Officials keep limited hours and only on weekdays, so plan well in advance. The marriage license is prepared by the minister who performs the ceremony.

English Language Radio

Tune to 1030 on the AM dial for a full-service radio station providing English language broadcasts from CBS, ABC, NBC, and the Wall Street Journal. Local news of events, new restaurants, sports, tours, festivals, and more is broadcast Monday to Wednesday at 8:30, 9:30 and 10:30am. On Thursday and Friday at these hours plus 3:30 and 5:30pm and on weekends at 9:30, 10:30 and 11:30am.

Chapter 15

u s V i r g i n i s l a n d s

On his second voyage to the New World, Christopher Columbus dropped anchor off the Salt River in **St. Croix** on November 14, 1493, and sent a boat ashore in search of fresh water. He named the island Santa Cruz before being driven off by hostile Caribs. Sailing on to **St. Thomas**, **St. John**, and Tortola, he named the group *Las Virgenes* in honor of the 11,000 virgins of St. Ursula who died at the hands of marauding Huns.

The first settlers on St. Croix were a motley group of Dutch, English, and French who could never quite get along and soon sailed on. By 1649, the English had a settlement near what is now Frederiksted, but they were driven out by Spaniards based at Puerto Rico. Finally, the island became St. Croix in 1639 when the governor of the French islands took it over as his private game park. When he died, he left it to the Knights of Malta, a group of French aristocrats who took possession of the island and planted sugar. Their debt-ridden effort ended in 1695 and France abandoned the island.

The Danish West India and Guinea Company surveyed St. Croix in 1733, sold plantations, and soared into a golden age of sugar riches. Planned on a grand scale equal to the city that is now Oslo, Christiansted emerged at a time when neo-classical architecture, with its graceful arches, was in vogue. Spurred by strict building codes and inspections, and built by exacting artisans, the city became a showplace.

Fearing German expansion during World War I, the United States bought the Danish West Indies in 1917, giving them territorial status and granting U.S. citizenship to their inhabitants. They were administered by the U.S. Navy, then by the Department of Interior until 1952 when

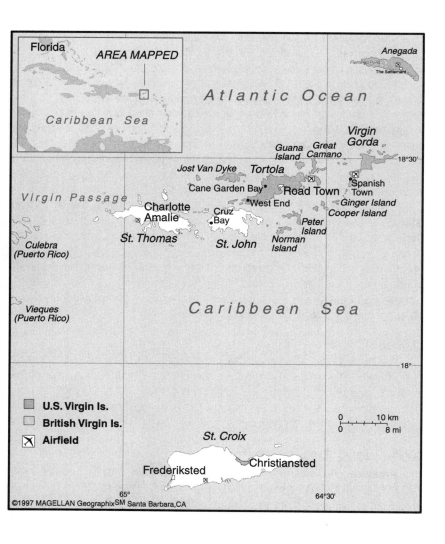

Florida
AREA MAPPED
Caribbean Sea

Atlantic Ocean

Anegada
Flamingo Pond
The Settlement

Virgin Gorda
18°30'

Guana Great
Island Camano

Jost Van Dyke Tortola

Cane Garden Bay
Spanish Town
Road Town
West End
Ginger Island
Cooper Island

Virgin Passage

Charlotte Amalie
Cruz Bay
Peter Island

Culebra
(Puerto Rico)

St. Thomas

St. John
Norman Island

Vieques
(Puerto Rico)

Caribbean Sea

18°

U.S. Virgin Is.
British Virgin Is.
Airfield

0   10 km
0   8 mi

St. Croix

Frederiksted
Christiansted

65°
©1997 MAGELLAN GeographixSM Santa Barbara,CA

64°30'

a governor was appointed. Islanders vote on their own government as well as their member of congress.

The Islands

St. Croix is 28 miles long and seven miles wide, the boyhood home of Alexander Hamilton and once dotted with more than 100 sugar plantations. Its terrain ranges from rainforest to dry desert.

St. Thomas, 13 miles long and three miles wide, is the capital of the U.S. Virgin Islands. Today known to cruisers as a Disneyland of duty-free and to yachties as a happy haven, St. Thomas has alluring beaches, resorts in all price ranges, a few historic sites, some notable dining, and lots of hidden pockets where the savvy visitor can find a quiet getaway only two hours from Miami.

Most of **St. John**, which is nine miles long and five miles wide, is a national park. Its settlement, **Cruz Bay**, looks like the setting for a South Seas movie. Its hills are threaded with hiking paths; its shining beaches and windex waters are unbeatable for unspoiled beauty. As leases expire on resorts, even more of the island will revert to national park status.

In 1996, the three U.S. Virgin Islands were joined by a fourth, **Water Island**, which was turned over to the territorial government by the U.S. Department of the Interior. Included are two docks, a beach, and public roads. A resort is being discussed but at press time has not been announced. Meanwhile, $3.3 million in government money is being spent to spruce up public areas. Take the five-minute ferry from St. Thomas to Water Island's Honeymoon Beach, which is open to visitors. As developments occur, they'll be announced in future editions of this guidebook.

Climate

The occasional "Alberta Clipper" cold front can come this far south to bring flag-fraying winds and temperatures in the 70s, but that's about the extent of the weather story here. Most days are 80-ish and sunny all year. During hurricane season, June through October, rain is more frequent and heavier and humidity can be cloying.

Arrivals & Departures

American Airlines flies into St. Thomas from JFK, San Juan, and Miami, *Tel. 800/433-7300*. **US Airways**, *Tel. 800/428-4322* flies to St. Thomas from Philadelphia and continues to St. Croix. **Delta Airlines**, *Tel. 800/221-1212* flies from Atlanta to St. Thomas and on to St. Croix. Service is also available via other air lines through San Juan.

Local airlines serving the U.S. Virgin Islands and other Caribbean points include:
• **Air St. Thomas**, *Tel. 590/277-7176, 340/776-2722* or *800/522-3084*
• **Air Sunshine**, *Tel. 888/879-8900* or *800/327-8900*

- **American Eagle,** *Tel. 800/433-7300 or 800/474-4884*
- **Bohlke International Airways,** *Tel. 340/778-9177*
- **Cape Air,** *Tel. 800/352-0714, www.flycapeair.com*
- **Delta Airlines** *Tel. 800-221-1212, www.delta.com*
- **Continental Airlines,** *Tel. 800/231-0856*
- **Isla Nena Air Service,** *Tel. 787/791-5110*
- **LIAT,** *Tel. 246/495-1187.* In St. Croix, *Tel. 340/778-9903;* in St,. Thomas, *Tel. 340/774-2313*
- **Seaborne Aviation,** *Tel. 340/773-6442 or 777-1227 or 866/359-8784.* Seaplane service is available between downtown Charlotte Amalie and downtown Christiansted.
- **US Airways Vacations,** *Tel. 800/455-0123*
- **United Airlines,** *Tel. 800/241-6522*
- **Vieques Air Link,** *Tel. 340/778-9858, www.ual.com*

Fly among the islands by **Seaborne Seaplane**. One-way fare from St. Croix to St. Thomas is $55. A 1 1/2-hour tour that includes 30 minutes of flight time is also available from St. Thomas for $99 per person, *toll-free Tel. 888/FLY-TOUR* or locally, *Tel. 777-1227.* Reservations are essential. Planes are found near the Edward Wilmoth Blyden IV Marine Terminal on Veteran's Drive, within walking distance of downtown Charlotte. Amalie. **Caribair** flies from St. Thomas or Fajardo to St. Croix, *Tel. 340/778-5044.*

A ferry operates every two weeks from St. Thomas and St. John to San Juan, Puerto Rico. The trip takes about two hours and the cost is $60 one way or $80 round trip, both including ground transportation to the San Juan Airport or Condado, *Tel. 340/776-6282.*

Ferries run between St. Thomas and St. John and from both islands to the British Virgin Islands of Tortola, Virgin Gorda, and Jost Van Dyke. Schedules vary according to time of year and day of the week, and can be curtailed by weather. Tours by air conditioned van, safari bus, bicycle or sailboat cost $95 to $140 per person. Lunch and a swim are included.

In season, **Virgin Islands Fast Ferry** operates between St. Croix and St. Thomas three times a day on weekdays and twice on weekends for a fare of $42 one-way or $75 round trip. *Tel. 877/733-9425.* Off season, frequencies are reduced.

Note: Check your local newspaper's travel pages for news of packages that include accommodations, some or all meals, and air service to one of the islands from your home town. During some seasons, more flights are added so, if your dates are flexible, ask about flights times for different weeks.

Orientation

St. Croix is only 28 miles long and seven miles wide, but it takes as long as an hour to get from **Christiansted** to **Frederiksted**. It's an impractical distance just for dinner, but a lovely drive for a day-long excursion with stops for shopping, swimming, and lunch. For such a small island it offers great diversity, from dry and cactus-rich landscape of the east to the craggy rainforest with its supersize ferns and the dramatically cliffy north coast.

St. Thomas is anchored by **Charlotte Amalie**, where ferries depart and cruise ships dock. **Red Hook** is at the east extreme of the island, and **Cyril E. King Airport** is just west of Charlotte Amalie. The island is 13 by three miles.

St. John is nine by five miles, with most activity centering around **Cruz Bay**, where ferries arrive from St. Thomas. Centerline Road goes from one end of the island to the other, allowing you to get from Cruz Bay to **Coral Bay** in about half an hour. Locals refer to the stretch of Centerline after Coral Bay as East End Road. Most of the best beaches and ruins are on North Shore Road; South Shore Road leads to Gift Hill Road, which connects to Centerline. The road is inland, but plenty of roads lead down to such beaches as **Great Cruz Bay** and **Chocolate Hole**.

Getting Around the Virgin Islands

Scheduled ferries make frequent trips among the U.S. and British Virgin Islands. A lengthy list of their schedules, which vary seasonally, is published in St. Thomas This Week (including St. John) and St. Croix This Week. Pick up free copies at any hotel. Routes go between Red Hook or Charlotte Amalie and Cruz Bay, St. John, St. Thomas, St. Croix, Charlotte Amalie and Tortola, Red Hook or Cruz Bay to Tortola, St. Thomas and St. John to Jost Van Dyke, St. Thomas to Virgin Gorda, and St. Thomas and St. John to Puerto Rico.

St. Thomas

Taxi fares are published by the Virgin Islands Taxi Commission, and range from $4.50 for one person traveling from the airport into Charlotte Amalie to as high as $10 for transport from the airport to the Red Hook area. The rate for each additional passenger is about 50 cents less than the primary fare. Additional charges are 50 cents per suitcase or box, $1.50 for trips between midnight and 6am and a 33% surcharge for radio dispatch. A two-hour tour for two costs $30 with $12 each for additional passengers. Waiting time after

Right Way, Wrong Way

For reasons we can't fathom, U.S. Virgin Islanders continue to drive on the left, English style, even though almost all vehicles have their steering wheels on the left, American style. It can be immensely confusing to visitors, especially in traffic circles. Be especially cautious, not just when driving, but when crossing the street.

ten minutes is 15 cents per minute. In town, there's a $2 minimum. Look for taxis that have a dome light and the letters TP on their license plates, indicating an officially licensed taxi. Others may not observe the official rates.

Taxi companies include:
- **East End Taxi Service**, *Tel. 340/775-6974*
- **Independent Taxi**, *Tel. 340/774-0394*
- **Islander Taxi**, *Tel. 340/774-4077*
- **Sunshine Taxi**, *Tel. 340/775-1145*
- **V.I. Taxi Association**, *Tel. 340/774-4550*
- **24 Hr. Radio Dispatch**, *Tel. 340/774-7457*
- **Wheatley Taxi Service**, *Tel. 340/775-1959*

If you have a problem or complaint, take it to the V.I. Taxi Commission, *Tel. 776-8294*. Note the driver's name and license number, which should begin with the letters TP.

Arrange an **Avis** rental car from the U.S., *Tel. 800/331-1084,* or in St. Thomas, *Tel. 774-1468*. **Budget Rent-a-Car** has seven locations around St. Thomas, *Tel. 776-5774* or *800/626-4516*.

Local car rental companies include:
- **Courtesy Car Rental**, *Tel. 340/776-6650*
- **Dependable Car Rental**, *Tel. 774-2253*
- **Discount Car Rental**, *Tel. 340/76-4858*
- **E-Z Car Rental**, *Tel. 340/775-6255*
- **Hertz Car Rental**, *Tel. 800/654-313, www.hertz.com*
- **Sun Island Car Rental**, *Tel. 340/774-3333*
- **Tri-Island Car Rental**, *Tel. 340/776-2879* or *775-1200*
- **VI Auto Rental and Leasing**, *Tel. 340/776-3616*

Buses on St. Thomas are roomy and air conditioned, but are not the fastest way to get around the island. Fares are 75 cents in town and $1 for other points on the island. Not all communities can be reached by bus. Catch a bus at Emancipation Garden or at bus stops around the island. Starting at 5:30am, buses travel about once every hour between Charlotte Amalie and Red Hook. Airport buses operate 6am-9:30pm. For bus information, *Tel. 774-5678*. Parking in Charlotte Amalie is a challenge but try the municipal parking lot east of the fort. Fees are 50 cents an hour or $4 daily; free on weekends and holidays. The lot is open 6am-6pm.

St. Croix

The airport is on the southeast shore of the island, about halfway between Frederiksted on the west coast and Christiansted, the island's main city, located mid-island on the north coast. Routes are numbered and are easy to follow if you keep track of your location on the map that comes with your rental car.

Thrifty rental cars are available at the airport on St. Croix, or can be delivered to a hotel or home. *Tel. 800/367-2277 U.S. and Canada.* When making reservations at a hotel, ask if rental cars are available on site, or if they have a package that includes a car. Prices in high season range from about $200 to $320 weekly, plus $8 daily Collision Damage Waiver.

For an **Avis** car, *Tel. 800/331-1084* from the U.S; locally *Tel. 340/778-9355.* For **Budget Rent-a-Car**, *Tel. 340-776-5774 or 778-0637;* **Hertz**, *Tel. 340/778-1402.*

Taxi companies include:
- **St. Croix Taxi Association** at the airport, *Tel. 340/778-1088*
- **Antilles Tax Service**, Christiansted, *Tel. 340/773-5020*
- **Caribbean Taxi & Tours**, Christiansted, *Tel. 340/773-9799*
- **Cruzan Taxi Association**, Christiansted, *Tel. 340/773-6388*

Taxi fares are posted and should be confirmed in advance. Round trip fare is double the one-way charge plus a charge for waiting time of more than 10 minutes. Between midnight and 6am, there is a $1.50 surcharge for rides out of town and $1 in town. Bags are 50 cents each; trunks are more. Minimum fare is $2. Lone passengers pay four times the rate charged per-person for two, e.g. the posted charged from the airport to Christiansted is $10 per person for two plus $5 each additional person. One person would pay $20; three people $25; four people $30.

Buses, *Tel. 340/773-7746*, go between Christiansted and Frederiksted every 40 minutes between 5:30am and 9:30pm every day. The route starts at Tide Village east of Christiansted and ends at Fort Frederik. By transferring at La Reine terminal, you can also get to and from the airport. Look for VITRAN bus stops. Fare is $1 for adults, 55 cents for seniors aged 55 and older. Transfers are 25 cents. Exact change is required.

St. John

If you are on a day trip and just want a tour of St. John, hop aboard one of the open air jitneys that meets every ferry. A tour is recommended, even if you're going to explore later on your own, because drivers have their own patter and style. Vitran buses run between Cruz Bay and Coral Bay. Fares are $1 adults; children under age 5 ride free.

Avis cars on St. John can be reserved at *Tel. 340/776-6374 or 800/331-1084.* **St. John Car Rental**, *Tel. 340/776-6103,* offers Vitaras, Sidekicks, Cherokees, Wranglers, and vans that hold up to eight people. Rental cars are available from **Conrad Sutton Car Rental**, *Tel. 776-6479;* **Courtesy Car Jeep Rental**, *Tel. 340/776-6650.* Jeep rentals are available from **Spencer's Jeep Rentals**, *Tel. 340/693-8784 or 888/776-6628;* **Delbert Hills Car Rentals**, *Tel. 340/776-6637.* **Varlac Car Rentals** offers Jeeps, Sidekicks, Blazers, and jitneys, *Tel. 340/776-6412.* Water taxis are available from **Inter-Island Services**, *Tel. 340/776-6282.*

Where to Stay

Add eight per cent government tax to all hotel tariffs in the U.S. Virgin Islands. In addition, a service charge is sometimes, but not always, applied in lieu of tipping. Rates quoted are for a double room in high season. Summer rates are lower.

Private villas can be booked through **WIMCO**, *Tel. 800/932-3222 or 401/849-8012.* Maid service and staff are available. Private pool villas and condos can be booked by the week through **Calypso Realty**, Box 12178, St. Thomas 00801, *Tel. 340/774-1620, Fax 340/774-1634; toll-free 800/747-4858, www.Calypsorealty.com.* On St. John book through **Vacation Homes**, Box 272 Cruz Bay, St. John VI 00831, *Tel. 340/776-6094, Fax 340/693-8455.*

Virgin Islands packages that include airfare, accommodations, and other features are offered by **American Airlines**, *Tel. 800/433-7300,* in four categories: moderate, superior, deluxe, and all- inclusive at savings of about 25 percent over piecemeal rates.

ST. JOHN
Expensive
CANEEL BAY, *P.O. Box 720, Cruz Bay, St. John, U.S.V.I. 00831. Tel. 340/776-6111, U.S. and Canada, Tel. 888/767-3966, www.caneelbay.com. Rates at this 167-room resort start at $450 double in high season. Ask about meal plans and packages.*

This is a resort that you'll either love or hate. Those who love it are so loyal that some rooms are booked years in advance; to stay in some areas, you have to wait for someone to die. Guests are met at the ferry dock in St. Thomas and brought to this legendary Rosewood resort and former Rockefeller hideaway. It was restored and reopened in the fall of 1996 without, by demand of its loyal clientele, the addition of television, room phones and other intrusions. Air conditioning has, however, been added.

On arrival you're welcomed with a chilled face cloth, then are taken by tram to your room, which will have its own patio, a mini-bar with refrigerator, coffee makings, and a wall safe. Two color schemes, one in coral and teal and another in sunny yellows and raspberry, set off handsome, handmade furniture from the Pacific Rim.

Trams make the rounds every 20 minutes and are the only way, except for more walking than is practical, around the far-flung grounds. For people whose workaday lives involve waiting for buses and trains, it can be less than amusing, especially in a tropical downpour. Picture yourself padding out to find the nearest phone to order room service or call home, and you see why some people are puzzled at this resort's mystique.

Cuisine here ranks with the best in the region. Eat at the Beach Terrace overlooking St. Thomas, Turtle Bay Estate House serving gourmet cuisine and fine wines, or in the Equator in the former Sugar Mill restaurant, where the brilliant menu is based on foods found around the equator from Brazil to Indonesia. The Caneel Bay Bar has live music nightly, and drinks are also served at the popular Breezeway/Starlight Terrace. After dinner at Turtle Bay, dance to live music.

For sloths, Caneel Bay offers sunning, seven grand beaches, shaded reading nooks under rustling palms, and sunset sails aboard a private yacht. at the Self Centre, practice yoga, t'ai and m'ai chi, meditation and massage. The Rhythm of Relationships program is designed to bring couples closer together. Hikers can explore the 170-acre resort's own nature trails or seek out advanced trails in the Virgin Islands National Park, which surrounds the resort, to see more than 500 species of plant life. Take an excursion to St. Thomas or to a sister resort, Little Dix Bay, on Virgin Gorda in the British Virgin Islands. Explore sugar mill ruins, snorkel the underwater trail, windsail, dive, or kayak. The Tennis Park has 11 all-weather courts, complimentary tennis clinics, private lessons, weekly tournaments, and an outstanding Pro Shop.

Children ages 16 and under stay free; add $75 for extra persons in a room. A full children's activities program is available.

THE WESTIN ST. JOHN, *Great Cruz Bay. Rates at this 285-room resort start at $329. Tel. 340/693-8000 or 800/WESTINS, www.westinresortstjohn.com. Ask about wedding and honeymoon packages and a Familymoon package for newlyweds and their children.*

Covering 34 acres of magnificently landscaped grounds, this resort has an enormous 1/4-acre swimming pool, restaurants, bars, entertainments, and plenty of bells and whistles. Rooms and suites are spread among ten low-rise buildings connected by gardens lined with flowers and palms and threaded with red brick walks. Play tennis on floodlit courts, dine in the restaurants, the deli or the pool bar and grill, shop the boutique for smart resort wear, and enroll the children in the Westin Kids Club. Work out in the fitness center or arrange fishing, kayaking, snorkeling, windsurfing, diving, sailing, or a golf game on St. Thomas' Mahogany Run course. You're checked in at dockside, so your vacation begins the minute you board the resort's own, 149-passenger *Westin Breeze* and are handed a rum punch and your room key.

Moderate

HARMONY RESORT *at Maho Bay, mailing address 17 East 73rd Street, New York NY 10021. Tel. 800/392-9004 or 212/472-9453, Fax 861-6210. Locally, Tel. 340/693-5855. Doubles are $95-$150 nightly plus $15 each additional person. A shuttle from the ferry costs about $5 per person.*

This is the place to rough it next to nature, without air conditioning, room service, or any other luxuries. This resort was once chosen the World's Most

Environmentally Friendly Hotel by 18,000 travel agents. In second place was a hotel in Bali. A step up from the same management's Maho Bay Campground, these tent-cottages are made from recycled materials and are sparsely but adequately furnished. Solar panels provide energy to heat bath water and operate the microwave. The design scoops in any trade winds, but on a calm day we wished for some high-voltage air conditioning. Furnished are kitchen gear and all linens. Your camp will have its own bathroom and deck. Use the same transportation, restaurant, cultural events and water sports as Maho Bay Campground.

While St. John has more luxurious resorts, this one is chosen for our Best Places listing because it's unique.

Selected as one of my *Best Places to Stay* – see Chapter 13.

GALLOWS POINT SUITE RESORT, *P.O. Box 58, St. John 00831. Tel. 340/776-6434 or toll-free 800/323-7229, www.gallowspointresort.com. Rates at this 60-unit resort start at $365 for a one-bedroom, one-bath unit with full kitchen, living room, and balcony. Don't bring children under age 5. You'll be met at the ferry dock and transported to the resort, which is a five-minute walk from "downtown."*

A cluster of two-story, plantation style buildings surround a cliffy coast and short strength of sandy beach on the outskirts of Cruz Bay. Units are privately owned and all different, but you can count on comfortable surroundings with everything you need to cook some or all of your meals. Sleep two in the bedroom, two more on the sofabed. Loft units, which sleep one or two more, have an additional half bath. The suites are air conditioned and have ceiling fans; some have cable television, and telephone. The resort has a pool and gift/gourmet food shop and is the home of Ellington's, one of the best restaurants on St. John.

CONCORDIA STUDIOS, *mail address 17 East 73rd Street, New York NY 10021. Tel. 800/392-9004 or 212/472-9453, Fax 212/861-6210; locally, Tel. 340/693-5855, Fax 776-6504, www.concordia-studios.com. Rates start at $135 double, plus $25 each additional person. A rental car is needed to get here from Cruz Bay, 40 minutes away.*

The views of Ram Head and the Salt Pond are breathtaking as you rough it easy in a hillside aerie with 20-foot ceilings, ceiling fan, and a full kitchen with dishwasher and microwave. Furnishings are spare but comfortable, with efficiencies and studios accommodating up to three and the duplex sleeping up to six in two twin beds, a queen-size sofabed, and roll-aways. This is the most remote corner of St. John, with superb shelling, snorkeling, and hiking. The nearest restaurants and shopping are in Coral Bay.

Budget

CINNAMON BAY CAMPGROUND, *P.O. Box 720, Cruz Bay 00831. Tel. 340/776-6330 or 539-9998, www.cinnamonbay.com. The park's 126 tent sites and cottages are $15 to $95 depending on how much equipment is provided. Ride the campground shuttle from the ferry for about $5.*

One of the most popular campgrounds in the world, this one is booked months in advance. Choose a plain campsite for your own tent and gear, a platform with tents, cots, cooker, ice chest and tableware, or a spartan cottage furnished camping style. This is roughing it in paradise, with the sea at your doorstep. There's a restaurant and a camp store where basic supplies can be purchased. The bathroom is communal, campground style.

CONCORDIA ECO-TENTS, *mailing address 17 East 73rd Street, New York NY 10021. Tel. 800/392-9004 or 212/472-9453, Fax 861-6210; locally, Tel. 340/693-5855, www.concordia-eco-tents.com. Rates are from $110. Rent a car at the ferry dock for the 40-minute drive to Coral Bay.*

Perched high in isolated hills just outside the national park boundary on the southeast corner of the island near Coral Bay, Estate Concordia is one of the Maho Bay Camps but is 25 minutes by car from the other camps and 40 minutes from Cruz Bay. A rental car is a must. Permanent tents are made of fabric supported by a wood frame, with such high-tech features as solar and wind energy and composting toilet. This is living next to nature overlooking the sea and intruding as little as possible on the hills.

Furnished are a refrigerator, cooking equipment, linens, and an ice chest you can supply from the office's ice machine. Guests can use the coin-op laundry. While the tents are built to catch the breezes, they can be warm when winds die. There's a big pool, or hike to the beach. Massage therapy is available for adults, infants, and youths. The registration office, where you can stop for information or to make a phone call, is only 8am-noon and 3-7pm.

THE INN AT TAMARIND COURT, *Box 350 Cruz Bay, St. John 00831. Tel. (430) 776-6378 or 800/221-1637, www.tamarindcourt.com. Single rooms with shared bath are $48; doubles with private bath start at $88. Continental breakfast is included. The Inn is in town within walking distance of the ferry dock.*

The flagstone courtyard of this unpretentious inn is one of Cruz Bay's most popular hangouts, with big shade trees, lively music, cheap food, good booze, and it's one of the few places in the VI where you can get sushi. The location in the center of things makes it popular with business travelers and a good headquarters for island The location in the center of things makes it popular with business travelers and a good headquarters for island excursions. It's not on the beach and doesn't have a pool, but room rates were the best we could find on St. John for amply furnished, air conditioned accommodations with daily maid service. Walk to tennis, beach shuttles, shopping, and a bunch of restaurants.

MAHO BAY CAMPS, *Tel. 340/776-6240, 340/776-6226, or 800/392-9004. Rates are $110 single or double. In summer children ages 16 and under sleep free in a parent's room. Visa and MasterCard are accepted. A shuttle from the ferry costs about $5 per person.* Permanently pitched tents on wood platforms are surrounded by thick, glossy, tropical foliage. They sleep up to four people in three rooms furnished with two twin beds and a sleep sofa. Bed linens, a propane stove, cooler, towels, and cooking and eating utensils are supplied. Each area shares a barbecue and water faucet. Toilets and pull-chain showers are communal. The camp has many special events ranging from recycling workshops to "meet the artist" demonstrations.

Eat breakfast and dinner in the outdoor restaurant if you like, or shop in the camp store for frozen foods, produce, canned goods, bread, milk, juices, beer, wine, and basic paper products. Leave your leftovers in the "help yourself" center for arriving guests to use. Take an art or education workshop, snorkel and swim, hike, and enjoy the sunsets from your own deck.

ST. THOMAS
Expensive
BOLONGO BAY BEACH CLUB, *7150 Bolongo, St. Thomas VI 00802. Tel. 800/524-4746 or 340/775-1800, www.bolongobay.com. It's seven miles east of the airport and four miles from downtown Charlotte Amalie. Rates are from $450 all-inclusive but many other plans and packages are available. Rates at this 75-room resort start at $270 per day single occupancy or $440 per couple including room, food, drink, activities, tax, gratuities, watersports, scuba, and airport transfers. Singles take note of the attractive singles plan.*

The all-inclusive concept has immense appeal to travelers weary of being charged every time they pick up a beach towel or book a tour. Everything here is exceptionally good quality from food and drink to snorkel cruises, tennis, fitness and aerobics, sauna, volleyball, basketball courts, an all-day sail, and nightly entertainment. It's a total vacation without having to open your wallet.

A semi-inclusive rate without meals and drinks is available for those who want to spend more time out on the island. All of the large, air conditioned bedrooms overlook the sea. They have television, ceiling fan, safe, private balcony with a view of the blue and telephone. Some have a kitchenette. Babysitters and cribs are available. Children under age 12 stay free with parents who are on the Continental (semi-inclusive) Plan.

MARRIOTT'S FRENCHMAN'S REEF RESORT, *Flamboyant Point, mailing address P.O. Box 7100, St. Thomas 00801. Tel. 340/776-8500 or 800/223-6288 for both resorts. Rates at this 501-unit resort start at $349; suites are priced to $1200. A meal plan is available and, in summer and fall, an all-inclusive plan. The resort is three miles east of Charlotte Amalie.*

This classy resort faces both the harbor and the Caribbean. Choose

Frenchman's Reef for a hilltop high-rise with a view or Morningstar for upscale accommodations on the beach. Top of the Reef suites have a loft bedroom and fabulous views of the harbor and the Caribbean beyond. Royal Suites have a spiral staircase, balcony, cathedral ceiling, and Jacuzzi. Rooms have voice mail and data line, individual climate control, cable television with pay-per-view, hair dryer, coffee maker, safe, ice maker, and mini-bar. This is also site of the 96-unit **Marriott Morning Star Beach Resort**, located directly on the beach with its own, beach-side swimming pool.

Together the hotels have shops, many restaurants and bars, a convenience store, a coffee bar, room service, in-room ironing boards and mini-bars, tennis courts, and a full range of watersports. The main swimming pool with its waterfalls and swim-up bar is a humdinger. Be sure to tell your driver where you're staying; the resorts' check-in desks are separate. Every day, a water taxi takes guests into town for shopping and sightseeing.

RENAISSANCE GRAND BEACH RESORT, *Smith Bay Road, mailing address P.O. Box 8267, St. Thomas VI 00801. Tel. 340/775-1510 or 800/314-3514. Rates at the 297-unit resort start at $329. A cab ride from the airport is $15 per person.*

This AAA Four Diamond resort on St. Thomas just keeps getting better, consistently boasting one of the highest Guest Satisfaction Index scores in the Renaissance chain. The 34 acres of grounds are groomed and gardened, providing restful views of sea and landscape. Units are spread over hill and dale but call a shuttle if you don't feel like walking. And if you can't walk at all, the resort's six wheelchair accessible units are a rare find in the Caribbean.

The beach is just off a huge pool area, so you can float the day away in the ocean, pool, sailboat or raft. The resort's Smuggler's Restaurant, where you can mix your own Bloody Mary on Sunday mornings, is an island favorite. The children's program is free, providing up to 12 hours a day of supervised fun and care.

One-bedroom suites have a balcony, coffee machine, refrigerator, wet bar, and a queen-size sofabed. High-tech equipment is furnished in the fitness center, which also has men's and women's steam, sauna, and extensive spa services. A plus is a comfortable lounge with rest rooms where travelers can hang out between checkout and a late departure. This resort has one of the most comprehensive choice of wedding packages on the island, or create your own wedding with the help of the resort's wedding planners and pay a la carte.

If you prefer to stay in self-catering accommodations on the resort property, book with **Pineapple Village Villas**, *Tel. 340/777-3985, Fax 775-5516; toll-free 800/992-9232; privately-owned villas start at $150 nightly.*

RITZ-CARLTON, *699 Great Bay, St. Thomas 00802. Tel. 340/775-3333, Fax 775-4444; toll-free 800/241-3333. U.S. and Canada 800/241-3333. High season rates start at $275 per room. Ask about packages. The 300-room hotel* with 80 residential units is 30 minutes from the airport or about $12 per person by taxi. Airport transfer by limousine can be arranged by the hotel, which is found on the island's eastern tip. Helicopter transfers from the airport can also be arranged through the hotel. Also available is the Ritz-Carlton Club, a six-story, 23-unit time share where guests can rent fully furnished residences. Tel. 800/278-0121, www.ritzcarltonclub.com.

Surely the ne plus ultra of St. Thomas resorts and the first Ritz-Carlton in the Caribbean, this one has all the five-star features of other Ritz-Carltons around the globe. From the moment you're welcomed at the portico and ushered across gleaming marble floors to the check-in desk, the coddling from perkily-uniformed staff is complete.

Built in the fashion of a grand palazzo, the property rims a fine beach and overlooks a brimming pool with an "infinity" edge that makes you think you're swimming on the horizon. From the main building, which houses some guest rooms, the lobby, meeting rooms, and The Cafe for fine dining, buildings cluster around a salt pond nature preserve filled with waterfowl. The rooms are spacious and come with all amenities. Specify sun or shade when you book; there's a choice of open or shaded balconies. Plan your days around swimming, the beach, sailing excursions aboard the resort's own catamaran, tennis, the fitness center,, diving, snorkeling, golf and more. The hotel has its own beauty salon, an 8,700 square-foot spa, and shops selling designer clothing and accessories. Jackets are not required at dinner, but this resort calls for your very best resort wear.

Selected as one of my Best Places to Stay – see Chapter 13.

SAPPHIRE BEACH RESORT & MARINA, Route 6, Smith Bay, St. Thomas 00801. Tel. 340/775-6100 or 800/524-2090. Rates at the 171-unit resort start at $395 for a suite with full kitchen. Rates are plus 8 percent tax, 7 percent resort fee and an energy surcharge of $4 per suite or $6 per villa per day. Suites sleep four; villas sleep up to nine. Ask about packages and meal plans. Children under age 17 sleep free in their parents' accommodations, and children up to age 12 eat free. The resort is 8 miles from the airport, 30 minutes from Charlotte Amalie and five minutes from the Red Hook ferry.

Check into a spacious suite decorated in cool whites and pastels. Each has a private balcony with ocean view, air conditioning, microwave, coffee maker, full-size refrigerator, satellite television, telephone, ceiling fans, air conditioning, and a living-dining area where the maid leaves fresh flowers daily. The beach is a picture postcard of white sand and turquoise water. In the Kids Klub, activities, crafts and meals keep little ones happy 9 a.m. to 4 p.m. for $20 per child, with a discount for multiple children. Leave kids for the evening, 5:30-10 p.m. for $25 and they'll be fed and entertained.

The resort is 15 minutes from the famous Mahogany Run golf course but, unless you're an ardent golfer, you won't want to leave the resort. It has its own gift shop, marina and dive center where you can connect with scuba

A Reminder About Rates

Rates quoted in this book are for a double room in high season. In shoulder and low seasons you will be able to get lower rates, more features, or both except during Carnival or other special events. Rates do not include room tax, which applies to all rooms, or service charges, which are charged by some hotels.

lessons or dives, a power yacht for excursions to the most colorful reefs for snorkeling, sea kayaking or deep sea fishing. Use of non-motorized watercraft is free. Play tennis or volleyball. For a small charge, shuttle service into Charlotte Amalie or Red Hook is available one way or round trip.

Casual dining is in the PrittyKlip Pavilion and Bar or dressier in the Seagrape Restaurant. Room service is available during breakfast and dinner hours. The bar, where live entertainers play most nights, is open until 2am. A Budget Rent-a-Car desk is in the lobby; a coin-op laundry is available for guest use.

Selected as one of my *Best Places to Stay* – see Chapter 13.

SECRET HARBOUR BEACH RESORT, *Nazareth Bay, St. Thomas 00802. Tel. 800/225-6510 or 340/775-6550, www.secretharborvi.com. Rates are from $155. The resort also offers one-and two-bedroom suites and villas. It's near Red Hook, a $12 taxi ride from the airport.*

The resort and the adjacent villas were merged in 1998 to form a grand complex. Units, which are air conditioned, have a full kitchen and private balcony or patio overlooking the sea. Two-bedroom suites have two baths, but even the studios are spacious with their own patio or balcony, bed-sitting room, and a bath with dressing room. Dine in the Blue Moon seaside café, work out in the fitness center, play tennis, sail the resort's catamaran, dive with the resort's five-star PADI center, browse the gift shop, and swim in the freshwater pool. All units get daily maid service. Babysitting can be arranged.

Moderate

BEST WESTERN CARIB BEACH, *70 Lindberg Bay, St. Thomas 00802. Tel. 340/774-2525, Fax 777-4131; toll-free 800/792-2742, www.caribbeachresort.com. Rates at this 69-room hotel start at 109 including continental breakfast.*

The perfect place for an affordable, weekend getaway in the sunshine, this hillside inn isn't fancy but it overlooks a flawless beach, serves modestly priced buffets nightly, and brings in entertainers often. Typical of this price-appeal chain, the hotel has television and telephones in the rooms, a swimming pool, air conditioning, tennis, and watersports rentals.

A sister **Best Western Emerald Beach** nearby has 90 rooms and is right on the beach, so rates are higher, starting from $209 with continental breakfast, *Tel. 800/223-4936.*

ANTILLES RESORTS, *Estate Smith Bay, St. Thomas VI 00824. Tel. 340/ 773-9150 or 800/524-2025, www.antillesresorts.com. Rates at this 68-suite resort start at $220 plus a 10 percent service charge for a suite with full kitchen.*

Check into a friendly apartment complex built for beachfront fun. Dine in whenever you like and enjoy the big living area and private balcony. Or, dine out, shop the resort's beach shop, and spend the day on or in the water. Suites are air-conditioned, have ceiling fans, and are handicap accessible. Children ages 12 and under stay free.

COLONY POINT PLEASANT RESORT, *Estate Smith Bay, St. Thomas, VI 00802. Tel. toll-free 800/524-2300, locally 340/775-7200, www.pointpleasantresort.com. Rates at the 134 suites, which range in size from studios to two-bedroom units, start at $255 nightly. Cab fare from the airport is $15.*

Spread atop a steep, cone-shaped hill like color on a snow cone, this all-suites resort has it all for the vacationing couple or family: three swimming pools, two restaurants including the renowned Agavé, a marina with motorized and non-motorized watersports, nature trails, and a tennis court. If you don't care to navigate the resort on foot, use the free shuttle service. In an unusual program, the resort allows each villa four hours use of a car daily at no cost except for a mandatory $12.50 fee for insurance and fuel.

The villas are individually owned so each is furnished differently but those we saw were fresh and attractive, with a hilltop overlook from the balcony, tile floors with jute area rugs, a welcome bottle of rum on the table, and a fully equipped tile kitchen. Suites are air conditioned and have ceiling fans.

WYNDHAM SUGAR BAY BEACH RESORT & SPA, *on Route 30, East End, mailing address 6500 Estate Smith Bay, St. Thomas VI 00802. Tel. 800/ WYNDHAM, www.wyndham.com. Doubles at the resort start at $375 per couple all inclusive. Ask about packages and, in summer, the kids-free program. The resort is a $12 cab ride from the airport.*

Once part of a sugar plantation, this 32-acre site has alternating strips of sugar beach and rocky headland, with views from your balcony of tireless surf. Every room has a television and refrigerator; furnishings have a mellow, colonial look accented with floral motifs. Dine outdoors and waterside at the Mangrove Cafe. Snorkel, play tennis, golf the Mahogany Run Golf Course, take a Jeep adventure, scuba dive, and swim in the interconnecting, freshwater pools where you can swim your way to from whirlpool to waterfall. Every evening, take in a boisterous revue in a cruise ship-like lounge, then dance afterwards until 1am. Everything is included in one fee except spa treatments at the spectacular, new (2002-03) $1.5 million Journeys Spa.

It's a plus that the resort has a heart defibrillator and has CPR-certified staff who can use it.

Budget

DANISH CHALET, *Charlotte Amalie. Mailing address Box 4319, St. Thomas 00803. Tel. 340/774-5764, Fax 777-4886; toll-free 800/635-1531, www.danishchaletinn.com. Rates at this ten-room inn start at $75. It's ten minutes from the airport.*

It's like going home to the folks when you stay with Frank and Mary Davis, former yachties who settled down here and opened an inn where drinks at the honor bar are only $1. Rooms are homey, with air conditioning or ceiling fan and telephone. The restaurants and shops of town are a five-minute walk away and it's 15 minutes to some of the island's best beaches. A continental breakfast is included and it is served in a pleasant setting where you'll meet other guests. You can also share the Jacuzzi and library with a nice mix of other guests.

HOTEL 1829, *Box 1576, St. Thomas 00801. Tel. 340/776-1829, Fax 340/776-4313; toll-free 800/524-2002, www.hotel1829.com. Rates at this 15-room inn start at $100; larger rooms are priced to $170.*

This charming inn was built as a home by a French sea captain for his bride. It took ten years and was completed in 1829, hence the name. Now a National Historic Site, the house has air conditioning, private baths with each room, cable television, and balconies in some rooms. A continental breakfast is included. The restaurant here is popular and the dark little bar is straight out of the 1950s. There is a tiny swimming pool, just large enough for a cooling splash. There's no elevator, so this isn't a good choice if you have a problem with stairs. Otherwise, we can't think of a lovelier, more relaxing place to stay if you want to be steeped in St. Thomas history.

ISLAND VIEW GUEST HOUSE, *Box 1903, St. Thomas. Tel. 340/774-4270, Fax 774-6167; toll-free 800/524-2023. Rates at this 15-room guesthouse start at $60.*

Located halfway between town and the airport, this is a good base for island exploring if you have a car. Parking is provided. Rooms are air conditioned and have television and telephone. The relaxed little inn has an arresting view of the sea far below from its own pleasant pool and breezy deck. In the foreground are acres of bright shrubs.

MAFOLIE, *Box 1506, St. Thomas 00804. Tel. 340/774-2790, Fax 774-4091; toll-free 800.525-7035, www.mafolie.com. Rates at this 23-room inn start at $197 including continental breakfast; weekly and month rates are available. It's 10 minutes from the airport.*

The view of the harbor 800 feet below is one of the great pleasures of this delightful small hotel. A free shuttle takes guests to famous Magens Bay beach, or you can spend your days in the freshwater pool with its big, sunny deck. Drink service is available at the pool all day. Rooms and suites (some with kitchenette) have air conditioning, ceiling fan, cable television, and all the comforts of a small, homey bedroom.

ST. CROIX
Expensive

BUCCANEER HOTEL, *Gallows Bay, mailing address P.O. Box 25200, Christiansted 00824. Tel. 340/773-2100 or 800/255-3881, www.thebuccaneer.com. Rates in this 150-unit resort start at $280 for a double room in season. Take East End Road east out of Christiansted for two miles. The resort is a $14 taxi ride from the airport.*

A historic treasure founded in 1653 by a French settler, this charming property is on ground that was once planted to sugar. Its lobby is in the remains of an old mill. The resort has been in the same family since 1947. Our deluxe beachfront room was as big as a ballroom, with cavernous closets, a big bathroom with double sinks, refrigerator and ceiling fans as well as air conditioning and remote control cable television. Butter yellow and Danish blue fabrics complement the blue and white tiles, vaulted pine ceiling, mellow rattan furniture, and mahogany woodwork. The window seat overlooking the beach is a bookworm's delight.

Swim in the pool, which has its own bar, or choose one of three surrounding beaches. Play the 18-hole golf course or eight tennis courts, choose from four restaurants, use the fitness center, or make an appointment in the spa. In addition to the beachfront units, other rooms, suites and a guesthouse are high on the hill with soaring views. Take a hike, or call for the shuttles that are always available.

Selected as one of my *Best Places to Stay* – see Chapter 13.

If You Hear a Hurricane Has Hit...

In all the years we have been traveling the tropics, one hurricane theme is repeated time and again. "Please tell them that we are open and operating," plead hoteliers whose guests have been scared away by over-dramatic press reports. Innkeepers are partly to blame because, when damage occurs, they invariably underestimate how long it will take to get things back in order. They don't reopen on time, or they claim to be running normally, and guests find themselves staying at Fawlty Towers. Even in the worst storms, some hotels don't close at all and others have only minor disruptions such as a brief or partial power failure. There's only one way to get the straight scoop and that's to call the airlines to see if you can get in and out. Then phone the hotel itself and ask, "Are you open and operating normally?" and then pin them down, "What services are unavailable or curtailed?" If the answer to #1 is "next week," call again and keep calling until you can be assured that the hotel is (not will be) operating fully. Better still, talk to someone who has just returned from the same hotel.

SUNTERRA RESORTS CARAMBOLA BEACH, *Estate Davis Bay, Kingshill, P.O. Box 3031, St. Croix 00851. Tel. 340/778-3800 or 888/503-8760, www.sunterra.com. Rates at this 151-unit resort start at $245. Take Route 69 north from the airport and turn left when it ends at Route 80. Cab fare from the airport is $12 for one or two persons.*

Looking down from Parasol Hill, a killer hill used in the annual St. Croix International Triathlon, the hotel complex looks like a bouquet of red hibiscus, each building roofed in crimson. Rooms are as spacious as suites, most of them with a private screened porch and a dim, wood interior that provides respite from the brilliant sunshine. Luxury features abound: air conditioning, a fitness center and spa, hair dryers and coffee makers in rooms, television, telephone, and room service. The Davis Bay Suite has two bedrooms and a private veranda that the Rockefellers once used to entertain groups of up to 100.

Robert Trent Jones, Sr. designed the golf course that is only a five-minute shuttle ride away. Tennis courts are lit for night play. The restaurants provide tony dining by candlelight or a lighter, deli experience. The beach was restored after the last hurricane and looks sandy and inviting despite a few rocky areas; just off shore, the 3000-foot wall is one of the island's best dive spots. Ask about the children's program, popcorn and movies, and activities for all ages. The site, aloof and scenic, is a popular one for weddings and the hotel has its own wedding planner who can make arrangements for everything from the cake and flowers to accommodations for the entire wedding party.

DIVI CARINA BAY RESORT & CASINO, *Grapetree Beach, St. Croix. Tel. 340/773-9700. Reservations: Tel. 919/419-3484, 800/823-9352, www.divicanna.com. Mail address: 25 Estate Turner Hole, Christiansted VI 00820. It's 30 minutes from the airport and 20 minutes from Christiansted. Rates at the 146-unit resort start at $225. Ask about packages, discounts for seniors, freebies for children, and perks for high rollers.*

Book a room, one- or two-bedroom suite, or a one-bedroom villa. Almost every window in the resort has a sweeping view of one of St. Croix' most breaktaking beaches. Dine in the Starlite Bar and Grill, play tennis, snorkel, sail, kayak and spend evenings in the Divi Carina Bay Casino. Rooms are done in a palette of sea tones and are equipped with air conditioning, satellite television, voice mail and dataport, VCR, hair dryer, safe, private patio or balcony, wet bar with mini-refrigerator, microwave, and plush robes. The villas have a full kitchen.

The resort has two freshwater swimming pools, two whirlpools, an air-conditioned fitness center, lighted Hard-Tru tennis courts, a beauty salon, massage room, two restaurants and three bars. If you bring the children, they'll love the Kid's Club. The casino, the first in the U.S. Virgin Islands, has 275 slot machines, 13 gaming tables and food and beverage outlets. High rollers get membership in the Beachcomber's Club, which can mean dis-

Virgin Islands Hotel Weddings

If you want to get married in paradise, a number of companies provide complete wedding planning including accommodations for the couple and their families, the ceremony, flowers, reception, photographer, and a honeymoon hideaway. Contact your hotel. If they don't have an in-house wedding planner, they can supply a list of professional wedding planners on St. Thomas or St. Croix.

counted or complimentary accommodations, free meals in the Starlite Bar & Grill, and invitations to private events.

HIBISCUS BEACH HOTEL, *4131 La Grande Princesse, Christiansted 00820, Tel. 340/773- 4042 or 800/442-0121, Fax 340/773-7668, www. 1hibiscus.com. It's 15 minutes from the airport and 10 minutes from Christiansted's shops. Rates at this 37-room hotel are from $170; add $80 per person per day for three meals. Children under age 12 stay free with parents.*

We fell in love with this hotel because of its half moon of perfect beach, and an early morning crowd of local beach walkers and passers-by. The restaurant is one of the best on the island, often with live music. Rooms have a patio or balcony overlooking Pelican Cove plus ceiling fan, air conditioning, color TV, telephone, stocked mini-bar and a safe. Fresh flowers greet your arrival. Guests have complimentary use of snorkel gear.

Moderate

CHENAY BAY BEACH RESORT, *P.O. Box 24600, Christiansted, St. Croix 00824. Tel. 800/548-4457 or 340/773-2918. Rates start at $215 for a cottage with full-size refrigerator, cooktop, and microwave oven. It's three miles east of Christiansted. Ask about meal plans.*

This lively, 50-unit resort has a big lap pool, a rim of beach, a locally popular restaurant with theme nights and parties, tennis, and good snorkeling just off the beach. Rooms are done in sunny colors, with air conditioning, ceiling fan, radio, television, microwave, coffee maker, dial telephone, small dining area, and mini-bar. For families traveling together, connecting cottages are available at family rates. Children are catered to with their own games and menu.

HOTEL CARAVELLE, *44a Queen Cross Street, Christiansted, 00820. Tel. 340/773-0687 or toll-free. 800/524-0410, www.hotelcaravelle.com. Rates at this 43-room, AAA Three-Diamond hotel are from $115. It's in the heart of downtown on the water, a $10 ride from the airport for one or two persons.*

A European-style boutique hotel has been transplanted in the tropics, blending the sunny airiness of a Cruzan resort with modern amenities. It has been generations since the Virgin Islands were Danish, but Danes continue to come to this user-friendly hotel. Rooms, many of them overlooking the harbor, are air conditioned and have mini-refrigerator and cable television. There's a freshwater pool, gift shop, and free parking—a plus if you want to spend a lot of time in parking-deprived Christiansted. The staff love innkeeping, and it shows. This hotel has the highest rate of repeat guests in the islands. The restaurant is a St. Croix favorite for locals and visitors alike. Golf is nearby; beaches and tennis courts are within walking distance. Ask about dive packages.

Selected as one of my *Best Places to Stay* – see Chapter 13.

TAMARIND REEF HOTEL, *5001 Tamarind Reef, three miles east of Christiansted and 25 minutes from the airport. Doubles are priced $160-$180 nightly including continental breakfast poolside; children under age six sleep free.*

Every room overlooks the sea in this neat-as-a-pin resort.. All rooms have air conditioning, ceiling fan, color television, clock radio, telephone, coffee maker, refrigerator, robes, hair dryer, ironing board and iron, and mini-bar service. The safe works on your own credit card, so there is no key to worry about. (Some hotels charge a key deposit for $50 or more). Spacious, airy rooms are done in sherbet pastels, with original art from a Florida artist and tiles from a Cruzan crafter. Kitchenette suites have two-burner stove, microwave oven, dishes and other galley gear. Junior suites have two queen-size beds and dining space for four. There's one suite, which connects to a deluxe-category room, so it's ideal for a family. Its roll-in shower is one of a handful on the island, making the entire suite wheelchair accessible. Dine casually in the Deep End, or elegantly in The Galleon. The beach is picturesque but rocky, so bring reef shoes. Diving, sailing, and watersports of all kinds can be arranged. The resort has tennis courts, six-wicket croquet, a marina and a big swimming pool surrounded by a sun deck. Ask about golf or dive packages.

THE WAVES AT CANE BAY, *P.O. Box 1749, Kingshill, 00851. Tel. 340/778-1805 or 800/545-0603. Rates start at $140 for a studio apartment with screened balcony and full kitchen. Cab fare from the airport is $13 for two.*

This 12-unit hideaway is a find for divers because owner-hosts have their own dive shop here plus a natural pool where beginners can take their first scuba or snorkel lessons. The beach is small and very attractive. Balconies hang right over the waves. The restaurant is an inexpensive hangout, popular with passers-by and a beauty spot for watching the sea.

INNPARADISE, *1 E Golden Rock, St. Croix 00821. Tel. 340/713-9803 or 866/800-9803, www.innparadisestcroix.com. Rates at this five-room inn are from $115 including breakfast. It's 10 minutes from the ferry dock and 20 minutes from the airport. Ask about a one-week package that includes inn stays on all three islands.*

Personal service is the hallmark of this small and gracious guest house, where free Internet access is available. Your day begins with a full breakfast served with a spectacular view of the surrounding bush and sea all the way to Buck Island. Rooms are individually furnished and are pictured on the website, so choose the one that fits your dreams.

CARRINGTON'S INN, 56 Hermon Hill, St. Croix 00820. Tel. 304/713-0508 or 877/658-0508, www.carringtonsinn.com. Rates at this five-room inn start at $115 including breakfast. It's five miles west of the airport and a mile west of the main road in Christiansted on the road to Queste Verde.

As comfortable as a private home and as service-oriented as a European inn, this B&B has a freshwater pool, private baths, and both air conditioning and ceiling fans. Rooms are all different, so discuss with your hosts what setting would be right for you and your travel partner(s). Rent a car for exploring, shopping, dining, and getting to the beach.

SAND CASTLE ON THE BEACH RESORT, P.O. Box 1908, Frederiksted, 00820. Tel. 340/772-1205 or 800/524-2018, www.gaytraveling.com/caribbean. Rates start at $115 per person. Cab fare from the airport is $8.50 for two. The resort is a half mile south of Frederikstad on the road to Sandy Point.

Although this inn bills itself as "proudly serving the homosexual and Lesbian community," all lifestyles are welcomed and our impression was one of a happy, homogeneous group of people having the time of their lives. Suites and villas overlook a seagrape-shaded sand beach, a warm cove with good snorkeling, and a seaside courtyard where breakfast is free and lunch and dinner are a delight. On the beach side, units have bedroom, living room, screened porch with pass-through to the kitchen, and an ocean view. Seafoam green fabrics are accented with iridescent amethyst; floors are Italian tile. A second unit across the narrow street has its own pool and two-bedroom suites.

Budget

FREDERIKSTED HOTEL, 442 Strand Street, Frederiksted, St. Croix 00840. Tel. 340/773-9150 or 800/524-2025. Rates at this 40-room hotel start at $85. Take a cab from the airport, which is about 10 minutes away, for $8 per couple.

The charm of a small, European hotel and the convenience of a downtown location add up to a fine value within walking distance of beaches, shopping, , and restaurants. The hotel has its own restaurant and sun deck; each room has a small refrigerator and a microwave oven.

KRONEGADE INN, 11 Western Suburb, Christiansted, St. Croix 00821. Tel. 340/692-9590, www.kronegade.inn. Rates at this 15-room inn are from $85. Children age six and under stay free. Ask about the six-day package. It's 20 minutes from the airport and ten minutes from the ferry/seaplane landing.

If you love walking the historic district of Christiansted with its shops, restaurants and churches, this is the perfect pied-a-terre. Better still, it's adjacent to the Harbormaster Beach Club with its watersports, funky restaurant and locally popular bar. Every unit has a fully equipped kitchenette.

HILTY HOUSE INN, *Questa Verde Road, Gallows Bay, mailing address P.O. Box 26077, 00824. Tel./Fax 340/773-2594, E-mail: hiltyhouse@worldnet.att.net. Rates at this five-room inn start at $95 including continental breakfast. A one-bedroom cottage is also available. Credit cards aren't accepted. Cab fare from the airport is $12.*

Hugh and Jacquie Haore Ware found this converted 1732 rum factory and have turned it into an enchanted inn. In a region where fireplaces are almost unknown, here is a huge one that is lit on Christmas Eve. Jacquie makes her own jams for breakfast from local fruits such as tamarind and mango. After a day of diving or exploring, relax in the old library with books and television. Or sign up for one of Jacquie's famous ethnic dinners held Monday nights, with authentic mood, music, and food. Rooms are all different, and all beguiling, with wonderful angles and crannies created by old walls that were built with another use in mind. There's no air conditioning, but ceiling fans augment the hilltop breezes.

PINK FANCY, *27 Prince Street, Christiansted, 00820. Tel. 340/773-8460 or 800/524-2045, www.pinkfancy.com. Doubles start at $85 including continental breakfast and Happy Hour drinks. Cab fare from the airport is $10 for two. Ask about the sailing package that includes accommodations and a three- or five-day sailing course.*

Dating to 1780, the buildings have been refurbished with rich mahogany pieces, reproduction art works, shiny mahogany floors, air conditioning and ceiling fans. An old hangout for show business folks, it is decorated with old showbiz posters and memorabilia. It's still popular with business travelers who, if they want only to crash and burn, take one of the small, inexpensive rooms. The heart of the 13-room inn is the cobblestone courtyard around the pool, where breakfast and cocktails are served. There's a gazebo for small weddings, and learn-to-cook weekends are offered in summer. Parking is on the street, but you won't need a rental car if you want only to hang out around the pool and enjoy Christiansted's shopping and dining.

Where to Eat

Dinner hours in the Virgin Islands seem awfully early when compared to French and Spanish islands but, even though kitchens close at 9 or 10pm, the drinking, dancing, music, and good times might go on for hours depending on the restaurant.

ST. THOMAS
Expensive

BANANA TREE GRILLE, *Bluebeard's Castle, Bluebeard's Hill, Charlotte Amalie. Tel. 340/776-4050. Main dishes are priced $18 to $28. It's open for dinner daily except Sunday and the month of September. Reservations are suggested. Hours vary seasonally, so call for information and reservations.*

In a menu it calls Caribbean Coastal Cuisine, the Grille offers such starters as pan-seared crab cake with golden apple and sesame salad or roasted quail stuffed with spinach and goat cheese. Have one of the very Caribbean soups or the Frisee Salad with Smoked Pineapple and White Peppercorn Vinaigrette or the organic greens with picked baby beets. Main dishes include pan-seared red snapper with roasted corn and tomato ragout, roasted rack of lamb with tamarind barbecue sauce and cassava fries, mahi-mahi grilled with crab risotto and pumpkin broth, or a delectable vegetarian dish made up of christophene with spinach pasta in a roasted red pepper sauce. Ask for a table with a view of the harbor, which becomes a sea of twinkling lights after dark.

HERVÉ RESTAURANT & WINE BAR, *Kongens Gade. Tel. 340/777-9703. Hours are Monday through Saturday for lunch and dinner and Sunday for dinner only. Find the restaurant between Zorba's and Hotel 1829. Plan to spend $30-$40 for a three course dinner; $25 for a two-course lunch.*

It's the buzz of St. Thomas. Hervé and Paulette put together a welcoming ambience and great food in a relaxed, bistro setting on Government Hill, the perfect place to take a break from downtown shopping. For a hearty meal, take the lamb shank braised with vegetables with fresh herbs and red wine. Or dine more delicately on chilled shrimp with papaya cocktail sauce, spinach and vegetables en croute, or a poached artichoke stuffed with crab and served with cold ravigotte sauce.

HOTEL 1829, *Box 1576, St. Thomas 00801, Tel. 340/777-7100. Hours are Monday through Saturday 11am to 2pm and 5:30-10:30pm. but they vary seasonally, so check ahead. It may not be open for lunch in summer. Reservations are recommended. Plan to spend $30-$40 for dinner.*

Dine in this prestige location on Government Hill in a local landmark known for its gracious service and West Indian ambience. Try the pan-fried snapper with mango compote, or lunch on a freshly grilled mahi-mahi sandwich served with roasted red pepper mayonnaise.

THE POINTE, *Villa Olga, Frenchtown. Tel. 340/774-4262. It's about a $5 taxi ride from town. Dine for about $50 per person. There's a fixed-price, three-course dinner for $42.75 each including coffee or espresso.*

If you're a St. Thomas regular, you'll remember this location when it was The Charthouse. If you like salad bars, you'll like the expansive Salad Bar feature of this restaurant, where aged prime rib, jumbo shrimp, grilled salmon, lobster tail, New York strip steak, or herb-crusted chicken complete the meal. The spinach dip makes a good opener, or have the coconut shrimp, sugarcane-skewered charred beef tenderloin, or a crab cocktail. You can visit the Potato Table and Salad Bar only for $16.95 as an entree or $3.95 with another entree. The burger is one of the best in the hemisphere, 10 ounces of tenderloin and aged sirloin ground together, cooked to order, and served on four-cheese bread with roasted red onions. The Danish baby back ribs are done in a bourbon molasses sauce. Order an aged steak, grilled to order, four choice of fresh fish, stuffed Caribbean lobster, or a combination platter. There's a tempting menu for children, or they can have just the salad bar for $6.95.

THE RITZ CARLTON DINING ROOM, *in the Ritz-Carlton Hotel, Great Bay, Tel. 340/775-3333. Open for dinner daily; reservations are urged. Plan to spend $100 for a three-course dinner for two.*

Dining at the Ritz can be expensive but the food is so splendid and the choices so many, even the most discerning diner will be dazzled. We started with the crisp, buttery foie gras Napoleon, served with mango chutney and faintly scented with balsamic vinegar. Then we had the Caesar salad for two, presented tableside, and went right on to dessert: the Spanish Hot Chocolate Soufflé. Only the hungriest trencherman will be able to tackle four courses but it's hard to resist trying one of the appetizers, a soup such as the velvety tomato bisque topped with a corn fritter, fresh fish or lobster, then the chocolate hazel parfait with candied cherries, or the trio of creme brulée featuring three custards, one vanilla, one lavender, and one lemon grass.

ROMANO'S, *97 Smith Bay Road on the north coast. Tel. 340/775-0045. Main dishes are priced $16 to $30. Dinner is served nightly except Sunday and during Carnival, when the restaurant closes for a week. Reservations are recommended.*

The pastas are not only the least expensive main dishes, they are invitingly different. Choose a simple pesto sauce, one of the seafood sauces, or the lasagna baked to creamy perfection with four cheeses. Carnivores will enjoy the veal marsala, osso bucco or a steak with a side of pasta. Fresh salmon is often on the board. Grilled to succulent perfection, it makes a toothsome meal with nothing more than a salad and a crusty bread. The desserts are homemade, and vary daily.

SEAGRAPE, *in the Sapphire Beach Resort. Tel. 340/775-9750. Reservations are suggested. Lunch and dinner are served Monday-Saturday; Sunday brunch is served 11am-3pm. Main dishes are priced $17-$26. Children's menu.*

Overlook a finest-kind beach while you dine on continental and American favorites such as grilled steak or chicken with mushroom relish, teriyaki, fresh fish, or roast lamb with a side dish of garlic mashed potatoes. The Sunday brunch is a feast featuring specialty waffles, salads, fresh fruit galore, and a galaxy of hot and cold dishes.

VICTOR'S NEW HIDEOUT, *103 Submarine Base. Tel. 340/776-9379. Reservations are urged, especially since you need to call for directions if you are driving (Victor's used to be at 32 Submarine Base). It's open for lunch and dinner Monday-Saturday and Sunday 5:30-10pm. Main dishes are priced $10-$50.*

Victor himself is from Montserrat, so his lobster is sauced with the style of his home island. Or, order it grilled in the shell without the cream sauce, and dip each luscious morsel into melted butter. Keep an eye peeled for celebrities of the television, movie, and music world who seek out this spot when they are on the island. Native Caribbean dishes here are done with flash and elan; the pies are like Mother used to make.

SMUGGLER'S *in the Renaissance Grand Beach Resort, Smith Bay Road. Tel. 775-1519. It's open for dinner nightly and for Sunday brunch. The room is best known for its Sunday brunch and for its open-air dining with live entertainers. Dine for $40-$50; brunch for under $20.*

Sunday morning is a gala time to brunch here. Make your own drink at the Bloody Mary bar, then feast from a groaning buffet board of meats, salads, cheese, breads, casseroles, and desserts to die for. After eating, take a leisurely stroll around this rambling resort and a beach that looks like it was created for a travel brochure.

OLD STONE FARMHOUSE, *Mahogany Run. Tel. 304/777-6277. Plan to spend $50 per person and triple that if you choose one of the rare wines or scotches. It's open Monday-Saturday 6:30-10pm. Reservations are recommended.*

Dine in the splendor of the old world in a stone mansion built out of native blue rock and rubble more than 200 years ago on a Danish plantation known as Estate Lovendal. The food is a fetching melange of international tastes ranging from Thai red curry to a great New York strip. Have pan-roasted chicken with artichokes, roasted lamb, duckling, and a lobster freshly plucked from the local sea. A comprehensive wine list features great vintages from around the world, and the single malt scotch choices go as high as $120 a drink.

Moderate

AGAVÉ TERRACE, *in the Point Pleasant Resort. Tel. 775-4142. The resort is found on the east end of the island between the Renaissance Grand Beach Resort and Red Hook. Plan to spend $10-$15 for breakfast and $20-$40 for lunch or dinner. Reservations are recommended. Dinner is served nightly from 6pm; brunch is served on Saturday and Sunday.*

The views from this all-villa resort overlooking Pillsbury Sound are awesome. Brunch starts with a morning Happy Hour drink and Eggs Florentine or a tropical fruit plate ringed with fresh, fragrant muffins. At dinner, appetizers in the $5-$9 range include a five-pepper dip with chips, conch chowder, or iced gazpacho. Choose a pasta specialty such as linguine with tenderloin medallions and Gorgonzola-walnut cream sauce, or one of the steaks. They come in two sizes.

Ask about the catch of the day, then fine-tune your order according to cooking method and sauce. If you've had fisherman's luck today, bring your own fish and let the chef serve it to you. Dinners came with a special salad tossed table side, fresh bread, and the house pasta. It takes an entire menu page to describe the desserts, after dinner drinks, coffees and teas; the wine list won an Award of Excellence from Wine Spectator magazine. Dress is resort-casual and kids are welcomed with their own menu. Full Moon Jazz, concerts on the night of the full moon, went into eclipse for a couple of years after the hurricanes, but at press time are making a comeback. Ask about them.

CRAIG AND SALLY'S, *22 Honduras Estate, Frenchtown. Tel. 777-9949. Open Tuesday-Saturday for lunch and Tuesday-Sunday for dinner. Closed Monday. Reservations are urged.*

Their ad promises a refreshing, convivial evening and it all comes true when you're greeted jovially by Craig while Sally creates cuisine magic backstage. Take time with the wine list, which is as daunting as it is tempting, and let a server suggest a choice. Choose from an inspired menu that tonight might feature lobster-stuffed potatoes, a butter-tender filet under a light sauce, roasted lamb drifted with fresh herbs, grilled fish, or a pasta invention.

THE CAFE IN THE RITZ-CARLTON, *Great Bay. Tel. 775-3333. Reservations are recommended. Dinner Main dishes are $24-$29; pizzas are $11.50-$17.50. The restaurant is open daily for breakfast, lunch and dinner.*

Even if you're not staying here, come for a dining experience that includes a walk through the palatial marble lobby, down the grand staircase, and into the pleasant, open-air Cafe. The pizzas are extravagantly topped with traditional pepperoni and trimmings, or try the guava barbecue chicken with shredded jack cheese. Have carmelized onion pizza or one topped with Thai shrimp, shiitake mushrooms, asparagus and cilantro. Choose from a menu that includes grilled basil shrimp in a banana leaf or Caribbean lobster and sweet potato stew. There's also a macrobiotic selection, and, for meat-and-potatoes eaters, a superb grilled sirloin with chunky whipped potatoes.

L'ESCARGOT, *12 Submarine Base. Tel. 774-6565. It's open for lunch and dinner Monday-Saturday. Closed Sunday. Main dishes are priced $15-$32. Reservations suggested.*

The name suggests French cuisine, which has been a St. Thomas staple here for as long as we can remember. Gaze out over a marina filled with bobbing yachts while you dine on snails, shrimp, lamb herb-roasted with rosemary, grilled fish or lobster, or a pasta dish. For dessert, have a pillowy mousse.

VIRGILIO'S, *Back Street, downtown Charlotte Amalie. Tel. 776-4920. Main dishes are priced $10-$20. Reservations are suggested. Hours are Monday-Saturday 11:30am-10:30pm.*

When you have a yen for northern Italian classics, you can't go wrong here. The setting is made for old-world Italian dining under a beamed ceiling echoing faintly with strains of favorite operas and other Italian classics. A specialty of the house is a five-fish stew chunky with mussels, lobster, scallops, clams, and oysters in an intoxicating saffron broth. Order fresh fish, dolma, lobster ravioli, or grilled or roast duckling, or lamb. For light diners there are individual pizzas made to order.

ALEXANDER'S CAFÉ, *Frenchtown. Tel. 340/774-4349. Main dishes are $20 and less. IT's open for lunch and dinner daily except Sunday.*

Grilled specialties are the stars of the show, so have a burger, steak, chop, chicken, or a piece of fish done on the grill. There's also chili, pasta dishes, cold sandwiches, and salads.

BLUE MOON CAFÉ, *Secret Harbour (south of Red Hook). Tel. 340/779-2262. Reservations are always recommended, so call ahead. Hours vary seasonally. Dinner appetizers and salads are priced $7 to $10.50; main dishes $13.50 to $30.*

This is one of the most romantic overlooks on the island, so wait until dark and take your date to one of the island's trendy, creative, contemporary eateries. Grilled scallops are served with a fragrant tomato-basil risotto and fresh asparagus. Swordfish is grilled and served on a Greek salad. Roasted duckling is bathed in orange tequila sauce. The vegetarian specialty is a delectable vegetable Napoleon.

SIB'S ON THE MOUNTAIN, *Mafolie Road. Tel. 340/774-8967. It's open for lunch and dinner every day. Plan to spend about $25 per person for dinner and a drink.*

A rousing sports bar and restaurant are a cool reason to get outta town on a hot day. Wrap yourself around a mountain of chicken, a two-fished burger, or a dinner featuring the fresh catch of the day. Cheer your home team at the bar, or eat more sedately on the restaurant side.

Budget

ASHLEY'S MOBILE RESTAURANT, *at Cyril King Airport. It's open daily for breakfast, lunch and dinner. Eat for less than $10. Tel. 340/774-1533.*

If you arrive hungry or want a meal before you fly away, this is the place for authentic local care such as patties, stew chicken, boil fish, and johnnycake.

BOBBY'S HARDWOOD GRILL, *in Drakes Passage and Trompeter's Gade downtown Charlotte Amalie. Tel. 340/774-6054. Eat for less than $10. It's open for breakfast and lunch, 7:30am to 5pm daily, although hours could vary seasonally.*

Locals like the straightforward American fare and follow the great smells drifting out of this hold-in-the wall. Start the day with an early breakfast or show up for a hearty lunch of a big sandwich or salad featuring something fresh and sizzling from the grill.

BUMPA'S SANDWICH AND ICE CREAM SHOP, *on the waterfront in Charlotte Amalie. Tel. 340/776-5674. Eat for less than $5. It's open every day for breakfast and lunch.*

Grab a sweet scone for breakfast on the go, an ice cream to cool you down on a hot afternoon, a cold drink to sip in a downtown park as you people-watch. Fresh salads and sandwiches are on the menu. Don't miss the brownies, cookies, cakes and other sweets as well as the creamy, tropical ice creams.

COCONUTS BAR GRILL, *between Back Street and Main Street, downtown Charlotte Amalie. Tel. 340/774-0099. Eat for less than $10. It's open every day; Happy Hour is 5-7pm.*

Leave your spouse here, with a cold drink, ladies, while you shop the temptations of the old city. The menu offers American specialties such as sandwiches and burgers, local seafood, fruity drinks, and snacks, especially a mouth-melting fried mozzarella.

CRAZY COW, *on Raadats Gade off the waterfront in Charlotte Amalie. Tel. 340/774-8518. It's open around the clock serving breakfast, lunch and dinner.*

It's your basic burgers and shakes place, with something on the menu around the clock. The coffee is hot and the drinks cold. Most of the cheapest places are open only for breakfast and lunch, so here's a place to get hot food during late hours when the big spenders are chowing down at the expensive spots.

DELLY DECK, *in the Havensight Mall. Tel. 340/776-9943. Open daily for breakfast and lunch.*

Everyone loves the hot, eat-from-your fist chicken, but there is also a good choice of hot and sandwiches, and eggs cooked to order. Eat here or stop in for takeout.

DOWNTOWN DELI, *in the Grand Hotel, downtown Charlotte Amalie. It's open for breakfast and lunch daily 7am-5:30pm and will delivery free within the downtown area. Tel. 340/777-4611. Dine for under $20.*

This is as close to a New York deli as you will find in the islands. Start the day with a sweet roll and a flavored coffee or order a cold fruit juice and a mile-high sandwich for lunch.

DUFFY'S LOVE SHACK, *in the Red Hook Plaza. Tel. 340/779-2080. Open daily for lunch and dinner. Eat for under $10; drinks can add a lot to the bill.*

This is wacky and fun, so don't rush your meal. Start with one of the tropical drinks in a take-home glass that will be the talk of your town. There's a Polynesian accent in the menu, especially in the lavish pupu platters, flaming drinks and barbecue platters. The hamburgers are always a good bet too.

ST. CROIX
Expensive

DUGGAN'S REEF, *on Route 82, Teague Bay. Tel. 340/73-9800. The restaurant is open for dinner every day, lunch Monday through Saturday, and Sunday brunch 11am to 3pm. Main dishes start at $14.50; appetizers at $6. Reservations are suggested.*

This outdoor eatery overlooks the water and Buck Island. The house specialty is Irish whiskey lobster at $27, which can be served with a five-ounce filet mignon for $4 more. Priced by weight are baked or stuffed lobster. There's a choice of pastas, soups, and salads, with new temptations daily. The catch of the day can be served baked, grilled, island style (in vegetables and tomato sauce) or blackened, or choose the prime rib, sesame chicken, veal Parmesan, or chicken stir-fry. Desserts are homemade, or finish your meal with a fancy coffee.

THE GALLEON, *Green Cay Marina, Estate Southgate. Tel. 340/773-9949. The bar opens at 5pm and dinner is served nightly 6-10pm. Main dishes start at $17.50; pastas at $15; chateaubriand for two is $50. Reservations recommended. Five minutes east of Christiansted, the restaurant is a $12 cab ride for one or two.*

Start with gravlox or the baked brie crusted with almond crumbs, then the tossed salad with the house herb dressing and a large or small pasta such as Beef Fedora – the house fettuccine tossed with wild mushroom cream sauce and skirted with thin strips of grilled sirloin in a bleu cheese demi glace. Salmon is served with dill butter; rack of lamb can be carved at your table. A house specialty is grilled filet mignon topped with lobster meat and bearnaise sauce. Everything is served with freshly baked bread, rice and vegetables. Check out the cognacs and after-dinner drinks too. Dress is resorty but elegant.

INDIES, *55-56 Company Street, Christiansted. Tel. 340/692-9440. Plan to spend $30-$40 for dinner. Dinner is served nightly. Lunch is served Monday through Friday; sushi is served Wednesday and Friday 5pm-8pm only. Reservations are essential. Park free on Company Street.*

A cozy crowding of tables on the old stones of an ancient courtyard adds up to an intimate setting surrounded by greenery and cooled by ceiling fans. The effect is magical, whether you're with a group of friends or it is just the two of you with eyes only for each other. Chefs hand-write their menus daily, so choices vary widely according to what looks best at the market. Start with a lobster corn quesadilla or the grilled vegetable antipasto. Follow with a soup or salad such as the mixed lettuces with citrus, then one of the brilliantly inspired main courses: cumin-lime grilled dolphin with mango chutney, mixed grill of lamb and chicken with roast shallots and tamarind glaze, penne with grilled vegetables, or a West Indian seafood curry bursting with mussels, shrimp and fresh mahi-mahi.

KENDRICK'S, *Quin House, King Cross Street, Christiansted. Tel. 340/773-9199. Main dishes cost $21-25; pastas $18-$22; appetizers $7 to $8.50. It's open daily in season for lunch and dinner. Reservations are advised. Hours are 6-9:30p.m. Monday-Saturday.*

Dine upstairs with the fine dining menu in a yacht club setting or downstairs at the clubby bar where salads and burgers are in the $8-$10 range. Chef David and Jane Kendrick are enthusiastic hosts in this big, two-story restaurant with a fine view of the harbor and lights of the city. Start with homemade eggplant ravioli in tomato-basil butter, proceed to chilled champagne gazpacho, then try a Roquefort Caesar or spinach salad. Chef David offers four pastas including homemade pappardelle with sauteed shrimp. Or order rack of lamp, filet mignon, pecan crusted roast pork, breast of duck, or a seafood specialty. The menu is inspired and extensive. Dine more formally upstairs or enjoy the pubby ambience downstairs.

MAHOGANY ROOM, *in the Carambola Beach Resort, Estate Davis Bay, Kingshill. Tel. 340/778-3800. It's open daily for lunch and dinner but days and hours vary seasonally. Reservations are strongly recommended. Plan to spend $20-$30 for lunch; $50 per person for dinner.*

Everything about the room and the setting spell relaxed elegance. Rich mahogany sets the scene; windows look out on the sea and the flower-filled grounds of this stellar resort. Wait staff are attentive and timely as you proceed through a three- or four-course feast served amidst snowy linens and gleaming tableware. Steaks and fresh seafood are a specialty and the desserts, always different and always showy, are worth saving room for.

Moderate

BOMBAY CLUB, *5A King Street, Christiansted. Tel. 340/773-1838. Main dishes start at $13 after 5pm, but appetizers, salads, and fajitas at $6-$10 are good value. Open Monday through Friday for lunch and dinner, the restaurant is open for dinner only on Saturday and Sunday.*

A great place to escape from the bustle of Christiansted shops is this courtyard where you can hang out in the bar to see major sports events on television or take a table far from the bar and linger over a meal. Order a two-fisted burger, sandwich or salad, or end your day with a 10-ounce filet mignon with a salad. The BBQ spare ribs are basted with garlic and honey; the signature King Street Seafood Pasta is a triumph of pasta tossed with shrimp, scallops, fish, roasted garlic, and Brandy Alfredo. A good selection of light alternatives includes peel-and-eat shrimp, a veggie sandwich, conch cocktail, spinach salad, and the chicken sandwich served on a kaiser roll with lettuce, tomato, and guacamole. There's always quiche of the day and beef brisket, served with rice and a salad.

KING CONCH'S COCONUT HUT, *at the Chenay Beach Bay Resort, East End Road, Route 82. Tel. 340/773-2918. Lunch for $10-$15; dine for $20-$30. Open daily 8am-9pm. Dinner reservations are recommended.*

Everyone ends up here at least once during a stay on St. Croix because of the special events such as a sunset lobster fest, Sunday brunch, the pig roast, the pasta pigout, a belly dancer, West Indies Night, Jump Up every Saturday, kick-back Sunday limin', and more. Live entertainers are on hand five nights a week to serenade diners on this pleasant outdoor terrace. Call to find out what's going on while you're here. Kids get their own menu.

COLUMBUS COVE, *at Salt River Marina, Salt River National Park. Tel. 340/778-5771. Open daily 8am to 11pm, the restaurant takes only American Express credit cards. Plan to spend about $15 for dinner; but luncheon fare is available all day in the $6-$10 range.*

The only restaurant within the national park, this wildly natural site is not far from the spot where Columbus first set foot on St. Croix. From the restaurant, catch a boat tour of the river and sea then stay on for a meal. For weekend brunch there are eggs Florentine or fresh fruit waffles. Lunch might be a chicken platter, fish plate, sandwich or burger. Dinners start at 6pm and feature steaks, pastas, shrimp, and fish. Homemade desserts are tempting: key lime pie, chocolate walnut pie, or raspberry Bailey's cheese cake. On Wednesdays there's a Caribbean barbecue of chicken or ribs with all the trimmings including corn on the cob.

COMANCHE CLUB, *Strand Street, Christiansted. Tel. 340/773-2665. Main dishes are $12.50 to $19; daily specials are $12.50 to $15.50. Reservations are accepted. The restaurant is open for lunch and dinner Monday through Saturday. Lunch guests may use the pool for a small fee.*

An ancient war canoe hanging from the ceiling sets the scene in this locally popular, second story restaurant overlooking the waterfront. Portions are brobdignagian, so show up with a huge appetite and tear into the unforgettable Beef Curry Vindaloo with 10 Boys (a cart brings the "boys", which are accompaniments). The mixed grill brings together lamb, filet of beef and calves liver. The lobster, says the menu, is "Always scarce; always expensive." Chicken is served with oyster stuffing and, if you're in a splurge mode, have the caviar with blinis at $50. Save room for the Rum Raisin Bread Pudding with your choice of caramel or fudge sauce.

BUCCANEER HOTEL, *Gallows Bay, Tel.340/773-2100 has four dining venues, but hours vary seasonally and not all restaurants are open in summer. Plan to spend $25-$40 for dinner. Fine dining is in a Thai restaurant and in the hotel's* **Terrace Restaurant**, *open for breakfast and dinner overlooking Christiansted; its* **Little Mermaid**, *which is at the beach, is an insider place to have lunch 11:30am-5:30pm. On Wednesdays have the West Indian buffet here. The hotel's* **Grotto** *serves lunch with salad bar 11am-3:30pm.*

Overlook the lights of Christiansted from this hilltop perch while dining on continental specialties at The Terrace. Order the rock lobster cakes with Creole mayonnaise and grainy mustard, then rum-planked salmon or an eggplant-tomato turnover in puff pastry. Or, order Asian favorites in the Thai restaurant in this fine, family-owned resort. Arrive early enough for a sundowner at the bar, with a spectacular view of the green flash while you sip icy rum drinks or one of the slushy fruit drinks.

HARVEY'S, *Company Street at King Cross Street, Christiansted. Tel. 340/773-3433. Open daily except Sunday from 11:30am to 9:30pm, Harvey's takes no credit cards. Eat for under $15.*

Goat stew, stewed fish, whelks, ribs and chicken, rice and beans, fungi, sweet potato and other West Indian specialties are dependable at this crowded, family style spot. The tropical drinks are dynamite, especially the

Whammy. Homemade pies made with tropical fruits such as pineapple or coconut are complimentary with your meal.

THE HIDEAWAY, HIBISCUS BEACH HOTEL, *4131 La Grande Princesse, on the beach west of Christiansted. Tel. 340/773-4042. It's open daily 7:30am; closing hours vary with special events. Main dishes are priced $13.50-$22.50 (or more depending on the market price for seafood). Reservations are suggested.*

Even though the official name is the Hideaway, your cab driver and other locals think of it only as the Hibiscus Beach, so ask for that. The setting, with a view of one of the island's best beaches, is too good to miss, so come here for breakfast or lunch, or come early enough before dinner that you can enjoy the sunset with cocktails and appetizers. The Hibiscus Hot Rocks are notorious for their gooey, fiery, crispy contrasts. Big shrimp are stuffed with cheese, wrapped in jalapeno, dipped in beer batter, and fried to a crusty brown. We loved the Hibiscus Chicken, a boneless breast floured with ground walnuts, sautéed, and baked in puff pastry with a brie sauce. Or, have fish or lobster, one of the pastas, baby back ribs, rack of lamb, or a steak. For lighter dining, try the grilled shrimp salad or chicken Caesar, or feast on a big burger with curly fries.

LE ST. TROPEZ, *Limetree Court 67 King Street, , Frederiksted. Tel. 340/ 772-3000. Reservations are suggested. Open for lunch weekdays 11:30am-2:30pm and dinner Monday-Saturday, 6- 10pm. It's closed Sunday. Main dishes start at $14.50. Lunches are $6.50 to $14.50.*

Daniele and Andre Ducrot are usually on hand with a personal welcome as guests are ushered into this crowded, fragrant bistro. At lunch, start with a glass of wine and then have the velvety lobster bisque or a California Salad, a toothsome blend of lettuces topped with tomatoes, hard-boiled egg, and freshly grilled chicken breast. On oilcloth-covered tables, blackboards announce tonight's soups, salads, seafood and specialties, all of them with a French accent starting with the escargot or homemade paté de compagne. The wine list is extensive. Ask them to put Edith Piaf on the sound system and imagine yourself in a torchlit Parisian courtyard on a moist June evening. End your meal with a selection from their imported cigars. Before leaving, visit the gift shop with its European imports.

NO BONES CAFE, *Flag Drive, Gallows Bay. Tel. 340/773-2128. Take a cab from Christiansted for $4. Dinners are in the $12-$15 range. Hours are Monday through Friday 11am to 9pm and Saturday 5-9pm.*

Po' boy seafood and chicken sandwiches are a favorite here, and so is the English-style fish and chips. More exotic is the marinated mussels with linguine and a colorful confetti of vegetables. Fresh seafood is always on the menu.

ON THE BEACH, *a mile south of Frederiksted on the shoreline. Tel. 340/ 772-4242 or 772-1205. Lunch and dinner Main dishes are in the $10-$15 range. Take a cab from Frederiksted for $3.50 or from Christiansted for $20.*

Part of a small resort that fronts on a beach fringed with palms and sea grapes, this open-air favorite has a magical friendliness kindled by loyal repeat guests. Order a huge mahi-mahi sandwich with remoulade sauce, roast vegetable pizza, or a vegetarian sandwich made with sun-dried tomatoes and basil bread. Don't miss the tiny, but imaginatively stocked, gift shop.

PICNIC IN PARADISE *at the Carambola Beach Club on the north coast west of Christiansted. Tel. 340/778-1212. Sunday Brunch is $10-$25; lunch under $10; dinner Main dishes start at $16.50. Hours are 5:30pm to 10pm Tuesday through Saturday. Sunday brunch 10am-3pm; dinner 5-9pm.*

In a setting where the rainforest meets the sea, use one of the changing rooms after an afternoon of snorkeling the North Star Wall, then have a sundowner overlooking the Ham's Bluff lighthouse. On cool nights take refuge indoors where there's a fireplace. Luncheons star imaginative salads and classic sandwiches plus omelettes and a couple of hearty main dishes. At dinner, the chef offers a terrific terrine of roast potatoes and goat cheese salad served on a bed of greens. Try the filet mignon topped with artichoke fritters, or a Caribbean pot pie crammed with lobster, shrimp, and conch. The Vegetable and Goat Cheese Napoleon could make a vegetarian out of the most ardent carnivore.

SOUTH SHORE CAFÈ, *on the southern shore southeast of Christiansted on Route 62 at Route 624. Tel. 340/773-9311. Dinner costs about $20. Reservations are suggested. It's open for dinner Wednesday through Sunday; the bar opens at 5pm. Only VISA cards are accepted.*

Overlook the Great Pond and the shoreline while you dine on vegetarian specialties or owner-chef Diane Scheuber's homemade pastas, bread and desserts, seafood, prime rib, or lamb. For dessert, try the black pepper ice cream.

STIXX, *in the Pan Am Pavilion between Strand Street and the harbor, Christiansted. Tel. 340/773-5157. Plan to spend $15-20 for dinner; under $10 for lunch. Open daily, Stixx serves breakfast from 7am and dinner to 10pm. Reservations are recommended for deck seating.*

Combine a memorable view of Christiansted Harbor with a jolly mix of divers, sightseers, vacationers, and local working folks in a place that's as perfect for a quick, early breakfast as it is for a leisurely dinner. The shrimp scampi pizza is a favorite or have a buffalo burger, steak, or fresh seafood. The champagne brunch on Sundays is served 10am to 2pm.

THE WAVES AT CANE BAY, *on Route 80 near Cane Bay Beach. Tel. 340/778-1805. Reservations are suggested. Hours are Monday through Saturday, 5pm to 9pm. Dinners are $17 to $25. Cab fare from Christiansted is $16; from Frederiksted, $20.*

Family-run and as friendly as a hometown pub, this open-air spot on the edge of the water offers frozen cocktails, fresh fish, steak, pasta, and vegetarian choices all served in generous portions suited to hungry scuba divers. Start with the Smokin' Shrimp, jumbo shrimp stuffed with cheese, wrapped with jalapeno and dipped in beer batter. The stuffed veal chop is filled with apple tarragon dressing, or try the roasted Cornish game hem with plum sauce. The catch of the day can be served blackened or with lemon dill butter sauce, creole sauce, or a tropical fruit chutney. Kids get their own, special menu.

TIVOLI GARDENS, *Strand Street in the Pan Am Pavilion, , Christiansted. Tel. 340/773-6782. Main dishes are $10.50-$19.50. It's open for lunch Monday through Friday and dinner nightly until 9:30pm. Reservations are suggested.*

The twinkling lights remind you of the other Tivoli overseas; the cool breezes are provided by its second floor porch location. At lunch have a sandwich or coquille St. Jacques. For dinner there are mushroom caps stuffed with lobster, broiled lobster tail, fresh fish and pastas. The've added some winsome oriental dishes including a Thai seafood curry and butterflied shrimp in soy-ginger sauce. End the meal with homemade coffee-crunch ice cream or their popular chocolate velvet dessert. The Guava Cream Pie is a luscious twist on the key lime theme. The wine list offers more than 100 choices.

RUMRUNNER'S and **THE PACIFIC GRILL**, *on the waterfront at the Hotel Caravelle, Christiansted. Tel. 773-6585 for Rumrunner's and 340/773-2100 for the Pacific Grill. Rumrunner's is less formal and is open breakfast through dinner until 10pm. Pacific Grill is open for dinner, 6-10pm. Also at the Caravelle, in the Arcade, is* **Tyrone's Place**, *serving West Indian food at moderate prices.*

Operated by the talented folks who founded Indies, this elegantly informal dining room is right on the water with a view of yachts anchored just off the docks and the chuckle of wavelets almost at your feet. This is the kind of tropical hangout where locals gather and travelers feel instantly at home in a nice mix of guests including a faithful following of Danes.

The only Bloomin' Onion on the island is served here, so it's a good spot for groups to gather for drinks and appetizers that also include hot wings, Cruzan fritters and a boffo seviche. Have a salad, quesadilla, salad for two served family style, or a pizza piled to your order. It's called the Do It Yo-Own-Bad-Sef. At dinner, ask about specials, which might be Steak Diane or freshly caught lobster. There's always a nice choice of pastas, seafood, chicken dishes, and a vegetarian dish. Island ice creams such as coffee or rum raisin are dessert favorites, but there's also a nice choice of cakes or pies plus creamy drinks. On Mondays, the West Indian buffet is one of the island's best deals.

BLUE MOON, *17 Strand Street, Frederikstad. Dine for $20-$25. It's open for dinner Tuesday through Saturday and for Sunday brunch. Tel. 340/772-2222.*

One of the most popular nightspots and restaurants on this end of the island is this hip and handy place along the Strand. Specialties include the chicken Dijon sandwich for lunch, fresh seafood any time, roasted pork or rumbera chicken for dinner, all the shrimp you care to eat on Tuesday, a lobster special on Thursday and grilled beef fajitas on Friday. Early bird specials are served 6-7:30pm so eat early and hang around the drinks and good times. Jazz plays hot on Friday nights and cool during Sunday brunch.

BLUE MARLIN, *in the Club St. Croix, Estate Golden Rock. It's open daily for breakfast, lunch and dinner. Tel. 340/773-9150. Plan to spend $10 for breakfast, $15 for lunch and $10-$25 for dinner.*

Have fresh seafood, one of the pasta dishes made with meat or fish, a vegetarian selection, a sandwich or whole-meal salad, a grilled steak, lobster, or one of the chicken dishes. It's part of a beachfront tennis resort, so ask ahead if court time is available before or after you eat.

Budget

ANTOINE'S, *in the Mill Harbor Condominiums north of Christiansted. Ask for directions when you call for reservations, which are recommended. Tel. 340/773-0263. It's open daily for breakfast and lunch. Eat for under $15.*

Start your day with French toast and bananas topped with whipped cream, or a choice of 15 luscious omelets. This is a favorite spot with cruising sailors, who may just dinghy in for a cup of coffee and a slab of the to-die-for Black Forest cake. At lunch have the kalalloo and a batch of Cruzan crab cakes. There's a children's menu and always good choices for vegetarians.

BAGGY'S, *on the waterfront at Gallows Bay in St. Croix Marina. Tel. 340/713-9636. Eat for $10-$15. No credit cards. Hours are Monday through Saturday 6am to about 9pm. Sunday brunch is served 7am-2pm.*

Locals come here for limin' in the breezes, especially evenings at sunset and on Tuesday nights for Trivial Pursuit. Try the cheese steak or the French melt with a frozen rum drink. A pot of homemade soup simmers on the stove, burgers are grilled to order, and chicken is served with sweet and sour sauce. Live entertainers are on hand most Friday and Saturday nights. Ask about daily specials at supersaver prices.

BREEZEZ, *in the Club St. Croix west of Christiansted. Tel. 340/773-7077. Hours are 11:30am-4pm daily except Sunday, 4-9pm daily, and Sunday brunch 10am-2pm. Sandwich prices average $6; dinner main dishes are $12.25-$19.50.*

Splurge on the Flaming Rum Lobster or blackened prime rib. The Zydeco salad is mixed greens with bleu cheese, and there's also a nice choice of sandwiches (try the shrimp po'boy) and melts. A specialty is the luscious Linguine Rickie, tossed with garlic butter, chicken, tomatoes, olives, and bacon. Ask for daily specials.

CHEESEBURGERS IN PARADISE, *Estate Southgate, near Green Cay Marina, East End Road, Route 82, 3.5 miles east of Christiansted. Tel. 340/773-1119. Lunch for under $10; dinners are under $20. It's open every day 11am until the crowd thins.*

This is a good-times, air conditioned place where cheerful pirates bring on the grilled chicken, nachos, chili dogs, hummus burritos, and margaritas to wash them down. The two-fisted burgers are a favorite on the island. Live music plays from 7pm Thursday through Sunday.

DEEP END BAR, *in the Tamarind Beach Hotel on East End Road at the Green Cay Marina turnoff. Tel. 340/773-4455. Light lunches and dinners are $10 or less. It's open daily from 11am. No credit cards.*

A popular, outdoorsy, grass-shack sort of hangout, it's very informal. Have a drink from the blender and a sandwich, salad, hot dog, or soup special such as conch chowder or black bean. For dinner, order a burger platter or a simple main dish such as meatloaf or fish and chips. On Fridays, local artists come to the Tamarind Beach to sketch, so it's a good time to stroll around and look over their shoulders. Vegetarian dishes are a specialty.

LUNCHERIA, *in the Apothecary Hall Courtyard off Company Street. Tel. 340/773-4247. Hours are Monday through Friday 11am to 9pm and Saturday noon to 9pm. Eat for less than $10.*

This longtime local favorite is a cluster of picnic tables in a courtyard where you can't always find full shade. Place an order at the bar and pick it up yourself. Mexican favorites prevail. We especially like the nachos with "the works". They're loaded with melty cheese, shredded lettuce, diced tomatoes, olives, and onions. Have a quesadilla, a choice or burritos or a burrito plate that includes rice and a salad, a choice of enchiladas, or chicken fajitas. There's a children's menu, and a full bar serving custom-built margaritas. Call ahead and your take-out order will be ready when you get here.

MONTPELLIER HUT DOMINO CLUB, *in the rainforest at 48 Montpelier, Route 76. No telephone nor credit cards. It's open daily for lunch and cocktails; evening hours vary. Eat for under $10.*

Every visitor comes here for the first time to feed one of the famous, beer-drinking pigs: Miss Piggy, Tony, Toni, or J.J. They go through four cases of non-alcoholic beer a day plus grains, providing a hilarious exhibition that they seem to enjoy even more than tourists do. It's all in good fun. You buy a beer, present it to the pig, and it is able to open and drink it and spit out the can in a few seconds. The Club is also a favorite stop for rainforest visitors who sit here under the palm frond roof for a cooling drink and a light meal of ribs or chicken with johnny cake, chicken or fish, or the rotis that are served on Fridays.

THE SALOON, *on the waterfront, Strand Street, Fredericksted. Tel. 340/772-BEER. Open daily at 11am until midnight; later on Friday and Saturday, when food is served until 3am. Sandwich baskets are in the $6-$8 range.*

This pubby hangout is popular with any sailors who happen to be in port—

the U.S. Coast Guard was here during our last visit—as well as with locals who like the air conditioning. There's also outdoor seating. The selection of beers is among the best on the island, and the menu of creamy drinks sounds like a candy store. Try the Peppermint Patty. The grill fires up daily at 11am, turning out chicken and burgers to be served with something simple like chips, slaw, or potato salad. Play darts, pool, or video games. Live entertainers are on hand some nights; other times there's the juke box, which sometimes plays free. There are always special events or Happy Hour specials.

SPRAT HALL BEACH RESTAURANT, *a mile north of Frederiksted on Route 63. Tel. 772-5855. Open daily from 9am to 4pm with lunch served 11:30am to 2:30pm, it accepts no credit cards.*

It's nothing fancy, but its location on one of the island's best beaches makes it a regular stop for locals and visitors like. For $2 you can use the changing rooms and showers, then have pumpkin fritters, conch chowder, tannia soup, fish salad, or some other old island specialty from the kitchen of island-born Joyce Hurd. Heartier fare includes ginger curried chicken, fresh fish steak, or a cooked vegetarian plate.

ST. JOHN
Expensive

ASOLARE, *Cruz Bay. Tel. 340/779-4747. Closed Tuesdays, the restaurant is open daily 5:30pm to 9:30pm. Reservations are recommended.*

Chef Carlos Beccar Varela presides over a kitchen where the specialties are from the Pacific Rim and Asia. Closed for most of 1997 for renovations, it is once again one of the island's premier dining spots.

ELLINGTON'S, *Gallows Point. Tel. 340/693-8490. Reservations are recommended. Dine for about $40. Open daily, the restaurant serves breakfast, lunch and dinner until 10pm.*

Get here before sunset to enjoy the views of Pillsbury Sound. Linger over cocktails, then pace yourself for an elegant evening featuring one of the best wine cellars on the island. Choose lobster, steak, the catch of the day, or a pasta specialty. Try Beef Ellington, which is prepared for two, or the chicken with honey mustard sauce. Ask about the restaurant's name (it has nothing to do with Duke Ellington) and the Richard Ellington who was an island character in the 1950s.

EQUATOR, *in the Caneel Bay resort. Tel. 340/776-6111. Reservations are essential for dinner, which is served 7pm to 9pm. Cars aren't permitted past the outer parking lot. Plan to spend $40-$60 for dinner.*

Dressy, elegant, and the picture of attentive service, this restaurant is in the grand, round, stone building that once housed Caneel Bay's Sugar Mill restaurant. The design, with a roof that rises several stories, is a marvel of 18th century engineering. Every dish is a still life painting: plump shrimp in miso, handmade tortillas wrapping tender cabrito, salmon under a drift of fresh herbs, and chocolate mousse garnished with candied Anaheim pepper and composed on a palette of sauces. Choose from a well-stocked cellar of good American and European vintages.

CHATEAU BORDEAUX, *Centerline Road, Bordeaux Mountain. Tel. 340/ 776-6611. It's open nightly for dinner. Reservations are strongly advised. Plan to spend $50 per person for dinner and drinks.*

The highest outlook point on the island is the setting for romantic dining. In summer, dine with the sunset; in winter come after dark and gaze out over a fairyland of lights while you and your love dine on lobster, fresh fish with a sassy sauce, chicken in wine, imported steaks or chops, or one of the chef's inspirations-du-jour. There's a full bar and a comprehensive wine list.

Moderate

FISH TRAP, *at the Raintree Inn, Cruz Bay. Tel. 340/693-9994. Have lunch for $10-$15 and dinner for $20-$25. It's open daily except Monday for lunch and dinner. Find it across from the Catholic Church.*

Outdoorsy and informal, this is a popular limin' spot for locals. It's an easy walk from the ferry dock, but just far enough that day-trippers miss it. Chef Aaron chops and steams away in his little galley, shoving out one fine chicken, fish, and pasta dish after another. Try the stir-fry shrimp and vegetables, the black bean tostada with three cheeses or the seafood sampler salad. Save room for one of the dessert specialties made by co-owner Laura Willis. Her Coconut Cake with Caramel-Rum sauce was featured in Bon Appetit magazine.

LIME INN, *Cruz Bay. Tel. 340/776-6425 or 779-4199. Two streets up from the ferry, turn right on the one-way street just past the Lutheran Church, walking against traffic. It's open Monday through Friday for lunch, daily except Sunday for dinner 5:30 to 10pm Dine for under $25.*

A latticed garden sets the scene for fish, steak or burgers grilled over an outdoor charcoal grill. Lobster is always a favorite when it's available, and the Wednesday night, all-you-can-eat shrimp is a bonanza for shrimp lovers. Try one of the homemade soups or choose from a long list of salads.

GLOBAL VILLAGE CUISINE ON LATITUDE 18, *in Mongoose Junction. Tel. 340/693-8677. Dine for under $20. Open seven days a week, the restaurant serves breakfast, lunch, and dinner. Reservations are accepted.*

A short walk from the ferry dock is this touristy but convenient bistro. Have a fruity drink then a deli sandwich or a Mediterranean main dish.

PARADISO, *Mongoose Junction, Cruz Bay is open daily for lunch 11am-3pm and dinner 5:30-9:30pm. After 10pm, it turns into a night club. Tel. 340/ 693-8899. Reservations are accepted. Lunch for under $10; dine for under $20.*

Pizza, piled with the goodies of your choice, is a specialty here but there are plenty of other choices at lunch too including soups, salads, and juicy cheeseburgers. At dinner, steak, fresh fish or chicken are served with fluffy stuffed or smashed potatoes. Bring the kids, and ask to see the children's menu.

SHIPWRECK LANDING, *34 Freeman's Ground, Route 107, Coral Bay. Tel. 340/693-5640. Main dishes are priced $12 to $16. Hours are 11am to 10pm daily; the bar stays open later. The restaurant is eight miles from Cruz Bay.*

Come here not just for the legendary kitchen overseen by Pat and Dennis Rizzo but for the ride to the east end of beautiful St. John. Start with a rum with lime and coconut milk and a bowl of conch fritters. Then try something Cajun such as blackened grouper or snapper, a burger or a taco salad, chicken tangy with ginger, fish and chips, or a juicy steak. Live entertainment plans several nights a week, with jazz on Sunday.

SOGO'S RESTAURANT, *in the heart of Cruz Bay. It's open daily except Sunday for lunch and dinner. Main dishes are in the $10-$12 range. Tel. 340/ 779-4404.*

West Indian classics and American favorites are what West Indians call finest kind in this popular, "in-town" restaurant. Have fresh fish cooked to order, a steak, chicken with peas and rice, one of the refreshing salads, or a heartwarming, homemade soup. For dessert, have one of the sweet and slushy drinks (with or without alcohol), or a piece of pie.

Budget
CHILLY BILLY'S, *at the Lumber Yard, Cruz Bay. Tel. 340/693-8708. Open for breakfast and lunch daily 8am to 2pm and on Sunday breakfast is served all day. Eat for $5-$8.*

It's cool and convenient when you're in town on errands, and worth a special trip when you want a great breakfast or lunch. Dine on standard breakfast and lunch fare: fluffy omelets, fish and johnnycake, toothsome sandwiches, burgers and fries, and a good choice of cold, fruity drinks. It's a great limin' place on Sundays, when you can do the eggs-and-bacon scene no matter how late you sleep.

SKINNY LEGS, *Coral Bay. Tel. 340/779-4982. It's open every day 11am to 9pm. Eat for under $10.*

Locals love this place for its homemade soups, grilled or cold sandwiches, ice-cold salads, and fresh fish specialties. It's busiest at lunch, cocktail hour, and for the dinner hour after 7pm, but it's also a great hangout spot for a cold drink and a snack in the heat of the day.

Seeing the Sights
ST. THOMAS
The **Paradise Point Tramway** is not just the island's most spectacular view, its hilltop destination is a favorite hangout for photographing the harbor

and watching the sunset. In seven smooth, pleasant minutes you're 700 feet above sea level with a panoramic view of the harbor. Board the tram, off Long Bay Road just above Wendy's, *Tel. 340/774-9809*. Fare for adults is $10, children $5. Once at the top you can shop for souvenirs, order a drink, or nosh on hot dogs, burgers or ribs. Sunset dinner specials are $13.95. *Tel. 340/777-1182*.

Seven Arches Museum is up Government Hill at Freeway Alley and King Street, *Tel. 774-9295*. Once the home of a Danish craftsman, it's furnished in antiques that offer a glimpse of colonial times. The $5 donation includes a guided tour and a drink in the walled, flower-filled garden. Hours are daily except Sunday and Monday 10am to 3pm.

Dive 90 feet deep to see the fish and coral off St. Thomas aboard the **Atlantis submarine**. During the two-hour tour you'll leave from Havensight Mall next to Yacht Haven Marine, then board an air conditioned submarine for a one-hour voyage that covers more than 1 1/2-miles of sea bottom. The dive can also be combined with a flightseeing seaplane tour, *Tel. 340/777-4491* or *776-5650* or, from the U.S., *800/253-0493*. **Coral World**, an outstanding water attraction that was destroyed by Hurricane Marilyn, has been restored. While you're on the island, *call 340/775-1555* for an update on hours and admission.

Allow at least half a day at **Mountain Top**, *Tel. 340/774-2400*, elevation 1,500 feet, for a look at tropical birds, a Caribbean village, and a museum of artifacts from pre-Columbian days through the swashbuckling pirate era. From Charlotte Amalie, take Route 30 (Veteran's Drive), to Mafolie Road (30 North) and turn left onto Route 33. Bear left at the "Y" in front of Sib's and follow the road to Mountain Top, which is said to be the home of the original banana daiquiri.

Take a self-guided tour of **Estate St. Peter Greathouse and Botanical Gardens** in the volcanic hills of St. Thomas, *Tel. 340/774-4999*. From the

Harbor Night

Every other Wednesday is **Harbor Night** at the pier in Frederiksted when the docking of a major cruise ship is celebrated with a street party attended by cruisers, locals, and land-based tourists galore. Stroll the blocked-off streets to sample homemade foods and buy local crafts. Explore the old fort, which is open and well lighted. Then dance to live music until midnight. Check with your hotel host about schedules. Also held on the waterfront in Frederiksted on the third Friday of the month, 5:30-7:30pm are **Sunset Jazz Concerts**. Admission is free. Check locally for schedules and names of visiting artists.

1000-foot-high observation deck on a clear day you can see 20 other islands. Sip punch while exploring the lush botanical gardens. It's open daily 9am to 5pm. From Charlotte Amalie, take Route 40 (Solberg Road).

ST. CROIX

To take a walking tour of Christiansted start at the **Old Scalehouse**, built in 1856 and cross to **Fort Christiansvaern**, 1738, which has dungeons and cannons. It's open every day, 8am to 5pm Look across the water to Protestant Cay, called that because Protestants, barred from the Catholic cemetery, were buried here. Cross Hospital Street and look at the **Steeple Building**, built as a Lutheran Church in 1735 and now a must-see **museum** of local history, *Tel. 340/773-1460*. It's open Monday through Friday, 9:30am to 3pm, with a one-hour closing from noon to 1pm.

Across the way, note the West Indian & Guinea Company Warehouse, built 1749. It was the site of slave auctions. It's now a post office and has rest rooms if you need some by now.

Walk up Company Street to the 18th century **Apothecary Hall**, then onto the Market Square and to Prince Street where Holy Cross Catholic Church dates to 1828. Heading down Prince Street to King, turn right to see the **Pentheny Building**, built as a private mansion in the 18th century. Walking east on King Street you'll see the library and a Lutheran Church dating to 1740. Across the street, **Government House** is a superb example of Danish colonial style dating to 1747.

To take a walking tour of **Frederiksted**, start at **Fort Frederik**, *Tel. 340/772-2021*, which dates to 1750. Its museum is good but it overemphasizes hurricane history when most visitors, we'd guess, are more interested in swashbuckling, battles, and pirates. Across the street see the **Old Customs House**, built in the 1700s and added to in the 1800s. It was here that local sugar was weighed for shipment. Continuing east on Strand Street, enjoy a pretty promenade of neo-classical and Victorian buildings. Turn back to King Cross Street and go two blocks inland to Old Apothecary Hall, another of the time-warp buildings that the visitor can ponder while imagining this as a swirling center of 17th century trade.

Asking as you go if necessary, move on to the Benjamin House on Queen Street. It's an elegant townhouse with a wrought iron balcony. Staying on King Cross to **St. Paul's Anglican Church**, built in 1812, you'll pass the old cemetery. Going west now to Market Street, you'll see **St. Patrick's Catholic Church** and rectory, with a cemetery dating to the 18th century.

Turn back towards the sea on Market Street, passing the old Market Square, once the heart of the city. On King Street you'll see more historic buildings. Note the **Flemming Building** on the corner of King and **Custom House**. It was built from dismantled sugar factory chimneys.

St. George Village Botanical Garden is not only a brilliant garden stuffed with greenery and good smells, it is a National Historic District. Built on the site of an Arawak village that became a Danish community, it once contained a rum factory, greathouse, lime kiln, cemetery, and aqueduct. Stroll through orchids, ferns, an orchard of tropical trees, a cactus garden, galleries, stony ruins, and a gift shop. It's just off Route 70, east of West Airport Road, Route 64; *Tel. 340/692-2874* for hours, which vary seasonally. Admission is $5.

Whim Plantation Museum on Route 70 near Frederiksted is a complete plantation with a superbly restored greathouse that offers tours led by elderly docents, some of whom actually worked here years ago. Thelma Clarke, now in her 70s, showed us the grand piano dating to 1866, the chairs donated by island resident Victor Borge, 18th century furnishings, and the famous planter's chair that served as a combination chair and boot jack. Have a sugary piece of Johnny Cake, browse the gift shop, and allow an hour or two for roaming the grounds to get the true, tropical flavor of this ancient place. For information, *Tel. 340/772-0598*. Admission is $5 adults and $1 for children. In summer, Whim is closed on Sundays. In winter, monthly candlelight concerts feature world class, overseas musicians. Unamplified music, played by candlelight in these ancient walls, makes for a magical evening. Tickets are in short supply, but try for admission if you're on the island at the right time.

A mile north of Frederiksted, the **Carl and Marie Lawaetz Museum** at Little La Grange can be found on Mahogany Road, Route 76. Explore the house and gardens of one of the Danish founding families. Guided tours are offered Tuesday-Saturday 10am-4pm. *Tel. 340/772-1539*. Admission is adults $5 and children $2.

Tours of the **Cruzan Rum Distillery** can be boring for little ones, but grownups like the samples and the gift shop. Admission is charged. Tours are offered Monday through Friday 9-11:30am and 1-4:15pm. For information, call the tourist bureau at *Tel. 340/772-0357*. Tour Santa Cruz Breweries, Estate La Grange, Frederiksted, to see where Santa Cruz beer is made. There's also a restaurant, gardens, theater, and museum, *Tel. 340/772-3663 or 772-2779*.

See the **St. Croix Aquarium** on the waterfront in Christiansted, *Tel. 340/773-8995*, and try to link up with one of the educational snorkel trips offered. The aquarium is open Wednesday through Sunday, 11am to 4pm.

One of the island's best nature preserves is in **Salt River National Historic Park and Ecological Preserve**, which you can find on Route 751 off Route 75. Once the site of Amerindian ceremonies and the spot where Christopher Columbus is said to have first landed, it is the home of one of the largest mangrove forests in the Virgins. The bird life is abundant and varied but otherwise there are no facilities at present.

While you're out on the island, you may also want to try running up **The Beast**, also known as Mount Eagle. It's the island's highest point, at 1,650 feet, found on Route 69. When you see the words "The Beast" in the pavement you know you have arrived. Each year it's the scene of the grueling American Paradise Triathlon.

The sightseeing buzz on the island, literally, is aboard a Waco biplane with pilot Bob Wesley, who will show you the island from the open cockpit of this 1993 reproduction of a 1930s-era airplane. Two passengers sit side by side in the forward cockpit, where the view of hillsides and rainforest, beaches and waters is a thrill that brings them back for seconds. The ride is $65 for two, $110 for one, for about half an hour. Wesley can also give you an aerobatics ride for an additional $36 per 10 minutes but most folks prefer the tamer, sightseeing version. Classic Biplane Rides, Inc., is at the airport, *Tel. 340/690-7433*.

Hour-long guided tours of Christiansted and Frederiksted are available through **St. Croix Heritage Tours**, *Tel. 340/778-6997*. The tours accent historic buildings, courtyards and market places connected with the island's Danish background.

A Blue Ribbon Day

Everything you love about an old-time county fair, done with a tropical twist, can be seen at the annual **Agrifest** held on St. Croix in mid-February. Always the Virgin Islands' bread basket, St. Croix is a major farming center and the home of Senepol cattle, which were bred for the island. Sample local foods, see a roast pig demonstration, enjoy rides and games, and see local agricultural exhibits.

ST. JOHN

Since much of St. John is national park land, explorations should begin at the National Park Service Visitors Center on North Shore Road in Cruz Bay, *Tel. 340/776-6201 or 775-6238*. Get maps and instructions for the many hiking trails and snorkeling sites including ranger-led hikes and swims. It's a real plus to go with guides or guidance not just because of the expert narration but because rangers often provide the necessary equipment or pick-up/drop-off at a remote site. The national park user fee is $4 per person, which covers access to Trunk Bay and the Annaberg Ruins.

The whole island is peppered with ancient ruins, some barely identifiable and others as exciting as **Reef Bay Great House**, which was inhabited as late as the 1950s when the lady of the house was murdered. Various stabs have been made at restoring the house, so we don't know what condition it will be in when you get there, but the park service tends to it as funds are available.

Also administered by the park service is **Annaberg Plantation**, an 18th century sugar mill complex that has been partially restored. The views are spectacular, the ruins extensive, the nature watching excellent. Sometimes local artisans set up their shops in the plantation to enrich the scene. It's on Leinster Bay off the North Shore Road. For serious explorations, rent a four-wheel-drive and snoop into every road you see. Most will lead you either to a great beach or a great view.

Nightlife & Entertainment
ST. CROIX
Spring Starving Artists' Fair
One of the liveliest arts events in the islands, this annual art fair is held at **Estate Whim Plantation Museum** on St. Croix in late March (usually the last Sunday of the month). Shop for arts and crafts, eat native foods, and discover local drinks such as maubi and banana frost. Volunteers do much of the work at this fund raiser, which benefits the St. Croix Landmarks Society. For information, contact the museum, *Tel. 340/772-0598.*

Clubs, Casinos & Dancing
DIVI CARINA BAY CASINO, *in the Divi Carina Bay Resort, Grapetree Beach. Tel. 340/773-9700.*

Open every day from 10am to 4am, except Friday, Saturday and holidays, when it's open to 6am, this is the first casino in the territory. Play 13 gaming tables or 295 slot machines. Have a drink in the Mongoose Lounge show bar or a snack in the Carina Café.

HIBISCUS BEACH HOTEL, *Tel. 340/773-4042.*

Friday nights feature live entertainers; Saturday evenings feature jazz. Arrive early enough for a sundowner overlooking the beach, then dinner from an inspired menu.

BLUE MOON, *on the waterfront at Frederiksted, Tel. 340/775-7084.*

The place for jazz, coffee, nursing a rum drink or noshing on bistro food. Open Tuesday through Friday for lunch, Tuesday through Saturday for lunch and dinner until 10pm and Sunday for dinner until 9:30.

THE SALOON, *just off Strand Street on Market.*

A block south of the pier in Frederiksted, this bar is not only air conditioned but nearly smokeless thanks to special smoke extractors. Or, sit outdoors. Live entertainment starts at 9pm. Darts start at 7:30 on Tuesday and Wednesday. There's plenty of food, free popcorn, a big beer menu, and the usual margaritas and coladas. Food is served until 3am on Friday and Saturday nights.

LOST DOG PUB, *14 King Street, Frederiksted, Tel. 340/772-3526.*

This pub features rock 'n roll on the jukebox, lots of brands of beer, and the most popular pizza on this end of the island. The fun goes on until 1am. Credit cards aren't accepted.

Support Your Local Beer

St. Croix' own beer, **Santa Cruz**, is brewed near Frederiksted and offered in draft or long necks. At press time, plans for the brewery include a museum, restaurant, gift shop and a theater where the Caribbean Dance Company will perform. Other brews on the Virgin Islands include: **Blackbeard's Ale** and **Captain Kidd's Golden Ale**.

At the **Buccaneer Hotel**, *Tel. 340/773-2100*, listen to a steel band on Sunday, calypso/reggae on Friday nights, and jazz on Saturday. **Chenay Bay**, *Tel. 340/773-2918*, has a steel band from 7pm on Saturday; **Hotel on the Cay** features a steel band Thursday through Monday 5pm to 9pm. Guitar and song start Thursday through Sunday at 7pm at **Cheeseburgers in Paradise** and nightly at **Tivoli Gardens**.

For crab races, an old wagering favorite since the days of the buccaneers, be at **King's Landing Yacht Club** Monday at 5:30pm or **Stixx** on Fridays at 5:30pm. For darts, try **King's Landing** or **The Saloon**.

Check the events schedule in *St. Croix This Week*, which is available free at any hotel for a listing of where and when to find steel bands, jazz, guitar and sing, Caribbean entertainment, calypso, reggae, or piano.

Yacht Club on Sunday evenings or **The Saloon** on Tuesdays and Wednesdays from 7:30.

ST. THOMAS

One of the best amphitheaters in the Caribbean for the presentation of concerts and Broadway shows is the **Reichhold Center for the Arts** in St. Thomas. Check local newspapers while you're here to see if anything is playing. It could be a star or show of international importance. Also check your hotel's Dining/Nightlife Channel 4 for the latest buzz.

Other places include:

HARD ROCK CAFE, *on the waterfront at International Plaza in Charlotte Amalie, Tel. 340/777-5555.*

Open all day and half the night for noshing and listening among a fortune in rock memorabilia. Come for a blimp-size burgers, a good salad, or to add to your collection of Hard Rock tee shirts. Live music plays Friday and Saturday nights.

SHIPWRECK TAVERN, *Al Cohen's Mall. Tel. 340/777-1293. Open until midnight, later on Saturday.*

This sports bar serves good food and drink while guests play pool, darts, pinball, air hockey, and Foosball. On Game Nights, winners (except for pool) get a free drink.

TURTLE ROCK BAR, *in the Wyndham Sugar Bay Resort, Smith Bay, Tel. 340/777-7100.*

Not far from Red Hook, this resort bar has a different drawing card every night. It could be live performances, karaoke, dancing, or reggae, If you want to eat here, find a good selection of dishes in the resort's Mangrove Restaurant. There's no cover charge in the bar. The fun starts with Happy Hour 4 to 6pm and continues to closing, which could be any time depending on the crowd.

For an offbeat night adventure, sign up for a Thursday night snorkeling excursion with Chris Sawyer. *Tel. 340/777-7804.* The outing, held 5:30-10pm includes dinner and costs $65.

Mocko Jumbies

A Virgin Islands traditional folk entertainment is **Mocko Jumbies**, stilt dancers in bright costumes who perform at every Carnival and parade. Mocko Jumbie dolls are catching on as collectible crafts.

ST. JOHN

The best bet for dining and nightlife on St. John is to go to downtown Cruz Bay and follow the sound of music. Hotspots include **The Back Yard,** *Tel. 340/693-8886* with music until midnight Wednesday through Saturday; **Global Village,** *Tel. 340/693-8677* for live music with dinner Friday until 9pm; **La Tapa,** *Tel. 693-7755* for soca and jazz, and **Tamarind Court Café,** also *Tel. 340/693-7755* for blues and country. **Pusser's Beach Bar,** *Tel. 340/693-8489* is one of the most popular spots in town for drinking, listening, crab races, and limin' into the wee hours.

At Coral Bay, try **Shipwreck Landing,** *Tel. 340/693-5640* for guitar, vocals, and light rock, **Skinny Legs,** *Tel. 340/779-4982* for jazz nightly except Sunday, or **Sea Breeze,** *Tel. 340/693-5824* for bands and light rock Fridays until 1am.

Sports & Recreation

Yacht brokers who can find the right boat and crew for your sailing vacation anywhere in the Virgin Islands include:
- **Admiralty Yacht Vacations,** *Tel. 800/544-0493*
- **Bajor Yacht Charters,** *Tel. 800/524-8292*
- **Easy Adventures,** *Tel. 800/524-2027*
- **Island Yachts,** *Tel. 800/524-2019*
- **Proper Yachts St. John,** *Tel. 776-6256*
- **Regency Yacht Vacations,** *Tel. 800/524-7676, local 340/776-5950.*

- **Stewart Yacht Charters,** *Tel. 800/432-6118*
- **Virgin Islands Charter Yacht League,** *Tel. 800/524-2061*
- **Virgin Islands Power Yacht Charters,** *Tel. 800/524-2015*

Book anything from a brief sunset or snorkeling sail to a week-long charter on which you'll share the storybook life of a crew, usually husband and wife, who live aboard the boat. The variety of boats and their comforts is enormous, so allow plenty of time for choosing and booking. Power and sailboats accommodating two to 20 people charter for $1,200 to $1,500 per person for seven nights, including food, drinks, sightseeing, and watersports. Some of the larger boats offered by Regency Yacht Vacations even come with a helicopter and masseur! You can also book a package that combines yachting and hotel stays; for more information, *Tel. 776-5950* locally or, in the U.S., *Tel. 800/524-7676 or 401/848-5599.*

Through **American Wilderness Experience**, book a sea kayaking and camping trip in the Virgin Islands for five or seven days or sail a tall ship on an eight-day Virgins voyage. *Tel. 800/444-0099.*

Offered on St. John and St. Thomas is **snuba**, a dive available to non-divers and even to novice swimmers. After a 20-minute training session, you'll dive to as deep as 20 feet while breathing through an attached air line. For information and reservations, *Tel. 693-8063.*

ST. THOMAS
Beaches

Sailboarders and snorkelers who have their own equipment like **Bluebeard's Beach** at the end of Bluebeard's Road, Route 322, which branches off Route 30 near Red Hook. Bring your own gear; no rentals are available here. **Coki Beach** is favored for its view of Thatch Key and the Leeward Passage. The beach has bathrooms, a food stand, and snorkel gear for rent. It's on the northeast Coast. Also on the north shore, just west of Magens Bay, is **Hull Bay**, a popular anchorage for local fishermen. Waters along the western tip can be frisky, which makes it popular with surfers when the surf's up, but usually the waters are calm and clear. The bay has a restaurant, appropriately named Bluebeard's. .

East of downtown, next to Morningstar Beach, is **Limetree Beach**, a picture-perfect beach on a natural cove. Come to walk the sands and photograph iguanas. **Magens Bay**, which is a public park owned by the island, has been named in top-ten lists of beautiful beaches. Admission of $1 per car, $1 per adult, and 50 cents per child gains access to covered picnic tables, showers, dressing rooms, boutique, snack bar, sailboat rentals, and snorkel rental. It's on the north shore at the end of Route 35.

Morningstar Beach is a busy, commercial place with gear and lounge chair rentals, bars, boardsailer instruction, and a good view of boats sailing past the east point of the harbor. It's near town at Marriott's Frenchman's Reef Beach Resort. **Sapphire Beach** on the east end of the island is enjoyed by snorkelers and boardsailers. It has a marina, restaurants, and a dive shop that rents equipment.

Bicycling

Water Island, the fourth of the U.S. Virgin Islands, will eventually be developed, but for now it remains a virgin Virgin where you can take a half-day bicycle tour with **Bike Water Island**, *Tel. 340/714-2186, www.waterislandadv.worldnet.att.net.* The price of $60 per person includes ferry transport both ways, refreshments, a guide, and use of bicycles. The ride is rated easy to moderate, but a liability waiver must be signed and no riders under age 16 are allowed.

Boating

Powerboat Rentals are available from **Nauti Nymph**, *Tel. 340/775-5066.* Power, sail, and sportfishing charters are available from **The Charterboat Center** at Piccola Marina in Red Hook, *Tel. 340/775-7990 or 800/866-5714.* Speedy Mako and Scarab powerboats for exploring or skiing are rented through **See and Ski** at American Yacht Harbor, Red Hook, *Tel. 775-6265.*

Ocean Runner Powerboat Rentals at Cruz Bay, *Tel. 340/693-8809,* offers Hydrasports boats from 22 to 25 feet.

Diving

The **St. Thomas Diving Club** on Bolongo Bay is your key to scuba diving St. Thomas. It's a five-star PADI facility, *Tel. 776-2381, Fax 777-3232; toll-free 800/LETS DIVE.*

Golf

Mahogany Run, *Tel. 777-6006 or 800/253-7103* is a fabulous Fazio-designed course overlooking the Atlantic. It's an 18-hole, championship, 6,033-yard, par-70 course feared and famous for its "devil's triangle" of devious holes. On the north side of the island, 20 minutes from Charlotte Amalie. A new irrigation network promises year-round play on pool table greens even during dry seasons. Greens fees are in the $55-$85 range.

Horseback Riding

Kerry's Northshore Horseback Riding offers tours of the trails and beaches for $20 per hour, minimum two hours. All-day packages include lunch. Lessons are also available. Reserve at least one day ahead. *Tel. 779-3578.* Rides can also be booked with **Paul and Jill's Equestrian Stables**, *Tel. 772-2627.* **Half Moon Stables**, *Tel. 777-6088,* offers horse and pony tours of the east end of the island for $45 per hour. Riding lessons and clinics are also available. **Carolina Corral** on St. John offers horse and donkey rides to the beaches and mountains, *Tel. 693-5778.*

Sea Kayaking
Paddle through unspoiled wetlands and mangrove swamps with **Virgin Island Ecotours**, *Tel. 779-2155 or 777-6200.*

Submarine Exploration
Atlantis Submarine operates out of Building VI, bay 1, in the Havensight Mall, *Tel. 776-5650 or 800/253-0493.* One-hour voyages explore the underwater mysteries of St. Thomas to a depth of 90 feet. Reservations are essential. The trip costs about $70.

ST. JOHN
Beaches
Caneel Bay can be reached through the plush resort of the same name, but it's also popular with boaters who anchor off its famous shores. If you arrive by land, stop at the front desk for a day visitor guide. If you arrive by boat, don't set so much as a toe above the high tide line or you are intruding on , very exclusive private property. The bay is on the north shore, close to Cruz Bay.

Hawksnest Bay on the north shore of the island near Cruz Bay is smaller and more quiet than Trunk Bay, so it's popular with locals. Changing facilities are available. The west side of the beach is part of Caneel Bay Resort. Again, don't trespass.

Trunk Bay is famed for its underwater snorkeling trail. The beach is picture-perfect with its talcum sands and luxuriant fringe of trees and shrubs. There's a place to change, and a small shop. If you'd like more advanced snorkeling, ask at the national park about a snorkel tour to Flanagan's Cay off the southeast coast.

Cinnamon Bay at the campground in the national park offers great snorkeling in clear waters, a store, restaurant, watersport rentals, and a fine sand beach. The island's great beaches also include **Maho Bay**, **Francis Bay**, and **Leinster Bay**.

Fishing
To find a fishing guide, charter boat rental, tackle, or other connections, call the island information center at *Tel. 340/776-6922.*

Hiking
Thunderhawk Trail Guides, *Tel. 340/774-1112*, offers guided trail tours for up to 50 people. Lasting about two hours, the hikes accent the history and culture of the Taino Indians. Rates are $20 to $40 including pick-up/drop-off at hotels.

Virgin Islands National Park is crisscrossed with miles of hiking trails, historic ruins, hills and dales, forests and flowers. When leaving the ferry dock, keep walking left and you'll come to a National Park Service information office. Since most of St. John is part of the Park, its hiking trails are abundant and well mapped. You can go it alone or join one of the guided walks with an environmentalist who can point out natural features you might miss on your own. Notices of upcoming hikes are posted at the interpretive center of the National Park.

Horseback Riding

Ride a horse or donkey through the **Virgin Islands National Park**, which covers most of St. John, *Tel. 340/693-5778.*

Underwater Exploration

Atlantis Submarine, based in St. Thomas, operates out of Cruz Bay one day a week, *Tel. 776-5650.*

ST. CROIX
Beaches

Let your hotel host suggest a new beach every day according to winds and sea conditions, keeping in mind that you're on your own without lifeguards. West of Christiansted, **Salt River Bay**, where Columbus first landed, offers a beach with frisky winds and waves, and no facilities. Continue along the North Shore Road to **Cane Bay Beach** and **Davis Bay Beach**, which offer excellent snorkeling about 100 feet off out. From Christiansted, take the ferry to the **Hotel on the Cay**, which has a beach, restaurant, and bar.

West of town, **Estate Golden Rock** has a beach a fifth of a mile long; **The Buccaneer** on Route 82 charges admission and rents beach chairs on its beach, which has food and drinks. The beach at **Green Cay** is remote and lovely, reached by rental boat from Green Cay Marina. Also east of town watch for Reef Condominiums and the **Reef Beach** opposite them, which is popular with board sailors. Off Route 60, find **Grapetree Beach** where seagrapes offer shade and a concession offers snorkel and sailboard rentals, drinks, food, and rest rooms.

Boating & Snorkeling

A trip to **Buck Island Reef National Monument**, which lies six miles from Christiansted, is a must. Skippers provide snorkel gear so you can explore the underwater trail.. Call **Llewellyn's Charter**, *Tel. 773-9027* or **Terero II**, *Tel. 773-3161* or *773-4041*. Personal watercraft and kayaks can be rented at **St. Croix Water Sports Center**, *Tel. 773-7060.*

Sails, trips to Buck Island, big game fishing, diving, windsurfing, parasailing and non-motorized watersports are available at Cutlass Cove Beach behind

The Mermaid restaurant. It's open daily 9am to 5pm. *Call extension 741 at the Buccaneer, Tel. 773-2100.* Jolly Mon, a 60-foot catamaran offers snorkeling, sailing, party sails, and weddings through **Mile Mark Watersports**, *Tel. 773-3434, 773-2638 or 800/523-DIVE.* **Caribbean Adventure Tours** does kayak expeditions based on history, snorkeling, or a moonlit paddle to view bioluminescent waters. Cost is $45 per person. *Tel. 340/778-2076.*

Bicycling

Ride mountain bikes over the rolling hills with **St. Croix Bike & Tours**, Pier 69 Courtyard, Frederiksted, *Tel. 773-5004 or 773-2343.* You'll climb Creque (pronounced Creaky) Dam Road if you're up to it, and explore the rainforest. Less hardy bikers can stay on flatter lands on a seashore tour to Hams Bluff.

Golf

All three golf courses offer instruction and equipment rental. The 18-hole course at **Carambola Golf Club**, *Tel. 778-5638*, was designed by Robert Trent Jones and has a Gold Medal Award from Golf Magazine. The par-72 course rolls past shining lakes surrounded by bougainvillea and palm trees. **Buccaneer Golf Course**, *Tel. 773-2100,* is a pretty 18-hole course on the seaside, said to be the prettiest course in the islands. The par-70 course has 5,810 yards of sloping fairways, water hazards, and challenging bunkers. It's designed by Bob Joyce.

A nine-hole course is on the east end of the island at **The Reef Golf Course**, Teague Bay, *Tel. 773-8844.* Greens fees start at $10; riding and pull carts are available for a fee.

Hiking

Link up with the **St. Croix Environmental Association**, *Tel. 340/773-1989,* for serious hiking or **Ay Ay Ecotours**, *Tel. 340/772-4079* for guided walks of historic areas. Hikers will enjoy Salt River National Park, Caledonia Valley, and Estates Mount Washington and Butler Bay. Both groups require reservations. It's always a plus to go with a guide who can point out unique plants or tell you local names for familiar tropicals.

Hike to **Castle Nugent**, a 300-acre working farm that was established on the south shore of St. Croix in the early 1700s. Hiking three or four miles of moderate to strenuous terrain, you'll see the area's cultural, historic, and agricultural significance. When you reach the "castle" you'll see the house, ruins of outbuildings and the slave quarters. For details contact the St. Croix Hiking Association, *Tel. 340/778-2076 or 778-2026.*

Horseback Riding

Ride horseback across strands of white sand through the surf with **Paul and Jill's Equestrian Stables**, *Tel. 340/772-2880.*

Kayaking

V.I. Ecotour, *Tel. 340/779-2155,* leads kayak expeditions through the mangroves.

Parasailing

Fly over the water by parasail, towed by a speedboat at **Hotel on the Cay**, *Tel. 340/773-7060.*

Scuba Diving

Hang around the **Aqua-Lounge Club** to learn about the underwater scene. Even the bartenders are divers, so everyone decompresses here from 5-7pm. Every night something new is sparking, such as bring-your-catch barbecue night, rap sessions, signups for dive buddies, and night dives. Located in an old Danish warehouse with easy access from King Street or the boardwalk, the air conditioned club offers free parking in the Anchor Inn lot. It's at 58A King Street, *Tel. 340/773-0263.* For a copy of the U.S.V.I. Dive Guide, *Tel. 800/372-8784.*

Dive operators offering scuba trips, instruction, refills and gear include:
- **Cap' Dick's Scubawest**, *Tel. 340/772-3701* or *800/352-0107.*
- **Dive Experience**, *Tel. 340/773-3307* or *800/235-9047*
- **Cane Bay Dive Shop**, *Tel. 340/773-9913,* Cane Bay, or *772-0715,* Frederiksted. *Toll-free Tel. 800/338-3843*
- **Cruzan Divers**, *Tel. 340/772-3701* or *toll-free 800/352-0107*
- **Anchor Dive Center**, *Tel. 340/778-1522* or *800/532-DIVE*
- **Mile Mark Watersports**, *Tel. 800/523-DIVE* or *340/773-3434.*
- **V.I. Divers**, *Tel. 340/773-6045* or *800/544-5911.* We can recommend Ed and Molly Buckley as congenial hosts ashore and afloat.

\Snorkeling

Guided snorkel trips are offered by the **St. Croix Aquarium and Marine Education Center**, *Tel. 340/772-1345.*

Tennis

In addition to the many courts at resorts, St. Croix has public courts at **D.C. Canegata Park** in Christiansted and **Fort Frederik Park** in Frederiksted.

Shopping

Even though Americans are still on American territory, customs limits must be observed and luggage is subject to search, either before leaving the islands or when changing planes in San Juan. Any purchases that total more than $1200 are subject to a five per cent tax and amounts over $2200 are subject to regular duty charges, even if you bought "duty free" in the islands. Island-made products in any amount are duty free, but be sure to get a receipt for any purchase of more than $25. In addition, you can ship home gifts of up to $100 per day.

Each U.S. resident over age 21 can bring back six bottles of liquor duty free as long as one of them is made in the U.S. Virgin Islands. Remember that plants and farm products can't be brought to the mainland, nor can protected products such as turtle shell and black coral. Customs questions? Locally, call *340/773-5650.*

ST. THOMAS

A popular cruise ship stop, St. Thomas is famed for stores packed with crystal, china, watches, jewels, cameras, perfumes, and liquors sold tax free. Cruise passengers come ashore clutching the maps and discount coupons given to them on board and swarm into shops whose hours are determined by when ships are in port. When they are, you can shop on Sunday mornings. Otherwise, plan to shop the other six days of the week.

An open-air market along the waterfront sells mostly tee shirts, sleazy rayon sarongs, and claptrap. Some booths are piled high with brand name leather goods, which may or may not be authentic, but nothing bears a price tag so you're on your own to make a deal. Even in the best shops we saw very few price tags, so St. Thomas is a place for shoppers who know exactly what model watch or camera, what carat jewel, or what brand perfume they want, and will recognize a good buy when they see it. If you're just browsing, you'll have to ask about prices one piece at a time.

Our favorite spot downtown is the **Native Arts and Crafts Cooperative** next to the Tourism Visitor's Bureau. Local artists pitch in to run the place as well as to display their wares. *Tel. 340/777-1153.*

In downtown Charlotte Amalie, most shops are along **Main Street** (Dronnigens Gade) and the waterfront, and on the narrow alleys that run between them. East of downtown nearer the cruise ships docks, **Havensight Mall** also has prestige shops such as Gucci, Little Switzerland, A.H. Riise, and Columbia Emeralds International as well as a pharmacy, beauty salon, and bank.

Look for such shopping meccas as:

Hibiscus Alley along Main Street has a **Coach, Cardow's Diamond Center, Local Color** for accessories, and the **West Indies Coffee Company** as well as a store selling memorabilia connected with the Virgin Island's America's Cup Challenge, which was sailed in the year 2000. **Lover's Lane** carries everything from exotic erotica to bridal and bath boutique items. It's on the waterfront at the corner of Raadets Gade, upstairs. **Palm Passage** is, between Main Street and the waterfront. Its stores include **Calvin Klein, BCBG, Ralph Lauren/Polo, Donna Karan, Nicole Miller, Diesel Jeans. Scandinavian Center** in the Havensight Mall has handmade products from Scandinavia including a complete line of Royal Copenhagen, Georg Jensen silver and precious gems. The center also has an art gallery filled with Caribbean and Danish scenes.

Cosmopolitan on the waterfront has Bally, Sperry Topsider, Sebago and other famous name shoes plus international sportswear brands. **Drake's Passage Mall** in the historic district is the only air conditioned mall downtown. Shops sell leather foods, clothing souvenirs, sweets, and clothing. If you're been inspired by the colonial mahogany furniture of the islands, you can buy greathouse furnishings at **Mahogany Island Style** in Al Cohen's Plaza on Route 38. Poster beds, armoires and planter's chairs are shown; international art works and accessories are also sold. On Raphune Hill, Route 38, look for **Mango Tango Art Gallery** for originals, limited edition prints, and gifts. It's open daily 9am to 5:30pm, Sundays 10am to 1pm.

Located downtown and around the island are such standout jewelry stores as **Amsterdam Sauer, Cardow, Little Switzerland, Diamonds in Paradise, Diamonds International**, and **Columbian Emeralds International**. For loose diamonds and jewelry at rock bottom prices, check out the **Diamonds International Liquidation Center** at the waterfront. At Red Hook, **Doucet Stanton Jewelers** is a family-owned business featuring handmade Scandinavian silver pieces as well as local art. It's in American Yacht Harbor Building C2-1.

If you need ordinary supplies at ordinary prices, St. Thomas has a **K-mart** in Tutu Park Mall, a ten-minute cab ride from the docks. Our favorite shopping haunt is a 25-stall arts and crafts mall opposite the **Renaissance Grand Beach Resort** in Smith Bay. Local vendors display their homemade wares.

Since every American over age 21 can take back five fifths of liquor or six fifths if the liquor is produced in the U.S.V.I., it's best to get island brews such as Cruzan Rum, Havensight Liqueur, Chococo, Clipper Spiced Rum, Old St. Croix, Estate Diamond, and Southern Comfort. Exemptions apply only on purchases made in the U.S.V.I. and not to the same brands bought aboard ship.

ST. CROIX

King's Alley, the brightest diamond in **Christiansted's** shopping tiara, re-opened in 1996 more brilliant than ever before. In one spot downtown, find twelve luxury hotel suites furnished in Danish West Indian style, *Tel. 340/773-0103*, plus restaurants including a Thai and a chop house, and 20 upscale shops. Its smaller sister in Frederikstad runs from Strand Street to King Street, handy to the pier. The hotel here, by the way, is right next to the seaplane pier so it's the perfect place to stay if you're just making a quick overnight trip to St. Croix.

The shopping game in St. Croix is to choose a **Crucian hook bracelet**. The unique designs rely on a hook or button latch. Each jeweler has its own designs in gold or sterling and some people make a collection of as many different models as they can find. Also featured here is the Caribbean gemstone *larimar*, a blue stone found only in the islands.

Local artist **Mark Austin Fine Art Gallery** is in the Caravelle Arcade downtown, offering hand-painted furniture as well as sculpture, original paintings and prints. Austin, a St. Croix native, is known for his depictions of local life. *Tel. 692-2301.*

For books try **Trader Bob's Bookshop and Gallery** at 5030 Anchor Way. It's a serious book store, with a good choice of fiction and nonfiction titles. Let Bob Elman suggest good beach reading for the Caribbean. It's also a good place to buy inexpensive trinkets for the kids and quality stationery or souvenirs, so come on a rainy afternoon for serious browsing.

ST. JOHN

It's fun to shop in little St. John because few here try to compete with the glitzy stores of St. Thomas. Stores feature folk arts, resort wear, crafts, seashells, custom jewelry, unusual gifts, and locally made foods and spice blends. Another St. John specialty is pottery featuring petroglyph motifs inspired by Arawak drawings. **Kareso Art Gallery** in Cruz Bay features oils by Karen Samuel, wood carvings, baskets, photography, prints and furniture. *Tel. 340/714-5511.*

It's worth a day trip to St. John on the ferry to shop **Wharfside Village**, **Mongoose Junction**, **Pink Papaya Gallery** in the Lemon Tree Mall behind the Chase Bank, and other shops, all of them a stone's throw from the ferry dock.

Columbian Emeralds, *Tel. 340/776-6007*, has a shop in Mongoose Junction and so does **Island Galleria**, *Tel. 340/779-4644*, with its crystals, perfumes, and collectibles. And if you can never carry home enough of your favorite Caribbean hot sauce, guava preserves or other treats, go to *www.eKalaloo.com* and place your order.

Excursions & Day Trips
ST. CROIX

Sweeny Toussaint, manager of **St. Croix Safari Tours**, *Tel. 340/773-6700* is a knowledgeable, attentive, and personable guide. He can arrange everything from airport transfer to sightseeing, car rental, and watersports. For a mystery trip out of St. Croix complete with lunch and champagne, let **Bohlke International Airways** set the pace, *Tel. 778-9177.* The line flies to St. Thomas, St. John, the British Virgins, St. Barts, or Puerto Rico. **Big Beard's Adventure Tours**, Christiansted, *Tel. 773-4482*, does sunset sails, private charters, and half- and full-day excursions.

Ras Lumumba, who moved to St. Croix from Dominica in 1964, leads wilderness tours. He's a practicing gardener and herbalist, offering hikes of two-four hours. Contact Ay-Ay Hike and Tours, *Tel. 340/772-4079.*

Buck Island Reef National Monument is St. Croix' most meaningful day trip. Sail, hike, snorkel, have a beach barbecue, or scuba dive. The uninhabited island is 6,000 feet long and half a mile wide, rising to 340 feel above sea level. It lies only one and a half miles off the northeast coast of St. Croix. Endangered species nesting here include the hawksbill turtle and brown pelican as well as leatherback and green sea turtles. On land, walk marked trails across the island through giant tamarind trees, hillsides covered with guinea grass, and lowland beaches. In the water, snorkel over a marine wonderland of elkhorn coral, brilliant sea gardens, and schools of darting fish. A marked underwater trail describes the sights.

Mile Mark Watersports offers dive expeditions, *Tel. 340/773-2628 or 773-3434*. Boats can be rented in Christiansted and half a dozen outfitters also offer half-and full-day excursions with time allowed in and out of the water. Snorkel gear is provided, *Tel. 773-1460.*

To take a self-guided driving tour, take Hospital Street out of Christiansted to East End road, Route 82 and note Gallows Bay on your left. Until recent years it was a busy port, now a good place for shopping and dining. Continuing on Route 82, pass the family-owned B**uccaneer** with its restaurants and 18-hole golf course and Green Cay Marina. Bear left, staying on Route 82 and keep a sharp eye for nesting blue heron. You'll pass **Chenay Bay**, **Coakley Bay**, the famous **Duggan's Reef Restaurant** and come to the **St. Croix Yacht Club**. Look up to your right to see a castle, which is privately owned. Ask locals about its story. Leaving from Christiansted harbor is the **Hail Mary Harbor Cruise**, sailing a silent, hour-long trip to Gallows Bay aboard an electric boat. The six-passenger boat sails 10am-2pm every Thursday. *Tel. 340/698-BOAT.*

Point Udall is the easternmost point under the United States flag, but don't try to drive to the beach. Roads wash out regularly and, at press time, are impassable. From here, take Route 82 back to Christiansted or go south on Route 60 along the coast. Stay along the water and you won't get lost as you pass **Great Salt Pond** with its waterfowl. Turning left at the Airport Market, Route 624 and left on Route 62, you'll continue along the south shore past farm fields filled with big Senepol cattle. The breed was developed on St. Croix. To return to Christiansted, turn right on Route 70, locally called Centerline Road, where most of the shopping centers, banks and other everyday commercial centers are found.

To take a tour of the north and west of St. Croix through the radically different terrain of the rainforest, start early in the day because there are many stops you'll want to make along the way. Take Route 75 out of Christiansted and turn right on Route 80. At the Salt River Marina sign turn right to the **Salt River National Park and Ecological Preserve**. See the place where Columbus is said to landed in 1493. Take time to look for birds, then return ro Route 80 and head west on the scenic North Shore Road with its views of the other islands in the hazy distance. At LaValle village, turn right to **Cane Bay Beach** for a swim, then stay on Route 80 to Route 69. Turn left and climb a steep hill leading to a view of Carambola. Route 76, Mahogany Road, leads to a stone quarry. On your left, watch for **LEAP**, an environmental project where items made from local woods are sold. At Route 63, turn right and follow the shore road past to Sprat Hall Plantation, which is closed to the public. Continuing along Butler Bay you'll pass the Coast Guard station and continue to Frederikstad with its shopping and dining. Leave town on Route 70, stopping **at Whim Plantation**, the **botanical gardens**, and the **rum distillery** on Route 64. Return to Christiansted via Route 66.

ST. THOMAS

Sail the *Lady Lynsey* out of the Ritz-Carlton on half day, all day, and sunset sails, *Tel. 340/775-3333.* Aboard the all-day sail and snorkeling expedition, you'll visit St. John or Jost Van Dyke and will be served a continental breakfast and gourmet buffet luncheon for $135-$145. A half day sail including continental breakfast (on the morning sail) and lunch costs $85 per person. The Sunset Sail is out for two hours and includes fruit, fresh vegetables, and finger sandwiches for $45. For a guided eco-tour of Magens Bay, book with **The Nature Conservancy/ V.I. Ecotours**, *Tel. 340/779-2155.* The tour lists 60-90 minutes, is moderately strenuous, and costs $60 per person. .

Whale Watching excursions are offered only for a few days in March by the Environmental Association of St. Thomas-St. John, but are worth waiting for. Tickets are $55. *Tel. 340/776-1976.*

Excursions from St. Thomas to the British Virgin Islands including the famous **The Baths** on Virgin Gorda and the hiking trails of Jost Van Dyke are available through:

• **Dohm's Water Taxi**, *Tel. 340/775-6501*
• **Inter-Island Boat Services**, *Tel. 340/776-6597 or 776-6282* Jost Van Dyke trips sail Friday, Saturday and Sunday.
• **Limnos Charters**, *Tel. 340/775-3203*
• **Stormy Petrel and Pirate's Penny**, *Tel. 340/775-7990 or 800/866-5714*
• **High Performance Charters**, *Tel. 340/777-7545*
• **Transportation Services**, *Tel. 340/776-6282 or 776-6597* Virgin Gorda trips sail Sunday and Thursday.

Take the ferry from Red Hook to St. John at 9am Tuesday, Thursday, or Saturday and catch the bus ($4.50) from Cruz Bay to the National Park Visitor Center for a three-mile downhill trail hike led by a park ranger. Wear walking shoes and a sun hat, and bring your own food and water. You'll be back in Cruz Bay by 3:30pm. Make reservations between 8:30am and 2:30pm. *Tel. 340/ 776-6330.* For bird watching hikes in the National Park, take the 6:30am ferry from Red Hook, and a taxi from Cruz Bay and the National Park Visitor Center. A taxi takes you to Francis Bay Trailhead where you're joined by a ranger. Reservations are essential. *Tel. 340/776-6201.*

ST. JOHN

When you arrive at the ferry dock in **Cruz Bay** you'll be met by nattering crowds of drivers, all vying for your sightseeing business. Even if you plan later to take off on your own scooter or rental car, take at least a short tour with one of these guides if only for the theater alone. Each driver has his own "shtick," each jitney its own decorations.

One "must-see" is **Annaberg Sugar Mill**, administered by the National Park Service, *Tel. 776-6201.* More than 140 windmill ruins dot St. Croix, but St. John had only five, all of them built between 1740 and 1840. The site is a knockout, with views far out to sea. Although it was farmed well into the 20th century, its use as a sugar plantation died with the freeing of Danish West Indies slaves in 1848. Take a half-hour, self-guided walking tour of the slave quarters, village, windmill, and gardens. To reach the site, take the North Shore Road, about five miles east from Cruz Bay. Through the National Park Visitor Center you can also make reservations for ranger-guided hikes, snorkels, and bird watching.

If possible, be on St. John the last Saturday of the month when "St. John Saturdays" feature kite flying, arts and crafts, local musicians, and booths selling island foods. Tours of St. John aboard a two-chair, wheelchair-accessible van are available from the **St. John Community Foundation**, *Tel. 340/693-7600.* The vehicle operates weekdays 8:30am to 4:30pm and costs $18 per person per hour for one or two, $12 per person per hour for four.

Practical Information

Area Code: At this writing 340 is the area code for all the U.S. Virgin Islands.
American Express: *Tel. 340/774-1855*
ATM: on St. Croix, an ATM is found in the Banco Popular in the Sunny Isles Shopping Center. At St. Thomas find an ATM at the airport and at banks downtown and in shopping centers. Banks on the island include Banco Popular, Chase Manhattan, Citibank, First Federal Savings, First Virgin Islands Federal Savings, and Scotia Bank. Chase Manhattan and Scotia Bank branches are in Cruz Bay, St. John.
Carnival: in the Virgin Islands Carnival is usually held in late April or early May.
Crime: when you're going to the beach, leave valuables in the hotel safe and not in the car, not even in a locked trunk. Take the same precautions you would at home. At press time, several major cruise lines have stopped calling at St. Croix because so many passengers and crew complained of street crimes. Police patrols have been expanded, some cruise lines

continue to serve St. Croix, and it's hoped that the troubles will be history by the time you reach the island.

Current: electrical service is the same as on the United States mainland.

Currency is the United States dollar.

Customs: No duties nor sales tax are charged on tourist purchases. U.S. citizens may bring up to $1,200 in merchandise (twice the allowance from non-U.S. islands) back to the mainland

Emergencies: dial 911 for police, fire, and ambulance.

Holidays: banks and government offices are closed on most of the same holidays celebrated on the mainland including New Year's Day and Christmas plus Boxing Day, Friendship Day on October 13, and the local Thanksgiving, which is in late October. Transfer Day is celebrated on March 31.

Immigration: Americans and Canadians need proof of citizenship such as a passport, green card, certificate of naturalization, or birth certificate plus a government-issued photo ID such as a driver's license. A driver's license alone won't do. Voter registration is no longer accepted. Britons need a passport and, to return to the United States or Puerto Rico, a passport plus green form, white form, crewmember form, or documentation of the Immigration Service indicating legal status in the United States. A pre-clearance inspection occurs in the U.S. Virgin Islands prior to a flight to Puerto Rico or the mainland. No further formalities occur after you return to the mainland.

Locals: are called Crucians if from St. Croix.

Pharmacies: in St. Thomas include the Sunrise Pharmacy, Red Hook, *Tel. 340/ 775-6600*; K-Mart in the Tutu Park Mall, *Tel. 340/777-3854*. On St. Croix, People's Drug Store in Christiansted, *Tel. 340/778-7355* and the pharmacy in the Sunny Isles Shopping Center, *Tel. 340/778-5537*. In Frederikstad, D&D *Apothecary, Tel. 340/776-6353*. The Drug Store has branches at 69 King Street, Frederikstad, *Tel. 340/772-2656* and at 184C Ruby, *Tel. 340/773-4775*. It's open Monday through Saturday 8am-7pm and Sunday 8am-1pm. In Cruz Bay, St. John, St. John Drug Center, *Tel. 340/776-6353*. The hospital in St. Croix is in Christiansted, *Tel. 340/778-6311*. The hospital in St. Thomas is in Sugar Estate, *Tel. 340/776-8311* and it has a 24-hour emergency room. In St. John, an emergency medical technician is on call at *Tel. 340/776-6222*. For fastest help, ask at the hotel's front desk for the names of nearby doctors, clinics, and drug stores.

Postage: the familiar American eagle delivers the mail in the U.S. Virgin Islands and U.S. postage stamps are used. No additional postage is required to send letters and post cards to the mainland.

Taxes: there's a departure tax but it's added to your airplane ticket, so you don't have to stand in line and pay it separately as is common on other islands. Hotel bills are plus eight per cent tax. There is no sales tax here, but a resort fee or service charge may be added to room rates. Some hotels also add an energy surcharge that may be a flat rate or a percentage, charged per person or per room per night. Ask.

Tourist information: *Tel. 800/372-8784 or 340/774-8784.* In Canada, *Tel. 416/233-1414.* Or write the U.S. Virgin Islands Department of Tourism, *Box 6400, St. Thomas VI 00804.* Visitor information offices are at the airports and in downtown Charlotte Amalie across from Emancipation Garden. Website, *www.usvitourism.vi.*

Weddings: to get married on St. Thomas or St. John, request a marriage license application from the Clerk of the Territorial Court, P.O. Box 70, St. Thomas VI 00804, *Tel.340/774-6680.* For a St. Croix wedding, contact the Family Division, Territorial Court of the Virgin Islands, P.O. Box 929, Christiansted, St. Croix USVI 00821, *Tel. 340/778-9750.* Allow plenty of time because you must both appear in person at the court to retrieve the paper work. After the application is received, filled out and notarized, it is sent back to the islands and an eight-day waiting period begins. Fees are $25 each for the application and license and $200 for a ceremony performed by a judge. (Courts are open Monday through Friday on St. Thomas and Monday through Thursday on St. Croix; if you want to get married on a weekend, arrive early enough to do the paperwork. Note holidays). Personal checks are not accepted. A number of professional wedding consultants plan weddings in the U.S. Virgin Islands. For a brochure listing them and the services they offer, *Tel. 800/372-USVI.*

Western Union: found at Pueblo Supermarkets on St. Thomas and St. Croix. For telegrams and money transfers on St. John, try Connections, *Tel. 340/776-4200.* Western Union is also available at St. Thomas Islander Services, *Tel. 340/774-8128.*

Chapter 16

Closely tangled with the U.S. Virgin Islands are the British Virgin Islands, a tiny, 35-mile-long sprinkling of cays including **Tortola, Virgin Gorda, Anegada, Necker Island** and **Jost Van Dyke**. All proudly fly the Union Jack but geographically they're much the same as their neighboring U.S. Virgin Islands – small and easy to get around, rimmed with remarkable beaches probing into hidden coves, and blessed with day-long sunshine.

Ports of entry are at Virgin Gorda, Jost Van Dyke, Anegada, Road Town, Beef Island, and at the west end of Tortola. Communities are found at **Great Harbour** on Jost Van Dyke; on Tortola at **Carrot Bay, Cane Garden Bay, Road Town, Sea Cow Bay, and Long Swamp**; on Virgin Gorda at **Spanish Town** and **North Sound**.

Most of the smaller islands are uninhabited. However, secluded, pricey resorts are found on **Peter Island** and **Guana Island**, on six-acre **Marina Cay**, and on **Necker Island** where a private estate house accommodates up to 24 guests.

Columbus first noted the islands in 1493 and it wasn't long before they, like the other islands of the Caribbean, were pawns in European battles that pitted Dutch against Spanish and English against French. The Dutch settled here at Soper's Hole in the 17th century, but the islands were claimed by the British in 1672 and remain today a British colony with its own, locally elected, government.

Among the famous swashbucklers who sailed through here was Sir Francis Drake, whose name lives on in the channel that separates the islands. Of all the legends, histories and half truths that have captured the public imagination, however, it is Robert Louis Stevenson's *Trea-*

british virgin islands

sure Island that travelers love most. The book's setting is believed to be Norman Island with its mysterious caves.

Do you remember the song about "Fifteen men on dead men's chest; Yo ho ho and a bottle of rum?" The story goes that the dreaded Blackbeard anchored in Deadman's Bay after a raid and got into a fight with his men while splitting the booty. He stranded 15 men on Dead Chest Island with a bottle of rum, their sea chests, and a sword. The rest is delicious speculation, conjuring up images of men fighting over the last of the supplies as they connived, killed each other or starved to death, taking to their graves the secret of where the treasure was buried. Some people are still looking for it.

Modern history began in the 1960s when the Rockefellers developed the resort at Little Dix Bay, Virgin Gorda. The Moorings followed by opening a charter yacht operation. The result is a booming, blooming island group fit for a queen. During her reign, Queen Elizabeth II has been twice to the tiny British Virgin Islands. They're a natural addition to any trip to the U.S. Virgin Islands.

Climate
The strongest North American cold fronts may push this far south, bringing stinging winds, but the climate in the BVI is a non-story except during hurricane season when storms may occasionally spin up. Plan on warm and sunny days in the 80s and 90s, and cool nights in the 60s.

Arrivals & Departures
Plan your arrival as early in the day as possible, especially if your trip will involve road and ferry travel after you've landed at the airport and gone through the customs and immigration gristmill. Sometimes the post-flight part of the trip is the most arduous.

By Air
Beef Island/Tortola, the main airport for Tortola and all the BVI, is served daily from San Juan by **American Eagle**, *Tel. 800/433-7300;* **Cape Air**, *Tel. 800/352-0714;* **LIAT**, *Tel. 246/495-1187,* **Virgin Islands Airways**, *Tel. 284/495-1972.* **Air Sunshine** (Seaburg Aviation), *Tel. 340/773-6442,* flies to **Virgin Gorda** from San Juan, a route also served by **Virgin Islands Airways**, and **Carib Air**, *Tel. 284/495-5965.* Air St. Thomas and Carib Air fly between Virgin Gorda and St. Thomas.

Clair Aero Service, *Tel. 284/495-2271,* flies three-four days a week from Beef Island/Tortola to Anegada and Virgin Island Airways flies daily between Virgin Gorda and Beef Island/Tortola. **Air Sunshine** serves the BVI, San Juan, and St. Thomas *(Tel. 284/495-8900;* in the U.S. and Canada, *Tel. 800/327-8900;* from Florida, *Tel. 800/435-8900).*

Inter-island service is available via **LIAT** daily from Beef Island to Antigua, St. Kitts, and Dominica. **LIAT** and **Winair** fly daily between Beef Island and St.

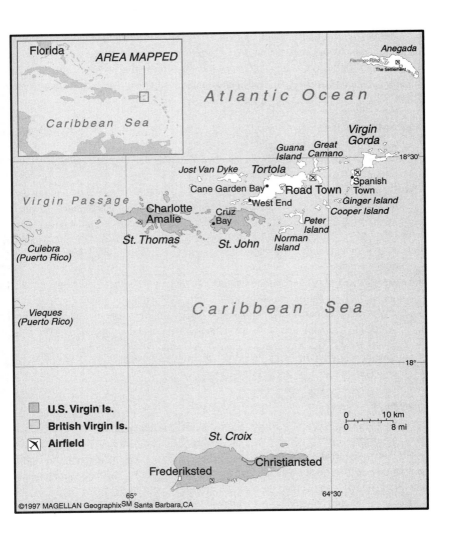

Florida

AREA MAPPED

Atlantic Ocean

Caribbean Sea

Anegada

Flamingo Pond

The Settlement

Virgin Gorda

Guana Island

Great Camano

18°30'

Jost Van Dyke Tortola

Cane Garden Bay Road Town

West End Spanish Town

Virgin Passage

Charlotte Amalie

Cruz Bay

Ginger Island

Cooper Island

Peter Island

St. Thomas St. John

Norman Island

Culebra (Puerto Rico)

Vieques (Puerto Rico)

Caribbean Sea

18°

☐ **U.S. Virgin Is.**
☐ **British Virgin Is.**
☒ **Airfield**

St. Croix

Christiansted

Frederiksted

0   10 km
0   8 mi

65°   64°30'

©1997 MAGELLAN GeographixSM Santa Barbara,CA

Maarten, St. Kitts, and Antigua. Charter flights are available through **Fly BVI**, *Tel. 800/1-FLY BVI (U.S.); 800/469-5955 (Canada) or 284/495-1747 elsewhere; www.fly-bvi.com; E-mail info@fly-bvi.com.* Gorda Air Services and Air St. Thomas also offer planes for charter.

By Ferry

Ferries are an important mode of inter-island transportation, always cheaper than flying and sometimes quicker if you want to go downtown-to-downtown. Schedules vary according to the day of the week and can be affected by sea conditions, so it's crucial to verify your time of departure by telephone.

Ferry companies include:

- **Inter-Island Boat Services**, *Tel. 284/495-4166*, operates between West End and Cruz Bay.
- **Jost Van Dyke Ferry Service**, *Tel. 284/494-2997*, operates between West End and Jost Van Dyke on schedule or on charter.
- **Native Son, Inc.**, *Tel. 284/495-461*, runs between Road Town, West End, and downtown St. Thomas. There's also daily service from West End to St. John and Red Hook, St. Thomas.
- **North Sound Express**, *Tel. 284/494-2745*, operates between Beef Island and North Sound, Virgin Gorda, with a stop at The Valley with four-hour notice.
- **Peter Island Ferry**, *Tel. 284//495-2000*, links Road Town at the Peter Island Ferry dock to Peter Island Resort & Yacht Harbour.
- **Smith's Ferry Service**, *Tel. 284/495-4495*, runs between Virgin Gorda and Road Town. Also from Road Town and West End to downtown St. Thomas/Red Hook.
- **Speedy's Fantasy/Speedy's Delight**, *Tel. 284/495-5240 or 5235*, operates between Virgin Gorda, Road Town, and St. Thomas.

Orientation

It's easy to get your bearings on any island if you can just remember where you are in relation to the ferry dock (except for Anegada, where the airport is the center of interest). If you're not being met by your hotel host, you'll find plenty of friendly, eager drivers at the airports and docks. If you choose a rental car or mo-ped, a good map will be provided. A Tourist Board office is on the waterfront at Wickham's Cay, near the main part of town.

Getting Around the British Virgin Islands

Taxis meet all flights. Taxi fare from Beef Island Airport to Road Town is approximately $6 per person, minimum three people. For more information, contact the **BVI Taxi Association**, *Tel. 284/494-2322*.

The town itself can be walked from one end to the other in half an hour. A leisurely tour, hitting all the high points, takes two hours or less. Waterfront Drive, home of **Pusser's Company Store and Pub**, follows the east side of the bay. Main Street and the settlement's shopping district plus the extravagant cruise ship shops are all packed into the **Wickham's Cay** area.

If you bring a bicycle, it must be registered with the Traffic Licensing Office in Road Town at a cost of $5.

Don't assume automatically that you can't manage without a rental car. Rental and fuel costs are high; roads are not good; driving is on the left; and you can probably find better uses for the $10 that they nick you for a driver's license. You can see a lot of these small islands on foot and by boat, then take a taxi or tour if you want to explore an island or try restaurants different from those at your resort.

The most popular rentals in the British Virgins are four-wheel-drive Jeeps ($35-$70 daily), with discounts for weekly rentals. Scooters, which rent for $30 a day or $170 a week are available on most islands. Insurance of $7-$10 may be additional. Collision damage waiver is optional, although a deposit of $500 or so may be required. Bicycles are available through rental agencies and many resorts. Most rental agencies pick up free at resorts or airports, but ask in advance to be sure about pick-up and drop-off requirements, which can be complicated if they involve meeting a ferry or private launch.

Auto and scooter rental agencies include:

Anegada
- **Anegada Reef Hotel**, *Tel. 284/495-8002*
- **D.W. Jeep Rentals**, *Tel. 284/495-8018*

Tortola
- **Alphonso Car Rentals**, *Tel. 284/494-3137*
- **Anytime Car Rentals**, *Tel. 284/494-2857*
- **Avis Rent-A-Car**, *Tel. 284/494-3322 or 494-2193; U.S. Tel. 800/331-1212, www.avis.com*
- **Budget Rent-a-Car**, *Tel. 284/494-8902; U.S. Tel. 800/527-0700, www.budget.com*
- **D&D Car Rental**, *Tel. 284/495-7676*
- **Dollar Rent a Car**, *Tel. 284/494-6093, U.S. Tel. 800/4000, www.dollar.com*
- **Hertz Car Rental**, *Tel. 284/495-4405, U.S. Tel. 800/654-313, www.hertz.com*
- **International Car Rentals**, *Tel. 284/494-2516, Fax 494-4715*
- **Itgo Car Rental**, *Tel. 284/494-2639*
- **National Car Rental**, *Tel. 284/494-3197, U.S. Tel. 800/328-4567, www.nationcar.com*
- **Tola Rentals**, *Tel. 284/494-8652*

Virgin Gorda
- **Hertz Car Rental**, *Tel. 284/494-5803,U.S. Tel. 800/654-313, www.hertz.com*
- **L&S Jeep Rental**, *Tel. 284/495-5297, Fax 495-5342*
- **Speedy's Car Rental**, *Tel. 284/495-5235 or 495-5240*

Where to Stay

Rates listed here do not include a seven per cent room tax and service charges, which are 10 to 15 per cent. Summer rates are usually 30-40 percent less than winter rates quoted here but some resorts add features and upgrades rather than lowering rates in the off season.

Private villas in the islands can be booked through **WIMCO**, *Tel. 800/932-3222 or 401/849-8012*. Maid service and staff are available. Guest houses, vacation houses and apartments are also available on arrangement with private owners. For a list call **BVI Tourism** in the US, *Tel. 800/835-8530*.

Mail sent here should be posted to the address, island, then British Virgin Islands, fully spelled out. Many of the hotels have mail drops in St. Thomas, where mail arrives quickly and at U.S. rates, in which case the address would end in VI, followed by the zip code. Ask.

ANEGADA
Moderate

ANEGADA REEF HOTEL, *Anegada. Tel. 284/495-8002, Fax 495-9362. Rates at this 20-room hotel, which is three miles west of the airport at Setting Point, start at $150 including three meals daily.*

So remote is the island that you're glad to find any place to lay your head, let alone a pleasant little hotel with its own restaurant and bar. In fact, the hotel is also where you can rent a car, find a taxi or bicycle, buy bait, tackle and ice, and have your air tanks refilled. Rooms are spacious and each has its own porch opening onto the beach. Be as private as you care to be, or let your host find you a deep sea fishing trip or a guide to take you out on the flats to hunt the elusive bonefish. There are just enough local characters, passing visitors, and yachties to justify the occasional barbecue or a festive evening with live music. Some rooms have telephones; all are air conditioned. Babysitting and car rental can be arranged.

Budget

OCEAN RANGE HOTEL, *in the settlement near the air strip, c/o General Delivery, Anegada. Tel. 284/495-2019, or radio VHF Channel 16. Rates start at $65 nightly.*

Ocean view rooms are plain vanilla, but you'll have a kitchenette and your own patio. Play Robinson Crusoe at bargain prices. Weekly and long-term rates can be arranged.

GUANA ISLAND

GUANA ISLAND, *booking address 10 Timber Trail, Rye NY 10580, Tel. 914/967-6050, Fax 914/967-8048, www.guana.com. The island's number is 284/494-2354. Rates start at $625 for two including three meals daily, afternoon tea, wine with lunch and dinner, and use of tennis courts and watersports equipment. Groups can rent the entire island, which has 15 double rooms and a cottage. For $35 per person round trip you'll be met at Beef Island Airport and taken by taxi to the dock for the ten-minute cruise to the island. Cash and checks are accepted, but not credit cards.*

They call this the only Virgin island that still is, an 850-acre piece of paradise plunked down in the dazzling sea north of Tortola. "You guessed it, teams of decorators were *not* flown in from New York," say the caretakers in explaining the furniture, which isn't Chippendale but looks just fine in an island setting. Wicker and woods complement white walls with accents of fresh flowers. Louvered doors admit the tradewinds.

The island's White Bay Beach is a stunner but if you want another beach all to yourself, take a boat and a picnic to one of the other six beaches on the island. Nature lovers will want to tramp the outback looking for wildlife and sea birds. See if you can find the rock outcropping that is shaped like an iguana, giving the island its name. Meals make use of fresh tropical fruits, vegetables and seafood; dinner is all crystal and candlelight, catered to your whim.

If you rent the cottage, which goes for $1200 to $1475 per night for two, depending on the season, take your meals in the dining terrace or have them brought in. It's a three-room hillside overlook with living room, kitchen, and bath, surrounded by decks and reached by walking a secluded trail past an ancient stone wall built by the Quakers who originally peopled the island.

JOST VAN DYKE
Moderate

SANDCASTLE HOTEL, *White Bay, mail address 6501 Red Hook Plaza, Suite 201, St. Thomas VI 00802. Tel. 284/495-9888, www.sandscastle-bvi.com. Rates are from $200 a day without meals; ask about a seven-night stay with breakfast and dinner included. Take the 20-minute ferry ride from Tortola.*

Four beachfront cottages and two air-conditioned rooms are garlanded with greenery and bright blooms to form the ultimate beach hideaway. Meals are served in the open air dining room. Have a Painkiller (the drink was invented here) at the Soggy Dollar Bar, a popular hangout. Shop the boutique, snorkel, beachcomb, and bring plenty of good reading to catch up on while you relax in a hammock.

Budget

PARADISE GUEST HOUSE, *BVI Customs, Jost Van Dyke, British Virgin Islands. Tel. 284/495-9281, Fax 284/495-9892. Rates at this guest house are from $100 double and $65 single.*

It's affordable, comfortable, and it has its own restaurant. This is a friendly, home-like place to stay in an "out island" atmosphere while you hike, snorkel and beachcomb. Maid service is provided.

NECKER ISLAND

NECKER ISLAND, *mail address Resort Management, Inc., 456 Glenrbook Road, Stamford CT 06906. Tel. 800/557-4255 or 203/602-0300, www.neckerisland.com. Rates for the entire island start at $15,000 per day for up to seven guests, $38,000 for 20-26 guests. One or two weeks a year, rooms or suites are available separately at $15,000 per couple per week.*

The rate doesn't seem so startling when you realize that you're renting an entire, private, 74-acre island owned by Virgin Group chairman Richard Branson. With it come a ten-bedroom villa and two private Balinese cottages. Included are all meals and drinks and everything else needed to pursue a grandly hedonist, out-island lifestyle. Use the boats, wind surfers, jet skis, books, music, a video library, games, an exercise room, swimming pool and tennis court, and let the staff of 42 cater to your every whim.

A tiny island rises out of a turquoise sea. It's rimmed with beige beaches and is topped by a mansion that looks out to sea from every direction. When you move in, you're lord and lady of the manor. There are no menus because you tell the cooks what and when you care to eat; no schedules unless you make them; no other guests unless you invite them. The island, in short, is yours to throw a house party, a reunion, a wedding, or just a vacation in paradise.

Interiors are airily raftered, rising to high ceilings that draw hot air from below, bringing fresh sea breezes through the windows. A 22-foot Brazilian table in the dining room seats everyone in elegance. The Bali influence turns up time and again in the hand-carved furniture, teak and stone surfaces, expanses of iron-hard Brazilian Ipé wood and Yorkstone floors, gauzy canopies over a four- poster bedstead, straw matting covering the rafters in some rooms, and wood balconies suspended over a view of the sea far below. When doors are flung open, it's easy to forget where indoors ends and outdoors begins. A waterfall spills into the swimming pool. Relax in the Jacuzzis, barbecue steaks around the pool or at the beach, use the floodlit tennis courts, play snooker, or use the workout equipment in the glass-walled gym.

PETER ISLAND

PETER ISLAND RESORT, *mail address Mailbox 4949, Duluth GA 30097, Tel. 800/346-4451 or 770/476-3723, www.peterisland.com. Rates at this 52-room, two-villa resort start at $530 for two; a four-bedroom Crow's Nest villa rents for $5,000-$7,250 for up to eight people. Rates include breakfast, lunch, dinner, and unlimited use of activities including water sports, scuba, tennis, fitness facilities, bicycling, and more. Ask about dive, romance, or ashore-afloat packages. The island is reached by private ferry from Road Town, Beef Island International Airport, or St. Thomas. Transfers are included in the room rate. Guests are discouraged from bringing children under age eight.*

It's an entire island, the home of resort so exclusive that, as bareboaters anchored in its harbor, we were once warned not to dry our tea towels on deck. You can rent the entire island, resort and all for $50,000 per day. Or just book a guest room or villa. The best one is the Crow's Nest, a four-bedroom showpiece high on a craggy overlook with a view of beaches and the sea. Dive on the Wreck on the Rhone. Dine casually in the Deadman's Beach Bar & Grill under the seagrape trees or in the elegantly laidback Tradewinds, where sumptuous Caribbean fare is served overlooking Drake Channel with Tortola in the distance. Take your choice of five white sand beaches around the island.

Although private land extends only to the tide line and visiting boaters can use the beaches, it's most likely you can find one to have all to yourself. Sail the bay. Hike nature trails and photograph wild goats. Take an island tour, go diving or deep sea fishing, or take an excursion to The Baths. Naturalists take guests on day sails to Norman Island. The resort has tennis courts and a health club.

TORTOLA
Expensive

FORT RECOVERY ESTATES VILLAS, *, P.O. Box 239, Road Town, Tortola. Tel. 284/495-4354 or 800/367-8455, www.fortrecovery.com. Rates start at $235 for two including breakfast. Ask about packages. From the airport, take the coast road west through Road Town about 40 minutes.*

Bring your family and settle into a villa with one, two, three, or four bedrooms. There's a manager on duty around the clock, a bar, restaurant, yoga and massages, and spectacular views of a half dozen islands across a crystal verdigris sea from your own private beach. The fort was built in the 17th century by the Dutch. Now it forms the core of this homey, British-style seaside community. Units are air conditioned and have fully-equipped kitchens, cable television, daily maid service and room service.

FRENCHMAN'S CAY, *Box 1054, West End, Tortola. Tel. 284/495-4844 or 800/235-4077 U.S. or 800/463-0199 Canada, www.frenchmans.com. Winter rates start at $225. The resort is on Frenchman's Cay, a separate island across from the ferry docks at West End.*

Each of the nine villas in this breeze-cooled beach resort has a full kitchen, dining and sitting areas, and terrace. When you're not eating "in," try the resort's bar and The Clubhouse Restaurant, featuring Caribbean flavors with a continental flair. Swim in the pool, play tennis, or just roam the 12 secluded acres to bask in the tradewinds. To get out on the water, rent one of the hotel's kayaks, Sunfish, boogie boards, or board sailers, or just borrow snorkel gear and go exploring. Horseback riding, scuba lessons, tours, and day sails are cheerfully arranged.

LONG BAY BEACH RESORT & VILLAS, *mailing address: P.O. 284, Larchmont NY 10538. Tel. 284/495-4252; in the U.S. and Canada, Tel. 800/729-9599; United Kingdom, Tel. 0800-898-379. Rates are from $749 per couple for a three-night package that includes breakfast daily and a candle-light dinner. Ask about family packages in the villas. From Road Town, go south and west on Waterfront Drive, then north on Zion Hill Road and west to Long Bay. If you arrive by ferry at West End, it's a ten-minute taxi ride. Meal plans are available. Children under age 12 can sleep free in a parent's room and pay a modest daily fee for a children's meal plan. Ask about packages.*

Hillside suites look out towards Jost Van Dyke over a strand of white sand that will be your private playground while you're here. Take a day sail on an 80-foot schooner, swim, and dine in the resort's highly-rated restaurant. Air conditioned rooms suites have high ceilings and a balcony that floats out over the tropical splendor, your own seascape. Designer prints are a dramatic black and white design, which is an effective foil for the sandy walls, tile, floors, and woody ceilings. Other rooms are done in sea greens and blues while still others are sunny ochres with accents of blue. Dine outdoors on linen-covered tables under the sun or stars, or indoors in the stony dining room with a greathouse look. The resort plays intensive tennis, and offers an attractive package for tennis players, but there's also plenty here for families, divers, beachcombers, and those who want to do nothing but veg out.

SUGAR MILL HOTEL, *Apple Bay, mail address P.O. 425, Road Town. Tel. 284/495-4355, Fax 495-4696; U.S. 800/462-8834; Canada 800/209-6874, www.sugarmillhotel.com. Rates at this 24-room boutique hotel start at $200. Suite and villa rates are from $620. Add $60 per person daily for breakfast and dinner. Ask about packages with and without dives. Children under age 11 are not accepted during high season. The hotel is about eight minutes from the West End ferry dock and 45 minutes from Beef Island Airport.*

Visitors flock to the famous restaurant here, so consider staying here among the ruins of a 17th century sugar plantation, eating all your meals at the acclaimed restaurant hosted by Jeff and Jinx Morgan. Breezy rooms with private terraces admit tropic breezes and look out over blue seas afloat with tropical greenery. Cool tile floors and filmy draperies are complemented by candy pastels or, in the deluxe villa, purple and peach. Some of the deluxe units have a bed or beds plus a queen-size sofabed, accommodating three or four. Standard rooms are poolside and have twin beds, refrigerator, hair dryer, ironing board, iron and coffee maker. Deluxe units have kitchens. All are air conditioned. Plantation House Suites, designed for one or two couples, have balconies so close to the sea, you're lulled to sleep by the sound of the surf.

Moderate

MOORINGS MARINER INN, *Box 139, Road Town. Tel. 284/494-2332. Fax 284/494-2226; U.S. and Canada 800/535-7289. Rates at this 26-room resort start at $170. Take Waterfront Drive northwest from Road Town and find the resort on Wickham's Cay 2.*

The Moorings charter yacht fleet is one of the most impressive in the world, and the inn was probably planned originally as a place for visiting yachtsmen to overnight before and after their cruises. Even if you're not a sailor, however, the yachtiness is part of the charm of the place. Every room has a galley, and provisioning is available in a well-stocked general store, so you can make your own meals when you don't feel like going out. The resort's dockside restaurant and bar are abuzz with sailing yarns shared by local liveaboards as well as fly-in charterers who are here for only a week or two.

NANNY CAY RESORT & MARINA, *Box 281, Road Town. Tel. 284/494-4895, Fax 494-0555, U.S. and Canada Tel. 800/866-BVI-HOTEL, www.nannycay.com. Rates at this 40-suite resort are from $115. Just three miles south of Road Town, the resort is 10 miles from the airport. Taxis are available, but ask about packages that include transfers.*

Twenty five acres surrounded by sea are home to a 42-unit resort and a 200-slip marina. The combination is a winning one in the BVI where liveaboards and charter sailors come ashore for evening grog with locals and guests. Your studio suite will be furnished in fading Caribbean colors and textures, with cable TV, direct-dial phone, kitchenette, and your own patio or balcony. There are two restaurants, Pegleg Landing and a poolside café, an Internet café, and two swimming pools. Tennis courts are lit for night play, and use of the volleyball court is free. The hotel can arrange a car rental, snorkeling equipment, dive trips, and anything else in watersports including board sailing lessons. It has its own, full-service marina.

PROSPECT REEF RESORT, *Box 104, Road Town. Tel. 284/494-3311, Fax 494-5595, U.S. 800/356-8937; Canada, 800/463-3608. Winter rates start at $150. Take Waterfront Drive south from Road Town through Fisher Estate.*

Spreading across a patch of waterfront overlooking Sir Francis Drake Channel and split by a tidal lagoon, this 127-unit resort has its own marina with sailing and diving trips, fresh and salt water swimming pools, tennis courts, an upscale restaurant, bars, shops, fitness center, and a pitch-and-putt golf course. All you need for a Caribbean getaway is right here just west of town. Take a studio or villa if you plan to do some of your own cooking; you can buy provisions at the resort. A courtesy bus runs to the beach and to town. A courtesy bus runs to town.

PUSSER'S FORT BURT HOTEL, *Box 3380, Road Town. Tel. 284/494-2587, Fax 494-2002. Winter rates start at $120 double. Take Waterfront Drive south from Road Town to Fisher Estate.*

A 300-year-old fort in the hills outside Road Town has been restored to provide seven rooms and a suite overlooking Sir Francis Drake Channel. Swim in the fresh water pool or walk to the marina for sailing, fishing, and other watersports. Each room has an ocean view, air conditioning, and television. The hotel's bar is a good place to meet locals; the restaurant features continental and West Indian favorites. Child care can be arranged.

PUSSER'S MARINA CAY, *Box 626, Road Town. Tel. 284/494-2174, Fax 494-4775. Rates start at $175 with breakfast. This is a small, private island north of Beef Island and reached only by boat.*

Bring friends and have the whole island resort to yourself. It has four rooms and two villas, a beach, a marina, a restaurant, and a bar that attracts a lot of passing boaters.

SEBASTIAN'S ON THE BEACH, *Box 441 Tortola. Tel. 284/495-4212, Fax 495-4466; 800/336-4870. Rates at this 26-room hotel start at $120. Eight luxury villas are from $300 nightly. From Road Town, go south and west on Waterfront Drive, pass Fort Recovery, and turn north (right) on Zion Hill Road, then left on Long Bay Road where the resort will be on ocean side.*

Choose a beachfront or garden room in a secluded hotel shaded by forests of palm trees. Some units are air conditioned. All have ceiling fans and refrigerator, and there's a commissary where you can stock up on snacks and cold drinks. The beach is a sugary strand, overlooked by the Seaside Grille where you can get lobster, fresh seafood, homemade soup or steak. It's open for three meals, but you're also close to other resorts and restaurants.

BEEF ISLAND GUEST HOUSE, *Box 494, East End, Tortola. Tel. 284/495-2303, Fax 284/495-1611. Rates at this four-room inn are from $85 including continental breakfast. Weekly rates are available.*

You're on the beach in this pleasant hideaway with its own beach bar and restaurant. Snorkel, windsurf and hike this end of the island. Maid service is provided.

Budget

JIP'S PLACE, *Cane Garden Bay, mail address General Delivery, Cane Garden Bay. Tel. 284/495-4543. Rates are from $60 nightly or $400 a week.*

The price is right for a simple place with a kitchenette near a great beach, restaurants and a beach bar. Maid service is included.

RHYMER'S BEACH HOTEL, *Tel. 284/495-4639, Fax 495-4820. Doubles start at $90 in winter, $55 in summer. From Road Town, take Joes Hill Road to Cane Garden Road. It's a 15-minute drive to the hotel.*

There's nothing fancy about this 24-room hotel but rooms do have telephones, air conditioning, and television, and the wind-sheltered beach is as wide and handsome as any found at pricier resorts. Meals at the hotel's restaurant feature star lobster, conch fritters, and other seafood; Rhymer's Beach Bar is a favorite hangout. Once you've arrived here you can manage without a car. If you choose to leave the hotel, several restaurants and bars with entertainment are within walking distance.

HOTEL CASTLE MARIA, *Box 206, Road Town. Tel. 284/494-2553 or 2515; Fax 494-2111. Winter rates at this 33-room hotel start at $90 double. Take Waterfront Drive south from the ferry dock and turn right on MacNamara Road.*

Stay snug in the heart of things (this is one of the closest hotels to Road Town) in a mansion-like setting surrounded by flowers and foliage. Private balconies overlook the sea; the hotel has its own swimming pool. Some kitchenettes are available; rooms have television, telephone, air conditioning or room fan, and refrigerator. Local art is used throughout. The hotel's restaurant and bar are locally popular, but you can also walk to town or the ferry dock. Babysitting can be arranged.

JOLLY ROGER INN, *Box 21, West End, Tortola. Tel. 284/495-4559, Fax 495-4184. Rooms at this 6-room inn, which is a few minutes walk west of the ferry dock in West End, start at $50.*

You're in the heart of a community with a dockside restaurant, bar, and shops. This modest hotel does have maid service and television, and watersports can be arranged, but don't count on using credit cards. It's a good budget choice if you have a rental car to get you to beaches and other adventures.

OLE WORKS INN, *Box 560, Tortola, located on Cane Garden Bay. Tel. 284/495-4837, Fax 495-9618. Doubles at this 18-room inn start at $150 in winter. From Road Town, take Joes Hill Road east to Cane Garden Bay Road, then south along the sea to the resort.*

Stay in a charming, 300-year-old sugar factory overlooking Cane Garden Bay. Your host, "Quito" Rhymer, offers air conditioned accommodations, each with refrigerator and oceanview balcony. Island music is played several nights a week in Beachfront Quito's Gazebo, which serves meals and exotic drinks, and Quito also has his own art gallery and gift shop.

VIRGIN GORDA
Expensive

BIRAS CREEK RESORT, *Box 54, Virgin Gorda, Tel. 284/494-3555, Fax 494-3557; U.S. and Canada 800/223-1108; United Kingdom 0800/894-057, www.biras.com. Arrange with the hotel for airport transfer. If you contact the* *resort at least 48 hours in advance, you'll be met at the Virgin Gorda airport and taken to the launch that will deliver you to the resort. If you arrive at Beef Island, take the scheduled ferry or Biras' private launch. Rates start at $525 per couple per day including breakfast, lunch, afternoon tea and dinner. For single occupancy, deduct $150.*

A small thimble of land is surrounded on all sides by the blue waters of the Atlantic, Caribbean, and Sir Francis Drake Channel. It's a secluded, 140-acre setting for nature trails for hiking and jogging, two lighted tennis courts, a private beach, and a beachside, freshwater pool. Bicycles are parked outside each of the 33 suites.

Unpack in a spacious suite done in happy Caribbean colors. Your room overlooks the real thing: a neon-hued sea, an incredibly white sand beach, and blue skies that are streaked with pink morning and evening. Each room has a sitting area, separate bedroom, ceiling fans, air conditioning, direct-dial telephone, a small refrigerator and a secluded, open-air shower. Private patios are tiled in terra cotta. In addition, Grand Suites have oversize terraces and sunken bathtubs. The meeting room is also the home of a little museum. Ask to see it. Watersports and instruction are all included, so you can snorkel, sail, spurt around in a motorboat, or board sail. Ask about the land-sea package that includes five nights in the resort and two romantic nights in a fully-provisioned, captained yacht.

BITTER END YACHT CLUB, *Box 46, Virgin Gorda. Tel. 284/494-2746, U.S. 305/468-0168 or 800/872-2392. Rates start at $450 including all meals. Airport transfers, which include a short taxi and/or ferry ride, are included with a five-night stay.*

Many of the resorts in the Caribbean are as yachty as they are landlubberly, but this one is especially salty because you can sleep on a boat or in one of the rooms for about the same price. You'll still get maid service, meals in the Yacht Club and, if you want to anchor off for a night, provisions to tide you over. Sea and sails are part of the scene everywhere, whether you're overlooking them from your hilltop villa, trading tall tales with sailors in the bar, or actually sailing one of the big fleet of Sunfish, Lasers, JY15s, Rhodes 19s and J-24s. Introduction to Sailing is a popular course for resort guests.

Zone out on your private veranda overlooking the verdant grounds, or plug into a carnival of good times: island excursions to The Baths and Anegada, snorkeling in reef-sheltered coves, swimming at the pool or one of the resort's three beaches, or joining a group to study marine science. A dive operator based at the Club can do a complete dive package from beginner to advanced, Ginger Island to the wreck of the *Rhone*. Dine in the Clubhouse Steak and Seafood Grille or the English Carvery, then dance under the stars at Almond Walk. Provision at The Emporium, which has staples as well as baked goods and takeout dishes.

Selected as one of my *Best Places to Stay* – see Chapter 13.

LITTLE DIX BAY, *P.O. Box 70, Virgin Gorda, British Virgin Islands. Tel. 284/ 495-5555, Fax 495-5661, U.S. and Canada 888/ROSEWOOD, www.rosewoodhotels.com. Rates start at $375 double and range to $1,110 for a one-bedroom suite. For $110 daily add three meals daily; add $90 for breakfast and dinner only. Children's meal plans are half that, and kids ages 4 and under eat free. Transfers from Tortola International Airport are $65 per person.*

Lying serenely behind a barrier reef, Little Dix Bay has a half-mile crescent of beach surrounded by 500 acres of forest, seagrape, tamarind, and palms. Founded in 1964 by the Rockefellers, it is now a grand resort with three employees for every guest, assuring a level of pampering that's impressive even in the service-savvy Caribbean.

From the moment you are met at the airport or ferry dock, you're in a world of seabreeze, sun, and luxury. Airy, spacious rooms are furnished with wicker and bamboo, soft pastels and brightly contrasting tropic bouquets. Most rooms are air conditioned but not all are, so specify AC if you want it. All have telephones, balconies or terraces. Hike nearby Gorda National Park or the resort's own nature trails. Walking sticks are provided in each room, and they come in handy on Cow Hill, the Savannah Trail, or the Pond Bay Trail.

Sightsee by boat or Jeep, play tennis, or enjoy a full menu of watersports. The resort has its own 120-slip marina where boats are waiting to take you sailing, deep sea fishing, or sunset cruising. Ferries run regularly to a sister resort, Caneel Bay on St. John, where you can eat if you're on the Little Dix meal plan. Dining here is elegant whether you choose the Pavilion, the Sugar Mill with its tropical bistro look and wood oven-baked pizzas, or the nautically themed Beach Grill featuring seafood and sandwiches. After dinner, dance to live music on the Pavilion Terrace and walk home along paths lit by tiki torches and scented with frangipani. Bonded, insured nannies are available by the day or hour and are welcome to participate with children at Children's Grove activities. Programs, including classes in etiquette and cooking, are offered for children and teens at added cost.

Selected as one of my *Best Places to Stay* – see Chapter 13.

Moderate
DIAMOND BEACH CLUB, *Box 69, Virgin Gorda. Tel. 284/494-8000, Fax 495-5875; U.S. 800/871-3551; Canada 800/487-1839. Rates at this 20-room inn start at $170. Located on the island's west shore, the resort is two miles north of the Virgin Gorda airport and also about two miles north of the dock where ferries arrive from Road Town.*

All patios in this clubby little resort view the ocean, where you can swim or snorkel over colorful reefs. Looming over its shoulder is Virgin Gorda Peak, surrounded by a national park where you can hike and birdwatch. Units have maid service and fully-equipped kitchens where you can cook supplies bought in the commissary. Ask about packages that include a Jeep.

GUAVABERRY SPRING BAY, *Box 20, Virgin Gorda. Tel. 284/495-5227, Fax 495-5283. Only a few minutes south of the airport and five minutes from The Valley. Rates at this 18-cottage resort start at $120. No credit cards accepted.*

Available by the day or week, this homey resort is fun to say. It's named for a local, cranberry-size fruit used in the making of liqueurs. Houses on stilts soar airily over a sea of boulders and bougainvillaea, catching sea breezes. Each unit has one or two bedrooms, kitchenette, and living/dining area. You can buy provisions at Yacht Harbour or in the little commissary that is operated here for guests. Diving, fishing, or island tours can be arranged by your hosts, or swim from the beach at nearby Spring Bay. These are the handiest lodgings to The Baths and the Copper Mine, close to Little Fort National Park, the airport, and the settlements of The Valley.

LEVERICK BAY RESORT, *Box 63, The Valley, Virgin Gorda. Tel. 284/495-7421, Fax 495-7367; U.S. 800/848-7081; Canada 800/463-9396; E-mail: leverick@surfbvi.com. Rooms start at $119.*

Stay in an air conditioned hotel room (there are 16) or rent the two-bedroom unit at this popular spot on Leverick Bay, a jump-off spot for out islands and for those Virgin Gorda resorts that can't be reached by road. The hotel looks out over Blunder Bay and North Sound toward Mosquito and Prickly Pear islands. Pass your days diving, playing tennis, water skiing, swimming or snorkeling off the beach, shopping the resort's own boutiques, or getting a massage or facial. Buck's Food Market at the marina sells everything you need to provision a villa or boat for a day or a week, including wines and liquors.

Pubby and popular, The Lighthouse bar here is a hangout for transient yachties, locals, and resort guests alike. Dine well, then dance the night away.

OLDE YARD INN, *Box 26, Virgin Gorda. Tel 284/495-5544, Fax 495-5986, U.S. 800/653-9273, www.oldeyardinn.com. A week-long stay is $1,375 per couple plus service charge and tax. Included are full breakfast daily, a bottle of champagne, a beach picnic for two, a two-day Jeep rent and other perks.*

What a find! Although there are only 14 rooms, the hotel has its own locally-popular bar and restaurant, health club, a gift shop, and entertainers three times a week. You're welcomed at check-in with a rum punch, and your vacation officially begins. Choose a book from the hotel's library and stake out a patch of shade on meticulously gardened grounds. Stroll into town, relax in the pool or whirlpool, rent a Jeep or a boat, go snorkeling or day sailing, or have a treatment in the beauty salon. Ride the complimentary shuttle to Savannah Bay Beach, and snorkel an underwater trail. Dine to classical music in the gourmet restaurant or more casually at the Sip and Dip Grill. Barbecue buffet and a local band are scheduled every Sunday night. Some rooms are air conditioned. Each has its own patio overlooking gardens alight with hibiscus, bushy palms, and bougainvillaea.

MANGO BAY RESORT, *Box 1062, Virgin Gorda. Tel. 284/495-5672, Fax 495-5674, www.mangobayresort.com. Rooms start at $100; villas are priced to $338. From the airport go north on North Sound Road, then left on Plum Tree Bay Road for less than a mile.*
Book your own cottage with a spacious porch, living area, fully- equipped kitchen and large porch, all just a seashell's throw from the sandy beach. If you like, the hotel will find you a cook. The hotel has its own bar and Italian restaurant. Wind surfing, kayaks, snorkel gear, floating mattresses and chaise lounges are provided at the beach.

Where to Eat

The international gourmet has nothing to fear when dining in the BVI's sophisticated restaurants. Here you can find the finest French, Italian, and Asian cuisine as well as Continental-Caribbean foods that blend the best of old and new worlds. However, you'll miss a lot if you don't try such local specialties as roti (curry-filled bread), boil fish (fish in tomato sauce with garlic and onions), peas and rice (beans and rice) or patties (pastry filled with spicy beef, salt fish, or lobster).

Except for local fish and lobster, just about every mouthful has to be imported, but hosts do a good job at providing fresh vegetables and preparing dishes with a West Indian flavor. Unless stated otherwise, these restaurants accept major credit cards. It's not unusual in small islands to ask you to make reservations early in the day and to order at that time.

TORTOLA
Expensive

THE CLUBHOUSE RESTAURANT, *Frenchman's Cay, is a short walk from Soper's Hole Marina. Tel. 495-4844. It's open daily for breakfast and daily except Monday for lunch and dinner. Reservations are suggested. Dinner entrees are priced from $17 or order the sumptuous Special Island Dinner with soup, salad, entree, rolls, dessert and coffee or tea for $30.*
Sea bass is prepared West Indian style, shrimp comes with spicy crab sauce, and the Caribbean chicken is done with chutney. Start with one of the soups, which come with hot dinner rolls. There's a good choice of appetizers, children's favorites, and desserts including a hot apple tart for two.

THE APPLE, *Little Apple Bay. Tel. 495-4437. Open for dinner daily. Main dishes average $20. Reservations are recommended.*
Just over the hill from Long Bay, Apple Bay is the surfer's beach, incredibly creamy and clear as waves boil ashore and keep the sands scrubbed clean. For a special dinner, seek out this quaint West Indian homestead framed in banyan trees. The food features local ingredients: whelk, soursop, conch, and fresh fish, all deftly seasoned and generously served by Liston Molyneaux, a Tortola native.

BRANDYWINE BAY RESTAURANT, *Brandywine Estate, three miles east of Road Town off the south shore road, Blackburn Highway. Tel. 495-2301. Reservations are requested. Main dishes start at $15.*

Popular for its Florentine-style dinner, this country inn serves guests on a romantic garden patio surrounded by birdsong and greenery. Lobster ravioli is a specialty. You're hosted by Cele and David Pugliese, whose restaurant was voted "our favorite in the Caribbean" by *Bon Appetit* magazine.

FORT BURT RESTAURANT, *in the Fort Burt Hotel, Fisher Estate, just south of Road Town. Tel. 494-2587. Dinner will cost about $50 with appetizer and dessert but without wine. An English breakfast is available in the morning, luncheon is served in the pub from noon to 2:00pm, and dinner is from 7:00pm to 9:00pm. For dinner, reservations are essential.*

The ruins of an ancient Dutch fort are part of the scene at this hotel and restaurant overlooking Careening Cove, Road Reef, and Burt Point. Dine in a seabreeze-cooled outdoor dining area with a million dollar view. Seafood with a Caribbean overtone is the rule, resulting in great sauced filets or seafood curries. The Brits being the Brits, there's also great roast beef. Desserts are made here so they're always worth a try.

SKY WORLD, *Ridge Road. Tel. 494-3567. Dinner with wine costs $50 or more for a six-course feast; lunch is in the $20 range. Reservations are essential.*

The best game plan for a celebration evening is to arrive here an hour before sundown to watch the sky streak with color and the sun sink into the sea. From this hilltop perch you're looking down on what seems like all of Tortola and across to all the other islands. When it's time to get serious about dining, pace yourself for a parade of courses that starts with an inventive salad and ends with a selection of meltingly flaky pastries. Dinner is dressy; lunch is resort-casual.

SUGAR MILL, *in the Little Dix Bay resort. Tel. 495-5555. Take the private ferry from the Beef Island airport to the resort. Plan to spend $60 for dinner. Reservations are essential.*

Dine in one of the Caribbean's most posh resorts, long a Rockefeller holding and completely refurbished under new management by the Rosewood chain of luxury hotels. Lunch is a buffet under the high-roofed pavilion. Dinner by candlelight in the Sugar Mill features simply grilled lobster, fresh fish, and steaks with dashing presentations and garnishes. Have a drink in the lounge, where live music plays just about every night. The restaurant is not air conditioned.

SUGAR MILL & PAVILION RESTAURANT, *Apple Bay. Tel. 495-4355, U.S. 800/462-8834. Fixed-price lunches start at $25; dinners at $40. Daily specials offer appetizers in the $7-$8 range and main dishes at $18-$25. Reservations are a must. Drive west from Road Town on Waterfront Drive,* *pass Fort Recovery, then turn right over Zion Hill and, watching for signs, turn right at the T.*

Celebrities Jeff and Jinx Morgan, columnists for *Bon Appetit* magazine and authors of several cookbooks, have owned this 300-year-old sugar mill since the 1980s, and their touch shows in the superb cuisine. The dining room is surrounded by original stone walls, now hung with Haitian art. The *Washington Post* called it "the island's best restaurant," but they were topped by *Business Week*, which called it "the best restaurant in the Caribbean." You might start, for example, with New Zealand Mussels in Dilled Cream or a terrine of smoked conch, followed by Tropical Game Hen in orange-curry butter or Fish with West Indian Creole Sauce.

Their signature dish is curry-banana soup, but everything here is freshly made according to whim, inspiration, and the best of what's available from the marketplace and the Morgans' own herb garden. A dress code applies at dinner, so ask about it when you make reservations.

Moderate

CAPRICCIO DI MARE, *Waterfront Road, Road Town. Tel. 494-5369. It's open daily except Sunday. No credit cards or reservations are accepted. Plan to spend $6 for breakfast, $10 to $12 for lunch, and $20 to $30 for dinner.*

Settle into a pleasant Italian bistro setting and start with a Mango Bellini, a mixture of mango juice and sparkling asti spumante. Then have one of the pastas with a choice of tomato, seafood, cream, or vegetarian sauces. Choose one of the pizzas, a hot or cold sandwich, or just snack on cappuccino with a sweet.

MRS. **SCATLIFFE'S RESTAURANT**, *Carrot Bay, North Coast Road, between Cane Garden Bay and Apple Bay. Tel. 495-4556. Reservations are essential . Prix fixe meals are in the $25 range. No credit cards are accepted.*

Mrs. Scatliffe and her family welcome you to their West Indies-style home where she cooks with locally raised goat and vegetables from her own garden. Dinner starts with a rum punch and proceeds through soup and salad, followed by a meat such as curried goat, chicken, or a fish (for example, West Indian boil fish). Dessert, usually featuring an exotic tropical fruit like coconut or guava, is followed by a lively *musicale* performed by Mom and the kids.

Budget

THE AMPLE HAMPER, *at Inner Harbour Marina next to the Captain's Table on Wickham's Cay. Pick up picnic makings at prices that start under $10. Hours vary seasonally.*

A popular gourmet provisioning spot for yachts, the Hamper is not an eat-in place but it has a full-service deli, imported English specialties, and delectable sandwiches made to order. It's the place to put together an elegant picnic to take to the beach or boat.

HAPPY LION, *next to the Botanic Gardens, Road Town. Tel. 494-2574. The restaurant serves breakfast, lunch, and dinner in the $10-$15 price range.*

Part of an apartment rental complex, this simple eatery is the place to get the real thing – johnnycake, goat mutton, and boil fish, as well as steaks, burgers, and sandwiches.

MR. FRITZ'S ORIENTAL RESTAURANT & TAKE AWAY, *on Wickham's Cay. Tel. 494-5592. Dine for under $10. Reservations can be made for lunch 11:30am-3:30pm and dinner from 5:30 pm.*

Barbara and Fritz keep the woks sizzling with Lobster Love Boat, Singapore chicken, and fiery Szechuan pork and beef. Try the Cantonese-style shrimp.

VIRGIN GORDA
Expensive

BATH AND TURTLE, *in the yacht harbor at Spanish Town. Tel. 495-5239. Reservations are important. Main dishes are priced $15 to $28. It's open every day 7:30am to 9:30pm.*

The breakfast crowd comes in early and the drinking begins with elevenses when the blender starts whirring with fruity margaritas or coladas. For lunch, have a chili dog, pizza, burger, Reuben, salad or a bowl of the four-alarm chili. Dine indoors or in the courtyard on fish fingers, coconut shrimp, lobster, grilled filet mignon, or chicken. Live music plays at least twice a week, never with a cover charge.

BIRAS CREEK RESORT, *North Sound. Tel. 494-3555. Plan to spend $50 for dinner and more if you order a vintage wine. The dining rooms are open daily for breakfast, lunch, and dinner. Call for early for reservations. You may be asked to make your dinner selection when you phone.*

A longtime guest liked the resort so much, he bought it and the well-liked restaurant that goes with it. The view is worth the trip. Ask for a table that looks down from the hilltop to the seas below. Fresh seafood and lobster are the top draw here, but the chef is also happy to sizzle a steak any way you want it. At lunch there's a nice choice of salads, burgers, sandwiches and light dishes, and sometimes there's a beach barbecue during the day. At dinner, start with a cocktail in the elegant lounge. The menu offers plenty of variety in meats and seafood, and the wine list is comprehensive.

BITTER END YACHT CLUB, *North Sound. Tel. 494-2746. Reservations are essential for dinner, so call early. Dinner at either of the restaurants, the Clubhouse or The Carvery, starts at $38. Open breakfast through dinner.*

The bareboat crowd comes ashore here for drinks and dinner but the breakfast buffet is also worth the trip. Everything from fresh fruit and yogurt to cooked-to-order pancakes and omelets is on the groaning board. At lunch, choose from a big buffet of cold meats, cheese, breads, and salads, or order a hamburger or grilled fish. Grilled lobster is the dinner specialty, served plain or with a Creole sauce. There's also a choice of chicken, steak, or chops.

Restaurants for Mariners

Some of these restaurants can be reached only by private boat; others have docks where you can tie up free for dining or overnight for a fee; others can be reached by launch or ferry. The voyage is part of the fun, and many visitors make a day-long project out of it. Most can be reached on VHF Channel 16. Always call ahead to see if they're open. Dinner reservations must be made early in the day.

Saba Rock Resort's dinner buffet is a West Indian treat served Sunday evening only. Call for information and reservations. *Tel. 495-7711.* **The William Thornton** is afloat off Norman's Cay; **The Last Resort** is on Bellamy Cay off Beef Island. On Anegada, which makes a good day trip, try the **Anegada Reef Hotel**, **Del's**, or **Pomato Point**. **Cooper Island Beach Club** is a restaurant and bar, and also offers beachfront cottages. Each has a kitchen, balcony, bathroom with open-air shower, and outdoor hammock, *Tel. 800/542-4624.*

On Jost Van Dyke look for **Harris' Place**, **Sidney's Peace** and **Love**, **Abe's Little Harbor**, **Club Paradise**, **Rudy's Mariner's**, **Ali Baba's** and **Foxy's**.

TOP OF THE BATHS RESTAURANT, *350 yards up the trail from The Baths. Tel. 495-5497. Lunch is less than $10.*

Restaurant patrons are offered a dip in the pool here, so it's a wonderful place to cool off after scrambling around The Baths. Food has a continental touch, always with a fresh fish dish and luscious salads.

OLDE YARD INN, *The Valley, Tel. 495-5544. Call ahead for hours and reservations; if you want Caribbean lobster, it has to be ordered before 4pm. Entrees are priced from $21.*

Start with scampi in garlic and wine sauce, jerk crab cakes, or the chef's pasta special of the day and serve as an appetizer. There's a hot or cold soup, a choice of salads, then a parade of main dishes such as the shrimp and chicken medley, breast of chicken drenched in rum, cream and pecans, or rack of lamb. For dessert, there's chocolate mousse of a fruit and cheese board served with a glass of port.

Seeing the Sights
ANEGADA

Anegada is as remote as the end of the world, a limestone and coral atoll rimmed with talcum powder beaches where you can walk for hours without seeing another human being. At its highest point, the island is only 27 feet above sea level. It's the quintessential nature sanctuary and the government is committed to keeping it that way.

Roam to your heart's content to see wild goats, donkeys and cattle, to look for 20-pound rock iguana (they look fierce but are harmless) and a host of heron, osprey, and terns. With luck you'll see some flamingoes too.

JOST VAN DYKE

Jost (yost) **Van Dyke** is the island that time forgot. Only 200 people live here, in West Indian wooden homes around Great Harbour.

NORMAN ISLAND

Famed for its caves and a port of call for boaters, it has a floating bar and restaurant off The Bight.

SALT ISLAND

This little island between Cooper Island and Peter Island has only one resident, and its only point of interest is its salt ponds. Once a thriving and even crucial industry in the Caribbean, harvesting salt from the sea goes on today as it did a century ago. The island is best known as the gravesite of the *Rhone*, which sank in 1867.

TORTOLA

Take off on your own in rental car or scooter if you want only to find a beach and spend the day there. However, if you want narrative and direction, hire a taxi by the day or take a safari tour with a knowledgeable guide. Island tours of Virgin Gorda aboard safari buses are offered by **Andy's Taxi and Jeep Rental**, *Tel. 284/495-5511,* **Speedy's**, *Tel. 495-5240* and **Mahogany Taxi Service**, *Tel. 495-5469*.

Sightseeing tours of Tortola are available from the **BVI Taxi Association**, *Tel. 494-2875*; **Nanny Cay Taxi Association**, *Tel. 494-0539*; **Travel Plan Tours**, *Tel. 494-2872*; **Travel Plan Tours**, *Tel. 494-2872 or 494-4000*. Flightseeing tours are available from **Fly BVI Ltd**, *Tel. 495-1747*. Quality Taxi Association, 494-8397 Waterfront Taxi Association, 494-3456.

North of downtown Road Town on Station Avenue, **J.R. O'Neal Botanic Gardens** are a four-acre oasis filled with native and imported tropicals plus a lily pond, waterfall, and orchid house. Bird houses attract an array of tropical birds. The gardens are open Monday through Saturday 8am to 4 p.m., *Tel. 494- 4557*. Admission is free. Shop your way down Main Street, pausing to look at the churches, 19th century post office, and the huge, shady ficus trees in Sir Olva George's Plaza.

The **Virgin Islands Folk Museum** is housed in an authentic West Indian house on Main Street. There's no phone but it's usually open in the middle of the day except Wednesday and Sunday. Admission is free. Of special interest are artifacts from the wreck of the *Rhone,* which you'll see during your visit if you're a diver, and bits of pre-Columbian pottery. Proceeding north on Main, take a picture of Cockroach Hall, built atop a huge boulder in the 1800s to serve as a doctor's dispensary. It's now a private business. Officially its name is Britannic Hall.

Next to it are two **churches**, the Anglican dating to 1746 and rebuilt in 1819, and the Methodist Church, which was rebuilt after a hurricane in 1924. Its congregation dates to 1789. Between them is Her Majesty's Prison, dating to the 1700s, where a cruel planter was hanged for killing a slave.

Climb **Fort Hill**, which is just below the roundabout at Port Purcell to see the remains of **Fort George**. It was built by the Royal Engineers in 1794 to stand sentinel against foreign powers, especially the French, and such pirates as Edward Teach, the dreaded Blackbeard. At the west end of Tortola at **Fort Recovery Villas**, you can see the well- preserved round tower that is thought to have been built by Dutch settlers in the mid-1600s.

Touring on your own, head east from Road Town, and you'll pass the ruins of **Fort Charlotte**. Now just a few walls, a cistern, and a powder magazine, it tops Harrigan's Hill. Continuing east you'll see a ruined church, which is all that remains of Kingstown, a community that was founded for free slaves in the 1830s. Along the road that runs from Ridge Road down to Brewer's Bay on Tortola's north shore, find **Mount Healthy** and a largely intact stone windmill, once part of a sugar plantation. It's the only such windmill on Tortola.

A ride 'round the island can take only three hours, but you'll want to spend days seeking out secluded beaches, trying restaurants, and hiking the hills. Don't rush it. Stop at the North Shore Shell Museum in Carrot Bay, the Callwood Rum Distillery, and Soper's Hole for shopping and to watch boats come and go.

Among the historic ruins to look for: Fort Burt, now a hotel, was built by the Dutch in the 17th century. The ruins of **Fort George** are on Fort Hill. Fort Recovery on the west end of Tortola dates, it is thought, to the first Dutch settlers in 1648. In Pleasant Valley, the ruins of the **William Thornton Estate** remain from the home of the designer of the United States Capitol. **The Dungeon**, actually a 1794 fort that has an underground cell, is halfway between Road Town and West End. Just east of Road Town, look for the ruins of The Church at Kingstown, once the center of a community of freed slaves.

VIRGIN GORDA

Just south of the Yacht Harbour, which is a beehive of sailing and sailors, **Little Fort National Park** is on the site of a Spanish fortress. Now a wildlife sanctuary, the 36-acre park still has remnants of the original fort and its powder magazine.

Between Little Fort and The Baths, **Spring Bay** is a smooth sand beach studded with enormous boulders, thrown up 70 million years ago by a volcanic eruption. They set the scene for your arrival at **The Baths**, where city-size boulders are flung about as if by angry gods. The scene changes constantly as the sun passes over and tides roll in and out, so it's a spot you can come back to time and again to explore, photograph, swim in, and commune with one of nature's great structures.

On Virgin Gorda's remote southwestern end, look for the ruins of the **Copper Mine**, which was worked by Cornishmen between 1838 and 1867. Remains of some of the buildings and works can still be seen (from a distance; they are not safe to explore). Also on the west coast is Nail Bay, where you can roam the ruins of an 18th century sugar mill made from brick, stone, and coral rock.

Fallen Jerusalem, a separate island off the south end of Virgin Gorda, can be reached only by boat and only on calm days. Its terrain is bold and dramatic, much like The Baths, a birdwatcher's mecca because of its many nesting sites.

Nightlife & Entertainment

It's likely that your hotel or the closest bar will have live music and it will be listed in one of the free magazines such as *Limin' Times* that you can pick up around the islands. If you want to venture off property, the hottest licks are at:

THE BATH AND TURTLE BAR, *Yacht Harbour, The Valley, Virgin Gorda. Tel. 495-5239.*

Inexpensive dinner fare is available until 9:30, so stoke up on burgers, pizza, or native dishes then stay on for live music on Sunday and Wednesday nights.

BOMBA'S SURFSIDE SHACK, *Cappoon's Bay, near Cane Garden Bay, Tortola. Tel. 495-4148 is Tortola's happenin' place, especially on Wednesdays, Fridays, and on nights when the moon is full.*

The decor is early beach bum and the sound system could wake the dead, but drinks are cheap, barbecue is plentiful, and the music is authentically Caribbean until midnight or later.

THE LAST RESORT, *Ballamy Cay, off Beef Island. Tel. 495-2520. Can be reached only by launch from Trellis Bay, which will be arranged for you when you make your (required) reservations. Dinner and the show cost about $35 per person, which you can charge to a major card.*

Tuck into an English buffet including roast beef, Yorkshire pudding, homemade soups and all the trimmings, followed by a hilarious, two-hour, one-man music and comedy show.

PUSSER'S LTD, *Marina Cay, reached by a causeway from Tortola's West End. Tel. 494-2467. It stays open until 2:30 a.m.*

This is the British Virgin Islands, which means pubs and pub grub, most notably at the yachty Pusser's where the Painkiller is not for the faint of heart (or liver). Made with the rum that was once the official grog of the Royal Navy, the drink makes great accompaniment for an evening of music listening, people watching, and good conversation until 2:30am. Pusser's serves a broad range of sandwiches, pizza, and a creditable shepherd's pie.

QUITO'S GAZEBO *at the Ole Works Inn, Cane Garden Bay, Tortola. Tel. 495-4837.*

Native-born Quito Rymer switches on his microphone at 8:30pm on Tuesday, Thursday, Friday and Sunday, sits on a stool with his guitar, and lets loose with his own ballads as well as reggae classics and popular tunes.

Sports & Recreation
Beaches

Tortola: Smugglers Cove on the western tip of Tortola has good snorkeling and children love its name. Try Long Bay on the north shore for white sand, Apple Bay for surfing and hanging out at Bomba's, Cane Garden Bay for picture postcard views, Brewer's Bay for beach bars, camping and snorkeling, Josiah's Bay for its scenery, and Elizabeth Bay for sands with a fringe of palm trees.

Virgin Gorda: The Baths is a spectacular arrangement of boulders and grottos, always changing but best in the morning before the hordes arrive; Spring Bay next to The Baths has good snorkeling and white sand; Trunk Bay

The BVI's Best Beaches

Some of these beaches can be reached by car, others only by boat. Find them on the road map that comes with your rental car, or on the marine chart that comes with your rental boat. They include:

Anegada: Loblolly Bay

Jost Van Dyke: White Bay

Sandy Cay: The entire island, which lies just southeast of Jost Van Dyke is rimmed with a picture postcard beach.

Peter Island: Deadman's Bay

Moskito Island: South Bay

Prickly Pear Island: Vixen Point

Tortola: Smuggler's Cove (where you'll see the Lincoln used by Queen Elizabeth when she visited the BVI in the 1950s), Long Bay, Apple Bay, Cane Garden Bay with its 1.5 miles of sifted sand shaded by towering palms, Brewer's Bay, Elizabeth Bay, and Long Bay for jogging or swimming. On Beef Island is Trellis Bay, loved for its good surfing and shelling.

Virgin Gorda: The Baths, Spring Bay, Trunk Bay, Savannah Bay, and Mahoe Bay.

can be reached over a path from Spring Bay or by boat; Savannah Bay is found just north of Yacht Harbour, and Mahoe Bay is a superb beach at the Mango Bay Resort.

Other Islands: Long Bay on Beef Island has a quiet beach, but enter from behind the salt pond so you don't disturb nesting terms. Loblolly Bay on Anegada has a beach bar; White Bay on Jost Van Dyke and Sandy Cay just off the island are reached by boat. Deadman's Bay on Peter Island can be reached by boat or ferry; Vixen Point in North Sound has white sand and a refreshment stand.

Camping

Camping on a bare site, or on a campsite with beds provided is available at **Anegada Beach Campground**, *Tel. 284/495-9466;* **Brewers Bay Campground**, *Tel. 284/494-3463;* **Neptune's Campground**, Anegada, *Tel. 284/ 495- 9439;* **Mac's Place Camping**, Anegada, *Tel. 284/495-8020;* and **White Bay Campground** on Jost Van Dyke, *Tel. 284/495-9312.*

Diving

Diving and snorkeling in the BVI is rewarding almost anywhere you fall off a boat, but the islands' most famous dive is the wreck of the *Rhone,* now crusted with corals and bright with darting fish in all colors of the rainbow. The pride of the Royal Mail Steam Packet Company, she hit Salt Island during a hurricane in 1867, broke in two, and sank in 80 feet of water. Best known as the site of filming for *The Deep,* the wreck still has an enormous propeller and a complete foremast with crow's nest.

Dive operators include **Baskin in the Sun**, *Tel. 494-2858,* **Blue Water Divers**, *Tel. 494-2847*, **Trimarine Boat Company Ltd**., *Tel. 494-2490* or *800/ 648-3393,* **Underwater Safaris**, *Tel. 494-3235,* and **High Sea Adventures** (snorkel tours), *Tel. 495-1300,* all on Tortola; and **Dive BVI Ltd.**, *Tel. 495-5513* or *800/848-7078* and **Kilbride's Underwater Tours**, *Tel. 495-9638* or *800/ 932-4286,* both based on Virgin Gorda.

Specializing in underwater photography is **Rainbow Visions** on Tortola, *Tel. 484-2749.* Book this service through one of the dive companies above to get a custom video of your dive or to rent an underwater camera or camcorder.

If you rent a boat to go diving on your own, you'll need a mooring permit. Anchoring in most of the best diving spots is illegal because it could damage the coral. Frankly, it's best to go with one of the outfitters listed above. They know both the rules and the best scuba and snorkel sites, such as:

Alice in Wonderland is a deep dive at South Bay on Ginger Island, where walls slope downward 100 feet to huge, mushroom-shaped coral heads.

Blonde Rock, found between Dead Chest and Salt Island, rises from 60 feet down to within 15 feet of the surface. Explore it to see ledges, tunnels, caves and overhangs alive with lobster and other sea creatures as well as a wonderland of gently waving fan coral.

Brewers Bay Pinnacle is a towering sea mountain abounding in sea life. Seas here can be rough, so this is a dive to take when conditions are right.

The Caves on Norman Island are so well known that they may be swarming with people, so try to arrive early in the day to see the place that is thought to have been Robert Louis Stevenson's inspiration for *Treasure Island*. The caves make for exciting snorkeling over dark waters; Angelfish Reef nearby is a good place to see rays and angelfish.

The *Chikuzen* is a 246-foot Japanese refrigeration ship that was sunk here in 1981 to form an artificial reef. It is in 75 feet of water six miles north of Beef Island and it's home to a huge aquarium of fish large and small.

Dead Chest Island, which is where Blackbeard is said to have marooned 15 of his men with a bottle of rum and a sword, offers good snorkeling over bands of sand and coral. Great Dog and The Chimneys lie in the "dog" islands between Virgin Gorda and Tortola. Underwater canyons, some of them shallow enough for snorkelers and rookie divers, are dazzling sea gardens.

Painted Walls is a shallow drive off the south point of Dead Chest. Four long gullies are crusted with colored coral and sponge only 20-30 feet down.

Santa Monica Rock, a mile south of Norman Island on the outer edge of the islands, lies close enough to deep water that it's a place to see pelagic fish (fish that roam freely rather than living in one reef), spotted eagle rays, and perhaps a nurse shark. The rock rises from the sea floor 100 feet deep to within about 10 feet of the surface.

Wreck of the Rhone, now a marine park, is the BVI's most popular dive. Broken in half and quickly sunk by a storm in 1867, she lies scattered and crusted, her innards open to view while coral and fish swirl through old cargo holds, the engine, and the immense propeller.

Sailing & Boating

Sailing courses including liveaboard cruise courses are available from **Offshore Sailing School**, *Tel. 800/221-4326* or *813/454-1700*. Board sailing rentals are available from **Boardsailing BVI**, *Tel. 495-2447* or *494-0422*.

Boating is best arranged through your hotel or condo host, who has rental boats or knows where to find them plus the best fishing guide, deep sea fishing charter, day sail, or sunset cruise. This is a crowded category that changes often as boats come and go.

Hiking

The most popular hiking trails in the British Virgin Islands are the path to Sage Mountain on Tortola and the walk to **Gorda Peak** on Virgin Gorda. Sage Mountain National Park is a vest pocket-size, 92-acre preserve that the serious hiker can cover in half a day. From Road Town, drive up Joe's Hill Road and keep climbing (4WD rental cars are popular here and this is why), watching for the small sign to Sage Mountain. The road ends at a small parking lot.

Take off on any of the three trails, which are connected, to enjoy moderately easy walking through bowers of elephant ears, cocoplum, and butter-yellow palicourea under a canopy of mahogany and manilkara trees and white cedars. In the open, find magnificent views of Jost Van Dyke across the sea to the northwest.

The islands' other popular trail is an easy walk in **The Baths National Park** on Virgin Gorda, where you'll find yourself surrounded by cathedral-size boulders catching a swirling sea. Go early in the day. By the time land-based visitors get up and passengers stream ashore from charter boats and cruise ships, The Baths can be too crowded. Another path from the same road leads lead off to **Devil's Bay National Park** on an easy, 15-minute walk through a cactus garden and a sand beach that is less crowded than The Baths.

The more rugged, half-hour hike to Gorda Peak, which is at 1,359 feet, is found off North Sound Road. Ask directions at the ferry dock. To stay on the right path, which leads to a small picnic area, follow the red blazes.

To climb to the 1,359-foot peak that tops **Virgin Gorda National Park**, drive the North Sound Road and look for a sign that points to stairs that climb up into the woods. You can make it to the observation tower in about 15 minutes.

Sportfishing

Offshore sportfishing or action-packed bonefishing on the flats you an be arranged through the **Anegada Reef Hotel**, *Tel. 495-8002*. Out of Tortola, the *Miss Robbie* is available for charter by the half day, day, or cruise for marlin fishing and other blue water sportfishing, *Tel. 494-3311*.

Shopping
TORTOLA

Crafts Alive in the heart of Road Town is a collection of West Indies-style booths selling dolls, straw work, crochet, pottery, and the inevitable tee-shirts. One of the shops, **BVI House of Craft**, claims that at least 75 per cent of its stock is produced locally including local bush teas, honey, and condiments. It's open daily, 9am to 5pm, but hours may vary seasonally.

Local artists show their work at the gallery at **Ole Works Inn** on Cane Garden Bay and at **Caribbean Fine Arts Ltd**. on Upper Main Street. The shop sells original art as well as antique maps, pottery, and primitives. For out-of-town newspapers and magazines try **Esmé's Shoppe** in Sir Olva George's Plaza behind the government complex on Wickham's Cay. It's open every day including holidays.

Samarkand on Main Street in Road Town has been here for 25 years selling handcrafted tropical jewelry including their own exclusive line of

Tortola green jasper. They're open daily 9am to 5pm and Saturdays 9am to 1pm.; closed Sunday. Nearby, **Caribbean Handprints** sells locally silk-screened printed fabrics by the yard. Island books and maps are at **Heritage Books and Arts** on Main Street.

For a large selection of island music, try **Bolo's** on DeCastro Road, Wickham's Cay. The shop can also repair leather and develop film, and it has a good selection of souvenirs and sundries. **The Shirt Shack** on Chalwell Street between Main and Waterfront has one of the island's best selections of tee shirts and also sells handicrafts. For handmade clothes made locally, try **Caribbean Handprints** on Main Street.

Pusser's Road Town Pub & Company Store on lower Waterfront Drive south of Wickham's Cay offers one-stop shopping for pizza, burgers, dinner pies, and all the popular Pusser's logo merchandise that captivates tourists. It's open daily, 9am to midnight, and accepts credit cards. **Sunny Caribbee Spice Company** on Main Street just below Chalwell is a company spice shop and gallery. Choose island seasonings and sauces to take home, then shop the gallery for locally crafted arts.

VIRGIN GORDA

Kaunda's Kysy Tropix, *Tel. 495-5636,* at the yacht harbor in The Valley is the place to get batteries, personal electronics, film, tapes, jewelry and perfumes. Kuanda will also pierce your ears.

Pusser's Company Store is another arm of the Pusser's empire, a holy name in British islands because Pusser's Rum is the official grog of the Royal Navy.

Practical Information

Area Code: 284

Alcoholics Anonymous meets regularly, *Tel. 494-4549 or 494-3125.*

ATM: the Chase Manhattan Bank in Road Town has a MasterCard/Cirrus ATM. Others ATMs are found at Banco Popular, Barclay's Bank, and Scotia Bank.

Banking: Road Town has a Chase Manhattan Bank with a 24-hour ATM machine, *Tel. 494-2662.* ATMs are also found at Banco Popular and Barclay's Bank in Road Town. Bank hours are generally Monday through Thursday 8:30am to 3pm, Friday 8:30am to 4pm.

Currency: U.S. dollars are the legal tender. American Express, VISA, Diners Club, and MasterCard are widely accepted.

Dress: it is offensive to locals when tourists appear in residential and commercial areas in bathing suits. Wear a cover-up.

Driving: a $10 temporary driver's license is required. Driving is on the left, with a maximum speed of 30 miles per hour on the open road and 10-15 miles per hour in settlements.

Drugs: stiff fines and jail sentences will be levied for possession or use of illegal drugs.

Emergencies: dial 999 for fire, police, or ambulance.

Government: British Virgin Islands are part of the United Kingdom. U.S. consular needs are provided from the U.S. Embassy in Bridgetown, Barbados, Tel. 246/436-4950.

Holidays: dates vary but public holidays generally include Christmas, Boxing Day (December 26), New Year's Day, H. Lavity Stoutt's Birthday on March 4, Commonwealth Day on March 11, Good Friday, Easter Monday, Whit Monday, the Sovereign's Birthday on June 8, Territory Day on July 1, August Festival in early August, St. Ursula's Day on October 21. When making business appointments or counting on finding a bank open, ask about upcoming holidays.

Immigration: citizens of the U.S. and Canada need only a birth certificate, citizenship certificate, or voter registration plus photo ID; others need passports, and visitors from some nations need a visa. For information contact the Chief Immigration Officer, Government of the British Virgin Islands, Road Town. Tortola, British Virgin Islands, *Tel. 284/494-3701.*

Medical care: can be found at the B&F Medical Complex, *Tel. 494-2196,* just off the cruise ship dock at Road Town. Open daily from 7am, it offers family doctors, specialists, x-ray, ultrasound, lab work and a pharmacy. Walk-ins are welcome. At the north end of Wickham's Cay at the traffic circle Medicure Pharmacy, *Tel. 494-6189, 494-6468 or 494-2346,* has prescriptions, a medical lab, x-ray and medical personnel on duty.

Permits: a Fishing Permit is required for fishing or the gathering of any marine organisms. Call the Fisheries Division, *Tel. 284/494-3429.* A Conservation Permit is required for mooring in any National Parks Trust moorings. If you'll be cruising the British Virgin Islands in a boat rented here or elsewhere, contact the National Parks Trust for information on permits and fees, *Tel. 284/494-3904.*

Pets: require advance permission and planning, so write well in advance to the Chief Agricultural Officer, Road Town, Tortola, British Virgin Islands.

Taxes: you'll pay a departure tax of $10 each. Hotel tax is seven per cent. A small tax or fee is charged to cash each traveler's check.

Telephone: the area code for the BVI is **284**; to access AT&T on your cellular phone dial 872, then Send. For Boatphone cell service dial O and Send, and an operator will take your credit card information. Cable & Wireless offices at Virgin Gorda and Road Town handle long distance calling, faxes, telegrams and telexes and also sell prepaid phone cards, which are used throughout the islands.

Time: add one hour to Eastern Standard Time.

Tourist Information: British Virgin Islands Tourist Board, 370 Lexington Avenue, Suite 1605, New York NY 10017, *Tel. 212/696-0400,* In North America, call toll-free, *Tel. 800/835-8530.* In Road Town, a tourist office is found on Wickham's Cay, *Tel. 284/494-3134.*

Weddings: you must be in the territory for three days before applying for a marriage license, which must be done in Road Town. For all details, write well in advance to or call the Registrar's Office, Post Office Box 418, Road Town, Tortola, *Tel. 284/494-3492* or *284/494-3701.*

index

Puerto Rico & Virgin Islands Guide

Things Change!

Phone numbers, prices, addresses, quality of food, etc, all change. If you come across any new information, we'd appreciate hearing from you. No item is too small! Drop us an email note at: Jopenroad@aol.com, or write us at:

Puerto Rico & Virgin Islands Guide
Open Road Publishing, P.O. Box 284
Cold Spring Harbor, NY 11724

open road publishing

U.S.
America's Cheap Sleeps, $17.95
America's Most Charming Towns &
  Villages, $17.95
Arizona Guide, $16.95
Boston Guide, $14.95
California Wine Country Guide, $12.95
Colorado Guide, $17.95
Disneyworld With Kids, $14.95
Florida Guide, $16.95
Hawaii Guide, $18.95
Las Vegas Guide, $14.95
Las Vegas With Kids, $14.95
National Parks With Kids, $14.95
New Mexico Guide, $16.95
San Francisco Guide, $16.95
Southern California Guide, $18.95
Spa Guide, $14.95
Texas Guide, $16.95
Utah Guide, $16.95
Vermont Guide, $16.95

Middle East/Africa
Egypt Guide, $18.95
Israel Guide, $17.95
Jerusalem Guide, $13.95
Kenya Guide, $18.95

Eating & Drinking on the Open Road
Eating & Drinking in Paris, $9.95
Eating & Drinking in Italy, $9.95
Eating & Drinking in Spain, $9.95

Latin America & Caribbean
Bahamas Guide, $13.95
Belize Guide, $16.95
Bermuda Guide, $14.95
Caribbean Guide, $21.95
Caribbean With Kids, $14.95
Central America Guide, $21.95
Chile Guide, $18.95
Costa Rica Guide, $17.95
Ecuador & Galapagos Islands Guide, $17.95
Guatemala Guide, $18.95
Honduras Guide, $16.95

Europe
Czech & Slovak Republics Guide, $18.95
Greek Islands Guide, $16.95
Holland Guide, $17.95
Ireland Guide, $17.95
Italy Guide, $21.95
Italy With Kids, $16.95
London Guide, $14.95
Moscow Guide, $16.95
Paris Guide, $13.95
Portugal Guide, $16.95
Prague Guide, $14.95
Rome Guide, $14.95
Scotland Guide, $17.95
Spain Guide, $18.95
Turkey Guide, $18.95

Asia
China Guide, $21.95
Japan Guide, $21.95
Philippines Guide, $18.95
Tahiti & French Polynesia Guide, $19.95
Tokyo Guide, $14.95
Thailand Guide, $18.95